The Psychology of

MEMORY

BASIC TOPICS IN COGNITION SERIES

Sam Glucksberg, *Editor*

THE
PSYCHOLOGY
OF
MEMORY

Alan D. Baddeley

Basic Books, Inc., Publishers

New York

Library of Congress Cataloging in Publication Data

Baddeley, Alan D.   1934–
    The psychology of memory.

    (Basic topics in cognition series)
    Bibliography: p. 379
    Includes index.
    1.   Memory.   I.   Title.
BF371.B23   153.1′2   75–36769
ISBN: 0–465–06736–0 (cloth)
ISBN: 0–465–06737–9 (pbk.)

To Hilary

CONTENTS

CHAPTER 4

CHAPTER 5

CHAPTER 6

CHAPTER 7

CHAPTER 8

CHAPTER 11

CHAPTER 12

CHAPTER 13

CHAPTER 14

CHAPTER 15

PREFACE

THIS BOOK began life in a London pub called the "Friend at Hand." It was January 1970; I was due to spend a sabbatical year in California; and Sam Glucksberg, who was himself on sabbatical in Britain at the time, suggested I write a short text on memory for a Basic Books series that he was editing. This seemed to be a useful way of spending part of a sabbatical year, and I promised the first part of the book for the following January. Some six years later, however, the book that has finally emerged is rather different from the short text that we both envisaged. Had I stuck firmly to my lecture notes when writing and left the checking of references till later, a brief text would no doubt have emerged more or less on time. Instead, however, I decided to take the opportunity of reading in some of the areas of memory with which I was less familiar; as a result, the writing of this book proved to be a much more enjoyable, but much slower, business than I ever anticipated. I suspect it may also have emerged as somewhat longer and more idiosyncratic than either Sam Glucksberg or I originally intended. For that reason, a few words on its organization and structure might be appropriate.

There are a number of logical ways of structuring a book on memory. One might, for example, divide memory into its three major aspects: the input, storage, and retrieval of information. Anyone who has tried to separate the three experimentally will understand why I rejected this structure: the three are so interdependent that it is rarely possible to isolate one stage from the others. Different ways of encoding material during learning produce differences in the information remembered or stored, which in turn will determine what method of retrieval strategy can be used. Hence, although it is conceptually useful to distinguish these three aspects of memory, as a general framework for a book such as this they present more problems than they solve. An alternative approach might be to follow the flow of information from the periphery inward, beginning with the brief sensory memory systems which Neisser has termed echoic and iconic memory, proceeding to short-term memory, and from there to long-term and semantic memory. This approach has the drawback, at least from a teaching point of view, of beginning with one of the most complex and difficult areas of memory, one which can be understood much better if earlier work on short-term memory has already been covered. Work in the area of short-term memory itself can best be understood in the light of earlier views of memory as a unitary system, and of the view that forgetting is caused by interference between traces rather than trace decay. For that reason, I have adopted a broadly chronological framework, beginning with relatively simple conceptualizations of human memory. These become more elaborate as the reader learns more about the complexities of the subject.

The first part of the book considers memory as an overall system. Chapter 1 outlines the work of Ebbinghaus and Bartlett, who were important in setting the two traditions in memory, represented by the need on the one hand to simplify the problem of memory in order to make it experimentally tractable, and on the other to avoid oversimplification, trivialization, and the exclusion of all that is most characteristic and interesting in human memory. The next three chapters are concerned with the operation of the memory system considered as a whole: Chapter 2 is concerned with the input limitations of the system, Chapter 3 with the storage and consolidation of the memory trace, and Chapter 4 with the loss of information from memory and, in particular, with the phenomenon of interference. The attempt to explain all forgetting in terms of interference between associations is examined in Chapter 5.

The remainder of the book is concerned with the attempt to break down human memory into separate subsystems or components and to try to understand these, typically using a cognitive or information-processing approach. Chapter 6 is concerned with the arguments for and against a distinction between long- and short-term memory. Chapter 7 deals with the principal phenomena and theoretical controversies within the general area of short-term memory, and Chapter 8 reexamines the concept of a simple dichotomy between long- and short-term memory in the light of more recent evidence. Until comparatively recently, work on memory has been dominated almost exclusively by studies of verbal memory. This extreme bias is fortunately beginning to change, and Chapters 9 and 10 attempt to cover recent work on visual, auditory, kinesthetic, tactile, and olfactory memory.

The final subsection of the book is concerned with the role of meaning in memory. It begins with a chapter on organization and memory, relying principally on evidence from experiments studying the retention of lists of unrelated words. Chapter 12 attempts to understand memory for prose in terms of interference theory, information theory, and the transformational approach to grammar developed by Noam Chomsky; it is followed by a chapter on the currently very active field of semantic factors in memory. Chapter 14 examines cases in which memory is abnormally good and attempts to explain the performance of mnemonists and the functioning of mnemonic systems in terms of what is known of normal memory. Finally, Chapter 15 attempts a brief overview and some speculations on future trends.

In writing such a book, one can choose either to present the information and views as objectively as possible or to present a personal view. I have attempted the latter. Consequently, although I have made every effort to ensure that my descriptions of experiments and results are fair and accurate, my selection of topics, degree of emphasis, and theoretical interpretations are, I am sure, somewhat idiosyncratic. No doubt anyone reading this book will find interpretations and views which he thinks are wrong; indeed, by the time the book is published, I suspect I myself will disagree with some of the things I have said. In some cases these aberrations probably stem from my willingness to write about areas of which I have no firsthand experience; the chapter on consolidation is a case in point, and I have no doubt that the views expressed in it were heavily influenced by some very stimulating discussions with Tony Deutsch, whose views in this field are, I am sure, by no means the accepted norm. The chapter on visual memory presents another example of this type, as it relies heavily on a paper by Michael Turvey that, in my own case, made intelligible a field which had in recent years grown increasingly obscure. It would have been preferable to have been able to devote enough time to such areas in order to present a more balanced picture, but given the breadth of work on memory, the rate at which new work is appearing, and the amount of writing time available to me, such an approach was just not practicable. I have therefore opted to give a partial and inevitably biased view of a relatively wide range of topics.

A second type of bias which runs throughout the book derives from my own approach to psychology. This probably shows up most clearly in my treatment of the verbal-learning tradition and interference theory, toward both of which I have distinctly ambivalent feelings. My intellectual background is British, but with strong North American links. My doctoral research was concerned with the very practical question of designing postal codes, and I discovered somewhat to my horror that the types of experiment demanded by this problem were very much in the verbal-learning tradition so roundly condemned by Sir Frederic Bartlett, the founder of the unit in which I was working. As Chapters 4 and 5 suggest, I find much of the verbal-learning tradition stultifyingly dull, but at the same time I have considerable respect for it on several counts. For many years it was the only serious attempt to understand the crucially important area of human learning and memory; its capacity for self-criticism and its willingness to attempt to increase the generality of its findings seem to me admirable, although the quality of this criticism and the success of the attempt are, I think, rather more questionable. I believe that both of these shortcomings stem from the isolation of the verbal-learning tradition. The tendency either to subscribe wholeheartedly to the interference theory position or to ignore it entirely has, I believe, proved harmful both for the study of memory in general and for the understanding of the very real and possibly quite crucial issue of the role of interference in forgetting. Hence my inclusion of a section which noninterference theorists will regard as excessively long and interference theorists as excessively biased.

Perhaps the most difficult problem presented in writing a book of this type lies in the enormously rapid rate of change in the field. This would have been a difficulty even with a rapidly written book, but with a book that has taken so long to write the problem is acute. It is particularly so in an area in which one is actively engaged; for example, my own views on short-term memory have changed very considerably since I began this book in 1971. Thus, the question arises: to what extent should one rewrite? In the case of short-term memory, I have opted to leave the earlier chapters relatively untouched. They possibly do not describe experimental results in quite the same way as I would if I were currently giving my own best guess at a probable interpretation. However, I know from bitter experience that my present conceptualization may well change yet again before this book reaches the bookshops. I have therefore decided to leave the chapter on the two-component view of memory in the form in which it was originally written (which does, at least, have the advantage of describing the experiments within the conceptual framework that stimulated them), while leaving for the chapter on working memory my subsequent doubts as to the adequacy of a simple dichotomy between long- and short-term memory.

There is a temptation to feel that at the end of each draft of a book one should go through and update it; the fact that the book has appeared at all is evidence that I have managed to resist this temptation. The end result, though inevitably uneven and idiosyncratic, hopefully may still convey some of the richness and excitement that I myself derived from producing this very personal review of the current state of research into one of the central problems of psychology.

It will, I hope, be apparent to the reader that I have profited from discussions with far more colleagues than it would be feasible to list here. I have attempted to acknowledge the source of the ideas derived from colleagues and friends, but since I rely on my memory for such information, I am sure that at least some of my intellectual debts will go unacknowledged; I hope they will be attributed to forgetfulness and not ingratitude. I am exceedingly grateful to George Mandler and Donald Norman, who acted as such generous hosts during my sabbatical year at the University of California, San Diego, Center for Human Information Processing. The intellectual stimulation I derived from my year at La Jolla will, I hope, be obvious to the reader. This book was in fact written in four different locations, and I am grateful for many useful discussions with colleagues at La Jolla, Sussex, Stirling, and the Applied Psychology Unit, Cambridge. The chapter on working memory owes a particular debt to Graham Hitch and Neil Thomson, and I would like to thank Bill Phillips for his comments on the visual memory chapter and Roy Patterson for his assistance with the section on auditory memory. I am particularly grateful to Karalyn Patterson, who read the penultimate draft of the book and offered many useful comments. I would like to thank Sam Glucksberg and Herb Reich for their valuable editorial advice, Derek Simmonds for his help with illustrations, and Lillian Astell, whose help in both preparing and typing the manuscript was invaluable. I am grateful for financial support provided during the writing of the book by the National Institute of Mental Health (N.I.M.H. Grant No. MH/5828), the Social Science Research Council, and the Medical Research Council. Finally, I would like to thank my wife, Hilary, for her continued encouragement and support during the book's long gestation.

The Psychology of

MEMORY

CHAPTER

1

The Ebbinghaus Tradition
and the Bartlett Approach

THE EXPERIMENTAL STUDY of human memory began in 1879 when a German philosopher, Hermann Ebbinghaus, initiated an experimental program that revolutionized the study of cognitive psychology. As a scholar of independent means, he had studied in Germany, England, and France, and it was in a secondhand bookshop in Paris that he found a copy of Fechner's *Elements of Psychophysics*. Impressed by the application of the experimental method to the study of sensation, he conceived the idea of applying the same approach to the study of memory. This was a somewhat daring notion, since the new experimental psychology was not considered a suitable tool for attacking such "higher mental processes" as memory even by its founders, Wundt and Fechner.

The Ebbinghaus Tradition

As a topic of philosophy, memory had already stimulated theories that were clearly not testable with the simple techniques available to the new psychology. Ebbinghaus (1885) described three major theories of forgetting: one, which would now be termed an interference theory, in which "the earlier images are more and more overlaid, so to speak, and covered by the later ones"; a second, corresponding to trace decay, in which "the persisting images suffer changes which more and more affect their nature"; and a third, in which forgetting involves "crumbling into parts and the loss of separate components instead of general obscuration." Such a view has recently been revived by Gordon Bower (1967), who terms it a multicomponent theory of the memory trace. The difficulty comes, however, not in formulating such theories but in testing them. Ebbinghaus himself made the point very clearly:

> Each of these opinions receives a certain, but not exclusive, support from the actual inner experiences, or experiences supposed to be actual. . . . If one considers the limitations to direct, unaided observation and to the chance occurrence of useful experiences, there seems but little prospect of improvement in conditions. How will one for example determine the degree of obscuration reached at a certain point, or the number of fragments remaining? Or how can the probable course of inner processes be traced if the almost entirely forgotten ideas return no more to consciousness (1885; 1913 ed., pp. 64–65)?

The orthodox reaction to this dilemma was to avoid the topic of memory altogether; Ebbinghaus's solution was to simplify it into a more tractable problem, one that could be attacked with a reasonable chance of success. He proposed to study the factors governing the learning by heart and retention of very simple material by a disciplined and motivated subject under rigidly controlled conditions. This allowed him "a possibility of indirectly approaching the problem just stated in a small and definitely limited sphere and, by means of keeping aloof for a while from any theory, perhaps of constructing one" (ibid., p. 65).

This involved creating a set of completely new techniques, since no one had previously attempted such a task. Because he wished to study new learning and to minimize the effects of previous knowledge, he used as his material separate nonsense syllables, each comprising a consonant followed by a vowel and another consonant (e.g., *wux, caz, jek*). These were made into lists which the subject (Ebbinghaus himself) read out loud at a rate of 150 per minute. He continued to read through the list with occasional tests until he could reproduce the list correctly without hesitation. It is notable that his rate of reading (2.5 syllables per second) was very much faster than is common in modern verbal-learning studies, in which the presentation rate rarely exceeds 0.5 nonsense syllables per second, and that Ebbinghaus explicitly avoided the use of meaningful associations and mnemonic aids. Finally, Ebbinghaus was scrupulously careful to hold external factors as constant as possible. He always tested at the same time of day, since this proved to affect learning capacity; he kept the activity preceding the test constant and discontinued the tests whenever "too great changes in the outer or inner life occurred." On resumption, he was always careful to train himself up to his previous level of performance before resuming experimentation. Finally, his results were always based on a large number of tests and evaluated statistically. Such zeal for controlling extraneous variables may seem excessive to the modern psychologist, who typically tries to obtain reliable data by using large numbers of quasi-randomly selected subjects. There are, however, very few modern studies that produce data as clear and regular as Ebbinghaus's original experiments.

RATE OF LEARNING

In order to evaluate any system for storing information, three very basic questions must be answered: How rapidly can information be registered? How much information can be stored? How rapidly is information lost? In the case of human long-term memory, the capacity is clearly enormous, and limits are therefore set by the rates of learning and forgetting. Both of these were investigated by Ebbinghaus using the *saving method,* a technique he devised for estimating the amount of material retained by measuring the difficulty of relearning it. Learning the same list for a second time will require fewer trials if it has been well retained than if it has been largely forgotten. The difference between the number of trials required for original learning and relearning can then be used as a measure of how much has been remembered.

Using this technique, Ebbinghaus asked the following questions: What is the relationship between the number of repetitions of a list and the degree of learning? Is the relationship like that between amount of heat and the height of mercury in a thermometer, in which each increment in temperature produces an *equal* rise in the height of the mercury, or is it more like the effect of an electric current on a magnetic needle, with each successive increment in current producing a *smaller* angular displacement of the needle? In order to investigate this, he employed lists of 16 nonsense syllables which he practiced for 0, 8, 16, 24, 32, 42, 53, or 64 repetitions, and then relearned the list to a criterion of one perfect recall 24 hours later. Figure 1–1 shows the results of this experiment, based on one subject, Ebbinghaus himself, and 70 lists. In this situation, human memory behaves more like a thermometer than like a magnetic needle. Each repetition during the original learning saves about 12

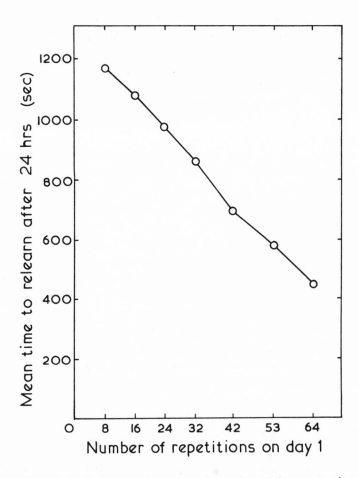

Figure 1–1   Influence of number of learning trials on retention after a 24-hour delay. Ebbinghaus 1885. Source: Data taken from H. Ebbinghaus, *Memory* (New York: Teachers College Press, 1913).

seconds on relearning the next day. This is a particularly good example of a characteristic of human memory which has only recently been redis-covered and which is currently known as the *total time hypothesis* (see Cooper and Pantle 1967 for a review). According to this hypoth-esis, the amount of learning is directly proportional to the total time spent in learning, regardless of how the time is distributed. This rela-tionship applies to rote learning but probably breaks down if the sub-ject switches from a strategy of simple repetition to one of reorganization based on visual imagery; nor does it apply to a search for meaningful relationships within the material (Paivio 1971c). The very clean results obtained by Ebbinghaus probably reflect his rigid adherence to a single, consistent strategy.

An intriguing feature of Figure 1–1 is the fact that a single repetition lasting less than 7 seconds gives a saving of over 12 seconds on relearning 24 hours later. We shall return to this point when we discuss the possible role of a memory trace consolidation process.

RATE OF FORGETTING

The second limit is the rate at which information is forgotten. This was studied by means of 169 double tests. Each of these double tests involved learning eight lists of 13 syllables, which were then relearned after an interval ranging from 20 minutes to 31 days. The amount forgotten was measured by expressing the number of trials required for relearning as a percentage of the number required originally. The difference between this and 100 percent thus represents the percentage retained and is shown in Figure 1–2. Unlike the learning rate, rate of forgetting is clearly not linear; it is in fact a logarithmic relationship. Figure 1–3 shows these data plotted on a logarithmic scale, together with data from a number of later studies which also used nonsense syllables. There is in all cases a clearly linear relationship when plotted on a logarithmic scale.

What conclusions did Ebbinghaus draw about theories of memory from his experiments? Unfortunately, after the two years of intensive and highly original empirical work that went into his book on memory, Ebbinghaus moved on to other topics, leaving a body of beautifully executed experiments and a set of highly original techniques that are still widely used, but no theoretical conclusions.

Ebbinghaus has clearly had an enormous influence on the subsequent development (or lack of development) of our understanding of human memory. Unfortunately, the negative features of his work appear to have been easier to imitate than its positive virtues. He consciously chose to ignore much of the complexity of human memory in order to demonstrate that it could be studied objectively, and he also chose to postpone the discussion of theoretical issues until adequate techniques were developed. Regrettably, much subsequent work in the Ebbinghaus tradition has tended to continue this atheoretical preoccupation with technique. While such an approach was admirable at a time when no one believed that objective experiments on memory were possible, it is a

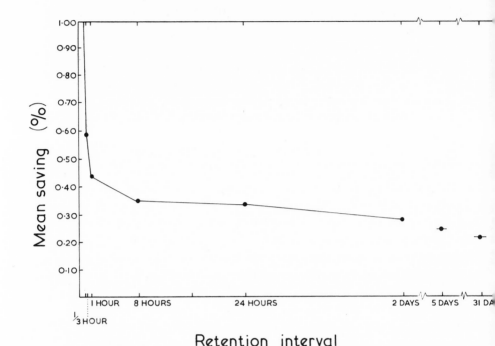

Retention interval

Figure 1–2   Rate of forgetting nonsense syllables observed by Ebbinghaus. Retention is measured using the saving method, in terms of the number of trials required to relearn a list after varying intervals. Source: Data taken from H. Ebbinghaus, *Memory* (New York: Teachers College Press, 1913).

very sterile long-term strategy for a developing science. Ebbinghaus's more conservative characteristics have been extensively copied in the intervening years, but his flair for devising new techniques and his ability to see the essentials of a problem and to express it in clear and vivid prose have unfortunately proved much harder to imitate.

Ebbinghaus's great contribution to the study of memory was to show that an apparently intractable problem could be attacked experimentally, provided the experimenter was prepared to simplify the situation with sufficient ruthlessness. The danger of such an approach is that of excluding all that is most central to human memory. This criticism of Ebbinghaus was made very strongly by Bartlett in his classic book *Remembering,* published in 1932. It represents very clearly the second major tradition, an approach which emphasizes the central importance of the subject's active search for meaning rather than his passive response to the stimuli presented by the experimenter.

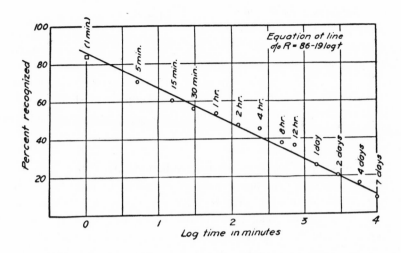

Figure 1–3   Rate of forgetting plotted on a logarithmic scale.
Source: R. S. Woodworth, *Experimental Psychology* (New York: Holt, Rinehart and Winston, 1938), p. 55.

The Bartlett Approach

Bartlett criticized Ebbinghaus's work on memory on the grounds that in attempting to avoid the difficult problem of meaning by using non-sense material, it confined itself to a highly artificial situation. He argued that the "repetition habits" studied in the verbal-learning laboratory had very little to do with memory in everyday life. This was probably true of Ebbinghaus's own studies, which used a rapid presentation rate and attempted to exclude any mnemonic aids or associations that might assist learning. However, although a determined and single-minded subject such as Ebbinghaus was probably successful in blocking out helpful associations and confining himself to simple repetition habits, this was certainly not the case with subsequent studies using slower presentation rates and untrained subjects. As Glaze (1928) observed, most nonsense syllables suggest real words, and the greater the number of meaningful words a syllable suggests, the easier it is to learn. Bartlett criticized the Ebbinghaus tradition for being too stimulus bound, for ignoring the subject's attitudes and prior experience and assuming that an impoverished stimulus would produce a simple learning situation. Bartlett later argued that the "effort after meaning" was central to human learning, in which case relatively meaningless material could present the subject with a particularly complex learning task. Such a

9

view is supported by Prytulak's (1971) recent study of the complex recoding strategies employed by subjects learning nonsense syllables. Ebbinghaus had succeeded admirably in demonstrating that human memory could be studied experimentally, but his experiments had excluded meaningful material of the type that makes up the vast majority of remembering in everyday life. Bartlett attempted to show that despite its complexity, such meaningful material also could be studied in the laboratory.

Bartlett's book describes a series of experiments using stories, passages of prose, pictures, and American Indian picture writing to investigate the retention of meaningful material. His most characteristic experimental method was that of serial reproduction, in which a subject would attempt to recall the same material on several occasions. In another form of the method a chain of different subjects would be used, with the first being shown the original stimulus material and then recalling it for the second subject, who would pass it on to a third, and so forth.

Bartlett's results are best illustrated with a concrete example; the following is an American Indian folk tale used extensively by Bartlett.*

The War of the Ghosts

One night two young men from Egulac went down to the river to hunt seals, and while they were there it became foggy and calm. Then they heard war-cries, and they thought: "Maybe this is a war-party." They escaped to the shore, and hid behind a log. Now canoes came up, and they heard the noise of paddles, and saw one canoe coming up to them. There were five men in the canoe, and they said:

"What do you think? We wish to take you along. We are going up the river to make war on the people."

One of the young men said: "I have no arrows."

"Arrows are in the canoe," they said.

"I will not go along. I might be killed. My relatives do not know where I have gone. But you," he said turning to the other, "may go with them."

So one of the young men went, but the other returned home.

And the warriors went on up the river to a town on the other side of Kalama. The people came down to the water, and they began to fight, and many were killed. But presently the young man heard one of the warriors say: "Quick, let us go home: that Indian has been hit." Now he thought: "Oh, they are ghosts." He did not feel sick, but they said he had been shot.

So the canoes went back to Egulac, and the young man went ashore to

* Permission to reprint the following excerpts from *Remembering*, by F. C. Bartlett (Cambridge: Cambridge University Press, 1932) is gratefully acknowledged.

his house, and made a fire. And he told everybody and said: "Behold I accompanied the ghosts, and we went to fight. Many of our fellows were killed, and many of those who attacked us were killed. They said I was hit, and I did not feel sick."

He told it all, and then he became quiet. When the sun rose he fell down. Something black came out of his mouth. His face became contorted. The people jumped up and cried.

He was dead (Bartlett 1932, p. 65).

This was reproduced by one subject on the first recall after an interval of about 15 minutes as:

War Ghost Story

Two young men from Egulac went out to hunt seals. They thought they heard war-cries, and a little later they heard the noise of the paddling of canoes. One of these canoes, in which there were five natives, came forward towards them. One of the natives shouted out: "Come with us: we are going to make war on some natives up the river." The two young men answered: "We have no arrows." "There are arrows in our canoes," came the reply. One of the young men then said: "My folk will not know where I have gone"; but, turning to the other, he said: "But you could go." So the one returned whilst the other joined the natives.

The party went up the river as far as a town opposite Kalama, where they got on land. The natives of that part came down to the river to meet them. There was some severe fighting, and many on both sides were slain. Then one of the natives that had made the expedition up the river shouted: "Let us return: the Indian has fallen." Then they endeavored to persuade the young man to return, telling him that he was sick, but he did not feel as if he were. Then he thought he saw ghosts all round him.

When they returned, the young man told all his friends of what had happened. He described how many had been slain on both sides.

It was nearly dawn when the young man became very ill; and at sunrise a black substance rushed out of his mouth, and the natives said one to another: "He is dead" (ibid., p. 70).

In a second recall four months later this became:

I have no idea of the title.

There were two men in a boat, sailing towards an island. When they approached the island, some natives came running towards them, and informed them that there was fighting going on on the island, and invited them to join. One said to the other: "You had better go. I cannot very well, because I have relatives expecting me, and they will not know what has become of me. But you have no one to expect you." So one accompanied the natives, but the other returned.

Here there is a part I can't remember. What I don't know is how the man got to the fight. However, anyhow the man was in the midst of the fighting, and was wounded. The natives endeavored to persuade the man to return, but he assured them that he had not been wounded.

I have an idea that his fighting won the admiration of the natives.

The wounded man ultimately fell unconscious. He was taken from the fighting by the natives.

Then, I think it is, the natives describe what happened, and they seem to have imagined seeing a ghost coming out of his mouth. Really it was a kind of materialisation of his breath. I know this phrase was not in the story, but that is the idea I have. Ultimately the man died at dawn the next day (ibid., pp. 70–71).

Another subject, when tested six months after reading the original, recalled:

> Four men came down to the water. They were told to get into a boat and to take arms with them. They inquired "What arms?" and were answered "Arms for battle." When they came to the battle-field they heard a great noise and shouting, and a voice said: "The black man is dead." And he was brought to the place where they were, and laid on the ground. And he foamed at the mouth (ibid., pp. 71–72).

The most obvious change over time involves the progressive shortening of the passage, together with a tendency for it to become more coherent from the subject's point of view. Bartlett describes a number of characteristic ways in which such passages are changed, including:

(1) *Omissions.* Not only are details omitted but also features of the passage that do not fit in with the subject's prior expectations. The supernatural element in *The War of the Ghosts* was frequently omitted by Bartlett's subjects, who tended to find it puzzling and illogical.

(2) *Rationalization.* Subjects would sometimes introduce material in an attempt to "explain" incongruous features of a passage. Thus *Something black came out of his mouth* becomes *foamed at the mouth*.

(3) *Dominant detail.* Certain features of the passage often become central and appear to serve as an anchor point for the rest of the passage. In *The War of the Ghosts* the death scene often played this role.

(4) *Transformation of detail.* Words and names are often changed so as to become more familiar (e.g., *canoes* may become *boats*).

(5) *Transformation of order.* The order of events may change considerably, although this is much more likely in a descriptive passage than in a well-structured narrative. Narrative material in general tended to be better recalled than descriptive passages.*

---

* One lengthy and very vivid description underwent almost complete distortion in one experiment described by Bartlett in which the passage was recalled by a sequence of subjects. The passage described an air raid which occurred when the narrator was taking a family, the Bothams, to catch a train at a seaside resort.

(6) *Importance of the subject's attitude.* In trying to remember a passage, the first thing the subject tends to recall is his attitude toward the material. "The recall is then a construction made largely on the basis of this attitude, and its general effect is that of a justification of the attitude" (ibid., p. 207).

In attempting to explain these and other results, Bartlett borrowed the concept of a *schema* from the neurologist Sir Henry Head, who used the concept to refer to the body image or model which essentially keeps track of the relative position of our limbs. While such a body schema clearly draws on kinesthetic and visual information, it also goes beyond such information to include the limits of the car we are driving or, for that matter, the feather on top of a hat we might be wearing. Bartlett suggested that our knowledge of the world comprises a set of models or schemata based on past experience. When we attempt to learn something new, we base our learning on already existing schemata. When these conflict with what is being remembered, distortions occur, as in the case of the Indian folk tale modified by Bartlett's subjects to make it more consistent with their own view of the world. Both learning and remembering are viewed as *active* processes involving "effort after meaning." The process of recall involves a considerable constructive component: we use what has been retained together with our preexisting schemata to try to re-create the original.

Curiously enough, although *Remembering* was published over 40 years ago, it is still difficult to assess its importance. It is certainly important in attempting to bridge the gap between the laboratory and real life; at the very least, it provides interesting observational data at the level of natural history. However, it can be argued that the method of repeated reproduction is itself somewhat artificial or at least restricted in generality. It is certainly not a particularly convenient analytic tool, since accurate scoring is difficult. There is the further problem that when a passage is recalled more than once, it is difficult if not impossible to know to what extent the subject is basing his recall on the original learning or

---

By the eleventh recall it had been transformed into the following brief and somewhat bizarre episode:

I went to see the Bothams off by train. I found a carriage with several older people and some toys and put them in. I heard the sirens and the engines throbbing. I paced down the platform in disgust, took the Bothams out of the carriage and threw them into the ditch. I saw four puffs of smoke. I have forgotten whether I was holding my head in my hands . . . (ibid., p. 164).

This particular subject said that he visualized the scene in terms of a concert platform and a public entertainer, and regarded the "Bothams" as a name for some unknown objects!

on the memory of his own earlier recall (Kay 1955). Furthermore, although it is possible to demonstrate most of the phenomena described by Bartlett, it is difficult to make specific predictions with any degree of certainty. For example, it is difficult to predict whether a bizarre detail will be well remembered as a "dominant detail" or will be omitted as irrelevant to the basic theme.

Bartlett's theory could be criticized as being too vague and complex to be testable; it is probably fair to say that for 30 years following the publication of *Remembering,* relatively little theoretical development occurred along the lines he suggested. Nevertheless, Bartlett has continued to have an important influence on the study of human memory, not only through his own students, such as Broadbent, Brown, and Conrad, but also through such U.S. psychologists as G. A. Miller and Neisser. In the introduction to his stimulating book *Cognitive Psychology,* Neisser (1967, p. 10) describes his approach as "more closely related to that of Bartlett than to any other contemporary psychologist." With the current trend away from the study of isolated words and with the growth of interest in meaningful material such as prose and pictures, Bartlett's work is likely to become increasingly influential. To give just one example, Bartlett's work on the recall of pictures has been largely neglected, and yet his technique of cued recall, in which he would ask the subject for specific details (e.g., "What, if anything, was the sailor smoking?"), would allow a much finer analysis of visual memory than is typically obtained in many current studies.

Furthermore, the development of the electronic computer, with its enormous capacity and flexibility, has made Bartlett's theoretical ideas seem much more viable. As early as 1954, Oldfield pointed out the analogy between Bartlett's account of human memory, in which existing schemata are used to store new information, and that of a computer, which must store patterns of events that have basic common elements. In both cases it is more economical to store a new event on the basis of an existing pattern, together with any deviations from that pattern, than to use a completely new set of storage locations for each item. A similar view was suggested by Miller (1968) and is incorporated into recent models of semantic memory discussed in Chapter 13, such as those of Quillian (1968) and Rumelhart, Lindsay, and Norman (1972).

The study of memory continues to be torn between Ebbinghaus's insistence on simplification (with its attendant danger of trivialization) and Bartlett's emphasis on the complexities of human memory (with its danger of intractability). As the ensuing chapters will show, the study of memory is repeatedly influenced by this tension, which is sometimes reflected in open conflict between theoretical positions, at other times in drifts in fashion from one approach to the other. Given the richness and complexity of human memory, such conflict is both inevitable and healthy; neither approach is uniquely correct, and an approach which is productive at one stage of conceptual and technical development may be sterile at another.

CHAPTER

2

The Limits of Memory:
Input Limitations

ANY DEVICE for storing information, including memory, must have at least three facets. One of these is responsible for the input of information; in the case of memory, this process is usually termed *learning* or *acquisition*. The second is responsible for storing the information; this is the stage to which the term *memory* itself most frequently refers. Finally it is necessary to have a means of accessing the information in the memory store; the term *retrieval* refers principally to this process. The present chapter is concerned with the characteristics of input to memory, though no attempt will be made to cover this vast topic comprehensively, the aim being simply to examine the broad question of what limits the input into long-term memory.

Total Time Hypothesis

The experiment by Ebbinghaus described in the previous chapter (see Figure 1–1) suggested a simple linear relationship between time available to commit something to memory and amount retained. In recent years, this relationship has been studied in a wide range of experiments. Bugelski (1962) had five groups of subjects each learn a list of eight pairs of nonsense syllables (e.g., *bev–yij*) until, given the appropriate stimulus syllable, they were able to recall the correct response syllable (e.g., given *bev,* the subject responds *yij*). A learning trial involved presentation of all eight pairs at a rate of 2, 4, 6, 8, or 15 seconds per pair, depending on the group. As would be expected, groups given longer presentation times needed fewer trials to learn the list. However, the total amount of time to learn the list (number of trials × duration of item presentation) remained constant. Amount of learning was a function of time spent, regardless of how the time was made up.

This relationship has been shown to hold across a surprisingly wide range of changes in learning procedure. Thus, Jung (1964) has shown that time to learn a list of pairs is constant whether the list is presented as a whole or cumulatively (i.e., trial 1 involves the first pair; trial 2, pairs 1 and 2; trial 3, pairs 1, 2, and 3, etc.). Similarly, the amount of time taken to learn a list is not affected when the list is learned as a series of shorter sublists which are then combined to give the whole list (Postman and Goggin 1964; 1966). Nor does it appear to matter whether the distribution of learning and test trials is determined by the experimenter or is left to the subject; here, too, the amount learned seems to be a simple function of the total time spent on learning (Zacks 1969). Bloom (1974) has extended this finding to the classroom situation, where again there appears to be a clear and simple relationship between time on task and amount learned.

Limits of the Total Time Hypothesis

NOMINAL AND COVERT PRACTICE

While the total time hypothesis does seem to give a good account of a very wide range of results, it is essentially a rule of thumb rather than a law of nature. To give an extreme example: If I present the first item in a 20-word list for 5 minutes and the following 19 words for 1 second each, the subject is unlikely to learn as much as if all words had been presented for an equal amount of time, simply because there is no way in which the 5 minutes on the first word can be efficiently used. What the total time hypothesis says is that subjects are extremely adept at distributing their learning time, often despite the efforts of the experimenter. Zacks points out, for example, that the majority of her subjects spent more time rehearsing difficult items than easy ones, even when presentation time was constant for all items. Like Cooper and Pantle (1967), she points out the need to distinguish between the *nominal* distribution of learning time set by the experimenter and the *covert* distribution actually adopted by the subject. It is what the subject actually does that is crucial, and the experimental constraints are important only insofar as they determine this. Once again, this applies to the classroom as well as the verbal-learning laboratory (Bloom 1974).

CODING

A second constraint on the total time hypothesis is the need to consider the subject's method of learning. For instance, the subject is likely to learn much more of a list of word pairs if he attempts to combine the words constituting each pair into a composite visual image than if he spends the same amount of time repeating them to himself (Paivio 1971c). Verbal material that has been processed in terms of its meaning will generally be recalled better than material processed in terms of its letter structure or sound (Hyde and Jenkins 1969). In short, the total time hypothesis is dependent on this further constraint: the manner of *coding* the material to be learned must be held constant.

NATURE OF THE MATERIAL

The total time hypothesis states that the amount learned is a function of the total time spent learning. This does not mean that the rate of learning is invariant across different types of material, and there is, of course, abundant evidence that this is not so. A detailed consideration of factors influencing rate of learning would be beyond the scope of the present book; however, no consideration of memory could be complete without some discussion of the determinants of the learning rate. The present section will therefore consider briefly some of the factors which influence the learning rate for lists of unrelated verbal material.

Nonsense syllables. Although Ebbinghaus devised the nonsense syllables with the specific aim of minimizing the role of meaning in memory, nevertheless it became increasingly obvious that syllables were not all equally meaningless. Glaze (1928) attempted to measure the meaningfulness of nonsense syllables by presenting each of 2,019 consonant-vowel-consonant syllables (CVCs) to a panel of 15 subjects, who were allowed a limited period of time to state for each syllable whether or not it suggested an English word. Syllables were then classified on the basis of the percentage of subjects producing a response. It has subsequently been shown in many studies that the greater the number of subjects producing an association (i.e., the greater the *association value* of the syllable), the easier it is to learn. Consequently, sequences of syllables like *cef, yim, zoj,* which evoked meaningful associations in none of Glaze's subjects, are very much harder to learn than sequences like *bal, vac, duc,* which evoked responses in all of Glaze's subjects. Paired-associate learning is similarly dependent on meaningfulness, with meaningfulness of the response playing a more important role than that of the stimulus (Cieutat, Stockwell, and Noble 1958).

More recently, Archer (1960) and Noble (1961) have reevaluated the association values of all possible CVC syllables, employing a rather larger sample of subjects and considerably more sophisticated scaling techniques. Other measures which broadly predict the ease with which lists of syllables will be learned are rated ease of pronouncing the syllable, frequency of occurrence of the three letters in the CVC syllable as a sequence in the English language (Underwood and Schulz 1960), and predictability (Baddeley 1963a; 1964). The predictability of a syllable represents the closeness with which its letter structure approximates the letter structure of English; the criterion is based on the frequency of occurrence of each pair of letters making up the syllable. These variables are, of course, all highly correlated; provided that correlations are based on large samples of syllables, there is a very clear relationship between each of them and the rate of learning, although when an attempt is made to correlate performance across individual syllable pairs, the relationship becomes much weaker (Baddeley 1963a).* Performance appears to depend on the subject's ability to bring into play a wide range of possible strategies operating both at the level of phoneme or letter structure and at the deeper level of meaningful associations. Largely as a

---

* As Coleman (1964) and Clark (1973) have pointed out, in order to draw general conclusions about types of material, it is necessary to test for the reliability of effects across material as well as across subjects. For example Baddeley (1963a) studied the recall of pairs of syllables that were matched for predictability, but differed in association value (Glaze 1928), and observed that nearly all subjects found the higher association value pairs easier. However, this was not characteristic of all pairs; there were several inconsistencies, and the difference was not significant when tested across pairs rather than subjects. While most experimenters were prepared to show that mean differences in performance were not due simply to a few atypical subjects, only a few (e.g., Baddeley 1963a; 1964; Coleman 1965) bothered to demonstrate that effects were not attributable to one or two atypical items. This neglect is discussed in detail by Clark (1973), who terms it the *language-as-a-fixed-effect fallacy.*

result of the variability in performance resulting from this complex array of strategies, work using nonsense syllables has become less and less common over the past 10 to 15 years. It seems likely that this trend will continue.

Words. As in the case of nonsense syllables, there is an overall correlation between the mean number of associations evoked by a word and its ease of learning in either a serial list or a paired-associate task (Noble 1952). Similarly, there is a broad correlation between ease of learning and the frequency of occurrence of a word in the English language. However, in a wide range of studies, Paivio (1969) has shown that subjects' ratings of *concreteness,* or the ease with which a word evokes a visual image, provide a much more powerful predictor of ease of learning. Unlike both meaningfulness and familiarity or frequency of occurrence, which affect the response rather than the stimulus, the imageability of the stimulus seems to be much more important than that of the response. This issue, together with the factors determining the ease with which more complex materials (such as prose) are learned, will be discussed in later chapters.

Intra-list similarity. Similarity among the items comprising a list will tend to make learning more difficult, particularly if the retention of order is required. Of course, similarity only influences performance if the subject is coding the material along the dimension in question (i.e., using it to learn the material); if he is ignoring the meaning of the words comprising a list, semantic similarity will not impair learning. Consequently, manipulations of similarity provide a useful technique for investigating which aspects of a word are being used by the subject. If he is coding the material in terms of the sound of the words, items like *court* and *caught* within the same list will produce problems; if he is coding visually, then words like *rough* and *dough* will confuse; and if he is coding in terms of meaning, *big* and *large* will tend to lead to confusions and impaired serial or paired-associate learning (Baddeley 1966*a*; 1966*b*).

LENGTH-DIFFICULTY RELATIONSHIP

A range of experiments from Ebbinghaus onward have shown that the length of the sequence to be learned is critical, with longer sequences taking disproportionately more time. This is illustrated in Figure 2–1, which shows the mean number of seconds per item required to learn sequences of digits as a function of sequence length. Each line is based on a separate subject; all except Lyon (1) were unusually expert in memorizing. The subjects tested by Binet and Muller were "lightning calculators," and even Lyon was very practiced at rote learning. The Lyon (dist) curve represents performance under *distributed practice,* when the list was read only once per day (see section below on distribution of practice). The length-difficulty phenomenon was subsequently studied in some detail by Thurstone (1930), who showed that the amount of additional time required to learn an item increased as the square root of the number of items in the list.

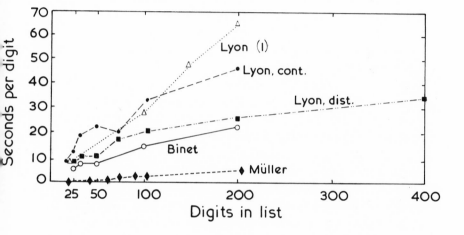

Figure 2–1   Increase in time per item to memorize digit lists of increasing length. Source: R. S. Woodworth, *Experimental Psychology* (New York: Holt, Rinehart and Winston, 1938).

However, although long lists are learned at a disproportionately slow rate, they appear to be better retained than short lists. This effect might be expected in view of the greater amount of practice required to learn a long list than a short one to the same criterion. An experiment by Woodworth (1938, p. 19), however, suggests that this is not the only factor. He presented his subjects with either 5, 10, 20, or 30 pairs of unrelated words at a rate of one pair every 6 seconds. They were then given a further three trials in which they were presented with the stimulus words of each pair and attempted to give the response. After 5 seconds the response was given, and the next stimulus followed. After the third presentation, the percentage recall scores were 100, 91, 84, and 71 for the lists of 5, 10, 20, and 30 pairs, respectively, showing better recall of the shorter lists. However, when subjects were tested again 2 days later, the pattern of recall was reversed, with the lists of 5, 10, 20, and 30 pairs showing mean recall percentages of 4, 16, 36, and 34, respectively, a result which Woodworth attributed to a tendency for the longer lists to be harder and hence to stimulate subjects to find meaningful relationships among the words. Further evidence for the better retention of longer lists has recently been produced by Ceraso (1967), and evidence that lists coded in terms of meaning are better retained has also appeared (e.g., Baddeley 1966a; Baddeley and Levy 1971).

DISTRIBUTION OF PRACTICE

It will be recalled that Lyon required less time per item to learn lists of digits when the list was read once a day than when all the learning was confined to one day (see Figure 2–1). The question of how practice should be distributed to enable a subject to learn most efficiently is a question of obvious practical importance which stimulated much research in the early years of the century. There are in fact two separate, though related, questions, one concerning how large a block of learning trials should be presented at any one session, the other concerning the optimal interval between blocks. A number of early experimenters studied both these questions in the same experiment. Thus Perkins (1914) had her subjects learn a list of 14 nonsense syllables for 16 trials in blocks of 1, 2, 4, or 8 trials, separated by intervals of 1, 2, 3, or 4 days. Retention two weeks later is shown in Figure 2–2, from which it is clear that the fewer trials per block, the better the recall. In contrast, the length of the interval between blocks was not a major factor, with recall percentages of 37, 50, 47, and 43 for intervals of 1, 2, 3, and 4 days, respectively. Although Perkins's experiment was based on only four subjects, the results are consistent with other studies. Thus, the tendency of large blocks of trials to produce slow learning has been shown by a wide range of studies, from Ebbinghaus's investigation of his own nonsense syllable learning ability to Yerkes's (1907) study of maze learning in the dancing mouse.

Data on the inter-trial interval effect are less consistent. Although Perkins's data suggest that a 2-day interval is best, an earlier study by Piéron (1913), using a single, well-practiced subject, found an improvement when the inter-trial interval was increased from 30 seconds to 10 minutes but no difference between 10 minutes and 2 days. The early work in this field therefore suggests a clear and marked effect of block size and a more variable and complex effect of inter-trial interval.

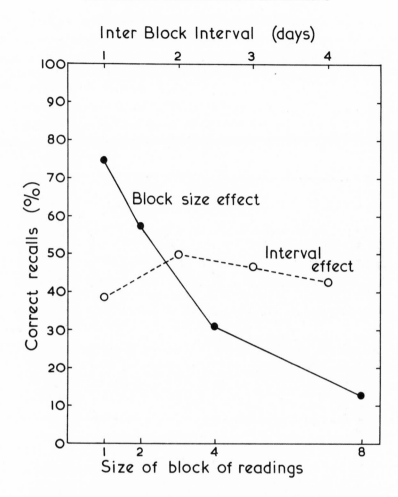

Figure 2–2   Retention of lists of 14 nonsense syllables as a function of the number of list presentations per trial block and the interval between successive blocks. Source: N. L. Perkins, The value of distributed repetitions in rote learning, *British Journal of Psychology* 7 (1914): 253–261.

Curiously enough, modern work has been concerned almost exclusively with the less consistent inter-trial interval effect, so much so that the trial block effect has virtually been forgotten. The greater interest that developed in inter-trial interval effects in the 1940s and 1950s probably stems largely from its apparent implications for Clark Hull's theory of learning, which included two inhibitory or fatigue components, Ir and sIr, which seemed likely to explain inter-trial interval effects very neatly (Hull 1943).

The most popular technique for studying these effects employs the pursuit rotor, a rotating turntable with a small brass disk in one section. The subject is given a rod with a joint in the middle and is instructed to try to keep the tip of the rod in contact with the rotating brass disk, success being measured automatically by a clock that indicates the amount of time on target. A typical result is shown in Figure 2–3. When given a sequence of several trials on the pursuit rotor in quick succession, subjects show rapid improvement on the first few

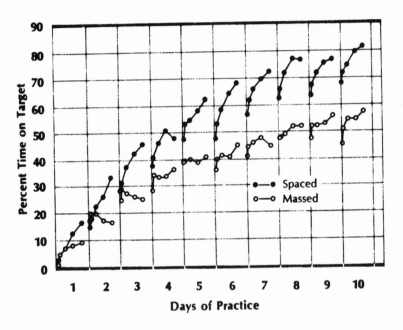

Figure 2–3   Performance on a pursuit rotor under massed and distributed practice. Source: R. S. Woodworth, *Experimental Psychology* (New York: Holt, Rinehart and Winston, 1938), p. 788.

trials but relatively little on later trials. They are then allowed to rest for a few minutes; on the very first trial of subsequent learning, they show much better performance than on any previous trial (the reminiscence effect), as if their earlier performance had been artificially depressed by fatigue. An ingenious experiment by Adams (1955), however, shows that this effect is not simply related to muscular fatigue, since it does not disappear if, during the interval, the subjects are required to observe the performance of a fellow subject and report when he is off target.

Despite its reliability and apparent simplicity, the reminiscence effect proved remarkably difficult to explain convincingly. It has become clear that although short inter-trial intervals led to poorer performance at the time, they did not lead to impaired motor skill learning as tested by performance after a delay, and in recent years there has been a general loss of interest in the topic (see Bilodeau and Bilodeau 1961 for an excellent discussion). Apart from the work of Eysenck (1964), who was interested in relating the size of the reminiscence effect to individual differences in temperament, distribution of practice has virtually ceased to be a live issue in the field of motor skills.

The second area in which inter-trial interval has been investigated in some detail is that of verbal learning. Hovland (1938) studied the serial learning of a sequence of nonsense syllables with inter-trial intervals of either 6 or 126 seconds. During the longer interval, subjects were required to name colors to discourage them from using the time to rehearse the list. When trials were massed (6 seconds between trials), learning took twice as many trials as when they were distributed (126 seconds between trials). This result has been followed up by Underwood in a marathon series of studies extending over more than a decade. Despite the apparent robustness of Hovland's result, the effect of inter-trial interval on verbal learning has proved highly unreliable, and in the words of Underwood, Ekstrand, and Keppel (1964), in "Studies in Distributed Practice Number 23," p. 212, "It must be concluded that the particular situations or conditions which will produce a facilitation by distributed practice in paired-associate learning still remain obscure." Fortunately, the 23 studies have produced a good deal of valuable information on topics other than the elusive inter-trial interval effect.

In the last few years there has been considerable interest in a rather different phenomenon which, using a task in which subjects were presented for one trial only with five pairs of words, has also been termed the distributed practice effect. Peterson (1966) showed that if the *same* pair of words is presented on two separate occasions during the single learning trial, the greater the separation between the two presentations, the higher the probability of subsequent recall. Hence, presenting the repeated items as the second and the fifth pairs leads to better retention than presenting them as the fourth and fifth pairs. This phenomenon is usually termed the *lag effect,* and a number of hypotheses have been proposed to account for it. They are reviewed by Melton (1970), who suggests that the phenomenon does appear to present an exception to the total time hypothesis, a view which is supported in a subsequent review by Hintzman (1974), who discusses seven different interpretations of the effect. He concludes that the phenomenon represents a very reliable effect which holds across a wide range of materials and test procedures but which is still open to a range of possible explanations.

During the period of intensive investigation of the inter-trial interval effect, the effect of the size of the trial block was largely ignored and, judging from many recent textbooks, appears to have been forgotten. Two exceptions were both experiments aimed at answering practical questions about job training. A study carried out by Keller during World War II was not published but is quoted by Woodworth and Schlosberg (1954, p. 812). Subjects were given a course in which they normally spent 7 hours a day for 5 weeks learning Morse code, followed by 3 weeks devoted to other topics. When learning time was reduced from 7 to 4 hours per day, thus allowing the other topics to be learned during the 5-week period, the level of performance at the end of the period was just as good, and after the full 8 weeks it was considerably better.

A more recent unpublished study by Baddeley and Longman on learning to type produced a similar result. With the advent of letter-sorting machines operated by a typewriter keyboard, the British Post Office was faced with the problem of training 10,000 postmen to type. Since these postmen could learn to type while performing at least part of their regular jobs, the Post Office had the choice of using each training facility either to train operators intensively a few at a time or to train larger numbers of operators more gradually. While the pre-1940 literature suggested the latter, since it would involve greater distribution of practice, the more recent literature (based principally on experiments which have manipulated inter-trial interval) seemed to indicate that distribution of practice might be principally a laboratory phenomenon occurring only under closely specified conditions involving simple laboratory tasks, and that even under these conditions its effects might be very short-lived. The dangers of extrapolating to a practical problem were stated very forcefully by Bilodeau and Bilodeau (1961, p. 263): "An aggravation to anyone who has varied distribution of practice on a standard piece of [laboratory] hardware is the knowledge that somewhere, someone is using his findings to urge an innocent consultee to distribute the practice of his trainees as widely as possible." Further work was clearly needed.

An experiment was therefore run using two lengths of lesson, 1 and 2 hours, and two frequencies of lesson, once or twice per day, giving four conditions, all of which were operationally feasible so far as the Post Office was concerned. Four groups of 18 postmen were trained, one group for one session of 1 hour a day (the 1 × 1 group), one for two sessions of 1 hour a day (the 2 × 1 group), a third for one session of 2 hours (the 1 × 2 group), and a fourth for two sessions of 2 hours (the 2 × 2 group). It was originally intended to train each group for 60 hours, which on a 5-day week schedule would take 12 weeks for the 1 × 1 group, 6 weeks for the 1 × 2 and 2 × 1 groups, and 3 weeks for the 2 × 2 group. Since level of performance after 60 hours was not so high as had been hoped, a further 20 hours training was given to all except the 1 × 1 group, for which the further 4 weeks of training was not practicable. The results are shown in Figure 2–4, which shows mean typing rate (in terms of correct keystrokes per minute) as a function of number of

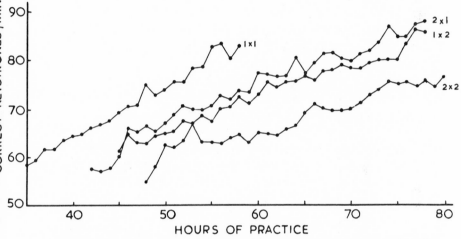

Rate of Acquisition of Typing Skill for the Various Training Schedules

Figure 2–4 Rate of acquisition of typing skill for a range of training schedules: 1 × 1 = 1 session of 1 hour per day, 2 × 1 = 2 sessions of 1 hour per day, 1 × 2 = 1 session of 2 hours per day, and 2 × 2 = 2 sessions of 2 hours per day. Source: Based on A. D. Baddeley and D. J. A. Longman, The influence of length and frequency of training session on rate of learning to type, unpublished (Cambridge: Medical Research Council Applied Psychology Unit, 1966).

hours of practice. The point at which each learning curve begins represents the time taken to learn the location of the keys sufficiently well to be able to touch-type material using the whole alphabet. There is a clear and statistically significant tendency for performance to be best in the 1-hour-a-day group, both in terms of time taken to learn the keyboard and in subsequent typing speed. Note also that the level of performance after 80 hours at 4 hours a day is lower than after 60 hours at 1 hour a day. The poorer performance of the 2 × 2 group was also reflected in a significantly higher rate of uncorrected errors. Finally, unlike the inter-trial interval effects discussed earlier, the inferior performance of the 2 × 2 group was not a temporary effect, since it continued to appear when retention of the skill was tested after layoffs of 1, 3, and 9 months, as Figure 2–5 shows. Levels of performance of the 2 × 1 and 1 × 2 groups were intermediate between those of the other two and did not differ

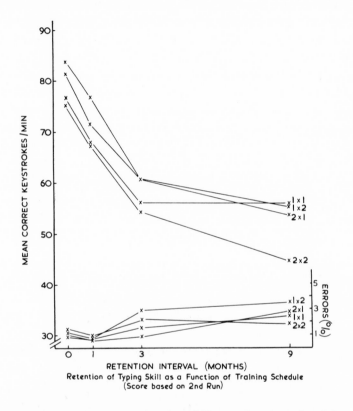

Retention of Typing Skill as a Function of Training Schedule
(Score based on 2nd Run)

Figure 2–5 Retention of typing skill as a function of training schedules in Figure 2–4. Warm-up effects are eliminated by omitting the subject's first run. Source: Based on A. D. Baddeley and D. J. A. Longman, The influence of length and frequency of training session on rate of learning to type, unpublished (Cambridge: Medical Research Council Applied Psychology Unit, 1966).

significantly from each other, suggesting that the crucial variable in this study is not length of session per se but rather the amount of training

28

given in a day. A similar observation had in fact been made by Keller from his code-learning study.

A number of conclusions can be drawn from the touch-typing experiment. First, it suggests that amount of training per day is a major variable which does not require the sheltered conditions of the laboratory to evidence itself. Note, however, that this does not mean that practice should always be distributed: measured in terms of number of days required to learn to type, an hour a day was least efficient, since it took the 1 × 1 group almost 3 months to reach the level attained by the 2 × 2 group in 4 weeks. The *optimal* distribution of practice will always depend on the operational constraints of the training situation, whether it is necessary to train people quickly or, if not, whether the time saved by reducing the length of the daily lesson can be used for other aspects of training. Morale is another factor to be considered: the 1 × 1 group became dissatisfied with having to spend 12 weeks acquiring a skill that others were learning in 4. Finally, of course, what is optimal for postmen learning to type may not, for example, be optimal for schoolchildren learning arithmetic, although the consistency of results across a range of both tasks and species (Woodworth 1938) suggests that the broad pattern of results will be the same.

If, as these results suggest, there is some basic limitation to the daily rate at which learning can take place, it is clearly important to know more about it. Is it, for example, different for different types of learning? Does the fact that one is learning to type affect the rate at which one can concurrently learn other things? If so, does efficiency of concurrent learning depend on the similarity of the things being learned? The implications of this type of question for education are clearly very great and were almost certainly recognized by the early investigators. Why, then, should subsequent efforts have been devoted almost exclusively to the smaller, less reliable, and (from a practical viewpoint) less important variable of inter-trial interval?

I think there are several reasons. First, inter-trial interval is a very much easier variable to study in the laboratory. Training experiments are laborious, expensive, and hard to control, whereas the inter-trial interval effect can be studied under rigidly controlled conditions with none of the problems associated with running a long-term training program. Basic research on optimal training rates could, of course, be done relatively easily with animals, as in many of the earlier studies. This approach was probably killed off by the development of learning theories which appeared to offer much more exciting problems to the animal psychologist in the 1940s. Furthermore, following the development of Hullian learning theory (Hull 1943), the inter-trial interval effect appeared to present a soluble problem of theoretical interest. To concentrate on such problems is, of course, a sensible strategy. It is unfortunate that in this case the problem turned out to be neither readily soluble nor theoretically productive. It is doubly unfortunate that the mass of relatively unproductive experimentation that followed effectively buried the more basic question of what limits the long-term rate of learning.

This limitation is one of the most obvious differences between the way information is registered in people and in electronic computers. If I want a computer to "remember" the sequence 7915642813, a single presentation will ensure error-free storage, provided I present the material in an appropriate form (i.e., the computer can "read" it) and that its memory store is not full. If I want a person to remember the sequence, it is likely to take a great deal longer, and retention will be much less reliable. In other words, learning is hard work or, if the learning situation has been well designed, hard play. Why should this be?

Current psychological theories have remarkably little to say about this obvious and important feature of learning. The nearest approach to an answer comes from experiments on the physiological basis of memory. These suggest that long-term learning demands permanent changes at a cellular or molecular level; such changes take time to *consolidate*. The idea that learning is limited by the rate at which memory traces consolidate dates back at least to Müller and Pilzecker (1900). Its subsequent influence has been much greater in the area of physiological psychology, but in recent years it has shown signs of becoming more important in the study of normal human memory, as the next chapter will show.

The Limits of Memory: Storing and Consolidating the Memory Trace

Traumatic Amnesia

A BLOW on the head leading to loss of consciousness is frequently followed by retrograde amnesia, a loss of memory for the events leading up to the blow. In a severe concussion, this amnesia will at first extend to events long before the accident; gradually, however, more and more is remembered, until finally everything except the events immediately preceding the accident can be recalled. The following case history, taken from Russell (1959), is a good example:

> A green-keeper, aged 22, was thrown from his motor-cycle in August, 1933. There was a bruise in the left frontal region and slight bleeding

from the left ear, but no fracture was seen on X-ray examination. A week after the accident he was able to converse sensibly, and the nursing staff considered that he had fully recovered consciousness. When questioned, however, he said that the date was February 1922, and that he was a schoolboy. He had no recollection of five years spent in Australia, and two years in this country working on a golf course. Two weeks after the injury he remembered the five years spent in Australia, and remembered returning to this country; the past two years were, however, a complete blank as far as his memory was concerned. Three weeks after the injury he returned to the village where he had been working for two years. Everything looked strange, and he had no recollection of ever having been there before. He lost his way on more than one occasion. Still feeling a stranger to the district he returned to work; he was able to do his work satisfactorily, but had difficulty in remembering what he had actually done during the day. About ten weeks after the accident the events of the past two years were gradually recollected and finally he was able to remember everything up to within a few minutes of the accident (Russell 1959, pp. 69–70).

Why should the few moments immediately before the accident never be recalled? Not simply because they are followed by a painful and traumatic experience, since bullet wounds in the head often do not cause this lasting amnesia. Nor is it the case that the patient fails to remember because he never took in the information necessary to answer questions about the accident.

This is illustrated by a study by Yarnell and Lynch (1970), in which American college football players who had been "dinged" (concussed) were questioned as soon as they could speak about what had happened. In each case, they could provide this information, together with the name of the particular play that had preceded the incident (e.g., "32 pop"). Yet, asked the same question 3 to 20 minutes later, they were completely unable to recall any of the relevant information. Unfortunately, only four cases were reported, no control group of players disabled by nonconcussive injuries was included,* and a more thorough investigation is obviously required. However, assuming the amnesia is associated with concussion rather than the mnemonic capacities of American football players, the evidence is consistent with the view that the information was registered in some temporary form which failed to be *consolidated,* or transferred into a more permanent form of storage.

The attempt to investigate this process of consolidation or transfer has generated a great deal of research, some of which will be outlined below. This is a difficult area to survey because it is characterized by

* A subsequent report (Lynch and Yarnell 1973) did include an appropriate control group.

a wide variety of approaches which, although concerned with a common problem, appear to have relatively few links. The situation is further complicated by the lack of agreement within the various areas as to which techniques are valid and which are subject to experimental artifacts. However, since I consider the question of consolidation to be an important one, potentially of considerable relevance to the cognitive psychologist, the present chapter is offered as a tentative survey of some of the work in this field. It represents the efforts of a nonexpert outsider to make sense of an area in which techniques are probably not yet stable enough to allow a clear overall picture.

Electroconvulsive Shock and Memory

Although concussion may produce dramatic effects on memory, it is not a convenient experimental technique. Quite apart from the difficulty in recruiting subjects, blows on the head are likely to have effects well beyond that of loss of memory. A technique which has better-controlled though somewhat similar effects on memory is that of electroconvulsive shock (ECS), in which a brief electric current is passed through the head, generally producing a cerebral seizure and temporary loss of consciousness. This technique, which is termed electroconvulsive therapy (ECT) when used to treat a range of nervous disorders, tends to be followed by a period during which patients show slightly poorer immediate memory and considerably poorer delayed memory for new material (Crönholm 1969). As in the case of concussion, the patient is said to be unable to recall events immediately preceding the shock, and again the extent of the preceding amnesia shrinks progressively. This is illustrated in Figure 3–1, which shows the results of an experiment by Crönholm and Lagergren (1959) in which the patient was given a three- or four-digit number to remember 5, 15, or 60 seconds before ECT. The graph shows the probability of recalling the number at various times after the shock. Note the gradual improvement over time, presumably reflecting shrinkage of the amnesia; note also that the closer the presentation was to the ECT, the poorer the retention at all delays. Unfortunately, the patient's activity between presentation of the number and ECT was apparently not controlled, so that it is impossible to discount the possibility that retention at 60 seconds before ECT is better because more rehearsal was possible. Nor are there adequate control

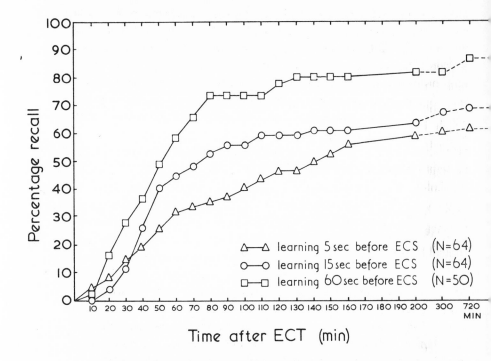

Time after ECT (min)

Figure 3–1 Cumulative percentages of patients recalling a number learned before ECT as a function of the time elapsing between ECT and test. Source: B. Crönholm and A. Lagergren, Memory disturbances after electro-convulsive therapy. 3. An experimental study of retrograde amnesia after electro-shock treatment, *Acta Psychiatrica Neurologia Scandinavica* 34 (1959): 283–310.

groups, so that we know neither how well a patient who had not had ECT would have remembered the digits, nor how much of the apparent shrinkage in amnesia is due to the gradual dissipation of the confusional state following ECT, rather than to a specific memory change. An experiment in which the patient performed a task involving recall of material learned long before (e.g., his own telephone number) might have thrown light on this question.

It is very difficult to do well-controlled human experiments in this field. The subjects are invariably suffering from some sort of mental disturbance, and if the ECT is successful, it produces changes in mood which may influence performance indirectly. Furthermore, the experience itself may be emotionally charged, which in turn will influence performance, as will whatever drugs the patient is taking at the time. Finally, the prime concern must be with the patient's welfare, and this is not always compatible with the degree of experimental control that is usual in laboratory studies.

An obvious alternative to the study of human patients is to use animals, and many experiments have indeed taken this approach. Perhaps the most common technique is to place an animal (usually a rat) on a platform a few inches from the floor of a box. When he steps down, an electric shock is delivered to his feet through the floor. After only one such trial a rat will show evidence of learning by hesitating much longer before stepping off the platform. When the foot shock is followed immediately by ECS, the rat appears not to have learned the association, and on the next trial he steps down just as quickly as if no foot shock had been given. This technique seems ideal for plotting the time course of memory trace consolidation, since with one-trial learning one knows exactly when the learning takes place. As the interval between foot shock and ECS is extended, the time available for trace consolidation will increase, and with it the probability of learning the association between stepping down and foot shock. When the interval is great enough for complete consolidation, no amnesia should occur, since the consolidated memory trace is assumed to be no longer vulnerable to ECS. Unfortunately, however, experiments have produced widely differing time constants, ranging from a few seconds (Chorover and Schiller 1965) through several hours (Kopp, Bohdanecky, and Jarvik 1967) to more than a month (Braun, Patton, and Barnes 1952; Stone and Bakhtiari 1956), while Lewis, Miller, and Misanin (1969) found that prior familiarization with the experimental apparatus reduced the period during which learning was vulnerable to ECS to less than 0.5 second.

A further difficulty is raised by the results of Hine and Paolino (1970), who simultaneously studied both the overt behavior and the heart-rate response of rats in a situation involving one-trial learning of a shock avoidance response. When the shock was immediately followed by ECS, the avoidance response was not learned. However, although these animals behaved like unshocked control rats, they gave the same heart-rate response as rats given shock without ECS, suggesting that the rats had learned to be afraid but were not able to make the appropriate response. Hine and Paolino suggest that this may be because the learning of the emotional fear response is so rapid as to be complete before the ECS is delivered.

The simple view that ECS prevents the storage of the memory trace, however, has been challenged in recent years by a range of new phenomena. Zinkin and Miller (1967) observed that although ECS caused amnesia on the first test trial, animals that were repeatedly tested began to remember. While there has been some difficulty in replicating this study (Luttges and McGaugh 1967), a related effect was observed by Koppenaal, Jagoda, and Cruce (1967) and by Riccio and Stikes (1969). In the Riccio and Stikes study, one-trial learning was immediately followed by rapid cooling of the rat. This grossly reduced retention in a test 24 hours later. However, when a second test trial was given, the animal showed as much retention as the uncooled control rats, indicating that the response had been learned but that cooling had in some way inhibited performance. Lewis, Misanin, and Miller (1968) showed that it was not even necessary for the second "reminder" to be a complete learning trial. They first trained their rats to avoid shock, then followed this with ECS, and having observed the standard ECS amnesia effect, then delivered a foot shock to the animal just prior to the test, but outside the test environment. When the animal was tested, the amnesia appeared to have dissipated. In subsequent studies, it was shown that the reminder need not be identical with the original aversive training stimulus; Miller and Springer (1972) trained rats to avoid immersion in ice water, and found that amnesia induced by ECS was dissipated when foot shock was used as a reminder. It appears, however, that the reminder must be a broadly similar stimulus to that involved in learning, since a habit learned for an appetitive reward was not reinstated by foot shock, although it did recover when an appetitive stimulus or exposure to the training apparatus were used as reminders (Miller, Springer, and Vega 1972).

On the basis of these and other results, Miller and Springer (1973; 1974) suggest that ECS affects not the storage of the memory trace but its retrievability. They use the analogy of a library and compare the memory trace to a book which is shelved very rapidly, but which is only catalogued relatively slowly. They suggest that ECS disrupts the filing system and hence makes it more difficult to find the appropriate item.

This view is countered by advocates of a consolidation interpretation who argue that "reminders" influence behavior by enhancing a weakened trace (Cherkin 1972; Gold and King 1974; McGaugh and Gold 1974), although just how such enhancement operates is far from clear. What is clear, however, is that the results of studies using ECS can no longer be regarded as providing unequivocal evidence of memory consolidation. The question is no longer one of whether any alternative to consolidation is possible but rather whether a consolidation interpretation is still viable.

Drugs and Memory

It has long been known that certain drugs may affect memory. In some cases the effect may be indirect; for example, sodium amytal is used in cases of "battle shock" to help the patient recall the traumatic incident that triggered his neurosis. The effect is indirect, since the drug acts by relaxing and tranquilizing the patient so as to allow him to explore an experience which is too charged with emotion to be handled without such help. As such, the drug presumably affects retrieval rather than the storage or consolidation of the memory trace.

Alcohol. One drug which, according to popular myth, does impair consolidation is alcohol; after a hard night's drinking, the drinker is assumed to have a very "thick" head the next morning and no memory of the previous night's revelries. One reason for this is that learning is to some extent state-dependent; in other words, recall is impaired if the stimulus situation is different from that experienced during learning. Since the subject was drunk when he experienced the events of the prior evening and is (presumably) sober when he tries to recall them next morning, the contextual stimulus situation will have changed, making recall more difficult (see p. 72 for a more detailed discussion). If this is the case, then getting the subject drunk again should improve his recall. Goodwin, Powell, Bremer, Hoine, and Stern (1969) have shown this is indeed the case; what you learn when drunk is best recalled when drunk.

It has often been suggested that, in addition to this state-dependent failure to retrieve, alcohol may have an adverse effect on consolidation of the memory trace. A recent study by Goodwin, Othmer, Halikas, and Freemon (1970) attempted to investigate this by recruiting ten drinkers from the local employment exchange, all being able and willing to drink more than a pint of whiskey in a few hours; perhaps not surprisingly, eight of the ten were alcoholics. The tests, which were limited to what a drunken subject was willing and able to do, involved simple arithmetic and other measures. Questions about the subject's early life were used to test remote memory; a child's toy, shown for a minute, and a minute-long scene from an erotic film were used to test more recent memory. Recall of the toy and the film was perfect in all subjects tested 2 minutes later, indicating that the information had been registered in at least a temporary form, and in five of the ten subjects recall was also intact after 30 minutes. When tested 24 hours later, these subjects recalled 60 percent of the items presented (control subjects recalled 80 percent) and recognized the remaining 40 percent. The other five subjects, although able to perform mental arithmetic, answer questions about their early life, and remember items after 2 minutes, all reached a point during drinking at which items could not be recalled after 30 minutes. Since the subjects were still drunk, this was presumably not a state-dependent retrieval failure; and since such items were never recalled or recognized the following day, it seems likely that no long-term memory trace had been formed. These subjects were all alcoholics who reported frequent previous blackouts during drinking.

Protein-synthesis inhibitors. It is possible to attack the question of consolidation of the memory trace more analytically with animal experiments using drugs which have a known effect. For example, it has been suggested that long-term memory storage depends on the synthesis of proteins in the neurons concerned, and experimenters have tested this hypothesis by injecting substances which are known to inhibit protein synthesis.

A series of experiments of this type is described by Barondes (1970), who injected the brains of mice with either a saline solution as a control or with a protein-synthesis inhibitor, acetoxycycloheximide. Five hours later he taught the mice a simple maze until they ran correctly three times out of four. Retention of the habit was subsequently tested after varying intervals, ranging from 3 hours to 7 days. The animals injected with the protein-synthesis inhibitor performed normally after 3 hours but showed significantly poorer retention at all delays of 6 hours or more. Barondes interprets this in terms of a short-term trace, lasting 3 to 6 hours, which does not depend on protein synthesis. It is assumed to serve as a template or pattern for the long-term trace, for which protein synthesis is essential.

In a further experiment, the rate of development of the long-term trace was studied by varying the time at which the inhibitor was injected. Mice who learned a simple maze to avoid a mild electric shock were injected with a protein-synthesis inhibitor at times ranging from 5 hours before learning to 24 hours after. Retention was then tested 7 days later. Animals injected either before or immediately after training showed impaired memory, but when the injection followed learning by 30 minutes or more, memory was not affected, suggesting that the protein synthesis necessary for a long-term trace in this situation is complete within half an hour. Hence, Barondes's results suggest the existence of two types of memory, one lasting for 3–6 hours, the other a more long-term system, with a transfer process based on protein synthesis which is complete within 30 minutes.

Barondes's explanation of his results was based on the assumed role of protein synthesis in memory consolidation. However, subsequent studies have shown that amnesia associated with protein-synthesis inhibitors may show both spontaneous recovery (Quartermain and McEwan 1970) and reminder effects (Quartermain, McEwan, and Azmitia 1970), suggesting that, as in the case of ECS, the amnesia may result from failure to retrieve a trace rather than failure to store or consolidate it. Furthermore, as McGaugh and Gold (1974) point out, it is still far from clear that the pharmacological agents used necessarily influenced memory through their effect on proteins rather than, for example, neurotransmitters.

Consolidation-enhancing drugs. A third method of investigating memory trace consolidation is to try to improve retention by using drugs which enhance consolidation. In one such experiment, Greenough and McGaugh (1965) gave rats two learning trials on a maze, followed a week later by five retention trials. The rats were injected with strychnine sulfate, a central nervous system stimulant, either 2 days before learning, immediately afterward, or 2 days before the retention test. The injection facilitated retention, but only when it immediately followed learning, as would be expected if its effect was to improve trace consolidation or transfer. An excellent discussion of alternative hypotheses, together with further experimental evidence, is given by McGaugh and Dawson (1971). This article includes experiments investigating the effect of delay of injection on subsequent retention. Maximum facilitation of memory occurred when the injection immediately followed learning, for each of a range of stimulants; but the longest delay at which facilitation still occurred varied from an hour with strychnine to less than 15 minutes with *d*-amphetamine, suggesting that this technique does not provide a simple estimate of the time taken for a memory trace to consolidate. A similar lack of consistency was, of course, found in studies using ECS.

A further link with the effects of ECS comes from studies showing that the adverse effects of ECS can be minimized by the injection of a central nervous system stimulant, such as strychnine, either before or even up to 3 hours after ECS (McGaugh and Hart 1973). This suggests that ECS may prevent consolidation by interfering with protein synthesis, while having no effect on the temporary trace, which, according to previously described experiments by Barondes, acts as a template for the more long-term trace. Further evidence for such a view comes from experiments by Essman (1970), who has shown that ECS inhibits the brain's production of RNA, a protein molecule which is often assumed to be necessary for the formation of long-term memory traces.

McGaugh and Dawson suggest tentatively that drugs that facilitate consolidation may do so by increasing the animal's level of arousal. The concept of arousal has been used very widely in psychology in recent years. It is assumed to reflect the animal's level of alertness, and to be associated with electrophysiological activity in the reticular formation of the brain. In support of their suggestion, McGaugh and Dawson cite evidence that retention is enhanced if learning is followed by electrical stimulation of the reticular formation, while disruption of memory occurs following lesions of the reticular formation. At present, the evidence is very far from conclusive, but an arousal hypothesis does have its attractions, particularly in view of the evidence for an effect of arousal on normal human memory described later in the chapter.

Consolidation and Synaptic Transmission

Some of the most intriguing evidence for consolidation has come from recent work on the role of the synapse in memory. The idea that learning and memory might be based on changes in conduction across synapses, the junctions between successive neurons, is an old one. Only recently, however, has knowledge of the biochemistry of synaptic conduction developed to a point at which it has been possible to test the hypothesis. In order to understand this work, it is first necessary to know a little about synaptic transmission.

The process of transmission is outlined in Figure 3–2. A nerve impulse releases a transmitter substance, acetylcholine, at the synapse; this substance causes transmission by stimulating the postsynaptic membrane. If too little acetylcholine is emitted, the nerve impulse will not be transmitted; if too much, a synaptic block in transmission occurs. In the normal course of events, the acetylcholine is rapidly destroyed by the enzyme cholinesterase. However, this process can be prevented by inactivating the cholinesterase with such anticholinesterase drugs as physostigmine and diisopropyl fluorophosphate (DFP). These inhibit

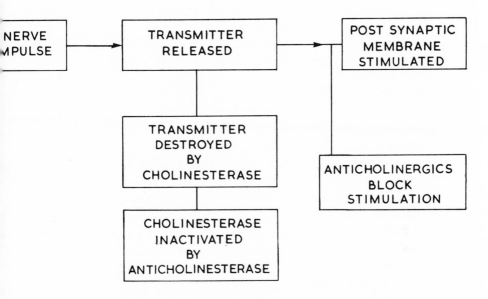

Figure 3–2   The process of transmission across the synapse. The nerve impulse releases the transmitter substance, acetylcholine, which, if present in the right amount, stimulates the post-synaptic membrane. If too little is present, stimulation does not occur; if too much is present, stimulation is blocked. The level of transmitter substance is influenced by the enzyme cholinesterase, which destroys the transmitter. If the cholinesterase is inactivated by an anticholinesterase drug, it can no longer destroy the transmitter. Finally, the process may be blocked at the post-synaptic membrane by means of anticholinergic drugs, which occupy the receptor sites at which the transmitter substance normally stimulates the membrane.

the effects of cholinesterase, thus indirectly preventing the breakdown of acetylcholine. This will increase the probability of transmission across the synapse if the amount of cholinesterase is relatively low but will have the opposite effect at high levels, when the increase in acetylcholine makes synaptic blocking more likely.

Just as the effective amount of the transmitter substance, acetylcholine, can be *increased* by means of anticholinesterase drugs, so its effective amount can be *decreased* by means of anticholinergics like scopolamine and atropine. These have their effect by occupying the receptor sites at which cholinesterase normally stimulates the post-synaptic membrane. If these sites are occupied by an anticholinergic drug, postsynaptic stimulation cannot occur; hence, the nerve impulse is not transmitted across the synapse.

Evidence for the importance of cholinesterase in learning and memory has been accumulating since the 1950s. Perhaps the most impressive set of results in this area comes from the experiments of Deutsch. In the first of these (Deutsch, Hamburg, and Dahl 1966), the destruction of acetylcholine was reduced by means of the anticholinesterase DFP, which was injected into the brains of rats that had learned to choose, to a criterion of 10 successive correct responses, the illuminated arm of a simple Y maze in order to escape from an electrified floor grid. They were injected with either DFP or an inert control substance after 30 minutes, 1 day, 2 days, 3 days, 5 days, or 14 days and were then required to relearn the maze 24 hours after the injection. DFP significantly impaired retention after the 30-minute delay and after the longer delays of 5 and 14 days. It had no effect on retention after 1, 2, or 3 days. Comparable results, obtained with a different anticholinesterase drug, physostigmine (Deutsch and Leibowitz 1966), and with food reward rather than escape from electric shock (Wiener and Deutsch 1968), are also shown in Figure 3–3. Similar results have been obtained by Hamburg (1967) and by Biederman (1970).

Deutsch interprets these results in terms of consolidation theory. He suggests that the amount of the transmitter substance present at the relevant synapses at first decreases between 30 minutes and 1 day and then gradually increases. Because of the high degree of learning, the effective increase in transmitter level produced by DFP will lead to synaptic blocking and hence to poorer apparent retention.

This somewhat counterintuitive interpretation can be tested by reducing the level of performance to a point at which facilitation rather than blocking should occur. This was done by extending the delay period to 28 days, by which time control animals were known to show considerable forgetting. Four groups of rats were tested as before, except that retention was tested after either 14 days or 28 days, with injection with either DFP or the control substance, peanut oil, preceding the test. After 14 days the controls required an average of five trials to relearn the maze, while the DFP group required about 44 trials. After 28 days, however, the picture was dramatically reversed: the control animals needed 45 relearning trials, while the DFP group needed less than 15 trials. Comparable facilitation of a partially forgotten habit has been shown in an appetitive reinforcement situation by Wiener and Deutsch (1968) and by Squire (1970) with physostigmine. Using pigeons,

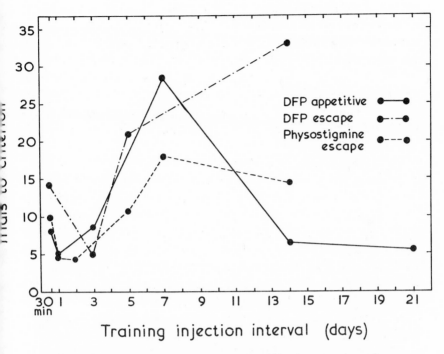

Training injection interval (days)

Figure 3-3   Effect of anticholinesterase injection on memories of different ages, as shown in three separate experiments. Trials to criterion during retest are plotted against the time which elapsed between retest and original learning. A larger number of trials to criterion during retest signifies a greater amnesia. The time between injection and retest was constant. The differences past the 7-day point probably represent different rates of forgetting. Source: J. A. Deutsch, The cholinergic synapse and the site of memory, *Science* 174 (1971), Fig. 1. Copyright 1971 by the American Association for the Advancement of Science. Reprinted by permission.

Biederman (1970) showed facilitation after 28 days of a partially learned discrimination of the orientation of a line, while finding no facilitation of an overlearned color discrimination. It is worth noting, however, that both the blocking and the facilitation effects are temporary and disappear as the injected drug wears off.

The experiments so far have studied the effect of increasing the level of the transmitter substance, acetylcholine. If the observed effects were indeed mediated by changes in synaptic transmission and were not merely the result of a chance side effect of the drug, it should prove possible to produce the opposite effects by means of anticholinergics, which *reduce* the probability of transmission of the nerve impulse by occupying postsynaptic receptor sites. Two experiments have been conducted with the drug scopolamine, one involving escape from shock, the other, food reward. In direct contrast to the anticholinesterase studies, performance was impaired by injections after delays of 1 or 3 days, but not after delays of 30 minutes or of 7 or 14 days. As predicted, reducing the effective level of acetylcholine produced results which were the mirror image of those produced by raising the acetylcholine level (J. A. Deutsch 1971).

All the experiments so far described are consistent with two assumptions: first, that the level of synaptic transmission is a crucial factor in memory and, second, that this level changes over time, decreasing between 30 seconds and 1 day, then increasing after 3 days, and beginning to decline again at some point between 14 and 28 days. If this is so, it should be reflected in simple retention scores. Huppert and Deutsch (1969) showed that when ceiling effects caused by overlearning are avoided, such a fluctuation in retention of a maze habit by rats does indeed occur, with rats taking only half as many trials to reach criterion after a delay of 7 or 10 days as they took after 1 or 3 days. A number of studies with similar results carried out in the early years of this century are cited in Deutsch (1971).

For the nonphysiological psychologist, one of the most attractive features of Deutsch's work is his use of the physiological techniques just described to ask questions of more general theoretical significance. One of these concerns the problem of whether learning involves a gradual increment in the strength of a *single* connection over a series of trials or an increase in the *number* of all-or-none connections as learning proceeds. On an incremental strength hypothesis, degree of training should increase the acetylcholine level of the synapse concerned, making it more susceptible to blocking by DFP as learning proceeds. No such effect would be expected if learning simply increased the number of synapses involved and left the acetylcholine level of already formed connections unchanged. The effect of anticholinesterase drugs on the retention of poorly learned and overlearned habits was studied in three experiments (see Deutsch 1971). All showed a clear facilitation of the partially learned habit, which produced much better retention than with the overlearned habit, a result giving clear support to the incremental hypothesis.

These techniques were also used to investigate the process underlying the extinction of a response. When an animal learns a response for a reward which is then withdrawn, does the response diminish because the underlying synaptic connection is weakened or because an alternative response is learned? This was investigated by comparing the effects of the anticholinesterase drug physostigmine on a habit learned 7 days before and extinguished either immediately or 4 days after learning. It is known that physostigmine blocks the retention of a well-learned habit after 7 days but improves retention of a weak habit. If extinction causes a direct weakening of the learned habit, physostigmine should enhance retention in both conditions. If, on the other hand, extinction involves the learning of a new and separate habit, the two conditions should differ. When both learning and extinction occurred 7 days before, both should be equally inhibited, and relearning should be relatively unaffected by the injection of physostigmine. When extinction occurred 4 days after learning, the original habit should be inhibited by the drug, while the later habit should be unaffected (since 3-day-old habits show normal retention). Since the rats will remember the extinction but not the original learning, relearning should be reliably slowed down. This is just what occurred; trained rats whose habit was extinguished immediately took about the same number of trials to relearn it as control animals did, while rats whose habit had been extinguished 3 days after learning took virtually twice as many trials. The result supports an interpretation of extinction as the learning of another habit rather than the weakening of an old one.

It is difficult to see how this sequence of experiments can be explained without assuming a process of consolidation in which transmission across the synapse is a crucial factor. It does not necessarily seem to require the assumption that storage itself occurs at the synapse, as Deutsch suggests. An interpretation in which synaptic transmission influences retrieval would seem to be equally plausible, particularly in view of the temporary nature of both the blocking and the facilitation effects. In view of the history of other approaches to the physiological basis of memory, such as work on ECS and on the biochemical basis of memory (Corning and Riccio 1970), in which a very promising start has led to a morass of claims, counterclaims, and experimental artifacts, it would perhaps be wise for the outsider to reserve judgment until enough critical work has been done to ensure that this too is not based on some pattern of unexpected artifacts. Meanwhile, it does appear to present an attractively coherent picture which, if it proves to be robust and replicable, has clear implications beyond the field of physiological psychology for any general theory of learning and memory.

Arousal and Consolidation

All the experiments discussed so far in this chapter have been concerned either with hospital patients or with animal studies, whereas experiments on normal human subjects have largely ignored the consolidation hypothesis. Osgood (1953), for example, discusses consolidation theory briefly but dismisses it because it is clearly not suited to explain all features of forgetting and thus cannot be the whole story. The general tendency in human experimentation has been to try to avoid the need for such a concept. An exception, however, is the work on arousal and memory stemming from the experiments of Kleinsmith and Kaplan.

In their first experiment, Kleinsmith and Kaplan (1963) presented their subjects with eight words, each followed by a digit. Subjects read out the word-digit pairs, and the galvanic skin response (GSR) evoked by each was measured.* The words were so selected that some would be expected to produce a strongly emotional response (e.g., *rape, vomit*), whereas others were expected to be more neutral (e.g., *swim, dance*). Recall was plotted separately for words evoking a higher than average GSR (and hence presumably arousing) and for those with a lower than average GSR. Digit responses to low-arousal words were initially well recalled but were subsequently rapidly forgotten; responses to high-arousal words were initially difficult to remember, but recall substantially improved over time. A subsequent study using nonsense syllables instead of words obtained similar results (see Figure 3-4): Responses to syllables evoking a high GSR were initially unlikely to be recalled but subsequently improved, while digits associated with low-arousal syllables were at first well recalled but were soon forgotten (Kleinsmith and Kaplan 1964), suggesting that the effect was not limited to meaningful words.

A number of studies have followed up these experiments using similar techniques (e.g., Walker and Tarte 1963; Corteen 1969; Butter 1970). Others have manipulated the subject's level of arousal by accompanying the visually presented material with bursts of white noise (e.g., Berlyne, Borsa, Hamacher, and Koenig 1966; McClean 1969). A third technique takes advantage of differences in level of arousal at different times of day (Blake 1967; Baddeley, Hatter, Scott, and Snashall 1970). While none of these results is quite so clear and dra-

---

* The GSR is a change in conductivity of the skin often used in "lie detectors" because it tends to indicate an emotional response on the part of the subject.

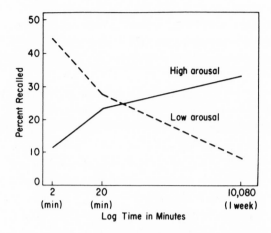

Figure 3–4 Differential recall of nonsense syllable paired-associates as a function of arousal level. High-arousal syllables were those evoking a high GSR during the initial learning presentation. Source: L. J. Kleinsmith and S. Kaplan, Interaction of arousal and recall interval in nonsense syllable paired-associate learning, *Journal of Experimental Psychology* 67 (1964): 125. Copyright 1964 by the American Psychological Association. Reprinted by permission.

matic as those of Kleinsmith and Kaplan, all show statistically reliable arousal effects, suggesting an interaction between level of arousal and delay: low-arousal items tend to be favored at short delays, high-arousal items at long delays.

This pattern of results is broadly consistent with the concept of a dual memory system of the type implied by the clinical evidence from human patients and by the animal studies using ECS or chemical stimulation. Looked at from this viewpoint, a high level of arousal facilitates consolidation or transfer to long-term memory but inhibits retrieval from the short-term system. The assumption of enhanced consolidation is a plausible one, especially in view of the evidence for an enhancement of consolidation following injection of drugs likely to increase arousal (McGaugh and Dawson 1971). Why high arousal should inhibit short-term memory is less obvious. Kleinsmith and Kaplan (1963) simply assume that high arousal increases the degree of activity in the neurons involved in storing the memory trace in question, and that this enhances consolidation but makes retrieval more difficult. I know of no other evidence that consolidating traces are

47

"protected" from retrieval in this way, and since the hypothesis does not appear to have stimulated any fruitful theoretical development, we should probably look elsewhere for an interpretation.

An ingenious alternative explanation is suggested by Hamilton, Hockey, and Quinn (1972) in terms of the subject's distribution of attention during learning. There is considerable evidence that an increase in level of arousal will narrow the subject's range of attention (e.g., Baddeley 1972), causing him to concentrate on a smaller number of environmental cues. Hockey and Hamilton (1970) found such an effect in a memory task in which subjects were shown a series of words in either quiet or noisy conditions and were subsequently asked to recall the words in any order. The words were projected at a range of locations on a screen, and degree of retention of this incidental feature of the material was subsequently tested. Hockey and Hamilton found no difference in number of words recalled between the quiet and the more arousing, noisy condition. However, noise had the effect of reducing the amount of incidental learning of word location but increased the tendency of subjects to recall words in the order presented. In the standard paired-associate procedure used by Kleinsmith and Kaplan, it is usual to ensure that the order of testing items differs from the order of presentation, so that any tendency to emphasize order of presentation under high arousal would tend to be counterproductive. Hamilton, Hockey, and Quinn (1972) went on to test this directly, using a paired-associate procedure in which pairs were tested in the same order as they had been presented or, as is usually the case, in a scrambled order. As predicted, they found that noise enhanced performance when recall was in the same order as presentation but impaired performance under the standard technique.

We are left then with a somewhat complex interpretation of the Kleinsmith and Kaplan result, based on the assumption that arousal biases attention toward order information, giving poorer immediate recall when the test order is changed, but enhances consolidation, leading to good long-term retention. Unfortunately, the picture is even more complex. Although this interpretation fits the available data based on temporary shifts in level of arousal, there is evidence that more long-term shifts (such as those due to diurnal variation or sleep deprivation) behave differently, with high arousal being associated with impaired immediate memory, even when recall is in the same order as presentation. The attentional hypothesis clearly requires a great deal of further experimentation before it can be regarded as anything more than a promising suggestion, but as a plausible alternative to the so far unproductive suggestion of Kleinsmith and Kaplan it clearly merits further exploration.

How necessary, then, is the concept of consolidation? The clinical evidence of posttraumatic and post-ECT amnesia clearly suggests some such process. Although attempts to explore the concept of trace consolidation using animals have proved disappointingly complex and equivocal, it nonetheless seems likely that the concept will continue to generate experimental work and that the gap between human and animal studies will eventually begin to narrow.

CHAPTER

4

The Limits of Memory: Forgetting and the Phenomenon of Interference

W̶E HAVE so far talked about the problem of putting information into the memory store, but we have said virtually nothing about the problems of getting it out again. The fact that we forget, however, indicates that information is either lost *from* the memory store (i.e., the trace is destroyed) or lost *in* the memory store, so that it becomes increasingly difficult to locate and retrieve the information when required.

In this chapter we shall be concerned with three theories of forgetting. Two, the Freudian and Gestalt theories, will be considered very briefly, since they currently have little influence on the experimental study of memory. The bulk of the chapter will be devoted to the phenomenon of interference, which has dominated theoretical approaches to memory for at least the last 30 years in the form of associative interference theory, which will be discussed in detail in the next chapter.

The Freudian Theory

Freud's theory of forgetting is based on the concept of *repression,* the unconscious blocking of information having painful or anxiety-provoking associations. Such information, though inaccessible, may, according to Freud, manifest itself as inadvertent slips of the tongue or pen, in which the speaker or writer makes an error which is said to reflect his underlying feelings rather than his intended meaning.* The concept of repression is based on Freud's observations of neurotic patients, and there is no doubt that it occurs, at least as a pathological type of forgetting. The clearest example of this is probably that of fugue, a condition in which a person under emotional stress may be completely unable to recall anything about his previous life (Nemiah 1969). The condition is frequently temporary, indicating that the defect is an inability to retrieve information about the past rather than a loss of information from the memory store.

The importance of repression in normal forgetting is, however, less obvious. In his *Psychopathology of Everyday Life,* Freud presents the case for motivated forgetting in normal subjects by means of anecdotes, of which the following, from an acquaintance of Freud's, is one of the most straightforward:

> "While taking an examination in philosophy as a minor subject I was questioned by the examiner about the teachings of Epicurus, and was asked if I knew who took up his teachings centuries later. I answered that it was Pierre Gassendi, whom two days before while in a cafe I had happened to hear spoken of as a follower of Epicurus. To the question how I knew this I boldly replied that I had taken an interest in Gassendi for a long time. This resulted in a certificate with a *magna cum laude,* but later, unfortunately, also in a persistent tendency to forget the name Gassendi. I believe that it is due to my guilty conscience that even now I cannot retain this name despite all efforts. I had no business knowing it at the time" (Freud 1914, p. 45).

While it seems likely that repression does occasionally occur in everyday life, it can surely not account for more than a minute fraction of the vast amount of information we process and forget every day. Can you, for example, remember the first word of this chapter? Probably not, but it seems unlikely that this is the result of its repression

---

* An intriguing example occurred in a recent British Psychology Society Bulletin (September 1975) where a list of forthcoming events on the back cover referred to the "Fraud Memorial Professorship." It appears that typesetters, at least, still have their doubts about Freud's views!

for emotional reasons! The fact that repression is not the most common reason for forgetting is not, of course, a reason for ignoring it, and a number of attempts have been made to produce convincing repression effects in the laboratory.

One technique that has often been cited as producing evidence favoring the Freudian repression hypothesis is based on the word-association task. In this, the subject is given a series of words and asked in each case to produce the first associated word that springs to mind. As Jung (1906) pointed out, certain emotionally toned words tend to produce very long latencies. Jung suggested that this is because they are linked to anxiety-laden complexes which the subject is unwilling to reveal, a view which is supported by the tendency of long associations to be linked with the type of high GSR response that is typically associated with emotion. A study by Levinger and Clark (1961) required subjects to produce associations to a total of 60 words ranging from emotionally toned items like *fear, angry,* and *quarrel* to relatively neutral words like *tree, cow,* and *window.* As expected, the emotionally toned words tended to evoke longer latencies and to be associated with higher GSR responses. Immediately after the word-association test was completed, subjects were given the same list of stimulus words once again, but this time they were instructed to remember the association they gave previously. Under these conditions, subjects tended to recall reliably more of their associations to the neutral words than their responses to the emotional stimuli.

Levinger and Clark suggested that their results were consistent with the psychoanalytic model of repression. However, alternative explanations are possible. Eysenck and Wilson (1973) suggest an explanation in terms of the results of Kleinsmith and Kaplan (1963; 1964), discussed in the previous chapter, in which the highly arousing items were poorly retained after a short delay but showed better recall than neutral items after a one-week interval. An unpublished study at the University of Cambridge by Bradley and Morris (1975) tested this interpretation by repeating the Levinger and Clark study using two groups of subjects, one of which recalled immediately, while the second did not recall until 28 days later. There was evidence for impaired retention of associations to emotional words when tested immediately, but after 28 days this effect had reversed to produce a strong advantage in favor of the recall of emotional associations. Such a result clearly supports an interpretation of Levinger and Clark's results in terms of the effects of arousal in memory and is inconsistent with an interpretation in terms of repression, since this would presumably predict that emotional responses would be difficult to recall on both occasions.

A second approach is illustrated by a study by Zeller (1951) in which subjects first learned a list of syllables, which they subsequently recalled. They were then split into a control group, which performed an emotionally neutral task, and a series of experimental groups, which performed a block-tapping task which was so arranged that they always failed to respond correctly. In the crucial experimental condition, everything was done to discourage the subject and make him feel anxious and inadequate:

> Great concern was expressed by E over S's level of mental ability. He was asked if he had not considered the possibility that he could not get through College and was informed that he probably would not. On the other hand, it was pointed out his mechanical ability was so poor he probably couldn't succeed in any of the trades. Nothing was omitted which would serve to make S feel insecure and inadequate (Zeller 1951, p. 34).

Following the interpolated task, the subject was again required to try to remember the original list of items. Subjects given the peculiarly nasty feedback just described remembered significantly fewer items than subjects given no such feedback. When the two groups were re-tested 48 hours later, the difference between them remained. The block-tapping task was then repeated, and the subjects given anxiety-provoking feedback on the previous test were allowed to succeed, were reassured, and were told that their previous bad performance had in fact been arranged by the experimenter. They then had a further retention test, on which their performance dramatically improved. After a further interval of 48 hours, a final recall test was given, and on this test their performance was only slightly poorer than that of subjects who had consistently had neutral feedback from the block-tapping task. This study is cited as evidence of repression, since it is suggested that the anxiety-provoking feedback from the interpolated block-tapping task was generalized to the list of syllables learned in the same situation, causing the verbal items to be associated with anxiety and thus repressed. Removal of the anxiety is said to be analogous to the relief of repression in psychotherapy.

Quite apart from the dubious ethical status of an experiment of this kind, its interpretation is by no means clear. It is difficult, for example, to rule out the possibility that the negative feedback impaired performance by changing the subject's willingness to produce items unless he was absolutely sure they were correct. Such a change in criterion would influence performance, although it might not reflect any difference in the information available and accessible to the subject. Erdelyi (1970) has demonstrated criterion effects of this type in the recall of pictures. Another possibility is discussed by Holmes (1972), who shows that the retention of previously learned material may be reduced by interpolated emotionally toned feedback, with the effect being just as great for positive, ego-boosting feedback as for negative, ego-deflating feedback. This suggests that it is the distracting effect of the emotionally toned feedback that impairs retention, rather than its capacity for provoking anxiety.

A more convincing laboratory analogue of repression was produced by Glucksberg and King (1967). Their study relied on the use of remote word associations. In an association test a word (e.g., *memory*) tends to evoke a second word (e.g., *mind*), which in turn may suggest a third word (*brain*). Hence, *brain* can be regarded as a remote associate of *memory*. *Justice–peace–war* is another such associative chain, with *war* being a remote associate of *justice*. Glucksberg and King first taught their subjects a list of nonsense syllable-word pairs (e.g., *dax–memory, gex–justice*). The subjects were then shown a list of words comprising the remote associates of the words learned, and some of these were accompanied by an electric shock. The subject's task was to learn which items were associated with shock. Hence, one subject might have *brain* associated with shock, while a second might have *war* associated. In a third stage of the study, subjects were tested for the retention of the initial pairs. There was a clear tendency for subjects to show poorer retention of words whose remote associates had been linked with shock; none of the subjects was able to verbalize the relationship between the shocked words and the initial learning, although all of them could remember which words had been shocked.

While this is a much better controlled study than that of Zeller, it is still open to an interpretation in terms of the adverse effect of arousal on immediate recall. It would be rather interesting to replicate Glucksberg and King's study with a delayed recall condition. If their result is indeed due to repression, the inhibitory effect should still be present after a delay, whereas if it is due to the adverse effect of arousal on immediate recall, the delayed effect should be reversed, with retention of the words remotely associated with shock enhanced rather than impaired. Whatever the result, however, it seems unlikely that laboratory-based studies will ever really settle the issue of the importance of repression in human memory. In a detailed review of studies on repression, Mackinnon and Dukes (1962) describe the difficulties encountered in attempting to derive a clear prediction from psychoanalytic theory. Indeed, there appears to be considerable resistance to the suggestion that there is any need to test the repression hypothesis. Kubie (1952) refers to "the uselessness of making pallid facsimiles in the laboratory of data which are already manifest in nature, merely to get around the human reluctance to look human nature in the eye" (p. 64). Considered at this level, the concept of repression appears to represent an article of faith, rather than a scientifically testable hypothesis.

Gestalt Trace Theory

The German school of Gestalt psychology that flourished in the 1920s and 1930s was initially concerned mainly with form perception. However, it influenced the study of memory in two ways: first, in its emphasis on the role of organization in memory (this will be discussed in Chapter 11) and, second, in its hypothesis of autonomous change in the memory trace, which long provided virtually the only active alternative to interference theory.

The hypothesis was a direct application to memory of principles based on the perception of form, and its experimental test was confined mainly to memory for shapes. It predicted that the memory trace for a shape would change progressively over time toward a "better," more regular, symmetrical figure. The most popular shape for testing this prediction was a circle with a gap, the prediction being that the memory trace would spontaneously tend more and more toward the good *gestalt* of a perfect circle. In other words, the gap should progressively close —not, one might think, a difficult hypothesis to test. I can, however, think of no question that has been attacked with more ingenuity and less success.

The Gestalt position on memory for form was initially presented by Wulf (1922), who showed subjects a series of 20 figures, which they were subsequently required to reproduce by drawing after intervals of 30 seconds, 1 day, and 1 week. Wulf interpreted his results as supporting the Gestalt view, but subsequent accounts both of Wulf's data and of other results using comparable techniques claim that they are at best equivocal (Woodworth, 1938). Part of the difficulty in interpreting Wulf's data stems from the problem of deciding exactly what changes Gestalt theory should predict, but even if one limits consideration to figures where prediction should be relatively straightforward, Wulf's technique is open to several basic objections.

The first objection stems from evidence that when a subject is required to remember many different figures, at least some of the forgetting is due to confusion among the items themselves, rather than to spontaneous changes in the memory trace (Gibson 1929). This has led to subsequent workers using far fewer items, and ideally only one. A second problem involves deciding whether trends are or are not progressive; this has led to a concentration on figures within which the change can be objectively measured, as in the case of a circle with a gap. The third problem was raised by Zangwill (1937), who pointed out that some of the errors which were attributed to changes in the memory trace could in fact be due to limitations in the subject's ability to draw the figure accurately. He argued that if changes in the subject's drawing represented changes in the underlying memory trace, then this should also be revealed in a recognition test. He therefore tested the same subject using both reproduction and recognition, and ensured that the recognition set contained a tidied-up version of the subject's own reproduction. Zangwill found little consistency between the subject's performance when measured by drawing and when measured by recognition and concluded that the evidence did not support the Gestalt view. Subsequent studies have therefore tended to avoid the difficulty of separating drawing errors from memory errors by using recognition testing.

Hebb and Foord (1945) reported a study which for many years was regarded as definitive. They presented their subjects with two highly dissimilar figures, a circle with a gap and an arrowhead, and tested each subject only once, either 5 minutes after presentation or 24 hours later. Subjects were presented with a pack of cards containing a range of figures resembling those presented and linked by a ring. A set might contain a range of circles with gaps varying from considerably narrower than that presented to considerably wider. Since the cards were on a ring, the subject could start at any point in the series and go through the pack looking for the figure most closely resembling the item he was asked to remember. Hebb and Foord failed to find any consistent trends in the case of either the circle or the arrowhead and concluded that their results did not support the Gestalt prediction.

In due course, however, the Hebb and Foord study was itself shown to have a basic flaw. Carlson and Duncan (1955) carried out a similar experiment using the same recognition procedure. They took care to note where each individual subject began his search through the set of alternatives, and discovered that this was crucial. If he began searching through circles with gaps which were smaller than that presented, then he tended to select a smaller gap, whereas if he started with circles which had larger gaps, he tended to select a larger gap. In short, his performance was being determined not only by the item presented but also by the interpolated test items. This makes the task of testing for changes extremely difficult, since any interpolated recognition item is likely to distort the subject's retention. If genuine autonomous changes in the memory trace had been occurring in either Hebb and Foord's or Carlson and Duncan's study, they could well have been masked by such interference effects.

Fortunately, one technique remained which avoided this problem. In an ingenious study, Irwin and Seidenfeld (1937) tested retention first by showing the subject a series of six figures and subsequently by showing the subject a single example of each and asking him about specific changes. Unbeknown to the subject, the recognition items were in fact identical with those presented originally; for example, a 5° gap in a circle would be followed by a second circle also with a 5° gap, and the subject was required to decide whether the second gap was smaller or larger than the first. If he were comparing the second stimulus with the memory trace of the first, and the gap in the memory trace had tended to close, then there should have been a consistent tendency for subjects to make "larger" judgments. Irwin and Seidenfeld reported evidence favoring Gestalt predictions in the case of three of their figures; their study can, however, be criticized both on the grounds that they used more than one figure and on the grounds that they tested the same subject repeatedly; a subsequent attempt by Hanawalt (1952) to repeat the study using a single test and other stimulus material was unsuccessful.

More recently, however, a number of studies using the method of identical stimuli and testing over brief retention intervals (from 2 to 30 seconds) have reported consistent trends (e.g., Crumbaugh 1954; Brown 1956; Karlin and Brennan 1957; James 1958). This suggested that in the case of short-term retention, autonomous changes in the memory trace can be detected. However, a subsequent study by Baddeley (1968d) showed that even the method of identical stimuli may be subject to a crucial flaw. He tested retention after a 15-second delay of a figure comprising a circle with a gap. Retention was tested using either the method of reproduction, in which a subject's original copy of the figure was compared with his drawing from memory 15 seconds later, or the method of identical stimuli. While the method of reproduction showed no consistent trend, the method of identical stimuli showed a tendency for subjects who had observed a 60° gap to judge a second 60° gap as larger, implying that the gap in their memory trace had decreased. A subsequent experiment, however, included a further condition which was intended to estimate the subject's guessing pattern. This was done by instructing the subject that the second item would be presented so briefly that he might not be aware of the stimulus; he was told that under certain conditions one is able to take in information without being aware of this (subliminal perception) and was urged to make a decision, if necessary, by guessing. In fact, a blank card was briefly presented, thus ensuring that responses were based on the subject's guessing habits and not on the recognition stimulus. Under these conditions, the pattern of responding was just what it had been in the previous study: subjects shown a 60° gap tended to classify the second (nonexistent) circle as having a larger gap. It appears that in the absence of real differences in the stimulus, a subject will base his response on guessing habits. A similar pattern of results was observed in a subsequent unpublished study in which subjects were shown a line on a card. When a very long line was followed by an identical long line, subjects tended to judge the second as longer, while no such effect occurred when two shorter lines were presented. Why this should be is not clear; it may be that subjects assume that the sequence of items will be random, and hence expect an extreme item to be followed by a less extreme. Be that as it may, it seems likely that although the method of identical stimuli produces consistent effects, these may be attributable to the guessing strategy adopted by the subject rather than a change in the memory trace.

In conclusion, although the Gestalt hypothesis of autonomous change in the memory trace has produced a splendid crop of unexpected experimental artifacts and biases (see Woodworth 1938; Riley 1962; and Baddeley 1968d for a more detailed review), it has so far proved both experimentally and theoretically sterile.

Trace Decay or Interference?

We know from Ebbinghaus's classical experiment on the forgetting curve (see Figure 1–2) that amount lost is a function of time. The simplest interpretation of this is the *trace decay hypothesis,* which suggests that the memory trace will spontaneously deteriorate over time, rather as a mark made in a pat of butter will gradually disappear in a warm room. The major alternative is the *interference hypothesis,* which suggests that forgetting occurs because the memory trace is either masked or obliterated by other events. A greater delay produces more forgetting simply because it allows more opportunity for such interfering effects to occur. A strong version of the trace decay theory would argue that the length of the delay between learning and recall is the only factor governing the amount of forgetting, while the strong version of interference theory would claim that time itself is unimportant and that if intervening activity can be prevented, no forgetting will occur.

A number of attempts have been made to test these predictions directly. One approach is to use animals which can be immobilized in some way between learning and subsequent test. A number of studies have used drugs to anesthetize animals between learning and retention; in general, they have found no difference between anesthetized animals and controls (e.g., Russell and Hunter 1937; Plath 1924). Other studies have attempted to control amount of activity by manipulating environmental temperature for insects or fish, which, being cold-blooded, tend to become more active as the temperature increases. Hoagland (1931) found no effect of temperature on the retention of a maze by ants at temperatures ranging from 15° to 25° C; temperatures above 28° C did impair retention, but since original learning at these temperatures was also impaired, factors other than increased interference from greater activity were probably responsible. French (1942) studied the retention of a maze by goldfish at temperatures of 4°, 16°, and 28° C. He found reliable differences in retention, but these were not correlated with amount of interpolated activity. In general, these results do not support interference theory. All of them can, however, be criticized on the grounds that the method of manipulating degree of activity almost certainly had additional, uncontrolled physiological effects which make interpretation very difficult.

Minami and Dallenbach (1946) attempted to avoid these problems by devising a technique that induced inactivity with no apparent deleterious side effects. They used cockroaches and found that these insects can be induced to remain immobile and quiescent for long periods of time if they are led to crawl into a narrow, cone-shaped box lined with tissue paper. The Minami-Dallenbach learning procedure was based on the fact that cockroaches spontaneously avoid a brightly lit area; they placed the insects in a lighted learning box and shocked

59

them whenever they entered a dark compartment. When the cockroaches had learned to avoid the previously attractive dark compartment, they were removed and induced to enter either the paper-lined cone (where they would remain immobile) or a cage; both the cone and the cage were placed in dark cupboards until retention was tested at periods of time ranging from 10 minutes to 24 hours. The results are shown in Figure 4–1, from which it is clear that the amount of forgetting was considerably reduced by inactivity.

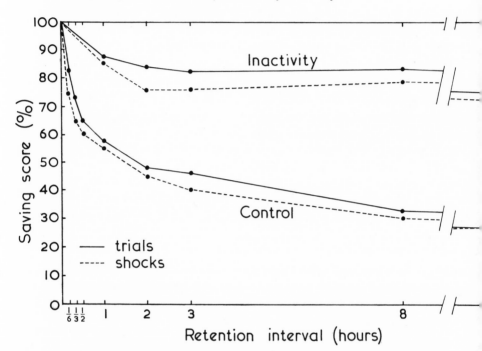

Figure 4–1   Retention of an avoidance response by cockroaches as a function of activity between learning and test. When insects were kept inactive, they relearned the task in fewer trials and obtained fewer shocks. Source: H. Minami and K. M. Dallenbach, The effect of activity upon learning and retention in the cockroach, *American Journal of Psychology* 59 (1946): 52. Reprinted by permission.

While the results of the Minami-Dallenbach experiment are consistent with interference theory, at least in its weak form, the question arises as to whether it is valid to generalize from the memory processes of cockroaches to those of man. A number of studies have attempted to bridge this gap by using sleep as a way of reducing the amount of activity between learning and retention in human subjects.

Jenkins and Dallenbach (1924) required their subjects (two students) to learn lists of ten nonsense syllables to a criterion of one perfect recitation; they then tested recall after delays of 1, 2, 4, or 8 hours, filled either by waking activities or sleep, and found a substantial advantage in favor of recall after sleep. This study has been criticized for confounding time of learning (morning or evening) with type of interpolated activity; when this factor is controlled, the difference becomes less dramatic (Van Ormer 1932). However, it seems clear from subsequent studies (Lovatt and Warr 1968; Ekstrand 1972) that retention is in fact better after sleep than after an equivalent waking period, at least during normal nighttime sleep conditions. However, Hockey, Davies, and Gray (1972) have shown that when sleep occurs during the day, it does not reduce the rate of forgetting, suggesting that simple cessation of activity is not the crucial factor. Coleman (cited in Ekstrand 1972) has suggested that sleep aids learning because it facilitates consolidation. She showed that a given amount of sleep benefits learning most when it comes immediately after learning, the most crucial period for the consolidation of the memory trace, rather than later in the retention interval.

Yet another possibility is suggested by recent speculation about the possible role of dreaming in memory. Two studies have investigated this. One, by Empson and Clarke (1970), attempted to control the amount of dreaming during a night's sleep by waking the subject up every time he exhibited REM sleep (sleep accompanied by rapid eye movements that characterize periods of dreaming), while control subjects were awakened the same number of times at random. REM sleep-deprived subjects showed poorer retention of prose material learned the previous evening, a result that the authors interpreted in terms of the hypothesis that REM sleep is a process that aids the consolidation and, possibly, the organization of the previous day's learning. However, the REM sleep-deprived subjects tended to sleep rather less than the controls; since there have also been claims that REM sleep deprivation may have adverse stress effects (Dement 1960), which could themselves presumably impair recall performance, interpretation of this finding is problematic.

A study by Ekstrand (1972) avoided this problem by taking advantage of the fact that most REM sleep occurs during the latter part of the night. He had his subjects either learn paired associates in the evening and recall in the middle of the night or learn in the middle of the night and recall the following morning. The latter group, as expected, showed more evidence of dreaming during the retention interval, as well as *poorer* retention, a result opposite to that shown by Empson and Clarke but one which Ekstrand also interprets in terms of consolidation, which he assumes to be *reduced* during REM sleep. Unfortunately, however, this study confounds the amount of intervening REM sleep with (1) time of learning and (2) time of awakening and recall. Stones (1974) has shown that subjects aroused from REM sleep are better able to recall material than if aroused from deep sleep; Ekstrand's result is therefore difficult to interpret. Subsequent work by Stones (1974) suggests that the type of material may be crucial, with REM sleep favoring the learning of meaningful material but not the rote learning of nonsense material, a possibility which further complicates an already confused pattern of results. Hence, although there is general agreement that retention is better after sleep than after waking, the intriguing but difficult question of why this is so remains unanswered. As a review of recent work on the question by Ekstrand (1972) suggests, trace consolidation and decay are probably at least as important as interference in producing the effect.

The attempt to support a strong interference theory position by showing that without interference no forgetting occurs thus runs up against two major problems: (1) it is difficult to find a situation in which intervening activity can in fact be avoided; and (2) any means of inhibiting activity is likely to have other effects (behavioral, biochemical, or both) which will inevitably make interpretation difficult. A more promising approach is to explore the weak interference theory position, that the amount retained will depend in part on the interpolated activity; in other words, interference influences forgetting but is not necessarily the only factor. There is a good deal of evidence for such a position, particularly from a vast range of studies which have shown that the amount retained is reduced if the learning of other material has occurred during the retention interval. Forgetting is particularly marked if the interfering material is similar to that originally learned.

McGeoch and MacDonald (1931) had their subjects learn a list of adjectives to a criterion of one perfect recall. They then spent 10 minutes either resting or learning new material varying in degree of rated similarity to the original list. Table 4–1 shows percentage recall on a subsequent test of the original list. It is clear that the more similar the interpolated learning, the greater the degree of forgetting. Such a result is inconsistent with the strong trace decay hypothesis, which regards length of retention interval as the only determinant of amount retained, and provides clear evidence for interference as a factor in forgetting.

TABLE 4–1

Effect of interpolated learning on serial recall and relearning of a list of adjectives.

INTERPOLATED ACTIVITY	MEAN RECALL (MAX = 10) ON TRIAL 1	MEAN TRIALS TO A CRITERION OF ONE PERFECT REPETITION
Rest	4.50	4.58
Learn 3-digit numbers	3.68	4.42
Learn nonsense syllables	2.58	4.50
Learn unrelated adjectives	2.17	5.17
Learn antonyms	1.83	6.67
Learn synonyms	1.25	7.33

Source: J. A. McGeoch and W. T. MacDonald, Meaningful relation and retro-active inhibition, *American Journal of Psychology* 43 (1931): 582. Reprinted by permission.

The Phenomenon of Interference

As we saw from the McGeoch-MacDonald experiment, a subject who has just learned a list of words is less likely to be able to recall it later if he has been required to learn a second list in the intervening period. Furthermore, if instead of retesting him on the first list, we wait a while and then test the second, we will find poorer list 2 retention as a result of the prior learning. The tendency for the second list to impair retention of the first is known as *retroactive interference* (abbreviated to RI), a term which implies that the interference is working backward in time (which is not, of course, literally true). The case in which the first list impairs recall of the list which follows is known as *proactive interference* (PI).

A great many experiments have investigated RI and PI, but for the purpose of illustration we shall use a series of experiments by Slamecka in which subjects were asked to learn and remember sequences of prose.

RETROACTIVE INTERFERENCE

In the first of these studies, Slamecka (1960) looked at retroactive interference with two basic questions in mind: (1) In what way is the retention of a sentence affected by how well it was learned originally? (2) How does the amount of practice on a second interfering sentence affect retention of the first? Although he used sentences, Slamecka's approach was very much in the classical Ebbinghaus tradition. The sentences were presented one word at a time at a strictly controlled rate of 3 seconds per word. Furthermore, although genuine sentences were used, they were written in a textbook style that seems to be striving to convey as little meaning as possible, e.g., *Communicators can exercise latitude in specifying meaning however they choose provided that such definitions correspond somewhat closely to regular usage.* After two, four, or eight repetitions, Slamecka's subjects were either tested immediately or presented with a second 20-word literary gem from the same source, which they were required to learn for either four or eight

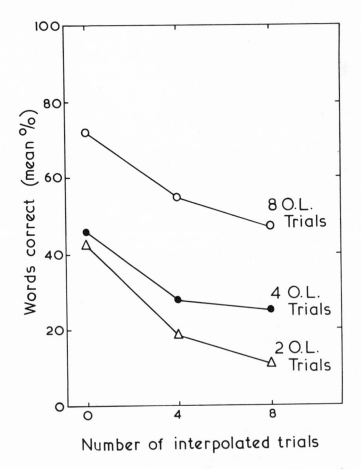

Figure 4–2   Effect of retroactive interference on the retention of prose. Recall is affected both by the degree of initial learning and by the number of interpolated trials with other material. Source: Based on N. J. Slamecka, Retroactive inhibition of connected discourse as a function of practice level, *Journal of Experimental Psychology* 59 (1960): 104–108.

further trials. Both learning and testing were carried out by the *antici-pation* method, which involves showing the subject the sentence one word at a time and then, on all trials after the first, asking him to try to keep one step ahead of the presentation. Thus, when the first word, *Communicators,* is shown, the subject should call out the second word, *can.* Three seconds later the word *can* will appear, confirming his response if he got it right, correcting him if he did not, and signaling him to produce the third word, *exercise.* This technique used to be very popular, since it both teaches the subject and tests him at the same time. In recent years, however, it has been used much less, since it confounds the effects of learning with those of recall by presenting the subject with a choice of whether he should spend the time available in trying to learn the present item or recall the next one.

The results of the experiment are shown in Figure 4–2, which shows the average number of words correctly anticipated on the first relearning trial following the interpolated learning. As one might expect, Figure 4–2 shows that the better a sentence is learned, the more resistant it is to subsequent interference, the relationship in this case being linear. The effect of amount of interpolated learning on subsequent retention (Figure 4–2) is again in the expected direction: more interpolated learning produces more forgetting.

PROACTIVE INTERFERENCE

In a study of proactive interference, Slamecka (1961) had his subjects learn one, two, three, or four passages of 20 words. He then asked them to recall the last passage after delays of either 15 minutes, 30 minutes, 1 hour, or 24 hours. The results of the experiment are shown in Figure 4–3. This shows two important features: first, the greater the number of prior interfering passages, the greater the forgetting; second, the adverse effect of prior learning increases over time. This tendency for PI to increase with increasing delay contrasts with the effects of RI, which tend to decrease over time (Briggs 1954). Possible explanations for this will be discussed in the next chapter.

Transfer of Training

The phenomenon of interference has traditionally been studied within the framework of *transfer of training,* the study of the influence of one task on the learning and retention of another.

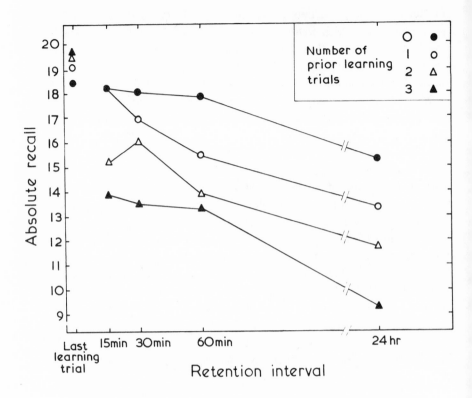

Figure 4–3   Effect of proactive inhibition on the retention of connected prose. Retention is affected both by the number of prior lists (PL) and by the retention interval. Source: N. J. Slamecka, Proactive inhibition of connected discourse, *Journal of Experimental Psychology* 62 (1961): 299. Copyright 1961 by the American Psychological Association. Reprinted by permission.

NONSPECIFIC TRANSFER

Nonspecific transfer is divided into two distinct phenomena, namely, *warm-up* and *learning to learn*. The term *warm-up* refers to the tendency for the learning of a task to be enhanced if the subject has performed a similar task immediately beforehand. The results of one such study, by Thune (1951), are shown in Figure 4–4. On each of five successive days, subjects were required to learn three lists of paired adjectives. As Figure 4–4 shows, on each day subjects learned the second list faster than the first and the third faster than the second, indicating an improvement in learning over the test session, despite the fact that the items in the successive lists were quite unrelated.

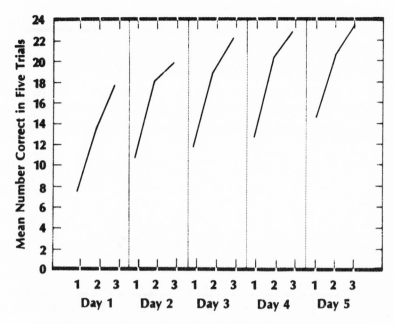

Figure 4–4   Warm-up and learning-to-learn effects: mean total number of correct anticipations on the first five trials for each of three lists learned on each of 5 days. Note both the gradual improvement in performance over days and the marked warm-up effect shown between the learning of the first and second lists on any given day. Source: Based on L. E. Thune, Warm-up effect as a function of level of practice in verbal learning, *Journal of Experimental Psychology* 42 (1951): 252. Copyright 1951 by the American Psychological Association. Reprinted by permission.

Two further features of Figure 4–4 are notable. First, note that the warm-up effect dissipates between each successive day, so that the performance on the first list of day 2 is reliably poorer than that of the third list on day 1. A study by Hamilton (1950) systematically varied the interval between successive lists and found that the warm-up effect declined rapidly over the first half hour and then leveled off, showing little difference between a 40-minute and a 24-hour interval. The second feature of Thune's study is the gradual improvement in performance over the five successive days. This probably represents a *learning-to-learn effect,* whereby the subject improves his learning skills over successive days of practice.

A much more clear-cut learning-to-learn effect was shown in a study by Ward (1937) in which subjects were required to learn serial lists of 12 nonsense syllables. As Figure 4–5 shows, the number of trials

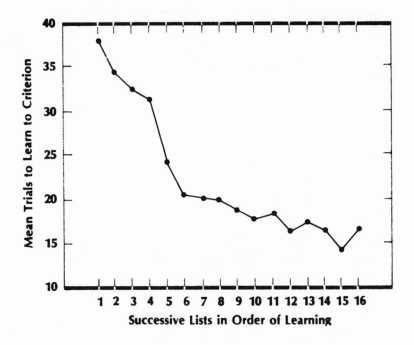

Figure 4–5   Learning-to-learn effect: subjects were required to learn a serial list of 12 nonsense syllables on each of 16 successive days. Source: L. B. Ward, Reminiscence and rote learning, *Psychological Monograph* 49 (1937).

required to learn the list declines dramatically, with the later lists requiring less than half as many trials as the first list. As we shall see in the next chapter (p. 82), this tendency for subjects to learn later lists faster than earlier ones has a critical bearing on studies of PI and should be borne in mind in interpreting such studies.

SPECIFIC TRANSFER

So far, most of the experiments we have described have used serial learning to study transfer. The paired-associate technique, however, allows the phenomenon to be analyzed in more detail by separating out the respective roles of the stimulus and the response. Table 4–2 shows the four most characteristic transfer-of-training designs. In each case the first list is referred to as the *A–B* list, where *A* represents the stimuli and *B* the associated responses. In condition 1 the *A–B* list is followed by a list comprising pairs of items unrelated to the *A–B* list (the *C–D* list). This serves as a control condition. Condition 2 represents

TABLE 4–2

Four characteristic transfer-of-training designs.

CONDITION	LIST 1	LIST 2	TRANSFER EFFECT
(1) Control	A–B	C–D	
	(vicar-chilly)	(farmer-putrid)	—
(2) Same stimuli,	A–B	A–C	
different responses	(vicar-chilly)	(vicar-drunken)	Negative
(3) Different stimuli,	A–B	C–B	
same responses	(vicar-chilly)	(farmer-chilly)	Positive (?)
(4) Stimuli and responses	A–B	A–Br	
re-paired	(vicar-chilly,	(vicar-ancient,	
	soldier-ancient)	soldier-chilly)	Negative
(5) Similar stimuli,	A–B	A'–C	
different responses	(vicar-chilly)	(parson-drunken)	Negative

Note: Examples of pairs are given in parentheses.

the classical RI design, in which the original *A–B* list is followed by an interfering *A–C* list where the same stimuli are associated with quite different responses. Condition 3 (*A–B, C–B*) represents the effect of holding the responses the same but changing the stimuli, a condition which may lead to positive transfer under certain circumstances. Condition 4 (*A–B, A–Br*) is one in which the same stimuli and responses are used in both the first and second lists, but they are paired in a different way. This typically gives rise to a very strong negative transfer effect. Finally, condition 5 (*A–B, A'–C*) represents a modification of the negative transfer design, with the stimuli in the second list similar in some respect to those in the first. If they are similar along a dimension that the subject is using to encode the material he is learning, negative transfer and forgetting of the original *A–B* list are the likely results.

The range of transfer designs is very great, and the pattern of empirical results complex (see Postman 1971 for a more detailed discussion). However, a good deal of the data can be described reasonably efficiently in terms of the transfer-of-training surface devised by Osgood (1949) on the basis of the data existing at that time. This is shown in Figure 4–6, which is a two-dimensional representation of a three-dimensional surface. The effects of different degrees of stimulus similarity are shown along the width of the surface, and the effects of response similarity along its length. The height of the surface above the zero line represents positive transfer, and the depth below represents negative transfer. Hence, with stimuli and responses identical the transfer will be maximal, since the second learning list will effectively

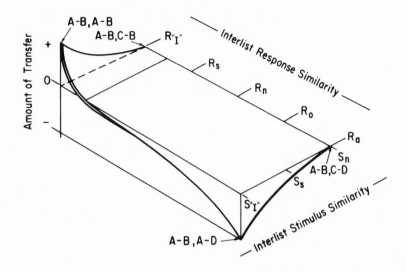

Figure 4–6   Osgood's transfer surface. The symbols S and R stand for stimulus and response, I = identical, S = similar, N = neutral, O = opposed, and A = antagonistic. The lower dashed curve represents the evidence of Bugelski and Cadwallader (1956). Source: Based on C. E. Osgood, The similarity paradox in human learning: a resolution, *Psychological Review* 56 (1949): 140.

be further training on the original list. On the other hand, with identical stimuli but very different responses, negative transfer will occur. Note that, according to the surface, there will be neither positive nor negative transfer when stimuli are unrelated, since the surface does not deviate from the zero point.

While subsequent tests of the surface (Bugelski and Cadwallader 1956; Dallett 1962; Wimer 1964) broadly support Osgood, they do suggest that his conclusions about response similarity may well be an oversimplification. For example, when the stimuli in lists are identical and the responses antagonistic (e.g., *sailor-good* followed by *sailor-bad*), maximal negative transfer need not result; in fact, subjects in some studies have found the second task particularly easy. The reason is probably that they are able to devise a rule whereby the responses in the second list can be derived from those they have already learned in the first.

The second reason why the role of response similarity is complicated stems from the separability of paired-associate learning into two stages. In order to perform a paired-associate task adequately, subjects must be able both to produce the response and to associate that response with the appropriate stimulus (Underwood and Schulz 1960). To give an extreme example, if subjects were required to associate single-letter stimuli with nine-digit responses (e.g., f–791063285), learning to produce the responses would constitute a major source of difficulty in mastering the list; whereas if the pairs were reversed, with the nine-digit sequences as stimuli and single letters as responses, response learning would be a relatively minor component in the task. Since similarity between the responses in list 1 and those in list 2 may serve as an aid to response learning, the question of whether transfer would be positive or negative becomes a relatively complex one, depending at least in part on the contribution of response learning to the total difficulty of the task.

This point is illustrated rather clearly in a study by Horowitz (1962) into the effects of intra-list similarity on paired-associate learning. Horowitz compared the effects of similarity among the various stimulus items and similarity among the responses. Many studies had shown that intra-list stimulus similarity impeded learning, but the results for response similarity had varied considerably from one study to another. Horowitz demonstrated that this was because response similarity had two separate effects. On the one hand, it made the subject's task of discriminating among the appropriate responses more difficult, and hence impaired performance. On the other hand, the similarity among the items made them easier to learn as responses, an effect evidenced in a study where subjects were simply given all the responses from the list and required to remember them in any order they wished. Under these free recall conditions, similar responses were consistently easier to learn than dissimilar responses.

In a third condition, termed *associative matching*, the response-learning aspect of the paired-associate learning task was removed by presenting the subject with all the stimuli and all the responses on separate cards and simply requiring him to match up each response card with the appropriate stimulus card. Under these conditions, response similarity impaired learning just as much as stimulus similarity, as would be expected on the assumption that similarity has a negative effect on the associative stage and a positive effect on the response-learning stage.

Apart from the complications of response similarity, however, the Osgood surface does represent a reasonable empirical summary of the evidence on transfer of training. Its interpretation in terms of associative interference theory will be discussed in the next chapter. Be-

71

fore moving on to theoretical interpretations, however, we will describe one more empirical phenomenon, termed *context-dependent memory*.

Contextual Stimuli and State-Dependent Learning

The role of the environment in which learning and recall take place has long been recognized as potentially important. The seventeenth-century British associationist philosopher John Locke cited a number of instances of such factors, including a curious anecdote about a young gentleman

> who having learned to dance, and that to great perfection, there happened to stand an old trunk in the room where he learned. The idea of this remarkable piece of household stuff had so mixed itself with the turns and steps of all his dances, that though in that chamber he could dance excellently well, yet it was only while that trunk was there; nor could he perform well in any other place, unless that or some other such trunk had its due position in the room (Locke 1690; Everyman's Library Edition [1961], vol. 1, pp. 339–340).

There are, of course, somewhat better-controlled instances of this type of phenomenon, including a study by Greenspoon and Ranyard (1957) of the role of the immediate environment on RI. They required their subjects to learn a list of ten nonsense syllables, followed by a second list, which in turn was followed by recall of the first list. Learning took place in one of two contrasting laboratory environments, which they refer to as the "drum room" and the "card room." In the drum room, the subject sat in a comfortable chair in a quiet, dimly lit area and was presented with the lists on a memory drum (hence the name), while the experimenter remained discreetly out of sight. Card room subjects had a much less comfortable time. They were required to stand and learn the list from cards presented by the experimenter in a brightly lit room filled with bits of old apparatus. A mistuned radio played loudly, and the door to an adjacent rat-running room was left open so as to lend a distinctive odor to the experiment. Greenspoon and Ranyard were interested in answering two basic questions: (1) Does additional material cause less interference if it is learned in a distinctly different environment? (2) Is subsequent recall better when it occurs in the same environment as the learning took place (as Locke's dancing gentleman would suggest)? The rigors of the card room did not affect the subject's rate of learning, and results from the two rooms are therefore combined in Table 4–3, which uses *A* to represent the initial learning room and *B* to represent the alternative room. Thus, for example, the *AAA* group learned lists 1 and 2 and recalled list 1 all in the same room, while the *ABA* group learned and recalled the first list in the same room but learned the second list in the other room. It is clear from Table 4–3 that RI was indeed minimized when the interfering list was learned in a distinctive context

TABLE 4–3

Influence of the environmental context on interference and recall.
A *represents the learning environment and* B *a contrasting environment.*

GROUP	ORIGINAL LEARNING CONTEXT	INTERPOLATED LEARNING CONTEXT	RECALL CONTEXT	SYLLABLES RECALLED ON TRIAL 1
1	A	A	A	3.47
2	A	A	B	1.79
3	A	B	A	7.12
4	A	B	B	3.91

Source: Data taken from J. Greenspoon and R. Ranyard, Stimulus conditions and retroactive inhibition, *Journal of Experimental Psychology* 53 (1957): 55–59.

and that recall was helped by returning to the environment where the learning took place.

It should perhaps be pointed out that despite a number of demonstrations of context-dependent memory, there have also been failures to observe an effect over and above that due to the distracting effect of actually moving from one environment to another (Strand 1970). However, subsequent studies by Godden and Baddeley, using both artificial laboratory environments and, with divers as subjects, contrasting underwater and land environments, have shown clear context-dependent recall effects which are not attributable to the disruption of moving from one environment to another. In one of these experiments (Godden and Baddeley 1975), 16 divers learned lists of 40 unrelated words either on the shore or 10 feet under the sea and were subsequently asked to recall them in either the same or the alternative environment. Mean free-recall scores are shown in Table 4–4, from which it is clear that what is learned underwater is best recalled underwater, and vice versa. A further experiment tested the interruption hypothesis by requiring subjects to learn and recall on dry land under two conditions: in one, they rested between learning and

THE PSYCHOLOGY OF MEMORY

TABLE 4-4

Recall of words by divers as a function of learning and recall environment.

LEARNING	RECALL ENVIRONMENT		TOTAL
ENVIRONMENT	DRY	WET	
Dry	13.5	8.6	22.1
Wet	8.4	11.4	19.8
Total	21.9	20.0	

Note: "Dry" involved learning on the shore; "wet" involved learning under-water. Words were best recalled in the environment in which they were learned.
Source: D. R. Godden and A. D. Baddeley, Context-dependent memory in two natural environments: on land and underwater, *British Journal of Psychology* 66 (1975): 328.

recall; in the second, they were required to enter the water and dive to a depth of 20 feet before returning and recalling. Disruption had no effect on subsequent recall, a result which supports the contextual cue interpretation of the first experiment.

A phenomenon which is probably related to that of contextual memory is *state-dependent memory,* in which learning that occurs under the influence of a changed physiological state, usually drug induced, is best recalled in the same physiological state. There are many examples of this phenomenon in both animal and human learning (Kumar, Stolerman, and Steinberg 1970), but one example should suffice. Goodwin, Powell, Bremer, Hoine, and Stern (1969) studied the acquisition and subsequent retention of a series of tasks including rote learning, avoidance learning, free association, and memory for pictures—both "neutral," from a mail-order catalog, and "emotional," from a nudist magazine. They found that for all except the picture recognition task, what had been learned under alcohol was best re-called under alcohol. They cite clinical evidence of heavy drinkers who, when sober, are unable to find alcohol and money which they hid while drunk but who remember the hiding places once they are drunk again. The absence of a state-dependent effect with recognition is interesting, since it implies that the state-dependent memory phenomenon may be a retrieval effect (as interference theory would suggest) and that recognition testing, which reduces the retrieval problem, may provide a means of confirming that an effect is actually state-dependent. A similar result has been observed in the case of context-dependent memory by Godden and Baddeley (unpublished): divers tested underwater or on land showed a clear context-dependent effect in recalling word lists but no effect with a recognition measure.

We have in this chapter sampled some of the vast amount of evidence pointing to the existence of interference as a reliable phenomenon. We shall be concerned in the next chapter with attempts to explain the phenomenon of interference and to generalize such an explanation to account for all forgetting.

C H A P T E R

5

Associative Interference
Theory

ASSOCIATIVE INTERFERENCE THEORY has its roots in the doctrine that all memory is based on the association of ideas, a view originating in classical times and further elaborated in the seventeenth century by the British associationist philosophers Hobbes and Locke. It was first applied to experimental data in the 1890s by the German psychologist G. E. Müller and was introduced into American psychology by L. W. Webb (1917). In its modern form, however, associative interference theory stems largely from the Chicago functionalists Carr, Robinson, and McGeoch, and it was for many years dominated by the "dust-bowl empiricist" approach to science that characterized functionalism, with its emphasis on the collection of data to the almost complete exclusion of theoretical development. (For a more detailed account of the origins of modern interference theory, see Irion 1959, pp. 540–544). In recent years, however, interference theory has become less rigidly functionalist, as it has attempted to expand beyond the traditional topics and techniques of verbal learning. Nevertheless, there is still a sense in which the term interference theory is a misnomer, since it suggests a single unified theory. In fact, it is less a theory than a pragmatic attempt to produce a set of general principles based on two assumptions: (1) that the essence of learning is the association of stimuli and responses, and (2) that the phenomena of transfer of training are basic to the process of learning and forgetting.

The approach is illustrated most clearly by the *A–B, A–C* transfer paradigm (see Table 4–2), which involves teaching the subject first one list of pairs, the *A–B* list (e.g., *vicar-chilly*), and then a second list (*A–C*) in which all the stimulus words are the same but the response words are different (e.g., *vicar-drunken*). This causes more forgetting of the first list than would be caused by a *C–D* list which is completely unrelated (e.g., *farmer-putrid*). The effect of interference from subsequent learning (retroactive interference) tends to diminish over time as the delay between learning and recall is increased (Briggs 1954), whereas the effect of prior learning (proactive interference) tends to increase with delay between learning and test (Greenberg and Underwood 1950). The retroactive interference (RI) effect was observed by Webb (1917), who attributed it to two factors. He suggested, first, that learning *A–C* caused the active disruption of the previously learned *A–B* list and, second, that when the *A–B* list was relearned there was a tendency for stimulus *A* to reinstate competing response *C*.

Response-Competition Hypothesis

Subsequently, McGeoch (1932; 1936) dispensed with Webb's assumption of the disorganization of *A–B* and attempted to explain all forgetting in terms of the single principle of response competition. He assumed very simply that the *A–B, A–C* situation caused two responses, *B* and *C*, to be attached to a single stimulus, *A*. When *A* is presented, the subject will make the stronger of the two responses. Note that this assumes that the associations *A–B* and *A–C* do not directly interfere with each other; *A–C* does not weaken *A–B*, it simply competes, and when *A–C* is stronger, the *C* response will be made in place of B. This has been called the "independence-dominance hypothesis" (Postman 1969).

One feature of a simple response-competition hypothesis is that it makes clear predictions about the mistakes that subjects will make. When the subject relearns the *A–B* list, his errors should consist mainly of intrusions from the interpolated list (i.e., *C* responses). Furthermore, the number of such intrusions should be closely related to the amount of interference, as measured by the difficulty of relearning *A–B*. This was examined directly in a study by Melton and Irwin (1940) using the serial learning of lists of nonsense syllables. After learning the first list to a criterion of one perfect anticipation trial, subjects then either rested (the control group) or learned a second list for 5, 10, 20, or 40 trials. One day later, they relearned the original list, and the amount of retroactive interference was estimated by subtracting the number of relearning trials required by the control group from the relearning scores of the various RI groups. The experimenters then used prior list intrusions to obtain a second estimate of RI. On a simple response-competition hypothesis, the two estimates should agree, since it is assumed that the reason the *B* response does not occur is because the *C* response is dominant. Results of the two estimates, shown in Figure 5–1, are clearly inconsistent with the hypothesis on two counts: first, the absolute number of intrusions is much smaller than would be expected; second, the shapes of the two RI functions differ markedly. Total RI estimated from the relearning scores increases

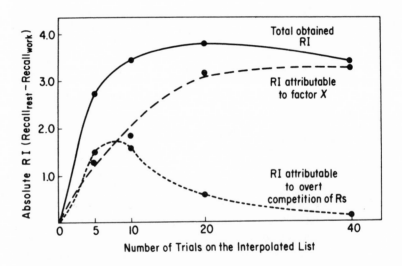

Figure 5–1   Amount of RI as a function of the degree of learning of interpolated material. The lower curve represents the amount of RI attributable to overt intrusions. The middle curve represents the discrepancy between the observed amount of RI and that expected on the basis of intrusions and attributed to "factor X." Source: A. W. Melton and J. M. Irwin, The influence of degree of interpolated learning on retroactive inhibition and the overt transfer of specific responses, *American Journal of Psychology* 53 (1940): 185. Reprinted by permission.

systematically with the number of interpolated trials up to ten and then levels off, whereas the number of intrusions at first increases but then *decreases* with the number of interpolated trials. Melton and Irwin suggest that some other process, which they term "factor X," must be responsible for the considerable amount of RI that could not be attributed to overt intrusion errors. They suggest that this factor may be analogous to the extinction of responses in classical conditioning when reinforcement is discontinued. Melton and Irwin suggest that *A–B* responses continue to be made during *A–C* learning but, being incorrect, are not reinforced, and hence are extinguished. This position was further developed by Underwood (1948*a*; 1948*b*), who assumed two factors, response competition and the unlearning of *A–B* associations during *A–C* learning, a view somewhat similar to that of Webb (1917).

New techniques were devised in the attempt to produce direct evidence of unlearning. Briggs (1954) devised a technique known as Modified Free Recall (MFR), in which the subject was allowed to give either the *B* or the *C* response; this in turn was adapted by Barnes and Underwood (1959) into a technique known as Modified Modified Free Recall (MMFR), in which the subject attempts to give both the *B* and the *C* responses when presented with stimulus *A*. It was assumed that response competition is a "momentary dominance of one associative response over another or the equally transitory mutual blocking of two responses of approximately equal strength" (Postman 1969, p. 196). Since such blocking was assumed to be transitory, and since in MMFR the subject may take as long as he wishes to make his responses, it was claimed that this technique eliminated the effects of response competition, thus providing a pure measure of unlearning. Whether this is a plausible assumption will be discussed in due course.

Barnes and Underwood performed an experiment closely analogous to that of Melton and Irwin. They first required their subjects to learn an *A–B* list of eight nonsense syllable-adjective pairs (e.g., *yig-hopeful*) to a criterion of one perfect trial. They then required them to learn an *A–C* list with the same stimuli but different responses (e.g., *yig-lovely*) for 1, 5, 10, or 20 trials. Recall was then tested using the MMFR technique; the subject first tried to recall the two responses associated with each stimulus and subsequently indicated which response came from which list. Figure 5–2 shows the mean number of responses recalled and assigned to the appropriate stimulus and list as a function of the amount of interpolated *A–C* learning. As the *A–C* list is learned, the probability of recalling the *B* responses decreases,

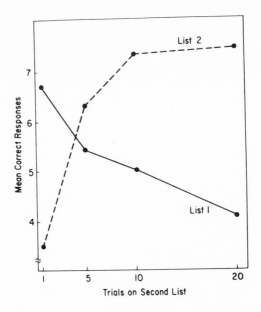

Figure 5–2   Mean number of responses recalled correctly in an RI experiment as a function of degree of list 2 learning. Although subjects were requested to produce both list 1 and list 2 responses, a greater degree of list 2 learning produced a decrement in list 1 recall. Source: J. M. Barnes and B. J. Underwood, "Fate" of first-list associations in transfer theory, *Journal of Experimental Psychology* 58 (1959): 101. Copyright 1959 by the American Psychological Association. Reprinted by permission.

although responses recalled were almost always assigned to the correct list. This forgetting of the *B* responses in a situation regarded as free from response competition was interpreted as strong evidence for the unlearning of the *A–B* association. Unfortunately, Barnes and Underwood did not include *C–D* control groups who learned unrelated pairs for 1, 5, 10, or 20 trials, so it is not possible to decide how much of the effect is due to specific *A–B, A–C* interference and how much to more general factors.

Proactive Inhibition and the Forgetting of Single Lists

Interference theorists have classically concentrated their attention on transfer-of-training experiments in which one set of material can be assumed to interfere with the retention of another. The forgetting of a single list was generally assumed to be caused by RI from subsequent verbal activity. However, such an interpretation has difficulty in accounting for the considerable forgetting that still occurs when interpolated activity is minimized, for instance by sleep (e.g., Jenkins and Dallenbach 1924) or hypnosis (Nagge 1935).

A solution to this problem was suggested in an influential paper by Underwood (1957), who emphasized the importance of PI in such forgetting. He plotted data from 16 studies, all of which involved learning to a criterion of one perfect trial and recall 24 hours later. He plotted the result of each study as a function of the number of prior lists that had been learned by the subject (see Figure 5–3). There is a very marked tendency for amount retained to decline with successive lists. Since it was at that time common for experimenters to use the

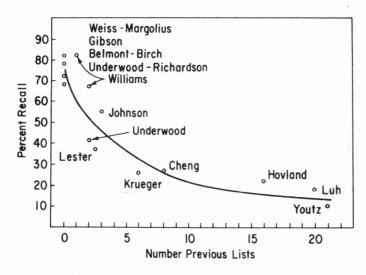

Figure 5–3 The role of PI in the recall of single lists. Each point represents the recall of a list learned 24 hours previously; the more previous lists the subject has learned, the poorer his retention. Source: B. J. Underwood, Interference and forgetting, *Psychological Review* 64 (1957): 53. Copyright 1957 by the American Psychological Association. Reprinted by permission.

same subjects repeatedly, Underwood's results suggested that the degree of forgetting typically cited in the literature was almost certainly inflated by the effects of PI. It further suggested that considerable interference with recall from prior language habits (*extra-experimental interference*) might also be likely. Hence, forgetting would be expected even if the interval between learning and subsequent recall were completely free of interfering activity. Before going on to consider the question of extra-experimental interference, however, an alternative reinterpretation of Underwood's results by Warr (1964) should be discussed.

Warr pointed out that the more lists a subject learns, the more rapidly he reaches the criterion of one perfect recitation. (See the section on learning to learn in the previous chapter.) In early lists, subjects are often close to criterion for several trials before eventually reaching it. Since some responses are learned very quickly and are subsquently recalled on every trial, the *average* number of times a response has been made correctly will be greater on the early lists, which require the most trials to learn. Consequently, although each list is learned to the same criterion, the average degree of learning of the individual items is likely to decrease over successive lists. This being so,

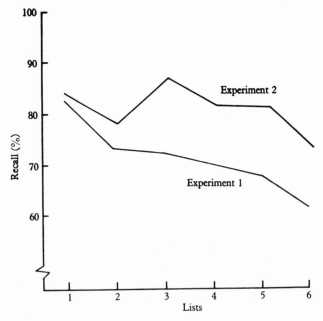

Figure 5–4   Mean percentage of items correctly recalled after 24 hours from each of six paired-associate lists. Experiment 1 involved learning each list to a criterion of one perfect recall; later lists were learned more quickly but also forgotten more quickly. Experiment 2 involved presenting each list for the same number of learning trials; here PI effects were much reduced. Source: P. B. Warr, The relative importance of proactive inhibition and degree of learning in retention of paired-associate items, *British Journal of Psychology* 55 (1964): 23. Reprinted by permission.

82

the forgetting observed by Underwood (1957) may be grossly exaggerated by the differential degree of learning of individual pairs in early and later lists. In order to test this, Warr first repeated Underwood's basic experiment, in which subjects learned a series of paired-associate lists to a criterion of one perfect recall and subsequently recalled each list 24 hours later. As the lower line in Figure 5–4 shows, the amount retained over 24 hours declined with each successive list, as Underwood had demonstrated. Warr also obtained the characteristic decrease in the number of trials needed to reach criterion with successive lists. In order to eliminate this confounding variable, Warr categorized each pair in each list on the basis of how often it had been correctly recalled during learning; he then plotted separately the items at each level of learning, a technique devised by Underwood (1945). Items matched for degree of learning showed slightly poorer retention on later lists, but the degree of this PI effect was considerably reduced. A subsequent study by Keppel, Postman, and Zavortink (1968), in which five subjects learned 40 successive lists, also used the control of matching items for degree of initial learning and found rather more substantial PI effects. There is, therefore, general agreement that the phenomenon of PI does occur and is not entirely attributable to differences in degree of initial learning. However, its effects are almost certainly less than might appear from the studies which are usually quoted.

Extra-Experimental Interference Hypothesis

Although Underwood's estimate of the importance of PI in forgetting was probably exaggerated, it is still possible that the much greater degree of prior learning comprising a subject's language habits may form a major source of interference.

Such a hypothesis was advanced by Underwood and Postman (1960), who suggested two main effects of prior language habits, *letter-sequence interference* and *unit-sequence interference*. Letter-sequence interference stems from the subject's experience with the letter structure of written language. When he is required to learn infrequent letter combinations, his learning will be impaired because of his need to unlearn prior associations; forgetting will be accelerated by the spontaneous recovery of such associations. Hence, learning the letter pair QI will involve unlearning the prior association between Q and U; the Q–U association will subsequently recover and cause forgetting. Unit-sequence interference is based on the prior associations among words. When a list of unrelated words is learned, the new associations will require the unlearning of prior competing word-word associations; these, in turn, will recover and cause forgetting based on PI. Unlike letter-sequence interference, which is assumed to be greatest with sequences of low probability, unit-sequence interference is assumed to be maximal with high-frequency words, since these are likely to have more and stronger prior associations.

The extra-experimental interference hypothesis thus predicts that with a comparable level of initial learning, improbable letter sequences will be forgotten faster than probable sequences and lists of high-frequency words faster than lists of low-frequency words. A number of experiments have tested these predictions with almost uniformly negative results. (See Keppel 1968 for a survey of these studies.) Given the same degree of initial learning, amount retained seems to be unaffected by either letter-sequence probability or word frequency.

One explanation for the failure of the extra-experimental interference hypothesis was explored by Underwood and Ekstrand (1966), who pointed out two ways in which prior language habits differ from prior lists in the classical PI paradigm. First, language habits are learned gradually over a period of years—that is, the learning is based on distributed practice. Second, the degree of learning is much greater than typically occurs in verbal-learning experiments. Experiments investigating these two variables showed little effect of degree of list 1 overlearning but a marked influence of distribution of practice. When the learning of list 1 was distributed over several days, its tendency to interfere with the subsequent recall of a second list learned under massed practice was markedly reduced. When retention of list 1 was subsequently tested using the MMFR technique, retention was almost perfect. While the explanation of this result is far from clear, it provides a strong indication that extra-experimental language habits, learned under conditions of widely distributed practice, are unlikely to interfere with the retention of lists of words learned under the standard laboratory conditions of massed practice. While this may go some way toward explaining the complete failure of the extra-experimental interference hypothesis, it provides little comfort for interference theory, since it emphasizes the gap between the highly artificial conditions from which the principles of interference theory are derived and forgetting in everyday life.

Interference and Recognition Memory

There has in recent years been considerable concern among interference theorists over the apparent absence of interference effects in studies testing retention by recognition. Garskof and Sandak (1964) and Postman, Stark, and Fraser (1968) have shown that massive interpolated learning (enough to produce an RI decrement of 50 percent with the MMFR technique) produces a drop in performance of only 10–15 percent when the need for response recall is avoided by providing the responses and requiring the subject to match them with the appropriate stimuli. When the response-learning phase is eliminated from both original learning and subsequent recall by using multiple-choice recognition instead of recall, the amount of RI is reduced even further (Postman and Stark 1969).

In terms of the widely accepted interference theory interpretation of response learning as based on contextual associations, this implies that RI effects reflect the extinction of such associations between environmental cues and responses, a view which Postman (1969) has shown to raise some serious problems of interpretation. First, since response learning is generally assumed to occur *before* the formation of associations between stimulus and response words, responses would be expected to be *better* learned, hence *more* resistant to forgetting and not less, as this interpretation of the recognition data would suggest. Second, if RI effects are attributable to the unlearning of responses, comparable effects should occur with *A–B, A–C* and with *A–B, C–D* designs, since both involve an equivalent amount of response learning, with different responses required in the two lists. But, in fact, the *A–B, A–C* paradigm does produce much more RI.

General Response-Set Interference or Specific Response Competition?

Postman (1969) attempts to avoid these problems by proposing that in learning a second list, the subject applies a "rule" restricting his responses to those present in that list. He suggests that the rule relies on a selector mechanism which typically responds on the basis of relative recency and frequency of occurrence, and that its task of excluding responses from the wrong set is made more difficult if the two sets are similar. Since the selector mechanism is not perfect, intrusions will occur and will be particularly frequent (1) early in learning, when the rule is still being "learned," or (2) when the two sets of responses are similar, or (3) when the two sets of responses are attached to similar stimuli, as in the *A–B, A–C* paradigm, in which *A* provides a common verbal context for the two sets of responses.

Immediately after interpolated learning, the rule for selecting list 2 responses will be dominant and will therefore interfere with any attempt to recall list 1, making any but the strongest responses unavailable. Postman further suggests that "the dominance of the most recent criteria of selection may be assumed to diminish over time" (Postman 1969, p. 201), leading to the relative recovery in availability of the first list, a phenomenon that has frequently been observed. The same process also accounts for the increase in PI with delay. PI is assumed to be the result of competition between two sets of rules; as time elapses, the relative dominance of the later rule will diminish, producing an increased tendency for responses from the first set to intrude.

It is possible, however, that interference theory may not need to resort to Postman's response-set hypothesis after all. Anderson and Watts (1971) point out that all the recognition studies cited by Postman are so designed as to avoid specific competition between responses attached to the same stimulus. They do so either by limiting recognition alternatives in an *A–B, A–C* paradigm to responses from the *A–B* list (Postman and Stark 1969) or by indicating the list from which the various response alternatives are drawn (Postman, Stark, and Fraser 1968). Anderson and Watts go on to show that when the recognition set includes both the correct (*B*) responses and the specific competing response (*C*), RI effects do occur with recognition testing. Recognition scores were lower for *A–B, A–C* groups than for the *A–B, C–D* control group when recognition sets contained both of the competing responses, but not when only one was included, as in the studies by Postman et al. Incorrect responses were much more likely to constitute the specific competing response (*C*) than responses that had been associated with other stimuli in either the *A–B* or the *A–C* list.

Further evidence for specific response competition comes from the observation of massive RI with the *A–B, A–Br* paradigm, in which the second list comprises the same stimuli and responses as the first, but paired differently. Since the same set of responses occurs in both the original and the interpolated lists, the response selector mechanism should require no modification, and hence should produce no response-set interference. Nonetheless, this paradigm produces even more RI than the $A–B, A–C$ paradigm (Postman 1972a). Similarly, when a mixed-list design is used, whereby both RI and control items appear within the same list, interference effects occur (Weaver, Rose, and Campbell 1971). This would not be possible if all interference effects applied to the list as a whole.

It should be pointed out, however, that Postman's claim that "the mechanism responsible for unlearning operates primarily if not exclusively on the entire repertoire of first list responses rather than on individual stimulus-response associations" (Postman 1969, p. 200) need not completely rule out specific response competition, and Postman and Underwood (1973) have subsequently claimed that their position was "misunderstood" by Anderson and Watts, since they did not "deny by any means that the second factor, namely specific competition, will come into play under appropriate circumstances" (Postman and Underwood 1973, p. 26).

It appears then that the concept of *specific* response competition is once more accepted. How good, then, is the evidence for *generalized* response competition? The recognition studies which have shown little or no RI appear to have eliminated specific response competition by excluding the specific competing responses (see Anderson and Watts 1971); is there then any clear evidence of RI which can *not* be attributed to specific response competition? Evidence cited by Postman and Underwood (1973) for general response-set interference includes work by Lehr, Frank, and Mattison (1972), who found that when $A–B$ learning is followed by the free-recall learning of a set of C responses, some RI occurs, although not so much as with interpolated $A–C$ learning. While this result is compatible with general response-set interference, the mixture of paired-associate and free-recall learning paradigms leaves the phenomenon open to a wide range of possible interpretations. For instance, if one regards the experimental environment as a stimulus with which free-recall responses are associated, then this becomes an $A–B, A'–C$ design in which each list 1 associate is followed by a series of list 2 associates, all of which bear some stimulus similarity with it (because the environment constitutes a common cue). Postman and Underwood also cite the finding that when responses in the $A–C$ list are very different from the B responses, RI is greatly reduced (Da Polito 1966). This is a potentially important result, but it does not necessarily imply response-set interference, since the phenomenon could presumably be operating at the level of the individual association.

The same authors discuss a good deal of additional evidence, but since it is compatible with both item-specific and response-set interference, it does not bear directly on the issue. Thus, although it seems intuitively very probable that subjects do on occasion derive retrieval rules governing the learning of particular lists (see Baddeley 1972), and although it also seems likely that interference between successive rules may occur, the evidence for this at present is equivocal. One cannot but agree with the conclusion of Postman and Underwood (1973, p. 26) that "it would clearly be premature to draw any definitive conclusions at the present time regarding the validity of the principle of response suppression." While interference between specific associations is clearly demonstrable, the case for general response-set interference remains unproven.

Unlearning and the Independent Retrieval Phenomenon

A further potential difficulty for classical interference theory is raised by what Martin (1971) has termed the *independent retrieval phenomenon*. He suggests that associative interference theory assumes that forgetting occurs because of direct competition between the $A-B$ and the $A-C$ associations. If this is so, there should be a negative correlation between the probability of recalling the B and the C responses; the greater the strength of the $A-B$ association, the smaller should be the probability of recalling the competing C response. However, Da Polito (1966) showed that this was not the case; the probability of recalling $A-B$ appears to be independent of that of recalling $A-C$, a result which has subsequently been shown by Greeno (1969) and Martin (1971) to hold across a large range of studies.

Postman and Underwood (1973) discuss the independent retrieval phenomenon in some detail and criticize Martin's conclusions on two counts. They argue, first, that Martin's claim that the phenomenon is inconsistent with classical associative interference theory is not justified and, second, that the evidence for the existence of the phenomenon is of questionable validity. The first of these criticisms is the more fundamental, since it bears on the basic concept of unlearning, and if it is conceded, the detailed technical arguments involved in the second criticism become far less crucial. Postman and Underwood suggest that unlearning does not necessarily involve the *weakening* of a response; it simply implies a reduced probability of its emission. Since this is essentially what Martin himself claims (e.g., Martin 1973), the conflict appears to be more apparent than real. The disagreement between Martin and Postman and Underwood over the interpretation of a concept as apparently basic as that of unlearning does, however, highlight the relative absence of agreement about even the most basic assumptions underlying associative interference theory.

Extinction and the Concept of Unlearning

For many years, unlearning has been assumed to be analogous to the phenomenon of extinction in classical conditioning, which is believed to reflect the progressive weakening of a conditioned response in the absence of reinforcement. Keppel (1968) discusses the extinction analogy in some detail and concludes that unlearning resembles counterconditioning, in which a new response is substituted for the old, rather than extinction. Unlearning differs from extinction in at least three ways:

(1) The omission of the response leads to extinction in conditioning but does not lead to forgetting in paired-associate learning. Indeed, Buttler and Peterson (1965) found that presenting the stimulus alone increased the probability of subsequent response recall.

(2) The spontaneous recovery of extinguished responses is a very marked effect in conditioning, whereas the absolute spontaneous recovery of the *A–B* associations in an *A–B, A–C* paradigm tends to be rare (Keppel 1968) and small in magnitude (e.g., Postman, Stark, and Fraser 1968).

(3) The extinction of a conditioned response requires the unreinforced elicitation of the response. In the RI paradigm, however, unlearning does not appear to require the overt performance of the *A–B* response. Of course, it can be argued that the response is covertly performed, and hence extinguished. Such a view is hard to test, and what indirect evidence is available is, in the words of Postman and Underwood (1973, p. 22), "far from impressive."

If unlearning is not analogous to extinction, then what is it? Is there indeed any need to assume a separate unlearning factor, over and above that of response competition? The major source of evidence in what Postman and Underwood (1973, p. 22) refer to as "the verification of the unlearning hypothesis" comes from the MMFR technique. List 1 responses tend to be forgotten as list 2 learning increases; since the MMFR task is assumed to be free of response competition, an additional source of forgetting must be invoked, that of unlearning. Note, however, that the contention that the MMFR task avoids response competition requires some very strong assumptions about the retrieval process involved. More specifically, it appears to assume that merely by allowing the subject to make both responses, competition is avoided. This may seem very plausible if one regards responses as discrete items; when one is emitted, it makes room for the next. However, this clearly cannot be an adequate model of retrieval, since it implies a process of sampling without replacement. In this model, retrieving an item should make subsequent recall of that item *less* likely, whereas there is considerable evidence that the opposite is true; a recall trial functions very much as an additional learning trial (e.g., Tulving 1967). Yet another problem is raised by Koppenaal's (1963) demonstration that PI effects may be detected using the MMFR technique; since PI is assumed to reflect only response competition, it is difficult to explain how an MMFR technique that is free of response-competition effects could produce such a result.

A slightly more plausible view of the retrieval assumptions underlying the MMFR technique is given by Postman (1969), who suggests that the MMFR technique would avoid response competition if one were prepared to assume that the blocking of one response by a competing response (1) is transitory and (2) fluctuates sufficiently rapidly to allow both responses to be dominant for part of the time during the recall period. He points out, however, that there is no evidence to support either of these assumptions, and hence no reason to suppose the MMFR technique to be free of response competition. Curiously enough, having made this very telling point, Postman (1969, p. 197) goes on to ignore it by discussing at some length the nature of unlearning as if it were a phenomenon, rather than a concept made plausible only by the dubious assumption that the MMFR technique is free of competition effects. Since the foundations on which the concept of unlearning is based are so shaky, it is perhaps not surprising that "attempts to specify the exact mechanisms of associative unlearning have met with only indifferent success" (Postman and Underwood 1973, p. 23). It would seem necessary to return to first principles and to consider the question of whether the assumption of an unlearning process is really necessary. We shall return to this point in the final section of this chapter, after considering a recent attempt to produce an alternative version of interference theory.

Martin's Interpretation of Interference

In a series of papers, Martin (1971; 1973) has suggested an alternative associationist view of interference. The core of Martin's position is the *stimulus encoding variability hypothesis*. This assumes that a given functional stimulus—for example, a word—may be interpreted by the subject in a range of different ways. Martin assumes that these alternative encoding features of the word are independent and that on any trial any one feature may be selected by the subject. However, the features differ in probability of being selected, and one source of difficulty in learning a paired-associate list is the variability in which particular features of each stimulus are sampled on successive trials. Hence, if the subject has learned to associate feature 1 of the stimulus with the correct response on the first trial but encodes feature 2 during the test, he will be unable to produce the appropriate response. The more varied and inconsistent the subject's encoding of the stimulus, the more difficult will be the learning. Hence, learning a paired-associate list requires the subject to modify his stimulus sampling up to a point at which the appropriate stimulus feature is very much more likely to be sampled on a given trial than are any of the inappropriate features.

One determinant of which feature of a stimulus will be selected is the response with which it is associated; consequently, during the interpolated learning of an *A–B, A–C* RI experiment, the subject will learn to encode a different feature of the *A* stimulus because of its association with a different response. RI is assumed to represent the persistence of the *A–C* feature-sampling bias during the attempt to recall the original *A–B* learning. Similarly, PI represents the persistence of the *A–B* feature-sampling bias during *A–C* recall. The independent retrieval phenomenon is explained in terms of the assumption that various features of a stimulus are independent. In an MMFR situation it is assumed that the probability of the subject's sampling the stimulus features associated during *A–B* learning will be independent of the probability of his utilizing the features of *A* encoded during *A–C* learning (although the assumption of an overall bias which produces the RI effect clearly constrains this independence).

Martin's position is criticized by Postman and Underwood (1973) on three counts. They claim that the evidence for the independence of the various components of the stimulus is far from strong, and they cite evidence from their own studies which conflicts with that observed by Martin. More crucially, they point out that attempts to produce direct evidence for encoding variability have been uniformly unsuccessful. There is apparently no strong evidence to suggest that subjects do encode the A stimulus differently in the $A–B$ and $A–C$ phases of a classical transfer experiment. While Martin may legitimately claim that techniques currently available are insufficiently subtle to reveal genuine changes in stimulus encoding, the absence of empirical evidence clearly weakens his position very considerably. Finally, Martin's approach is criticized for relying heavily on the standard $A–B$, $A–C$ negative transfer paradigm. It is far from easy to see how it would be applied outside this procedure; for example, what is the relevant stimulus in free recall, where clear RI effects are observed (Tulving and Psotka 1971)? When one moves outside the laboratory altogether, the question of identifying stimuli and responses becomes even more difficult, and the appropriateness of a model based so rigidly on S–R associations becomes still more questionable.

Nevertheless, although Martin's position does not currently present a convincing alternative to more classical approaches to interference, the concept of stimulus encoding variability is one which seems worth exploring in considerably greater detail. There is, for example, some evidence that a stimulus which has been encoded in a range of different ways is more likely to be recognized on a subsequent test (Bevan, Dukes, and Avant 1966). Similarly, the concept of stimulus encoding variability has been used in order to explain the distributed-practice effect in short-term memory (Melton 1970). It may be recalled that this phenomenon reflects the tendency for an item which has been presented twice to be better recalled if the two presentations are separated by several intervening items than if they are presented adjacently. The encoding variability interpretation of this result suggests that the two adjacent presentations are likely to lead to the encoding of the same feature on both presentations, whereas a separated presentation is more likely to lead to two different encodings. If one assumes that a larger number of encodings is likely to enhance the probability that one of these will be accessible at recall, then it follows that distributed presentations will be better than massed presentations. Note, however, that whereas Martin tends to emphasize the negative effects of encoding variability (the greater the range of possible encodings, the lower the probability of selecting the same encoding on presentation and recall), Melton's interpretation emphasizes the advantages of encoding variability. These positions are not inconsistent, of course; the first implies that the fewer the available encodings, the greater the probability that a particular encoding will occur at both learning and test trials; the second suggests that given a standard number of possible encodings, the greater the range of features of a stimulus which has been encoded during learning, the greater the probability that a learned feature will be sampled on recall. Hence, both suggest that the higher the proportion of possible encoding features that has been associated during learning, the greater the probability of subsequent recognition or recall. The concept of encoding variability is potentially a fruitful one, but it clearly needs considerably more empirical exploration if it is to assume the theoretical significance which both Martin and Melton suggest it deserves.

The Present State of Interference Theory

It is becoming increasingly clear that interference theory, once regarded as "one of the most successful and established theories in psychology" (Kintsch 1970), is now in a state of crisis. Interference theory has difficulty in demonstrating its relevance outside the rigid confines of the verbal-learning laboratory and faces increasing competition from more cognitive views of memory (e.g., Bower 1970a), which have in recent years produced a wealth of new and interesting experimental results (see Chapter 11). Why then does it continue to survive? Certainly not simply because of the conservatism of its defenders. Indeed, it is notable that virtually all the evidence against interference theory has been amassed by proponents of the theory, notably Postman and Underwood. In contrast to its dust-bowl empiricist origins, interference theorists have worried at the shortcomings and limitations of the theory with exemplary zeal and with what must have been discouraging effectiveness. Two papers by Postman provide good examples of the frankness and thoroughness with which interference theory has been criticized by its adherents. The first discusses most of the problems outlined in the present chapter and concludes: "While the shortcomings of existing formulations are beginning to be understood, it is fair to say that the principles of RI and PI established in the laboratory have thus far failed to generate a model of the forgetting process which can be shown to have general validity" (Postman and Keppel 1969, p. 406).

A second, subsequent paper (Postman 1972) gives an admirably fair and thorough review of the evidence for organizational factors in memory. It claims, with some justification, that the phenomena can be explained in the language of an associationist interference theory. But Postman goes on to admit that "during the last decade organization theorists have asked many important and imaginative questions about the conditions of learning and recall that association theorists have not asked. Whether the best in both approaches can be melded productively remains to be seen" (ibid., p. 29).

Postman in particular has gone to considerable lengths to maintain an interference theory position in the face of increasing difficulties (Postman 1963; 1969; 1972; Postman and Underwood 1973). In discussing his reluctance to abandon the extra-experimental interference hypothesis, Postman (1969) emphasizes (1) the evidence for the occurrence of PI and RI in the laboratory and his obvious reluctance to assume separate mechanisms for forgetting in everyday life and (2) the absence of any competing theory. As he points out, decay theory, the historical alternative to interference theory, has not generated testable alternative hypotheses. This is certainly true historically; the only recent attempt to apply decay theory to long-term memory was Brown's (1959) model, which was never developed beyond its original highly schematic form.

One reason for the lack of an alternative has been the trend during the 1960s away from global models attempting to explain large tracts of data in terms of a few simple principles. While I believe this to be a healthy development, I think there is still a use for simplified global theories, inasmuch as they give an economical description of a large amount of important data. In its primitive atheoretical form, interference theory served this function (though it did little else). Those who have attempted to develop it theoretically have run into many snags, and attempts to circumvent them have become increasingly complex and cumbersome. As early as 1963, Postman proposed five additional ways in which interference theory could "explain" deviations from the predicted result, and the intervening years have increased this number yet further (e.g., Postman 1969; 1971; Postman and Underwood 1973).

Interference theory no longer provides an economical description of the phenomena of normal forgetting, PI, or RI. The following section attempts to do so in terms of a simple trace theory, which aims to provide an economical description of the major phenomena of forgetting, pending the development of the more powerful and detailed information-processing models which an adequate account of human memory will probably demand.

A Modified Trace Theory

The theory will attempt to cover the following basic phenomena:

(1) Normal everyday forgetting;
(2) RI effects which
    (a) depend on amount and similarity of interpolated material and
    (b) decrease with delay between interpolated learning and recall; and
(3) PI effects which
    (a) depend on amount and similarity of prior learning and
    (b) increase with delay between learning and recall.

Recall is assumed to be based on a decaying trace and a retrieval process with two components, the first a search process which locates the trace, the second a process of discrimination of the trace against a background of "noise."

Traces are assumed to decay exponentially with time, although it is quite probably the quasi-random neural activity occurring during the delay, rather than time per se, which causes the decay of the trace. Recall first requires the location of the trace, and as Norman (1970a) has pointed out, the retrieval process may have more in common with problem solving than with the processes usually studied in connection with memory. Given the question "What were you doing 16 months ago?" subjects typically perform a good deal of preprocessing of the question before even beginning the actual memory search. As Tulving and Pearlstone (1966) have demonstrated, the problem of locating a stored item is a major factor in forgetting even with a recently presented word list. Tulving and Psotka (1971) have shown that interference effects in free recall are principally of this type. Their experiments demonstrate that RI effects occur with the free recall of a series of categorized lists but can be largely avoided by cuing the subject with the names of the categories comprising the list to be recalled. In paired-associate learning, however, it seems possible that interference occurs at the levels of both trace discrimination and trace location. With an $A–B$, $A–C$ interference paradigm, the B and C responses may be stored at the same or at least a similar location, making subsequent trace discrimination difficult.

Interference effects at the level of both search and trace discrimination are assumed to reflect a process somewhat analogous to McGeoch's concept of response competition. However, I would like to suggest that the process of selective attention may provide a more appropriate analogy than that of classical conditioning as used by interference theory. Discriminating two competing traces is analogous to attempting to listen to one of two simultaneous spoken messages. Deciphering the appropriate message becomes more difficult as the alternative message becomes louder or more similar to the crucial message in location, voice, or content (Moray 1969), just as recall difficulty increases with the degree of learning and similarity of the interfering material. Visual selective attention probably provides a somewhat more appropriate analogue, since it is more static than speech, which by its nature is continuously changing over time, although the basic principles are probably the same. This analogy is illustrated in Figure 5–5, which shows the

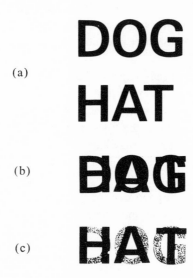

(a) DOG HAT

(b) BOG

(c) HAT

Figure 5–5   A visual analogue of response competition: (a) no competition; (b) competition between two equally strong stimuli; (c) competition between stimuli of unequal strength.

difficulty in interpreting two superimposed signals, each of which is readily discriminable on its own. Note that if one signal is much stronger than the other, it will continue to be discriminable. The discrimination problem is not solved by allowing the subject to make both responses, as is the case with RI, where requiring the subject to produce responses from both lists in the MMFR technique does not prevent interference effects. The selective attention analogy does not suggest that the MMFR will be free of response-competition effects, as interference theorists initially assumed. Thus it has no difficulty in accommodating the fact that the MMFR technique is also sensitive to the effects of PI (Koppenaal 1963; Postman, Stark, and Fraser 1968), a result which presents problems for interference theory, which regards PI as entirely attributable to response competition and MMFR as competition-free.

The visual analogue we have been using is, of course, oversimplified. The storage location of an item is probably represented by as many dimensions as the subject uses in coding the word during learning. One of these is probably a temporal dimension, and it may be the distinctiveness of the distributed-practice prior lists on this dimension that allowed Underwood and Ekstrand's subjects to minimize proactive interference between these and later lists learned under massed practice.

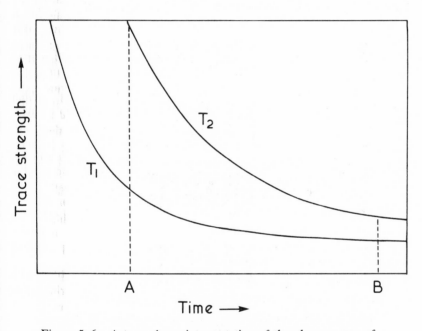

Figure 5–6   A trace decay interpretation of the phenomenon of interference. T_1 and T_2 represent the fading traces of two successive lists over time. Competition between the two lists is a function of the relative strengths of the two traces at the time of recall. At time A, list 2 has just been learned and T_2 will be substantially stronger than T_1. At this point, RI effects will be maximal (reflecting the difficulty of retrieving trace T_1 in competition with the much stronger trace T_2), while PI effects (based on the retrieval of T_2) will be minimal. At time B, when the two curves are both approaching asymptote, the ratio of T_1 to T_2 will be smaller. This will reduce the amount of RI observed (based on retrieval of T_2) but increase the amount of PI (based on T_1 retrieval).

If the two traces decay exponentially with time, their relative strengths will change as shown in Figure 5–6, in which T_1 represents the trace of list 1, T_2 that of list 2. When list 1 is recalled at point A, shortly after list 2 has been learned, RI will be considerable, since the strength of T_2 is much greater than that of T_1. By point B the discrepancy has diminished, and with it the degree of RI, as is the case empirically (Briggs 1954). In the case of PI, of course, the reverse is true; if list 2 recall is requested at point A, little PI will occur, since the competing list 1 trace is weak relative to the new and strong list 2 trace. As the delay between list 2 and recall increases, the *relative* strength of the competing trace T_1 will increase (although its absolute strength is decreasing); hence PI, the tendency for T_1 to compete with T_2, will increase over time, as is the case empirically (Greenberg and Underwood 1950).

The decrease in RI and increase in PI over time is explained by the two-factor interference theory by assuming that list 1 associations which have been unlearned during list 2 learning spontaneously recover over time. Curiously enough, theorists who claim to find the notion of traces decaying as a function of delay unacceptable, since they feel that time per se cannot influence memory, appear to find the concept of traces spontaneously recovering as a function of mere passage of time quite acceptable. The trace decay hypothesis just described differs from that of spontaneous recovery in predicting that the increase in the strength of T_1 over time should be relative rather than absolute. This does not, of course, mean that the probability of recalling T_1 may not increase over time. Recall depends in part on the relative strength of T_1 and T_2; provided T_2 declines at a sufficiently rapid rate, it is possible for the recall probability of T_1 to increase, although since the strength of T_1 is itself declining, such an effect is unlikely to be either large or reliable. This appears to be the case; most of the numerous experiments on spontaneous recovery have succeeded in showing a relative improvement, but few show an absolute increase in the probability of recalling list 1 items (Keppel 1968).

To summarize, we have assumed that traces decay exponentially with time and that recall involves first locating the trace, then discriminating it from background noise. The stronger the trace and the more discriminable it is from the background noise, the greater the probability of correct recall. This simple model provides an economical description of normal forgetting, together with the major features of PI and RI that have traditionally been regarded as the strongest evidence for interference theory. Whether it can ever become more than a simplified description will depend on whether the rather vague conceptualization of the search and retrieval process can be successfully elaborated.

We have so far been content to treat the memory system as a unified whole. We shall be concerned in the chapters which follow with the attempt to analyze memory into separate subsystems.

CHAPTER

6

How Many Kinds of Memory?
The Two-Component View

WHEN YOU LOOK UP a telephone number, remember it long enough to dial it, and then forget it, are you using the same memory system as when you recall your own familiar number? The question of whether there are separate memory systems underlying long-term memory (LTM) and short-term memory (STM) or only one system functioning at two different levels of learning was one that caused considerable controversy during the 1960s. It might be thought that the evidence from the consolidation studies discussed in Chapter 3 would preclude a unitary view of memory, but for a number of reasons this was not the case.

Limitations of the Unitary View

Relatively few people working on normal human memory were familiar with the more physiological approach to memory typically adopted by consolidation theorists, who based most of their conclusions on either experiments using animals or on hospital patients suffering from memory defects. The results of such studies were often conflicting, as in the ECS animal studies, which indicated a short-term memory component ranging in alleged durability from seconds to hours. In addition, it was far from clear that one could validly extrapolate from experiments in which rats were shocked for stepping off a platform to the very complex language habits involved in testing a human subject's verbal memory. For all these reasons, the question of whether human memory is a unitary system or involves two or more components was discussed in relative isolation from the research on consolidation.

The traditional S–R associationists did not distinguish between LTM and STM, although this was probably attributable largely to their almost exclusive use of LTM techniques in the 1940s and 1950s. Similarly, people working on STM at this time were not generally interested in LTM or in the traditional associationist approach. They were more often concerned with information theory (e.g., Miller 1956; Broadbent 1958) or with applied telecommunications problems (Conrad 1958), and they tended to conceive of forgetting in terms of trace decay rather than interference. In the 1950s there was no controversy mainly because there was virtually no communication between workers in LTM and in STM.

The situation changed dramatically following the discovery by Brown (1958) and Peterson and Peterson (1959) that a sequence of items well within the memory span will be forgotten within 20–30 seconds if the subject is prevented from rehearsing. Figure 6–1 shows the results of the study by Peterson and Peterson (1959) in which subjects were shown three consonants (a CCC trigram) and required to retain them for periods ranging from 3 to 18 seconds. In this technique, each subject is tested many times, and it is possible to obtain a smooth forgetting curve from a short experiment using relatively few subjects. These results attracted considerable attention for two reasons: (1) they appeared to illustrate an elegant new technique for studying in great detail the forgetting of individual items, and (2) both Brown and Peterson interpreted their results in terms of decay theory, not in terms of interference theory, which was then almost universally accepted by those working on LTM. If the new phenomenon did indeed reflect trace decay, then it implied either separate STM and LTM systems or else a unitary system based on the principles of decay theory, a view which was totally unacceptable to the S–R associationists who composed the vast majority of people working on human memory at that time. For

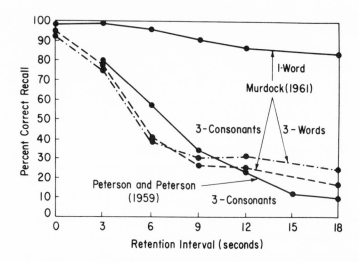

Figure 6–1 Short-term retention of CCC trigrams (Peterson and Peterson 1959) and one-word and three-word sequences (Murdock 1961). Source: A. W. Melton, Implications of short-term memory for a general theory of memory, *Journal of Verbal Learning and Verbal Behavior* 2 (1963): 9. Reprinted by permission.

this reason, the initial controversy focused on the question of whether forgetting in STM was based on trace decay or interference.

In 1963, Melton presented a strong defense of the concept of a unitary memory system obeying the principles of interference theory. He showed a range of similarities between the phenomena of LTM and STM and argued that, in the absence of convincing evidence to the contrary, it was more parsimonious to assume one system and one single set of principles. We shall postpone discussion of the nature of short-term forgetting till a later chapter. Suffice it to say at this point that Melton showed that it was far from obvious that STM reflected trace decay rather than interference; in doing so, he clearly demonstrated the need for further, more direct evidence before the unitary view of memory could be dismissed.

Melton's demonstration of the similarities between LTM and STM also helped make clear the need to distinguish between STM as an *experimental situation* and STM as a *labile memory system* which may be responsible for some, though not necessarily all, of what is recalled in such a situation. In order to minimize confusion, we shall henceforth use the term STM to refer to a *situation,* typically involving the presentation of a relatively small amount of material to be tested within a few seconds. We shall use the term *short-term store* (STS), as suggested by Atkinson and Shiffrin (1968), to refer to the *system* which is frequently assumed to contribute to STM performance. We shall use *long-term memory* (LTM) to refer to situations in which a large amount of material is typically presented for several trials and may be tested after a considerable delay. The term *long-term store* (LTS) will be used to refer to the memory system underlying recall in such a situation.

While Melton's paper presented a powerful attack on the view that STM was not explicable in terms of interference theory, it is open to a basic objection: the similarities shown between LTM and STM reflect the fact that most, if not all, STM techniques draw on both the STS and LTS systems. Since STM tasks have an LTS component, it is not surprising that similarities can be shown with LTM tasks having a similar, if somewhat larger, LTS component. Nevertheless, Melton's paper was extremely valuable in emphasizing the lack of convincing evidence against a unitary system, and it was without doubt influential in stimulating further work on the question and, possibly even more important, in helping bridge the communications gap between traditional S–R associationism and the information-processing approach to memory that characterized most of the work on STM.

Two-Component Tasks

In the mid-1960s, evidence against a unitary view of memory began to accumulate from a variety of sources. Several STM tasks were shown to comprise two separate components, one suggesting a labile STS system, the other implying a more stable LTS component.

FREE RECALL

The two components appeared to show up particularly clearly in the free-recall task, in which the subject is presented with a list of items which he subsequently tries to recall in any order he wishes. Probability of recalling a given item depends on when it was presented. When recall is immediate, the last few items presented tend to be recalled first and best (see curve *A* on Figure 6–2). This phenomenon is known as the *recency effect,* since it reflects enhanced recall of the most recent items.

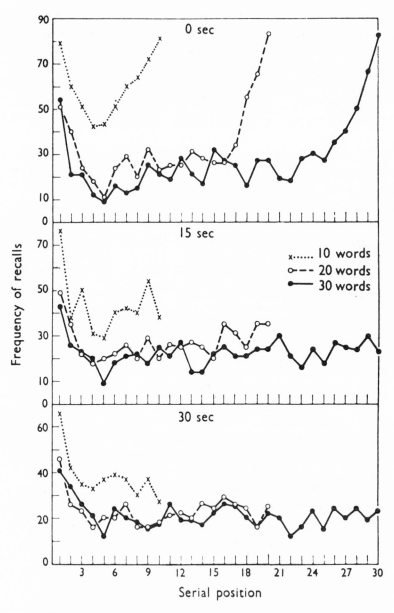

Figure 6–2   Serial position curve for lists of 10, 20, or 30 words recalled either immediately or after a 15- or 30-second delay. Note that for each list length the last few items presented are very well recalled on immediate test (the recency effect) but not after a delay. Source: L. Postman and L. W. Phillips, *Short-term temporal changes in free recall, Quarterly Journal of Experimental Psychology* 17 (1965): 135.

Both Postman and Phillips (1965) and Glanzer and Cunitz (1966) independently showed that when recall is delayed for a few seconds, during which rehearsal is prevented by a counting task, the recency effect disappears (see curve *B* on Figure 6–2), whereas performance on earlier items is virtually unaffected by the delay.

Provided recall is immediate, however, the recency effect is remarkably robust, being unaffected by virtually any of the characteristics of the words comprising the list, such as whether the words are similar to each other in sound or meaning (Craik and Levy 1970), how many syllables they comprise (Craik 1968*a*), how often each word is repeated (Glanzer and Meinzer 1967), or even, with trilingual subjects, whether they come from one, two, or three different languages (Tulving and Colotla 1970). In contrast, the earlier portion of the list, which is assumed to reflect the LTS component, is sensitive to all of these and, in addition, to virtually any variable that is known to influence LTM, including rate of presentation (Glanzer and Cunitz 1966), word frequency (Raymond 1969), the age of the subject (Craik 1968*a*), and many others (Glanzer 1972).

SERIAL PROBE TASK

Waugh and Norman (1965) devised a task in which subjects listened to a sequence of 16 digits. One of the digits from the sequence was then repeated, accompanied by a tone which indicated that the subject was to respond with the item that had followed that digit in the sequence. Thus, given 5719624809132957–tone–4, the subject should respond 8. This task shows a pronounced recency effect, attributed by Waugh and Norman to the STS superimposed on a relatively stable LTS component. As would be expected, if recall is delayed and rehearsal prevented, the recency effect vanishes, leaving only the relatively stable LTS component (Baddeley 1968*a*).

SHORT-TERM PAIRED-ASSOCIATE LEARNING

In short-term paired-associate learning, the subject is presented with a number of pairs of items (e.g., *dog-blue, cat-red, hen-gray, pig-black, cow-green*). The subject is then tested on one or more of the pairs by being given the first word and asked to supply the second (e.g., *cat-?* [*red*]) before going on to another, different list. Peterson (1966) showed that the last pair of items behaves as if registered in the labile

STS; if tested immediately, recall is very good, but recall declines rapidly if the test is delayed by a rehearsal-preventing task. However, recall of earlier pairs, although initially low, actually improves with delay (see Figure 6–3a). A further discrepancy between immediate and delayed recall is shown in Figure 6–3b; repeating a pair of items has a slight negative effect on immediate recall, reflecting both STS and LTS, but a pronounced positive effect when the recall is delayed for 8 seconds, at which time it is presumably based almost entirely on LTS.

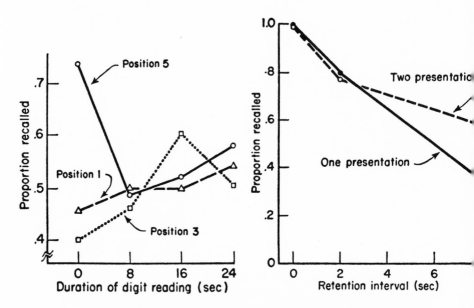

Figures 6–3a and 6–3b   Evidence for two components in minimal paired-associate learning. Figure 6–3a shows the retention of the first, third, and fifth pairs presented, following 0 to 24 seconds of interpolated digit reading. Note that only the last item shows forgetting. Figure 6–3b shows recall after one or two presentations of a pair. Note that the effect of dual presentation is evident only after a delay. Source: L. R. Peterson, Short-term verbal memory and learning, *Psychological Review* 73 (1966): 199, 201. Copyright 1966 by the American Psychological Association. Reprinted by permission.

SERIAL MEMORY SPAN

With the serial memory span technique, devised by Jacobs (1887), the subject is presented with a sequence of items which he attempts to recall in the presented order. Although this is the most traditional STM task, it has been claimed to have a large LTS component. Craik (1970) has shown that memory span correlates more highly with the LTS component of free recall ($r = +.72$) than with the STS component ($r = +.49$). When the STS component is eliminated by delaying recall, performance is impaired, but the decrement is not very great and is largely limited to the later items in the sequence (Baddeley and Levy 1971).

BROWN-PETERSON TASK

The Brown-Peterson short-term forgetting task is a particularly complex procedure which is still not fully understood but which will be discussed in greater detail in Chapter 7 (pp. 122–131). When LTS interference from prior items is avoided by testing each subject only once, the task appears to show a small STS component, which disappears within about 5 seconds, and a relatively large and stable LTS component (Baddeley and Scott 1971).

It appears to be the case that most, if not all, STM tasks contain a substantial LTS component. This should be taken into consideration in attempting to draw conclusions about STS from STM experiments.

Amnesia and the STS–LTS Dichotomy

It has been known for many years that patients suffering from Korsakov's syndrome may have a gross LTM defect together with an unimpaired immediate memory span. Korsakov's syndrome is an alcoholic condition which results from excessive drinking and inadequate diet; this is assumed to lead to a vitamin deficiency which produces permanent brain damage and may be associated with dementia, amnesia, or both. The amnesia is reflected in the patient's inability to recall such simple facts as what day or year it is, where he is, or how long he has been in the hospital. He has no apparent knowledge of current events and is quite unable to say, for example, who is the current British prime minister or U.S. president. On the other hand, he is generally able to talk about his early life, where he was born, his job and family, and events preceding his alcoholism, with no obvious impairment. In terms of performance on memory tasks, such patients have great difficulty in learning new material, such as paired-associate lists, but have an unimpaired immediate memory span either for digits or for words presented randomly or as sentences (Zangwill 1946).

Patients suffering from bilateral damage to the temporal lobes and hippocampus show a similar pattern of normal digit span and unimpaired general intelligence, coupled with a grossly defective ability to learn new things. The most extensively studied case is the patient H.M. (Milner 1970); after a bilateral operation on the temporal lobes and hippocampus aimed at reducing epileptic seizures, H.M. suffered from very pronounced amnesia.

Some of the best quantitative data on temporal lobe amnesia come from a study by Drachman and Arbit (1966) using a technique devised by Ebbinghaus in which subjects are presented with digit sequences of varying lengths, each sequence being repeated until correctly recalled. Their results showed that amnesic patients did not differ from control subjects in their memory span, but once this was exceeded, their ability to learn such sequences was grossly impaired.

So far we have presented evidence for a specific LTM deficit in amnesic patients who have normal memory span. What does this imply for the STS–LTS distinction that is assumed to underly the STM–LTM dichotomy? Baddeley and Warrington (1970) investigated this by testing a group of amnesic patients on tasks assumed to comprise differential STS and LTS components. In one experiment, subjects were tested on the free recall of lists of ten words, recalled either immediately or after a 30-second delay, during which rehearsal was prevented by a counting task. The results are shown in Figure 6–4. Although the amnesic patients performed very poorly after the 30-second delay, on immediate tests they showed a normal recency effect. When the two components were separately computed, the amnesic subjects were found to have very poor LTS but completely unimpaired STS, a result that is consistent with a serial probe study by Wickelgren (1968) on the patient H.M. described extensively by Milner (1970).

While it has been known for many years that amnesic patients may have normal STM, it has only recently been pointed out that the converse may also occur (Warrington and Shallice 1969; Shallice and Warrington 1970). Their initial work was performed on a single patient, K.F., but a number of further cases have subsequently been studied (Warrington, Logue, and Pratt 1971). K.F. suffered from damage in the left parieto-occipital region following a motorcycle accident. He was slightly aphasic and had occasional difficulty in selecting the appro-

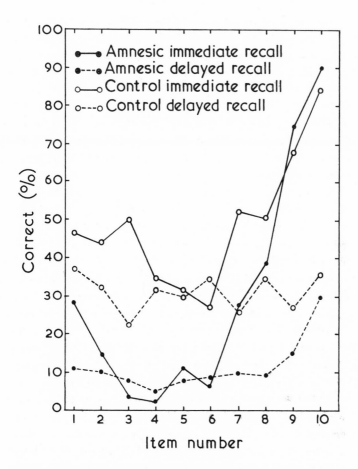

Figure 6–4   Immediate and delayed free recall in amnesic and control patients. Note that amnesics show a normal recency effect. Source: A. D. Baddeley and E. K. Warrington, Amnesia and the distinction between long- and short-term memory, *Journal of Verbal Learning and Verbal Behavior* 9 (1970): 179.

priate word when speaking and rather more difficulty in reading. He had no general amnesia; he was fully aware of his situation and could discuss events of current interest quite normally. He had, however, an auditory digit span of less than three items, although his span increased when the digits were presented visually. His long-term learning ability was good and his free-recall performance normal, except for a recency effect of only one item, suggesting a normal LTS but defective STS.

Hence, it appears to be the case that amnesic patients show a pattern of memory disruption that suggests a clear STS–LTS dichotomy.

Differential Capacity of LTM and STM

Wundt (1905) observed that the span of immediate memory was about six "simple impressions," whether these were digits, letters, words, or unrelated lines. When items were grouped, however, the span increased greatly; thus, the span for letters increased to ten when they were presented as CVCs (consonant-vowel-consonant nonsense syllables), and to between 20 and 30 when they formed part of a meaningful sentence. This point was emphasized in an influential paper by Miller (1956), who showed that span of immediate memory was only very slightly influenced by the amount of information per item. In this context, the term *information* is used in its technical sense, as defined by Shannon and Weaver's *Mathematical Theory of Communication* (1949). The amount of information conveyed depends on the amount of uncertainty present at the time of the message. A message telling you that 2 is an even number would convey no information, since you presumably already know this. If I flip a coin, my telling you that it came up heads does give you some information, although since there are only two possible outcomes, I would be giving you less information than if I rolled a die and told you which of the six possible numbers had come up.

Information is measured in terms of the *bit,* the number of binary yes/no questions that would be required to discover the outcome. In the case of the coin, the answer to a single question (e.g., *Was it a head?*) is enough to give me a complete answer and reduce the uncertainty to zero. A message describing the outcome of a single toss is thus said to convey one bit of information.

Suppose I were to take a pack of cards and select one; how much information would I convey by telling you whether I had selected a heart, club, diamond, or spade? As Figure 6–5 indicates, with four equally likely alternatives, two binary questions are required—*Is it a red card?;* if yes, *Is it a heart?*—and telling you that the card is a heart therefore conveys two bits of information. The measure is not of course limited to cases in which the number of alternatives is a power of two, as Figure 6–5 illustrates. This shows the mean number of binary questions involved in determining which of 10 numbers has been selected. In each case the amount of information conveyed is $\log_2 N$, in which N is the number of equiprobable alternatives. It should be noted, however, that although it is convenient to measure information in terms

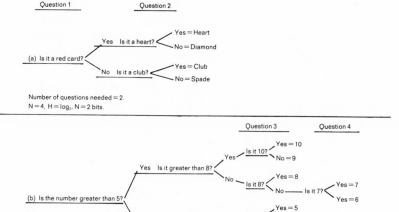

Number of questions needed = 2.
$N = 4$, $H = \log_2 N = 2$ bits.

Note: Mean number of questions needed = 3.4.
$N = 10$; $H = \log_2 N = 3.32$ bits.

Figure 6–5 Mean number of questions needed to discover (a) which of 4 suits has been chosen from a pack of cards and (b) which of 10 digits has been chosen. Note in the latter case that the mean number of questions in the example is in fact slightly greater than $\log_2 N$. This is because it is not possible on a single trial to distribute questions optimally, since 10 is not a power of 2. The optimal strategy could, however, be applied over a sample of trials by distributing the questions probabilistically.

of the base 2, the base of the logarithm selected is purely arbitrary; the base 10—or, indeed, any other base—would be equally valid.

In all the examples described so far, the possible outcomes have been equiprobable, but frequently this is not the case. The statement that it was sunny today is much more probable if I am talking about San Diego in the summer than if I am describing Wigan in the winter. The more probable the statement, the less the information conveyed. Suppose my pack of cards is biased so as to comprise 50 percent hearts, 30 percent diamonds, 10 percent clubs, and 10 percent spades. My optimal first question would then be *Is the card a heart?* On 50 percent of the trials the answer would be yes, and no further questions would be required. If the answer were negative, the optimal second question would be *Is it a diamond?* If I am unfortunate enough to be wrong again, then a third question would be required. Since on 50 percent of the trials one question would be required, on 30 percent two questions, and on the re-

111

maining 20 percent three questions, on average I would require 1.7 questions. The bias in the pack has thus reduced the information from 2.0 to 1.7 bits. (For further details see Attneave 1959.)

Miller (1956) pointed out that memory span for binary digits, each containing one bit of information, was only slightly longer than that for unrelated words selected from a population of 1,000, and hence conveying 10 bits per item. He concluded from this that the capacity of immediate memory was 7 ± 2 "chunks," regardless of how many bits of information each chunk contained. There is, however, still some disagreement about this. Crossman (1961) studied memory span using a range of natural vocabularies differing in size; their contents included directions (North, South, East, and West), digits, months, consonants, and words. By modifying the information measure so as to give increased weighting to the information conveyed by the order of occurrence of the items, Crossman was able to produce some support for the view that the information content of memory span remains constant, not the number of chunks. (See Welford 1967 for a sympathetic discussion of this view.) Crossman's position is, however, open to a number of objections. It can be argued that he is, in fact, counting order information twice in his estimate, and even then the span for words conveys more information than does the span for smaller vocabularies. It has also been pointed out by Conrad and Hull (1964) that the larger vocabularies used by Crossman, such as consonants, tend to contain many items that are similar in sound; Conrad and Hull demonstrated that the greater the acoustic similarity of the items comprising the sequence, the poorer the subject's performance. When vocabulary size and acoustic similarity were pitted against each other, acoustic similarity was found to be much the more potent factor. A subsequent experiment by Woodhead (1966) compared memory span for vocabularies of two and eight items with acoustic similarity controlled. She found a small advantage for the binary set; this was, however, entirely explicable on the basis of the higher probability of guessing correctly in that condition. It seems, then, that Miller is broadly correct in claiming that the main determinant of memory span is number of chunks rather than amount of information per chunk, although span *is* influenced by such additional factors as acoustic similarity (Conrad and Hull 1964) and word length (Baddeley, Thomson, and Buchanan 1975).

It follows from the chunk hypothesis that it should be possible to increase the memory span by combining items into fewer chunks. As letter sequences approach more and more closely to English, the span can be increased by combining several letters into a single speech sound;

hence a sequence such as *mucrup* becomes two chunks rather than six. A recent study by Slak (1970) applies a similar process to the recall of digit sequences by devising a recoding scheme which allows digit trigrams to be recoded as CVCs; for example, the sequence 265070193 would be recoded as *bafdiltun*. Once the code was learned (unfortunately, this took 20 hours!), it produced a dramatic improvement not only in digit span but also in serial learning, free recall, and recognition memory for three-digit numbers.

Although memory span is relatively insensitive to amount of information per chunk, this is not true of LTM. Nevelsky (1970) studied the effect of vocabulary size on both memory span and what he terms long-term memory span. This is computed by dividing the number of items learned by the number of trials required to learn that sequence. He used vocabularies of 2, 8, 64, and 512 three-digit numbers (i.e., 1, 3, 6, and 9 bits of information per item). In contrast to results for STM, long-term memory span was very sensitive to amount of information per item, with the 512-alternative set requiring 6.5 times as long to learn as the binary set. However, when the span was measured in terms of amount of information, it proved much more stable, showing only a 1.8-fold increase in learning trials. It is possible that this in turn may underestimate the amount of information contained in the 512-alternative set, since it seems probable that the subject may have been insufficiently familiar with the set to take full advantage of the restriction in size and may, in effect, have been operating on the basis of the full set of 1,000 possible three-digit numbers (000–999). In this context, it would be interesting to repeat Nevelsky's (1970) study using letter sequences and varying the information load by manipulating the degree of approximation of the letter sequences to English. In this situation, it is fair to assume that subjects will be sufficiently familiar with the statistical structure of the language to make full use of any reduction in information due to letter sequence redundancy.

So far, then, it appears that STM as measured by the memory span is limited to about seven chunks, whereas there is no obvious limit to the capacity of LTM. On the other hand, amount of information per chunk is important for LTM but not for STM. To what extent do these statements hold for STS and LTS?

Craik (1971) reviewed the evidence for the capacity of the STS component in free recall and concluded that it is between 2.5 and 3.5 words, considerably less than immediate memory span, a fact which he attributes to the LTS component in the memory span task. As we noted earlier, the STS component is not affected by word frequency, implying that, like memory span, it is probably not influenced by the amount of information conveyed by each word. The STS component is not affected by the number of syllables in the words being stored (Craik 1968a), whereas memory span is very sensitive to word length (Baddeley, Thomson, and Buchanan 1975). This suggests another possible reason why memory span may exceed the capacity of STS—namely, that it takes greater advantage of rehearsal. Consequently, the number of items recalled will be a function of the combined capacity of STS and the verbal rehearsal loop. It could be claimed that in free recall, where the number of items presented far exceeds the capacity of STS, using the available time for rote rehearsal is probably a much less efficient strategy than using it to encode material into LTS by organizing it semantically (Glanzer and Meinzer 1967).

Murdock (1965) studied the effect on free recall of a card-sorting task performed during the presentation of the list. He found that as the number of sorting alternatives was increased, the amount recalled decreased. In a subsequent study, Baddeley, Scott, Drynan, and Smith (1969) repeated Murdock's study, using both an immediate and delayed recall to allow separation of the STS and LTS components. The information load imposed by the sorting task was found to impair input into LTS but had no effect on STS capacity. This suggests that LTS has a much more limited input capacity than STS.

A recent study by Waugh (1970), using the serial probe technique, studied the time to retrieve an item from STS and LTS. She concluded that retrieval was faster from STS and that if an item is registered in both, it will be retrieved from STS in preference to LTS. It appears, then, that STS has a much smaller storage capacity than LTS but allows more rapid input and retrieval.

We have so far shown, first, that many tasks appear to have two separate components; second, that when broken down, these components appear to suggest two separate systems; and third, that the two suggested systems appear to differ in storage capacity. The next section presents evidence to suggest that the two rely on different coding processes.

Differential Coding in LTM and STM

In carrying out a study on memory span for consonant sequences, Conrad noticed that errors were often similar in sound to the correct letter (e.g., B for T, M for N), despite the fact that presentation was visual.

He investigated this further by collecting first a matrix of auditory confusion errors; this was obtained by requiring subjects to discriminate the relevant consonants when spoken against a background of white noise and recording the pattern of erroneous responses. He then produced an analogous confusion matrix for errors made in recalling visually presented consonant sequences. The two error matrices proved to be highly correlated ($\rho = .64$), strongly suggesting that subjects were translating the letters from their visual form and remembering them in terms of either their sound or the pattern of articulation used in vocalizing them (Conrad 1964).

There has been considerable discussion as to whether the coding is acoustic or articulatory, since the perception and generation of speech are so closely related that it is difficult to distinguish between the two alternatives (Wickelgren 1969). However, a more recent study by Conrad (1970) suggests that some, if not all, confusions have an articulatory basis. Conrad's experiment studied the recall of consonant sequences in congenitally deaf subjects. Analysis of confusion errors indicated that subjects fell into two relatively distinct groups, one showing "acoustic" confusions, the other showing a very different error pattern. When the subjects were subsequently rated by their teachers on how well they spoke, it was found that those showing an "acoustic" error pattern were consistently rated as better speakers. There is no doubt that some congenitally deaf subjects do articulate during memory tasks, and since they presumably do not receive any acoustic signal from this, it seems probable that the resulting confusion errors are articulatory in nature. Needless to say, the fact that articulatory confusions do occur does not prove that acoustic confusions do not. It should be noted at this point that the term *acoustic similarity* will subsequently be used operationally to refer to items which would be judged similar if presented acoustically. It does not, in the present context, imply that the basic encoding is acoustic rather than articulatory.

In another study, Conrad and Hull (1964) showed that acoustic similarity was an important determinant of memory span. They presented sequences of letters varying in the degree of acoustic similarity among the constituent letters. Highly similar sequences (e.g., *DCBTPV*) produced considerably more errors than dissimilar sequences (e.g., *LWKFRT*), although presentation was visual. Comparable results were shown by Wickelgren (1965), who also pointed out that acoustic similarity disrupted the retention of the *order* in which the letters occurred rather than retention of the letters themselves; item recall was in fact improved by acoustic similarity. This enhanced recall of item information is really not too surprising, since the fact that all the letters sound alike restricts the range of possible responses considerably, producing a reduction in information load which, in turn, is likely to facilitate guessing correctly. For this reason, when using similarity effects to study the dimensions on which subjects are encoding, it is usual to provide the subjects with displays showing the set of relevant responses, hence minimizing the need for item recall and maximizing the detrimental effect of similarity on the recall of order information.

The work of Conrad (1964) and Wickelgren (1965) showed that STM relies heavily on acoustic coding. Baddeley (1966a; 1966b) attempted to pursue the question further by asking, first, whether STM was more susceptible to acoustic than to semantic similarity and, second, whether the same was true of LTM. In order to compare acoustic and semantic similarity, it was necessary to use words rather than letters. In one study (Baddeley 1966b), subjects attempted to recall sequences of five words taken from each of four sets: acoustically similar words (*mad, map, man,* etc.), dissimilar control words (*pen, day, rig,* etc.), semantically similar words (*huge, big, great,* etc.), and semantically dissimilar words (*foul, old, deep,* etc.). Recall of each five-word sequence was tested immediately after its presentation. There was a massive effect of acoustic similarity, with subjects correctly recalling only 9.6 percent of the similar sequences, compared with 82.1 percent for the control sequences. In contrast, semantic similarity had an effect which, though statistically significant, was very small: 64.7 percent of the similar sequences, compared with 71.0 percent of the control sequences. However, the acoustically similar words were also, of course, visually and formally similar (i.e., they had many letters in common). This variable was studied by comparing a set of words that were visually and formally similar but different in sound (*cough, dough, through, bough,* etc.) and a set of words that were acoustically but not visually similar (*caught, sort, taut,* etc.), with appropriate controls. The results showed that the effects were indeed based on acoustic rather than visual or formal similarity.

In the equivalent LTM study (Baddeley 1966a), the same four basic sets of words were used, but sequence length was increased to ten words, and in order to minimize the role of the STS, a 20-second digit span task was interpolated between presentation and test. Four trials were given, followed by a fifth recall trial 20 minutes later. As in the STM study, the relevant set of words was continuously available, making the task one of recalling the order of the items. Results are shown in Figure 6–6. Whereas acoustic similarity had no reliable effect on

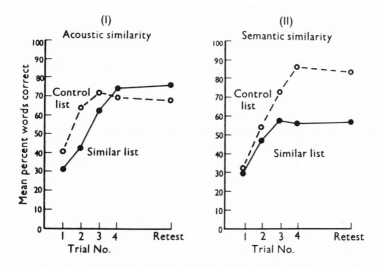

Figure 6–6   Effect of acoustic and semantic similarity on the learning and retention of word sequences, with STS controlled. Only semantic similarity has a reliable effect. Source: A. D. Baddeley, The influence of acoustic and semantic similarity on long-term memory for word sequences, *Quarterly Journal of Experimental Psychology* 18 (1966): 302–309.

performance, similarity of meaning markedly slowed the rate of learning. Studies using paired-associate learning showed substantially the same results—namely, that acoustic similarity affects STM and semantic similarity affects LTM (Baddeley and Dale 1966; Dale and Baddeley 1969; Baddeley 1970*b*).

Studies by Sachs (1967; 1974) suggest that this generalization extends beyond serial and paired-associate learning to the retention of prose passages. She presented her subjects with passages of text. Occasionally a sentence would be repeated, and the subject's task was to decide whether the repeat had been changed in any way. Sachs was principally interested in using this technique to test hypotheses about the encoding of grammatical features of the passage; consequently, a range of syntactic changes was studied, together with modifications in the meaning rather than the syntax. The results showed that most of the syntactic information was forgotten almost immediately, in contrast to the semantic information, which showed very little forgetting. Comparable results have been obtained by Wanner (1968), Johnson-Laird and Stevenson (1970), and Jarvella (1971).

Although there is now a great deal of evidence consistent with the generalization that verbal STM relies on acoustic coding whereas LTM is semantically coded (Baddeley, 1972), there are a number of exceptions. It is clear, in particular, that LTM may employ acoustic coding. As Aristotle pointed out (see Dennis 1948), when trying to remember a name, we often produce something which is similar in sound, even though we know it is not correct (e.g., *Mr. Garlick* for *Mr. Gulick*). Brown and McNeill (1966) demonstrated this in the laboratory in a study in which subjects were read the definitions of uncommon words and were instructed to attempt to produce the word. On occasion, subjects would feel strongly that the word was on "the tip of the tongue," although they could not retrieve it. Under these conditions, however, subjects could often report a number of acoustic features of the word, such as number of syllables and initial letter, indicating correct storage and retrieval of some acoustic characteristics of the word. Indeed, it is surely necessary to have a long-term acoustic memory in order to learn to speak and understand in the first place.

There is further evidence that subjects will employ acoustic coding in LTM if this allows them to simplify the learning task by applying a simple rule. Bower (1970*a*) has shown that if each response in a paired-associate list rhymes with its stimulus, the subject will use this acoustic feature to improve his performance. Similarly, McGlaughlin and Dale (1971) and Laurence (1970) have shown positive transfer with an *A–B, A–B'* design in which the second list involves the same stimuli as list 1 linked with homophones of the list 1 response (e.g., list 1, *fleshy-taught*; list 2, *fleshy-taut*). While this result might seem to suggest that subjects were storing list 1 acoustically, this is not necessarily the case. Even if they had stored it semantically, provided they recalled the list 1 word when presented with list 2, they would presumably discover the relationship, and from then on they would perform the appropriate transformation on their list 1 responses. A study by Bruce and Crowley (1970) on clustering in free recall is consistent with such a view. They studied the recall of groups of similar words embedded in a list of unrelated words. In the case of semantic similarity, recall was enhanced whether the words were presented as a block or were split up, whereas acoustic similarity facilitated performance only when the words were blocked. This is presumably because the acoustic features of the words were only used for retrieval from STS, so that if repetitions of similar words did not occur within the memory span, the similarity would not be noticed and used.

A second set of apparently conflicting results comes from a number of studies demonstrating semantic coding in STM. The bulk of these effects are probably attributable to the LTS component present in most STM tasks (see Baddeley 1972). This raises the more interesting question of the relationship between coding and the hypothetical STS and LTS systems. This question was studied by Kintsch and Buschke (1969) using Waugh and Norman's (1965) probe technique, which allows the separation of STS and LTS effects. In one study, the subject was presented with either 16 unrelated words or 8 pairs of synonyms (e.g., *polite-courteous*), the pairs being split up and presented in random order. One of the 16 words was then repeated, and the subject had to recall which word had followed it. In a second study, eight scrambled pairs of homophones (e.g., *night-knight*) were compared with a control list of unrelated words. Consistent with the two-component view, semantic similarity impaired LTS but had no effect on the STS component, while acoustic similarity had the opposite effect, depressing recall from STS but leaving LTS unaffected.

Unfortunately, such a clear relationship between STS, LTS, and coding is not always evident. For example, in a study (Baddeley 1970*b*) of coding in short-term paired-associate learning, three experiments all showed a clear effect of acoustic similarity, while no reliable semantic similarity effect was found. However, Peterson (1966) has shown that this task has a very large LTS component. Examination of the serial position curves suggested that the acoustic similarity effect was at least as great over the LTS portion of the task as for the STS component. While the occurrence of acoustic coding in LTS is no longer surprising, this result does raise the question of what determines whether or not material will be coded semantically.

One hypothesis is that semantic coding is relatively slow unless the material is highly meaningful; hence, subjects tend to encode acoustically in STM experiments because they are unable to process strings of unrelated words semantically, given a single rapid presentation. Baddeley and Levy (1971) tested this by using semantically compatible material (pairs of words such as *priest-pious, apple-delicious, lion-ferocious*). With compatible pairs a very reliable semantic similarity effect occurred, whereas when pairs were mismatched (e.g., *priest-delicious, apple-ferocious, lion-pious*), no evidence of semantic coding was found. A further experiment used serial recall and an immediate and delayed test to allow STS and LTS effects to be separated. The semantic similarity effect was only found after a delay, strongly suggesting that it was limited to LTS. A complementary study by Levy and Craik (1975) showed that effects of acoustic similarity with incompatible pairs of words disappeared when compatible pairs, allowing easy semantic coding, were presented.

Semantic coding presumably occurs in LTM studies using unrelated words mainly because presentation is usually slower and subjects have several trials with the same material. It is notable in this context that the semantic similarity effect found in Baddeley's (1966*b*) serial LTM experiment was not present on the first trial (see Figure 6–6). Presumably, semantic coding normally occurs in free recall because the subject is free to create his own meaningful relationships among as many of the words as he can encode and to recall the words in any way he wishes. However, as Eagle and Ortof (1967) showed, if the subject is required to perform a demanding supplementary task during presentation of a word list, evidence of acoustic coding does appear, implying that acoustic coding occurs when the subject does not have enough processing capacity for semantic encoding. A similar conclusion was reached by Poulton (1958) from a study in which subjects were required to read text at rates ranging from 37 to 293 words per minute. The forced increase in reading rate impaired recognition of statements about the *meaning* of the passage much more than it impaired the recognition of specific words. Poulton concluded that the rapid rates exceeded the subject's speed of comprehension, so that although he could process the individual words, he could not adequately encode the material semantically.

To summarize: STM frequently reflects acoustic coding simply because STM studies usually employ rapidly presented and often meaningless material. If the subject is not capable of encoding semantically under these conditions, both the STS and LTS components will show evidence of acoustic coding. When semantic coding is possible, it is likely to be apparent both immediately, in STM, and after a delay, in LTM (Baddeley and Ecob 1970). It appears to be the case, however, that a semantically coded sequence (and possibly even an individual item) will not be easily forgotten. In other words, semantic coding is equivalent to registration in LTS.

We have thus presented evidence for the existence of two memory components in a range of memory tasks. The two components appear to be differentially disrupted in certain amnesic patients and to reflect underlying storage systems with very different storage capacities which typically rely on different methods of encoding verbal material. It is not easy to see how the complex phenomena discussed in the present chapter could be explained in terms of a unitary system. The question of whether the dichotomous view is also too simple will be discussed in Chapter 8. First, however, we shall examine some of the characteristic phenomena of STM.

C H A P T E R

7

Short-Term Memory

ONE OF the dominant features of the field of human memory during the 1960s was the great increase in interest in short-term memory. As the previous chapter suggested, the question of a dichotomy between short-term and long-term memory stores was a dominant theme, but by no means the only one. The present chapter aims to discuss some of the other major theoretical issues and to explore some of the extensive empirical evidence accumulated since the early 1960s on the characteristics of STM.

Short-Term Forgetting

Much of the work on short-term memory has been concerned with the nature of short-term forgetting. This was initially regarded as a central issue because the claim that short-term forgetting is the result of trace decay was used as one of the principal arguments for a distinction between STS and LTS (Broadbent 1958). While the nature of forgetting is no longer regarded as an important argument in favor of a dichotomy, it remains an interesting question in its own right and provides a useful framework for exploring STM in greater detail. A wide range of techniques has been included under the general rubric of STM. Since they involve a range of different processes and differ widely in their degree of assumed reliance on STS, only the most commonly used techniques will be discussed.

BROWN-PETERSON TECHNIQUE

Much of the intial impetus for work on STM came from the independent discovery by Brown (1958) in England and Peterson and Peterson (1959) in the United States that sequences as short as three items would be forgotten within 20 seconds if the subject was prevented from rehearsing them during the retention interval. It seemed unlikely that this rapid forgetting was attributable to retroactive interference from the task used to prevent rehearsal during the retention interval, since Brown found that it made only a slight difference whether this distractor task involved the same or a different type of material. Similarly, the Petersons explicitly used a distractor task involving digits to avoid RI in their task, which involved consonant sequences. Further evidence against an RI interpretation was subsequently produced by Posner and Rossman (1965), who showed that the crucial feature of the distractor task was the amount of information processing it demanded, not the number of responses or their similarity to the material to be recalled. Both Brown and the Petersons interpreted their results in terms of a short-term memory trace that decays with time unless it can be maintained by active rehearsal.

An alternative interpretation based on interference theory was proposed by Keppel and Underwood (1962), who suggested that such forgetting might be due to PI from prior experimental items. To support this hypothesis, they produced evidence that the very first sequence on which the subject was tested showed little or no forgetting, whereas subsequent items showed the typical Brown-Peterson forgetting curve. They argued that learning a subsequent item involves unlearning the prior item. As time elapses, the prior item spontaneously recovers and causes forgetting by competing with the item to be recalled. The longer the delay, the greater the recovery; hence, the greater the amount of forgetting. Wickens, Born, and Allen (1963) subsequently showed that if, after a series of consonant sequences, the recall task is switched to digits, little or no forgetting occurs on the first trial with the new material, a result that fits neatly into interference theory, which predicts that interference only occurs between sets of similar material. This phenomenon is usually termed *release from PI* and can be shown to occur repeatedly if the material is changed every few trials. Figure 7–1 shows the results of a study by Loess (1968) in which subjects were required to remember three words selected from within a single taxonomic category (e.g., birds). Every seven trials, the category was switched (e.g.,

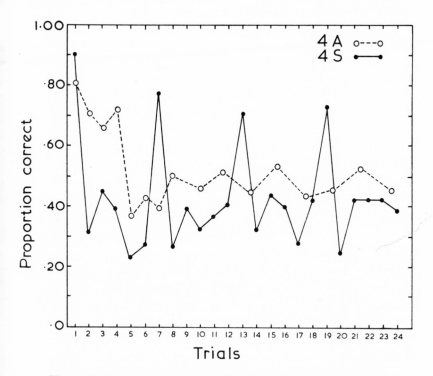

Figure 7–1   The release from PI effect. Group 4A received items alternately from four taxonomic categories. Group 4S received six items consecutively from each of four categories. Note that the first item of each new category in condition 4S shows excellent recall. Source: H. Loess, Short-term memory and item similarity, *Journal of Verbal Learning and Verbal Behavior* 7 (1968): 80. Reprinted by permission.

from birds to trees, then from trees to countries, etc.), producing an immediate improvement in performance (the release from PI) followed by a subsequent decline over the next six trials. Wickens (1970) has used this technique with considerable success as a means of investigating which aspects of verbal material subjects are encoding. It has been shown in this way that subjects are potentially sensitive to many aspects of the stimuli, ranging from their semantic characteristics to the nature of the background against which they are presented

(Wickens 1970). However, the implications of these results for the understanding of memory are much less clear, since there is currently no generally accepted explanation of the phenomenon of release from PI.

The most obvious interpretation of PI in the Brown-Peterson task is the classical interference theory view proposed by Keppel and Underwood. This assumes that the learning of new material causes the unlearning of prior items. Such items spontaneously recover over time and, by competing with the items to be recalled, cause forgetting; the longer the delay, the greater the spontaneous recovery and the lower the probability of recalling the correct item. Release from PI is assumed to occur because switching categories means that prior items are dissimilar; thus, they are not unlearned and do not spontaneously recover and cause interference.

However, the classical interference theory interpretation of PI in STM has difficulty in accounting for three phenomena. First, PI generally reaches a maximum within three trials; it does not build up gradually, as in LTM (Loess 1964). Second, Conrad (1967) observed that phonemically similar intrusion errors are more likely to occur after *short* delays than after long delays; according to classical interference theory, similar items should produce maximal unlearning, should be the last items to recover, and hence should produce such intrusions after *long* rather than short delays. Third, if trials are separated by a rest interval, PI is reduced (Peterson and Gentile 1965) and after 2 minutes virtually disappears (Loess and Waugh 1967); there is no reason to expect this on the basis of interference theory. A trace decay theory could, however, account for all these phenomena. The build-up of PI is maximal within a few trials because traces of items more than a few trials back will have decayed. Phonemic intrusions can be interpreted as based on partially decayed traces; after a brief delay, these still contain enough information about the initial item to allow a sensible guess. With further decay this information disappears, and intrusions approach random guesses. Finally, as the interval between successive trials is increased, the traces of prior items will decay more, making them less able to compete with traces of the correct items.

The trace theory implied in the last sentence differs in one important respect from earlier formulations (e.g., Brown 1958). It assumes that traces must be discriminated against a background of "noise," which in the Brown-Peterson task is made up from prior items. On this interpretation, release from PI occurs because the set of items to be recalled has a distinguishing feature which allows it to be discriminated from the background of partially decayed traces left by the prior items. Note that the crucial difference between this and classical interference theory is no longer the question of *whether* prior items interfere with recall but *how* they interfere. The classical theory claims that progressive forgetting is due to the spontaneous recovery of unlearned prior items; decay theory argues that prior items simply form a background of "noise" which exaggerates the spontaneous weakening of the trace over time.

A crucial question in deciding between this and a classical interference theory explanation then becomes: What happens when PI is avoided by testing on only one trial? Interference theory predicts no forgetting, while decay theory predicts a less pronounced version of the normal multitrial curve. Most of the existing data are uninterpretable, since performance is at virtually 100 percent at all delays on trial 1. When such ceiling effects are avoided, however, forgetting clearly does occur.

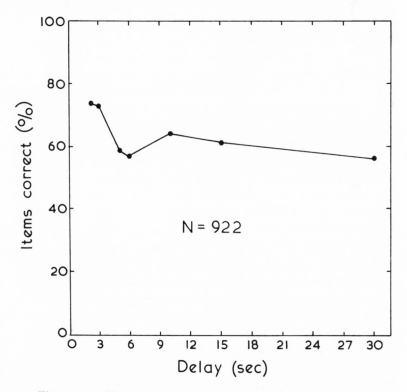

Figure 7–2   Short-term forgetting in the absence of PI. The data are taken from a number of studies involving a total of 922 subjects, each of whom was tested on a single sequence. Source: Data taken from A. D. Baddeley and D. Scott, Short-term forgetting in the absence of proactive inhibition, *Quarterly Journal of Experimental Psychology* 23 (1971): 275–283.

Figure 7–2 shows the combined data from a number of studies by the writer, in all of which the subjects were tested only once. Forgetting was consistently found but was virtually complete within 5 seconds; comparable results have been obtained both by D. Marcer and by A. W. Melton (personal communication). We also found comparable rates of forgetting for both high- and low-frequency words (Baddeley and Scott 1971, exp. 4), which rules out extra-experimental interference as an interpretation; provided that artifacts from ceiling effects were avoided, we found that length of sequence had no effect on rate of forgetting, suggesting that intrasequence interference (Melton 1963) was not responsible for the forgetting observed. This leaves either trace decay or displacement by items in the distractor task as the most obvious explanations.

Displacement might be expected to occur in any system which has a limited capacity, with subsequent items "pushing out" earlier items in some way. Although displacement could be regarded as a kind of interference theory, its advocates (e.g., Waugh and Norman 1965) tend not to subscribe to the assumptions of classical associative interference theory. Studies by Judith Reitman (1971) and Richard Shiffrin (1973) have claimed that displacement is the most probable explanation. They showed that when subjects were required to perform a difficult auditory detection task during the retention interval of a Peterson task, no forgetting occurred, despite the fact that subjects reported no rehearsal. However, a very careful further experiment (Reitman 1974) suggested that, despite precautions, subjects in the earlier studies probably were rehearsing. Her subsequent study suggests that subjects who do abstain from rehearsal show clear forgetting, suggesting that trace decay *was* occurring. However, interpolated tonal detection led to less forgetting than detecting changes in syllables (from *doh* to *toh*). This is presumably because of the greater similarity between the verbal material to be retained and the syllabic material to be detected; as such, it constitutes further evidence for an interference or displacement effect.

Figure 7–2 suggests that, in the absence of prior items, forgetting levels off within 5 seconds. Why, then, should forgetting in the multitrial procedure continue for 20, 40, or even 60 seconds (Baddeley and Warrington 1970)? It seems possible that the Brown-Peterson task comprises two components: an STS component, which occurs in the absence of prior items and reaches asymptote within about 5 seconds, and a much larger LTS component, which is subject to forgetting over longer intervals when recent prior items are present. One possible interpretation of this latter forgetting is in terms of time tags. This hypothesis is

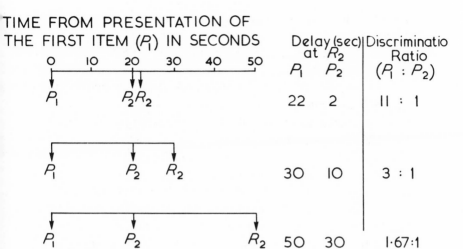

TIME FROM PRESENTATION OF THE FIRST ITEM (P_1) IN SECONDS	Delay (sec) at R_2		Discrimination Ratio
	P_1	P_2	($P_1 : P_2$)
P_1 ... P_2R_2	22	2	11 : 1
P_1 ... P_2 ... R_2	30	10	3 : 1
P_1 ... P_2 ... R_2	50	30	1·67:1

= Presentation of item 1
= Presentation of item 2
= Recall of item 2

Figure 7–3 Temporal discrimination hypothesis of short-term forgetting. P_1 represents the presentation of the first item, P_2 the presentation of the second, and R_2 the recall of the second item. It is assumed that if the two items come from the same general class of material, then the only cue which the subject has in recalling the appropriate item is its time of occurrence. It is further assumed that the discriminability of this temporal cue will determine recall probability. When the critical item is tested after a short delay and the prior item is separated by a long delay, this discrimination will be easy and recall probability will be high. As the delay increases, the relative discriminability of the two items will decrease and recall probability will drop.

illustrated in Figure 7–3. It assumes that a major source of difficulty in the Peterson task is that of locating the appropriate items (the last one presented) among a mass of earlier items. Under standard multitrial testing, time or order of occurrence will be the only cue allowing the correct item to be selected. If one assumes that the discrimination among temporal cues behaves very much as would any other psychophysical judgment, then Weber's law suggests that the discriminability of the cue will be determined by the ratio of the temporal intervals in question. Let us assume that the prior item was presented some 20 seconds before the item to be remembered. After a delay of only 2 seconds, the subject will be faced with a temporal discrimination which involves separating 22

THE PSYCHOLOGY OF MEMORY

seconds from 2 seconds, a ratio of 11:1. After 10 seconds, the relevant delays will be 30 and 10 seconds (a ratio of 3:1), while after a 30-second delay, the relevant temporal discrimination will be that between 50 and 30 seconds, a ratio of less than 2:1.

Increasing inter-trial interval will increase the discrimination ratio by adding to the temporal interval associated with the prior item but not the wanted item, and hence will minimize forgetting (Loess and Waugh 1967). The temporal discrimination hypothesis can also account for the otherwise puzzling observation by Turvey, Brick, and Osborne (1970) that when items were tested at constant delay intervals, with all items for a given subject being tested after the same delay, the subjects who were always required to retain items for 25 seconds showed no more forgetting than subjects who were always tested after 5 seconds. Subjects were then switched to a uniform 15-second retention interval. As would be expected on the basis of the temporal tagging hypothesis, perform-ance proved to be a direct function of the prior retention interval, with subjects who had previously experienced short intervals (and who would consequently have relatively low temporal ratios between the wanted and the prior, unwanted items) performing at a much lower level than subjects who had previously experienced long delay intervals (producing relatively large temporal ratios of wanted to unwanted items).

Baddeley, Ecob, and Scott (1970) attempted to estimate the relation-ship between probability of recall and mean discrimination ratio by searching the literature for appropriate published data. Figures 7–4a and 7–4b show the data they obtained, which tend to suggest separate functions, depending on whether the subject was or was not aware of the time delay in question. An attempt was then made to predict the data from the study by Peterson and Peterson (1959) on the basis of the discrimination ratios to be expected from their subjects, on the assump-tion that the order of delays was randomized, so that each delay was likely to precede each other delay equally often. Figure 7–5 shows the mean recall percentage which would be predicted on the basis of the previous figure. When it is compared with the results obtained by Peter-son and Peterson and by Murdock in a subsequent study, the degree of fit is remarkably good. While it is clearly unwise to base too much on the post hoc analysis of data collected for other purposes, neverthe-less the temporal tagging hypothesis does appear to merit further investigation.

The phenomenon of release from PI can also be accounted for quite neatly in terms of a discrimination hypothesis. If the subject is given an additional cue to supplement the temporal tag, then it will facilitate the

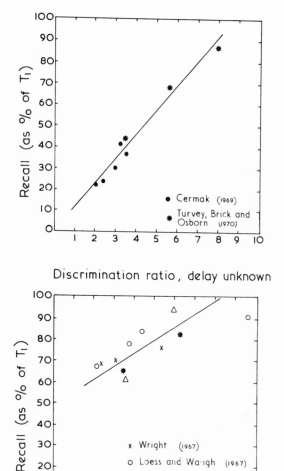

Discrimination ratio, delay unknown

Discrimination ratio, delay known

Figures 7–4a and 7–4b   Recall probability as a function of discrimination ratio from a range of studies. In each case, recall is expressed as a percentage of performance on the very first trial of the study. The discrimination ratio represents the ratio of the delay between presentation and test of the critical item to the delay since the presentation of the immediately prior item. Figure 7–4a represents studies in which subjects were unaware of what the delay would be; Figure 7–4b represents data from studies in which subjects knew the relevant delay in advance. The lines are fitted by eye. Source: A. D. Baddeley, J. R. Ecob, and D. Scott, Retroactive interference effects in short-term memory, paper presented at the annual meeting of the Psychonomic Society, San Antonio, Texas, November 1970.

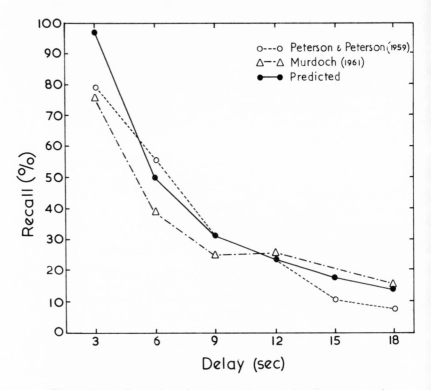

Figure 7–5 Forgetting functions observed by Peterson and Peterson (1959) and Murdock (1961), together with the function predicted on the discrimination hypothesis. The prediction is based on the relationship between discrimination ratio and recall probability observed in Figure 7–4a. The relevant discrimination ratios were obtained on the assumption that each delay was preceded equally often by each of the delays used, thus allowing an average discrimination ratio to be estimated. Source: A. D. Baddeley, J. R. Ecob, and D. Scott, Retroactive interference effects in short-term memory, paper presented at the annual meeting of the Psychonomic Society, San Antonio, Texas, November 1970.

discrimination of the appropriate item from the background of prior items. Such a view thus interprets the release from PI in terms of retrieval rather than differences that occur during learning. Evidence that the build-up and release from PI effects operate at the level of retrieval rather than learning comes from a recent study by Olga Watkins (1975). She ran a standard experiment demonstrating build-up and release from PI, with one modification: subjects were asked for final free recall (FFR)—that is, they were requested to recall as many of the words used in the experiment as possible. If the PI effect was operating at the level of learning or forgetting, one would expect the items which had been well recalled (because of the absence of PI) to be better recalled than subsequent items which had suffered from PI. This proved not to be the case; initial and release items were no better recalled than subsequent items, suggesting that the degree of learning and forgetting involved was the same, and hence implicating retrieval as the source of the PI effect in this paradigm. Further evidence for the view that the build-up and release from PI and STM reflects the discriminability of retrieval cues comes from an ingenious study by Gardiner, Craik, and Birtwisle (1972) in which subjects were required to recall successive triads of flower names. After several triads of garden flowers, a triad of wild flowers was presented. Subjects did not appear to notice this change, and they showed no release from PI when tested. However, when the feature was pointed out after presentation but before recall, a substantial release occurred, suggesting that the phenomenon is not automatic but rather involves a retrieval strategy whereby a discriminating cue is used to select among a range of available items.

What other techniques are available? Work by Peterson (1966) suggests that paired-associated learning may comprise only a small STS component, represented principally by the last pair presented. It is hence unsuitable for studying STS, although it has been used very effectively by Atkinson and Shiffrin (1968) to study the role of what they term the "rehearsal buffer" in STM. Two techniques which do appear to have clearly separable STS components, however, are free recall and the serial probe technique devised by Waugh and Norman (1965).

FREE RECALL

As we saw earlier, free recall has what appears to be a clear and easily separable STS component represented principally by the recency effect. The interference theory explanation of the characteristic serial position curve in free recall assumes a combination of PI and RI effects. The last few items presented are initially well recalled, since they have few items following them, and hence little RI. They do, however, suffer from PI, which builds up when recall is delayed, causing the recency effect to disappear. On the other hand, earlier items are affected by RI; the longer the list, the greater the RI and the lower the overall probability of recall (Postman and Phillips 1965).

An alternative to the RI explanation of the reduction in recall probability as list length increases is offered by Shiffrin (1970), who suggests that recall involves a recursive random search through the relevant set of traces in LTS. The longer the list, the larger the set of traces and the smaller the probability of finding and retrieving any given item before the search terminates (see Chapter 11, p. 288). To test this hypothesis, Shiffrin had his subjects recall a series of lists, half of them short and half long. However, instead of having the subjects recall the list most recently presented, he required them to recall the penultimate one. This technique allows list length to be separated from number of words interpolated between presentation and test. A short interpolated list should produce less RI than a long list but should not affect the size of the retrieval set, which should be dependent on the length of the list to be recalled and should be unaffected by the length of the interpolated list. There were thus four crucial conditions: *short*-long (where the list in italics is the one recalled), *short*-short, *long*-long, and *long*-short. The results are shown in Figure 7–6. It is clear that the important factor is the length of the list recalled, not the number of interpolated words. Thus, it appears that a word is less likely to be recalled from a long list because the relevant retrieval set is larger, presenting a more difficult memory search, not because of greater RI from interpolated words.

We have so far been concerned with the LTS component of free recall. What causes forgetting in the STS component? This was investigated by Glanzer, Gianutsos, and Dubin (1969) in a series of experiments in which the recency effect was studied following a series of manipulations of the task interpolated between presentation and recall. Results suggested a simple displacement model, whereby items in STS are pushed out by subsequent filler items; because of the limited capacity of STS, it is assumed that five or six words are sufficient to obliterate the recency effect. The degree of forgetting is unaffected by similarity between the recent items and the filler words, suggesting that classical interference theory is not appropriate. Neither the information load imposed by the interpolated task nor elapsed time were major factors, suggesting that trace decay is not the principal cause of forgetting. A similar conclusion was suggested by a study by Baddeley and Hitch (1976), which attempted to avoid rehearsal by using an incidental

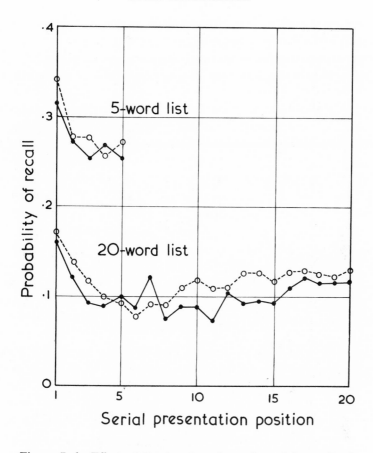

Figure 7–6 Effect of list length and number of interpolated items on free recall. Dotted lines represent items recalled after the presentation of an interpolated list of 20 items; solid lines represent the recall of lists following an interpolated list of 5 items. It is clear that list length is a much more powerful determinant of recall than the number of interpolated items. Source: R. M. Shiffrin, Forgetting: trace erosion or retrieval failure? *Science* 168 (1970): 1602. Copyright 1970 by the American Association for the Advancement of Science. Reprinted by permission.

learning task in which subjects were given a sequence of 12 names to classify as male or female at a rate of 2 seconds per name. Subjects were not told to memorize the names but were subsequently asked to recall them either immediately or after a 30-second delay, which was either filled by a digit-copying task or left empty while the experimenter shuffled papers as if looking for material for the next experiment. The results are shown in Figure 7–7. The recency effect is just as great after

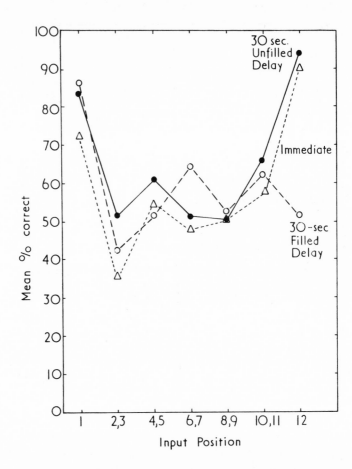

Figure 7–7 Recall of items presented under incidental learning conditions. Recall is either immediate or after a 30-second filled or unfilled delay. Note that an unfilled delay does not abolish the recency effect. Source: A. D. Baddeley and G. Hitch, Recency re-examined, in S. Dornic (ed.), *Attention and Performance VI* (forthcoming).

30 seconds as on immediate test, provided there is no interpolated activity. There is no evidence to suggest either trace decay or the obliteration of the recency effect by spontaneously recovering prior items (Postman and Phillips 1965), so this result appears to suggest that forgetting in STS is the result of displacement by later items.

What constitutes an item in STS? An item seems to involve a single integrated unit, such as a word or even a sentence (if it is sufficiently well integrated), regardless of the number of syllables; Craik (1968a) has shown that the recency effect is just as great for words of four syllables as it is for monosyllables, and Glanzer and Razel (1974) have shown that a complete proverb may function as a single unit so far as the recency effect is concerned. However, STS does not appear to be sensitive to clustering among words either on the basis of sound or meaning (Craik and Levy 1970), suggesting that the system can handle a large but well-integrated sequence as a single unit but cannot use similarities and relationships between items to integrate them into a single unit, as occurs in LTS.

SERIAL PROBE TASK

In their initial study using the serial probe task, Waugh and Norman (1965) were concerned with the question of whether forgetting in STS was a function of elapsed time, as trace decay theory would suggest, or was attributable to displacement by subsequent items. They therefore compared the retention of digits presented at two different rates, 0.5 or 2 digits per second. The procedure involved presenting 16 digits, followed by a seventeenth probe digit. The subject had to say what digit had followed the probe in the presentation sequence. The results are shown in Figure 7–8. It is clear that forgetting is more dependent on the number of digits separating presentation and recall than on amount of elapsed time, since rate of presentation does not have a major effect. However, as Shallice (1967) has pointed out, there is *some* effect of rate; although rapidly presented items start at a lower level of initial recall, indicating a lower degree of learning, they show less forgetting per interpolated item than the slowly presented digits. A recent study by Hockey (1973) suggests that the subject's strategy is an important factor in determining the effect of rate on probed recall. With an active rehearsal strategy, performance is better at slower rates, but when the subject is instructed to remain passive, performance is better at fast rates, particularly in the case of the later items, as would be expected on a trace decay hypothesis. Nevertheless, displacement appears to be the major factor with this technique, as indeed one would expect with a memory system of limited capacity. It appears to be the case that new items tend to displace old ones, so that the older the item, the smaller the probability of its survival in STS.

The question of what constitutes an item was also raised by Waugh and Norman (1968), who attempted to answer it by varying the nature of the items following the crucial probed item. They found that a repeated item functioned as a single unit, although it had physically

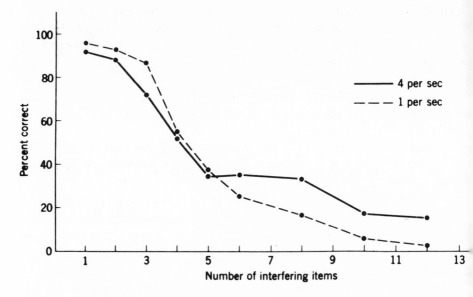

Figure 7–8   Short-term retention of digits using a probe technique, as a function of presentation rate and number of interpolated items. Source: Based on N. C. Waugh and D. A. Norman, Primary memory, *Psychological Review* 72 (1965): 89–104.

occurred several times. This suggests that the subject controls what is registered in STS and does not overload it unnecessarily by encoding redundant material. Glanzer and Meinzer (1967) observed a similar lack of effect of repetition on the number of different words registered in the STS component in free recall.

The Nature of Short-Term Forgetting

It should be clear by now that there is no simple, generally accepted explanation of short-term forgetting. The following is a tentative personal view of the issue. Forgetting may be due to either storage or retrieval factors; these will be discussed in turn.

STORAGE FACTORS

Coding effects. An important determinant of the durability of learning is the type of coding on which it is based. This is best illustrated using the technique of incidental learning, where type of coding can be manipulated by varying the nature of the cover task. A study by Johnston and Jenkins (1971) required subjects to perform a semantic cover task (e.g., supplying an appropriate adjective for each word presented), a nonsemantic cover task (e.g., supplying a rhyme for each word presented), or no cover task. Subjects were either warned that their recall would be tested (intentional groups) or given no such warning (incidental groups). On subsequent recall, subjects given the nonsemantic cover task, which presumably encouraged acoustic coding, recalled considerably less than the other groups, which did not differ among themselves. Provided semantic coding was required, instructions to learn were not necessary. When semantic coding was inhibited, instructions to learn were ineffective. Other evidence for this view was reviewed in the previous chapter.

Storage capacity limitations. Forgetting will clearly occur if the capacity of the short-term store is exceeded. This is reflected in the limit on span of immediate memory, which was also discussed in the previous chapter.

Trace decay. There is probably enough evidence to suggest that trace decay is a real phenomenon (Baddeley and Scott 1971; Baddeley, Thomson, and Buchanan 1975; Reitman 1974; Wickelgren 1970), though one which is usually swamped by the much more pronounced retrieval effects based on serial position and temporal cues.

RETRIEVAL FACTORS

Serial position cues. These can be divided into *fixed cues* and *variable cues*. Fixed cues are those associated with the beginning of the list, breaks in the rhythm of presentation, or items which stand out for some reason (the Von Restorff effect, described on p. 266). Since these cues are reasonably constant, they serve as "landmarks" during retrieval; hence, they tend to minimize retrieval failure as a cause of forgetting.

Varied cues are those which continuously change during presentation; by far the most important of these are recency cues. It seems likely that subjects can access items using the cue that it was the last item processed, or the last-but-one, or the last-but-two. The limit of this ordinal cuing seems to be five or six items, and since each recalled item will in turn take up the position of last item processed, moving all earlier items one place back, the recency effect is self-limiting. The use of ordinal cues of this type is probably responsible for the feature most commonly associated with STS, the recency effect observed in free recall, serial probe recall, and short-term paired-associate learning. In each case, about five interpolated items are enough to eliminate most of the recency effect. In the case of paired-associate recall, the recency effect tends to be particularly small, since each pair presented or tested comprises two items (a stimulus and a response) rather than one.

Temporal cues. Difficulties in discriminating cues of time rather than order of occurrence are probably the main source of forgetting in the Peterson task, with the exception of the first few seconds (or distractor items), for which ordinal retrieval cues are probably used. Time of occurrence is virtually the only cue which allows the subject to discriminate the set of items he is required to recall from those presented earlier. When an additional cue is provided, recall performance improves (the release from PI phenomenon).

To summarize: we assume that some of the phenomena associated with forgetting in STS are attributable to the inherent limitations of ordinal recency cues. The association between STS and acoustic coding may be because such coding leads to poorer trace durability. Because of their lack of durability, acoustically coded items form a much larger proportion of recent items than they do of older items. Since the ordinal cuing underlying STS is confined to recent items, it will tend to be associated with acoustic coding. (See Shallice 1975.)

Probe Recognition Studies

A more detailed analysis of STS is possible if recognition is used instead of recall, since this allows the application of techniques adapted from signal detection theory. Given a number of basic assumptions, these can then be used to compute a measure of trace strength that is free of criterion and response bias effects.

In a typical experiment, a subject might be presented with a sequence of 15 digits followed by a probe digit which he must classify as "old" if it occurred in the set of 15 or "new" if it did not. It is assumed that this decision is based on the trace strength or familiarity of the probed item. New items are assumed to vary in initial strength, presumably due to prior presentations or similarity to presented items. A presentation is assumed to add strength to this initial "noise" level,

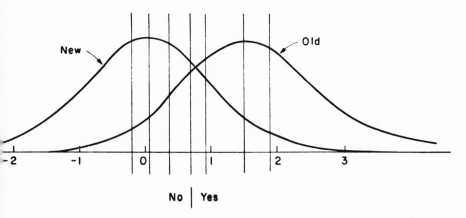

No | Yes

Figure 7–9   Hypothetical strength distributions for new and old items, with criteria for "yes" or "no" responses for each level of confidence.

giving a second distribution for old items. Figure 7–9 illustrates the two distributions.

Due to the variability of the noise distribution, some noise items will have more strength than some signal + noise items, so that perfect discrimination is not possible on the basis of trace strength. The subject can therefore only avoid falsely classifying some new items as old if he is prepared to fail to detect a relatively large number of genuine old items. As he relaxes his criterion by classifying items as old at a progressively lower strength level, he will initially make many more correct responses at the cost of relatively few false alarms. Gradually this will change; as he lowers his criterion still further, he will make more and more false alarms, while adding little to his detection score. This relationship is shown in Figure 7–10, which is based on a study of recognition memory for digits by Norman and Wickelgren (1965). Note that the relationship between the increase in detections and the increased false alarm rate is curved, whereas if the subject were simply guessing when uncertain, one would expect a straight line. (For further details see Kintsch 1970.)

The most common technique for obtaining readings at different criteria is to require the subject to rate his confidence in his decision, using, for example, a 7-point scale in which 1 means "certainly new," 7 means "certainly old," and intervening numbers indicate intermediate levels of certainty. The data can then be analyzed first by treating only responses of 7 as "old" responses, which will give a high

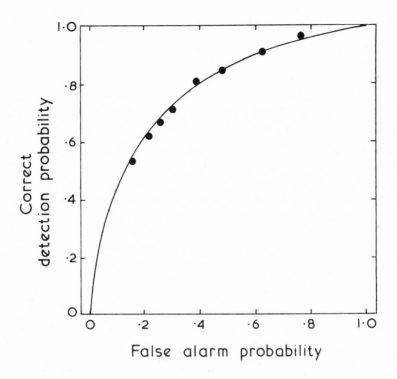

Figure 7–10   Memory operating characteristics for single digits. The data are plotted on regular linear coordinates. Source: Based on D. A. Norman and W. A. Wickelgren, Short-term recognition memory for single digits and pairs of digits, *Journal of Experimental Psychology* 70 (1965): 483.

criterion point. The second analysis, which treats responses of both 6 and 7 as "old," gives a slightly lower criterion. The third criterion point includes responses of 5, 6, and 7, and so forth, until all responses except those categorized as 1 have been treated as old responses. If the data fit the detection model, a curved relationship between detections and false alarm rate should emerge, resembling that of Figure 7–10. If this is the case, separate measures of trace strength (d') and bias (β) can be computed using the tables provided by Freeman (1973). If the assumptions of the model are valid, d' should not vary from one criterion to another within the same subject, whereas β should decrease as the criterion is relaxed.

Wickelgren and Norman (1966) have investigated forgetting in STM using this technique and have shown that trace strength declines exponentially with the number of items between presentation and test.

Norman (1966) demonstrated that this relationship holds whether an item comprises a single digit, a pair of digits, or a nonsense sound (a digit played backwards), although the absolute level of performance differs widely among the three types of items.

In a test of the retention of order information, Wickelgren (1967) presented subjects with sequences of 12 digits followed by a pair of probe digits. The subject's task was to decide whether the second digit of the pair had followed the first digit in the presented sequence. Again, Wickelgren found that trace strength declined exponentially with number of interpolated items. In order to study interference effects, he included a condition in which the first digit in the probe pair occurred more than once in the sequence, followed by a different digit in each case. Since this is essentially an $A-B$, $A-C$ paradigm, one might expect a reduction in trace strength because of unlearning. No such effect was observed; as in the case of LTM (Postman, Stark, and Fraser 1968), this suggests that interference effects may not show up as clearly with recognition memory as with recall (see pp. 85–87).

Hitch (1969) used signal detection theory to study the nature of PI in the Peterson paradigm. He did so by performing a recognition memory experiment in which trace strength was measured after a delay of either 5 or 18 seconds. Recognition items were either "old" (from the sequence just presented) or "new," and new items comprised both items from the immediately prior sequence (PI items) or control items which had not appeared previously. According to interference theory, PI effects are due to the spontaneous recovery of prior items, whereas a decay or displacement theory would interpret forgetting in terms of the weakening of the items to be remembered during the retention interval. Hitch's results very clearly showed that the increase in forgetting was attributable to the weakening during the filled retention interval of the trace strength of items to be recalled, not to spontaneous recovery of the prior items, which actually tended to become weaker rather than stronger as a result of the delay.

Reaction Time and Short-Term Memory

All the experiments we have so far discussed have studied memory in terms of errors, either quantitatively, by percentage of errors under various conditions, or qualitatively, in terms of the nature of the errors.

Such an approach has two drawbacks. First, it concentrates exclusively on memory at the point of breakdown. This may behave very differently from error-free memory, which probably constitutes a very important part of memory in everyday life. Second, the preoccupation with errors tends to focus attention on forgetting rather than on the equally important question of how information is successfully retrieved. For both these reasons, the demonstration by Sternberg (1966) that reaction times can be used to test quite specific models of error-free memory is particularly important.

STERNBERG'S SERIAL EXHAUSTIVE SCANNING MODEL

Sternberg's initial experiment involved presenting the subject with a sequence of from one to six digits, allowing 2 seconds for rehearsal, and then presenting a probe digit. The subject's task was to decide as quickly as possible whether or not the digit was in the presented sequence and to press a "yes" or "no" lever accordingly. Figure 7–11 shows the results of this experiment. Reaction time (RT) increases

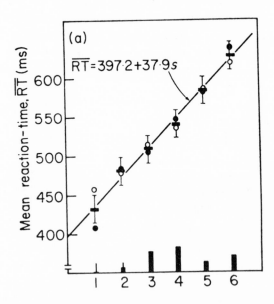

Figure 7–11   Relationship between response latency and number of symbols in memory for positive responses (filled circles) and negative responses (open circles). Source: Based on S. Sternberg, High-speed scanning in human memory, *Science* 153 (1966): 653. Copyright 1966 by the American Association for the Advancement of Science. Reprinted by permission.

linearly with number of digits presented, with positive and negative responses giving the same slope.

Sternberg suggests a model in which the items in memory are scanned very rapidly by a comparator which compares each item with the probe and decides in each case whether the two match. If a match occurs, the subject responds "yes," and if none of the items matches the probe, he responds "no." The linear increase in RT with size of set can then be explained by assuming that items are scanned serially, one at a time; hence, the greater the number of items, the longer the RT. The most obvious strategy might seem to be for the comparator to stop scanning as soon as it detects a match between the probe item and an item in STS. If this were the case, it would rarely have to scan the whole set before making a positive response. Sometimes it would detect the positive item at the beginning of the scan, sometimes at the end, but on average it would need to scan about half the items. This means that the increase in set size should have less effect on time to make "yes" responses than on "no" responses; since the comparator would always have to scan all items in the set before concluding that no match was present, the slope for "no" responses should be approximately twice as steep as that for "yes" responses. It is clear from Figure 7-11 that this is not the case. Sternberg suggests that this implies that the comparator scans all the items before a response is made in both positive and negative cases. He points out that such a strategy would be reasonable on the assumption that it is much quicker to scan an item than to make the decision that a match did or did not occur. The process Sternberg suggests is as follows: The digits are presented and read into STS. When the probe occurs, the subject performs a very rapid scan (38 msec. per item) through the list; any match between the probe and the items in the list will be registered by a comparator. When the scan is complete, the comparator is tested and a "yes" or "no" response emitted accordingly.

In a further experiment, Sternberg (1966) showed that an almost identical relationship holds with a fixed-set procedure in which the set of positive digits remains constant throughout a whole test session; for example, the digits 1, 3, 4, and 7 might be positive and the rest negative for the duration of that session. He argues that the similarity occurs because the positive set is fed from LTS into STS for high-speed scanning. Evidence that STS is involved comes from a study (Sternberg, Knoll, and Nasto 1969) in which the varied- and fixed-set procedures were combined by requiring the subject to hold a constant set of one, three, or five digits in memory throughout a session. On half the trials a probe digit would be presented, as in Sternberg's previous fixed-set study; in the other half the subject was presented with a sequence of seven letters which he was instructed to remember. On some of the trials on which the subjects were remembering the seven letters, immediate recall of the letters was demanded. On the remaining letter trials a probe digit was presented, and the subject was required to decide whether or not it was in the fixed set. The results are shown in Figure 7–12. In both conditions RT increased linearly with the size of the positive set, but when STS is filled up with

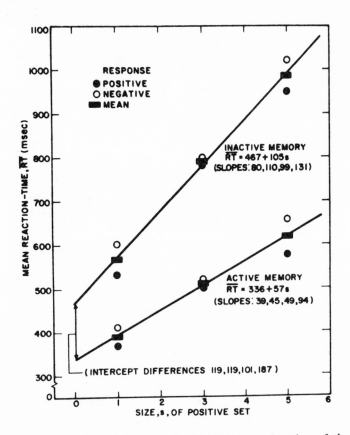

Figure 7–12   Mean time to classify digits as a function of the size of the positive set. When the subject is required to hold a sequence of seven letters in STS (upper function), the slope is approximately twice that observed when there is no additional memory load. Data are from four subjects. Source: S. Sternberg, R. L. Knoll, and B. A. Nasto, Retrieval from long-term vs. active memory, paper presented at the annual meeting of the Psychonomic Society, St. Louis, Mo., 1969.

letters, the slope is twice as steep, suggesting that active memory, or STS, plays an important role in retrieval from LTS. An initial hypothesis was that material must be transferred from LTS to STS before scanning can occur. If this were the case, it might be expected that subsequent recall of the letters would be grossly impaired, with each digit read into STS displacing a letter. Sternberg, Knoll, and Nasto (1969) examined this in a subsequent experiment, which showed that although larger positive fixed sets caused rather more forgetting of STM letters, this effect was much smaller than would be predicted by their displacement hypothesis.

Sternberg's technique has been applied across a range of materials (Sternberg 1969), and there is little doubt of the robustness of his original findings, although Briggs (1974) has suggested that the bulk of the data indicate a logarithmic rather than a linear relationship between RT and set size. However, a number of phenomena have recently been reported which do not fit easily into the serial exhaustive scanning model. The model assumes that information about individual items within the sequence is not preserved, since the comparator merely records whether or not one or more items matched the probe. There is, however, growing evidence that information about individual items does influence RT. A number of experimenters have found serial position effects, with later items evoking faster responses (Morin, Derosa, and Stultz 1967), the effect being particularly clear when the probe is immediate (Clifton and Birenbaum 1970) rather than separated by a 2-second delay, as in Sternberg's experiments. The delay presumably allows rehearsal, which disrupts the serial position effect. Baddeley and Ecob (1973) observed in a varied-set, STM design that repeated digits (e.g., 5 in 5359) produced faster RTs than non-repeats from equivalent sequences (e.g., 3 in 5359), a result which would not be predicted by an exhaustive scanning hypothesis. Using the fixed-set procedure, Krueger (1970) has shown that if certain digits are tested more often than others, they tend to evoke faster RTs.

Further evidence for the importance of the individual item in determining reaction time comes from a study by Morin, Derosa, and Stultz (1967), in which the positive set comprised sequences of four consecutive digits (e.g., 3, 4, 5, 6). Subjects responded consistently more slowly to both positive and negative items near the set boundaries (e.g., 6 and 7). This phenomenon has been explored in greater detail by Marcel (1976), who found a consistent relationship between RT and distance from the set boundary, a relationship which holds for both positive and negative responses. This result presents two problems for a simple exhaustive scanning hypothesis. First, how does the model account for different latencies for different responses, given a comparator which simply records whether or not a match has occurred? Second, how does the model account for variations among negative items? The exhaustive scanning hypothesis would suggest that negative responses occur because the positive set fails to produce a match; if this is the case, the nature of the negative item should be irrelevant. Further evidence that negative items are processed comes from a study by Theios, Smith, Haviland, Traupman, and Moy (1973), who showed that frequently occurring negative items are given a "no" response more rapidly than rarely occurring negatives. Marcel (1976) has shown that negative set-size effects do not operate when the positive set comprises only one item, indicating that with a set size of one, a different process of matching may occur, possibly based on a match of the physical properties of the item presented. (See the experiment by Posner and Keele described on p. 206.) Finally, Banks and Atkinson (1974) have observed that when different words from a set of 1,000 are used on every trial, both slope and intercept are less than if the items always came from a restricted set of 12 words. It is hard to see why such increased familiarity with the set used should *decrease* scanning rate, as the Sternberg model would presumably have to assume.

Given a range of phenomena which do not appear to fit naturally into the initial version of Sternberg's high-speed exhaustive scanning model, one is faced with the choice of attempting either to incorporate them into the model by assuming additional processes or to produce an alternative model which will account for both the original Sternberg results and the new phenomena. A wide range of models have been proposed, but they can be divided broadly into three categories: parallel comparison models, self-terminating search models, and trace strength discrimination models. These will be considered in turn.

PARALLEL COMPARISON MODELS

Parallel comparison models characteristically assume that the probe item is compared with the available memory set simultaneously and not serially, as the Sternberg model suggests. Most typically, the increase in reaction time with number of alternatives is then explained by assuming limited processing capacity, which means that the more items considered, the longer the processing of each item will take (Atkinson, Holmgren, and Juola 1969; Corcoran 1971; Townsend

1971). Probably the best known of these models is that of Atkinson, Holmgren, and Juola (1969), which assumes that available capacity is divided equally among those comparisons which have not yet been completed. As soon as one comparison is completed, the capacity used for that comparison is instantly reallocated to the others, and a decision is made only when all items have been processed. Although this model aims to account for Sternberg's results in a different way, it still assumes exhaustive processing of the positive set; consequently, it too has difficulty in accounting for the time taken to process different items within the sequence. It probably can be modified to account for serial position and repetition effects, but it is less easy to see how it can account for differences in processing time for items in the negative set. Sternberg (1975) also points out that when some of the available processing capacity is taken up by a concurrent task, this should change the slope of the reaction time function, whereas what evidence exists suggests either no change in either slope or intercept (Darley, Klatzky, and Atkinson 1972) or a change in intercept but not slope (Wattenbarger and Pachella 1972). In general, it would seem that the future of parallel comparison models will depend very much on their ability to generalize beyond the original Sternberg paradigm and provide a fruitful way of looking at other information-processing tasks which might be assumed to use the same limited-capacity system.

SELF-TERMINATING SEARCH MODELS

Theios (1973) has proposed a model which assumes that subjects search through a list comprising both positive and negative items, each associated with its appropriate positive or negative response. The search is serial but terminates as soon as the item matching the probe has been located, whereupon the response attached to that item is made. Items are assumed to be stored as a "push-down stack." The stack is searched from the top downward, and the position of both positive and negative items in the stack is determined by such stimulus events as recency and frequency. The model accounts reasonably well for set-size effects (provided the positive and negative sets are of equal size), and it can account for frequency and repetition effects without difficulty. However, Sternberg (1975) suggests that the model runs into difficulties in accounting for studies in which the sizes of the positive and negative sets are unequal, while Banks and Fariello (1974) have pointed out that Theios's model cannot be applied to situations in which very large stimulus sets are used. The model was designed essentially to account for results from the fixed-set procedure and runs into further difficulties when applied to the varied-set procedure; in particular, it is unclear how varied-set items which have not been presented have "no" responses attached to them. It is similarly unclear why frequently occurring negative items should be responded to rapidly in a varied-set paradigm (Marcel 1976). A final problem is raised by Sternberg (1975), who points out that the *minimum* reaction time observed for a given condition increases systematically with positive set size. On the Theios model, the fastest RT should always occur whenever the top item in the stack is sampled, and this will happen some of the time regardless of set size, although the frequency of its occurrence may, of course, be greater for smaller sets. Whether Theios can adequately counter these objections remains to be seen.

TRACE STRENGTH DISCRIMINATION MODELS

A third class of models attempts to extend the type of model used to account for probe recognition memory using error responses, as previously described (Norman and Wickelgren 1969), to account for Sternberg's results. Essentially, these models assume that when an item is presented, a trace is laid down at a location in a memory store. When the probe item occurs, the subject accesses the location corresponding to the probe and decides whether the amount of trace strength at that point exceeds a criterion. If it does, then he responds "yes"; if not, he responds "no." The difficulty with this type of model is to account for the *linear* relationship between RT and set size, together with equal slopes for positive and negative responses. A number of ways of deriving this relationship have been suggested (Baddeley and Ecob 1973; Corballis, Kirby, and Miller 1972; Nickerson 1972). However, the models proposed by Corballis et al. (1972) and by Nickerson (1972) appear to predict that the last item presented or rehearsed will give the fastest RT, with this minimum remaining constant regardless of set size. As mentioned in the previous section, Sternberg (1975) has shown that this is not the case.

Sternberg (1975) further claims that a recent study by Darley, Klatzky, and Atkinson (1972) is not consistent with the Baddeley-Ecob model. This study showed that when one item from a varied-set list is singled out as being the only item which will be tested by the subsequent probe, the size of the list in which it is embedded does not influence RT. Since subjects were subsequently required to recall the entire list, it is clearly not the case that subjects were simply ignoring the other items. However, the item singled out was always presented in a different modality from the rest of the items; as we shall see in Chapters 9 and 10, there is abundant evidence for separate sensory stores which are able to hold one or two items. This would allow subjects to make a particularly rapid match on the basis of the physical dimensions of the stimulus (Posner 1969; Kroll, Parks, Parkinson, Bieber, and Johnson 1970). In short, a result of this type would only be embarrassing for the Baddeley-Ecob position if the possibility of using a separate sensory store for the single item was eliminated and the same result obtained. Even then, it would be necessary to know the strategy that subjects were using before drawing any very general conclusions.

A trace strength approach is clearly compatible with repetition effects, serial position effects, the Banks-Atkinson familiarity effect, and bias effects in favor of more frequent items; this approach is not embarrassed by deviations from linearity. The Baddeley-Ecob model is, however, rather less comfortable in accounting for the results from fixed-set studies and, in particular, for the observation (e.g., Marcel 1976) that items which occur frequently in the negative set will tend to evoke a faster negative RT than those which occur infrequently. A simple trace notion might assume that frequency would always increment strength, which would enhance "yes" responses but interfere with "no" responses. A possible solution to this dilemma is suggested by the proposals of Simpson (1970) and Marcel (1976) that what is stored at a particular trace location is not simply "strength," indicating that the particular item has occurred recently, but also an association between that item and the appropriate "yes" or "no" response. In a varied-set procedure, this information may be largely disruptive, since it refers to the outcome of previous trials which are not strictly applicable to the decision in hand, whereas in the fixed-set procedure they will provide an important and valuable component; they will nevertheless be present and will affect RT in both. This view would certainly seem to merit further exploration.

One final problem facing all the models discussed so far is that of the *speed-error trade-off*. In general, subjects can increase their speed of response at the expense of making more errors. Sternberg attempted to avoid this problem by insisting that his subjects kept their error rate low, typically below 5 percent. However, if the relationship between speed and errors is at all analogous to the relationship between correct detections and false alarms in a discrimination task, where changes in error rate of a few percentage points may have a dramatic effect on hit rate (Green and Swets 1966), such a strategy may be very misleading. Whether or not this is the case, no model of the recognition process can be regarded as satisfactory until it can account simultaneously for both speed and errors.

To summarize: it is clear that phenomena exist which cannot be fitted into Sternberg's serial exhaustive search model without substantial additional assumptions. Other models, though lacking the elegant simplicity of Sternberg's, can nevertheless account for these phenomena, but such models have their own potential snags. Before deciding whether to elaborate the serial search model or investigate an alternative, I would like to suggest that we look very carefully at what Brunswik (1956) has termed the *ecological validity* of the task on which such models are based. Are the phenomena observed limited to this highly artificial laboratory task, or do they represent something of much greater generality? If the high-speed memory search is an important component of normal information processing, then it should be possible to take the concepts generated by the Sternberg paradigm and apply them much more generally. This does not, of course, mean simply carrying out Sternberg experiments under a range of different conditions with different types of subjects and simply reporting, for example, that schizophrenics have the same slope as normals but a different intercept. It requires, rather, a demonstration that the Sternberg paradigm tells us something of importance outside the limits of the paradigm itself.

It is not easy to see what function an exhaustive recognition scan could have outside the limits of Sternberg's task, in which a relatively small fixed set is held in memory and used to make yes/no judgments. It is possible that certain inspection tasks may be of this type, although Neisser's (1963) work on visual search suggests that the effect of positive set size may be very small with highly practiced subjects. Although it seems highly likely that retrieval from LTS may involve some form of scanning, it appears unlikely that the scanning is either serial or exhaustive, although such a scan could possibly form part of a more complex retrieval process. However, regardless of the fate of the high-speed exhaustive scan hypothesis, Sternberg's work is important. In demonstrating that sophisticated models of error-free memory can be devised and tested using purely RT data, Sternberg has enormously extended the range of potential work on human memory.

The Modal Model of Memory

Suppose we agree that memory does comprise a complex system and that some sort of distinction between long- and short-term memory is likely to prove useful. How should we conceptualize such a system? One of the most popular ways of conceptualizing the memory system in recent years has been the information-processing model. Since the 1950s when it was pioneered by Broadbent (1958), this approach has grown enormously in popularity, and in the late 1960s and early 1970s there was a proliferation of such models of memory. This tendency probably reached its high point with the publication of Norman's book *Models of Human Memory* in 1970, containing papers by no fewer than 13 contributors, each advocating a different model. In actual fact, many of these approaches were basically rather similar, and they all can be regarded as approximating, to a greater or lesser degree, what Murdock (1971) has termed the "modal model."

ATKINSON-SHIFFRIN MODEL

Perhaps the most influential information-processing model in recent years has been that devised by Atkinson and Shiffrin (1968), which is essentially a development of the original Broadbent model.

The model is illustrated in Figure 7–13, which is taken from a lucid and persuasive summary of their views presented in an article in *Scientific American* (Atkinson and Shiffrin 1971). Information from the environment first enters a series of sensory registers, temporary buffer stores that hold information in a relatively raw state. The information is further processed by being read into STS. The various sensory registers are each limited to a single modality, but when information is registered in STS, Atkinson and Shiffrin assume that the relevant associations in LTS are activated and the additional information registered in STS. Hence, a word presented visually will be joined in STS by its verbal name and its meaning. STS is equated with "consciousness"—that is, "the thoughts and information of which we are currently aware . . ." (ibid., p. 83). Hence, STS is conceived not as a simple repository of information but as a working memory, responsible for decision making and problem solving. It forms the center of the control system that is responsible for directing the flow of information; as such, it forms a crucial component of the memory system. As

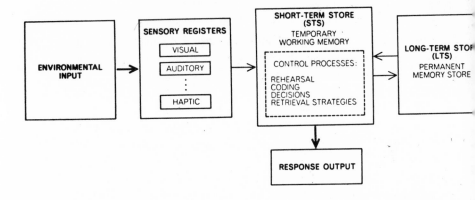

Figure 7–13 The flow of information through the memory system as conceived by Atkinson and Shiffrin. Source: R. C. Atkinson and R. M. Shiffrin, The control of short-term memory, *Scientific American* 225 (1971): 82. Copyright © 1971 by Scientific American, Inc. All rights reserved. Reprinted by permission.

Figure 7–13 illustrates, STS is essential in this model for the working of the long-term store; without STS, information can neither be put into nor retrieved from LTS.

The procedures whereby the subject governs the flow of information within the memory system are termed *control processes,* and it is the central role of such processes in learning, recalling, decision making, and problem solving that makes STS so important in this system. One control process that plays an important part in Atkinson and Shiffrin's system is that of *rehearsal,* the overt or covert repetition of information. This can be used to maintain information in STS, although the extent to which this is possible is constrained by the limited capacity of the short-term store. Hence, although most people can maintain six or seven digits in STM for as long as they care to rehearse, they cannot maintain ten digits in this way. Another important control process is that termed *coding,* by which Atkinson and Shiffrin mean the attachment of additional information from LTS to the incoming stimulus; the use of a visual imagery mnemonic would be an example of this. Other control processes include organizational schemes, retrieval strategies, and decision rules about such questions as whether an item retrieved from LTS is the one for which the subject is searching and, if not, whether the search should be abandoned.

The role of control processes is well illustrated by Atkinson and Shiffrin's account of retrieval from long-term memory, illustrated in

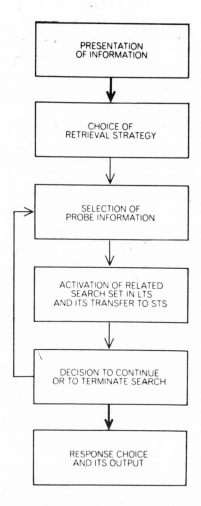

Figure 7–14 Atkinson and Shiffrin's conception of retrieval from LTS. Source: R. C. Atkinson and R. M. Shiffrin, The control of short-term memory, *Scientific American* 225 (1971): 83. Copyright © 1971 by Scientific American, Inc. All rights reserved. Reprinted by permission.

Figure 7–14. The information demanding LTS retrieval is presented (e.g., *What is the capital of Turkey?*). I then select a retrieval strategy (e.g., output names of Turkish cities). The relevant probe for accessing this information is selected, the set is activated, and the items retrieved are successively transferred into STS. Since my knowledge of Turkish cities is very limited, I might well begin by transferring the most available name into STS (e.g., Istanbul). I examine this, decide that it is not the correct answer (presumably because of associated information), and probe once again. This time I come up with Ankara, which I decide *is* correct. I then terminate the search and respond with *Ankara*. Note the crucial importance of STS throughout this process.

STS is also regarded as vitally important for transferring information into LTS, particularly via the process of rehearsal, the repetition of information in STS. Atkinson and Shiffrin support this claim by citing a series of experiments by Rundus (1971), who studied rehearsal by means of the simple but effective technique of requiring his subjects to rehearse aloud and tape-recording their rehearsal. In one experiment, Rundus studied the free recall of a list of 20 words and counted for each word in the list how many times it was rehearsed. His results are shown in Figure 7–15. The relationship between number of rehearsals and recall probability is very close over the early part of the list, with a marked primacy effect being associated with a

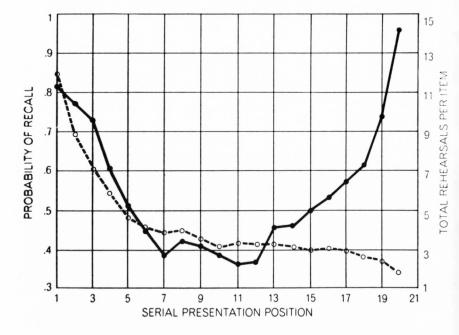

Figure 7–15   Relationship between mean number of overt rehearsals and recall probability. When subjects are required to rehearse aloud, more rehearsals lead to better recall for all except the more recent items. Source: Based on D. Rundus, Analysis of rehearsal processes in free recall, *Journal of Experimental Psychology* 89 (1971): 63–77.

cumulative rehearsal strategy. Subjects could rehearse about four items per presentation. A typical rehearsal pattern would be that shown in parentheses, with the items presented shown in uppercase letters: *DOG* (*dog, dog, dog, dog*), *CAT* (*cat, dog, cat, dog*), *HEN* (*hen, cat, dog*), *FISH* (*fish, dog, cat, hen*), and so forth. Early items not only tended to benefit during the original cumulative period but were also more likely to be rehearsed later in the series; presumably they are well learned and hence more accessible than later items. The association between number of rehearsals and recall probability breaks down completely over the recency portion of the serial position curve, suggesting that number of rehearsals affects the probability of an item's being transferred to LTS but is not a major factor in recall from STS.

CRITICISMS OF THE ATKINSON-SHIFFRIN MODEL

Atkinson and Shiffrin (1968) began by applying their model to paired-associate learning and have subsequently applied it to free recall and to the Brown-Peterson task, although they ignore the crucial factor of PI in this technique (Atkinson and Shiffrin 1971). Their model presents a coherent, plausible, and widely accepted view of memory. The degree of acceptance is reflected in the view of one prominent worker in the area of STM: "Now that we know all about short-term memory, it is time to move on to long-term memory." Unfortunately, however, I suspect this view is premature by at least a decade, since despite its obvious attractions, there are reasons to believe that the Atkinson-Shiffrin model may be fundamentally misleading. It is open to criticism on four counts: (1) its emphasis on rote rehearsal as the major process for registering information in LTS; (2) its suggestion that items in STS are automatically accompanied by their meaning; (3) its claim that STS is essential for input to and retrieval from LTS; and (4) its implication that STS is a unitary system. These will be discussed in turn.

Rote rehearsal and input to LTS. The Atkinson-Shiffrin model is potentially enormously complex, since it allows for an indefinite number of control processes. Such a model *could* prove completely sterile, simply postulating a new control process to account for any result that does not fit in with the existing system, but in the hands of Atkinson and Shiffrin this has not so far proved to be the case. The reason is that they have taken one control process, that of rote rehearsal, and have investigated it with considerable skill and ingenuity. As a result, we know considerably more about rote rehearsal. Unfortunately, however, rehearsal has tended to be taken as the paradigm case. Atkinson and Shiffrin freely acknowledge the importance of semantic factors in retrieval from LTS, but they tend to conceive semantic coding primarily as the attachment of a mnemonic tag to material; the tag is then rehearsed together with the material. The example they give is that of remembering the paired-associate *HRM-4* by recoding *HRM* as *homeroom* and *4* as *fourth grade,* and then thinking of one's fourth-grade classroom (homeroom). Coding tends to be regarded simply as a means of supplementing the basic process of rehearsal.

Rehearsal almost certainly is important if one is learning relatively meaningless paired associates presented only once for a short period of time, as in the original Atkinson-Shiffrin experiments. Subjects have great difficulty in coding semantically under these conditions (Baddeley and Levy 1971). However, when the material is meaningful or the conditions less constraining, subjects tend to process material semantically, since rote rehearsal appears to be a very inferior way of registering information in LTS. Bower and Winzenz (1970) compared the retention of paired associates after instructions to subjects to rehearse, to link the items with a sentence, or to combine the items as a composite visual image. Rote rehearsal proved to be much the least efficient learning strategy. The inadequacy of rote rehearsal as a learning procedure is emphasized even more strongly by a study by Craik and Watkins (1973), discussed in the next chapter (see p. 166).

In the case of free recall, the Rundus technique virtually forces the subject to adopt a strategy of rote rehearsal, a strategy which is almost certainly both atypical of normal free-recall learning and inefficient. Glanzer and Meinzer (1967) performed a free-recall study in which subjects read each word presented either once or four times. The two groups showed a comparable recency effect, but the repetition group showed reliably poorer overall performance. It might be argued that repetition of individual items is simply a less efficient rehearsal strategy than cumulative rehearsal; however, a study by Atkinson and Shiffrin (1971) suggests that this is not in fact the case.

Consequently, although the concept of a control process is very wide, in actual practice Atkinson and Shiffrin tend to interpret the process in a way that is applicable to the very restricted situations they themselves have studied. But this interpretation is atypical within the memory laboratory and even more unsuited to handling the memory of prose material or the incidents of everyday life.

One example of the dangers of extrapolation from a limited range of studies is provided by Atkinson and Shiffrin's (1968) interpretation of the recency effect in free recall as simply reflecting the contents of the rehearsal buffer. If this were so, an incidental learning task in which subjects have no reason to rehearse should show no free-recall recency effect. As Figure 7–7 suggests, this is not the case. Unfortunately, however, this particular study is not a convincing example, since the recency effect was small and no comparable intentional learning condition was included. The same incidental learning task was therefore repeated, again using the classification of names as "male," "female," or "either," but was modified by using a slower rate of presentation (10 seconds per name) and by including an in-

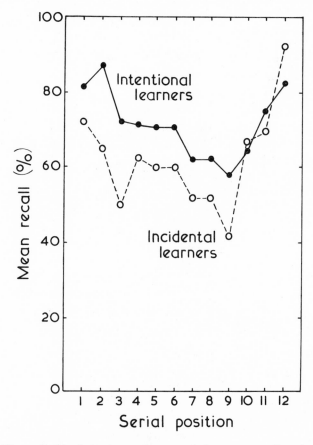

Figure 7–16   Intention to learn and the recency effect in free recall. Since subjects who are not trying to learn the items show an unimpaired recency effect, it seems unlikely that the effect is due to a specific learning strategy. Source: A. D. Baddeley and G. Hitch, Recency re-examined, in S. Dornic (ed.), *Attention and Performance VI* (forthcoming 1976).

tentional learning group which knew that after the classification was complete, recall would be required. The results are shown in Figure 7–16, from which it is clear that intention to learn has a marked effect on overall performance but has no influence on the recency effect, making a rehearsal buffer interpretation very implausible (Baddeley and Hitch 1976).

Semantic coding in STS. The available evidence tends to suggest that STS does not employ semantic coding. Since this view was elaborated in the previous chapter, however, it will not be discussed here.

Is STS an auditory system? A further problem with the Atkinson-Shiffrin model lies in its oversimplification of the relationship between the sensory registers, which hold material very briefly in a modality-specific form, and the STS system with which they connect. There is by now a considerable body of evidence for modality effects in STM. We shall illustrate this point briefly in the present section, leaving a more detailed analysis to Chapter 9.

Modality of presentation has a marked effect on the STS component of a range of tasks. It is well illustrated in a free-recall experiment by Murdock and Walker (1969) in which 20 words were presented either aurally or visually at a rate of two per second. The results are shown in Figure 7–17, from which it is clear that auditory presentation enhances recall from the latter part of the list, implying differential encoding of auditory and visual information in STS. An alternative way of studying the retention of auditory and visual material was used by Margrain (1967), who simultaneously presented two lists of four digits, one aurally, the other visually. Aurally presented lists were better retained than lists presented visually, but performance tended to be better when recall was written; on visual items the reverse was true, with spoken recall being better than written. This suggests separate visual and auditory storage systems, susceptible to different types of interference from the recall process. Both the studies described imply modality-specific storage over periods considerably longer than those typically associated with the sensory registers, a conclusion which will be explored further in Chapters 9 and 10.

Is STS essential for the operation of LTS? The emphasis of the model on rehearsal is not a necessary feature and can be modified fairly easily. A more fundamental feature, however, is the model's emphasis on STS as essential for the operation of LTS. One interesting and plausible feature of the model is its suggestion that STS is used to hold and operate retrieval strategies. The limited capacity of STS could then be used to explain the retrieval limitations on LTS to be dis-

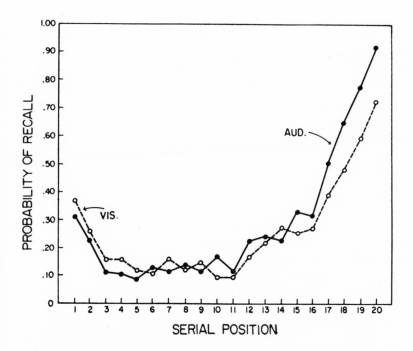

SERIAL POSITION

Figure 7–17   Effect of presentation modality on free recall. Auditory presentation enhances recall of the last few items presented. Source: B. B. Murdock, Jr. and K. D. Walker, Modality effects in free recall, *Journal of Verbal Learning and Verbal Behavior* 8 (1969): 668. Reprinted by permission.

cussed in Chapter 11. Such a view is consistent with the previously described study by Sternberg, Knoll, and Nasto (1969). A study by Martin (1970) required subjects to perform a manual tracking task during the learning and free recall of a list of words, on the assumption that the greater the attentional demands of the learning, the poorer the tracking performance would be. He found that tracking performance was poorest during recall, suggesting that a common system (working memory?) was involved in both retrieval and tracking.

An attempt was made to demonstrate the importance of STS in retrieval by Karalyn Patterson (1971), who presented subjects with lists of 20 either taxonomically categorized or unrelated words. The control condition involved normal free recall, whereas the experimental condition attempted to clear STS by requiring the subject to count backward for 15 seconds after each word recalled. Somewhat surprisingly, there was no reliable decrement in performance, as measured by either number of words recalled or degree of subjective organization shown for either categorized or random lists. It appears that the retrieval plan was probably held in LTS rather than STS; although it is possible that the plan was transferred to STS before each recall, there was no evidence to suggest this additional step in the retrieval process. A much simpler assumption is that the retrieval plan, being semantically coded, is not dependent on STS for either storage or utilization.

Once again, we have a result which would not be predicted but which, given a few modifications of the rather vague assumptions about control processes, could be accommodated without basically changing the model. A much more difficult case for the model to handle is that of K.F., the patient described in Chapter 6 with grossly impaired digit span, a recency effect of only one item, and hence, presumably, a defective STS system, who nevertheless shows quite normal long-term learning and recall (Shallice and Warrington 1970; Warrington and Shallice 1969). If STS is essential for long-term learning and retrieval, such patients should be grossly amnesic and have great difficulty in even conversing normally. This is certainly not the case with either K.F. or other similar patients (Warrington, Logue, and Pratt 1971); such patients can carry on a perfectly normal conversation with no evidence of any general memory defect. Indeed, after talking to such a patient, one is left wondering whether STS serves any function other than that of keeping experimental psychologists occupied! One can, of course, argue that the grossly impaired STS system is still sufficient to allow completely normal learning and recall, but if a fraction of the system is enough to maintain normal behavior, it can hardly be regarded as one of the major limitations on input and retrieval from LTS.

How does information get into LTS if not through the STS system? One alternative is that of parallel semantic coding, where information is assumed to enter directly into a semantically based long-term memory system without needing first to be held and processed in a short-term system, as is commonly supposed. How plausible is such a view? There is good evidence that the semantic features of a briefly presented word may be accessible before the word itself can be reported (M. Coltheart 1972), and there is evidence to suggest that semantic factors are important in determining whether a word can be read by certain types of aphasic patients, including K.F. (Shallice and Warrington 1975). Thus, a patient studied extensively by Marshall and Newcombe (1966; 1973) showed much better reading performance on imageable words than abstract words. He was able to read about

50 percent of the imageable nouns, but only 10 percent of the abstract nouns and virtually none of the prepositions, conjunctions, and other function words presented. His intrusion errors tended to be predominantly semantic substitutions (e.g., *speak* instead of *talk, pray* instead of *chapel*). In order to explain this and other types of dyslexia, Marshall and Newcombe (1973) propose a model of word storage which assumes separate and parallel phonological and semantic access routes. Preliminary evidence for independent semantic and acoustic coding in a memory situation has also been obtained (Baddeley and Ecob 1970), although further experimentation is needed before a rapid sequential processing hypothesis can be excluded.

What, then, is the use of the STS system? A clue is given by further experiments by Warrington and Shallice (1972) on their patients with defective STS. Although such patients do not have any difficulty in handling normal conversation, their performance can be made to break down if the rate at which information is presented is very high. This was done using the "token test," a task in which a series of plastic shapes of different colors and sizes is placed in front of the subject, who is given instructions of increasing complexity. The patients have no difficulty in obeying a simple instruction (e.g., *Touch the green circle*) but are quite unable to cope with instructions involving several steps (e.g., *Touch the large green circle with the small red triangle*). Presumably this is because the amount of information in the sentence is too great to be semantically coded during presentation. A normal subject can solve this problem by holding the sentence in STS while he decodes it at leisure. In the absence of an adequate STS, the patient is unable to understand or obey the instruction. In short, it seems likely that a short-term phonemic memory system is needed when direct semantic processing is not feasible; such a situation occurs with a high information rate and probably also in cases where the material is ambiguous, or when the listener is not paying attention and semantically processing the speech on first hearing. A phonemic STS allows the listener to do a "double take" and, by playing back the information, gain a second chance to process it semantically.

There does, therefore, appear to be some evidence that the STS may function as a working memory, although its role appears to be much less clear than the Atkinson-Shiffrin model might suggest. We shall return to this question in the next chapter.

C H A P T E R

8

Working Memory

A S WE SAW in the previous chapter, a great deal of the evidence available on human memory is compatible with the view that human memory comprises two major components: a short-term store of limited capacity, which relies on phonemic coding, and a long-term store of enormously greater capacity, which depends most heavily on semantic coding. The short-term store is seen as revealing itself most clearly in the recency component of STM tasks, a component which is present in amnesic patients, who nevertheless have grossly impaired LTS. Conversely, other patients whose LTM performance is unimpaired may perform at a grossly impaired level on STM tasks. Finally, the short-term storage system is assumed to function as a working memory, playing a central role in reasoning, comprehension of language, and long-term learning.

Problems of the Dichotomous View

While this dichotomous view continues to account for the bulk of the available evidence, there have in recent years been an increased number of results which can be fitted into this picture only with difficulty. We shall consider some of these before going on to look at alternative ways of viewing the human memory system.

CODING

As we saw in Chapter 6, it is certainly the case that phonemically coded material *may* be stored in LTM. Such storage is clearly necessary in learning a language or in recognizing nonspeech sounds, such as the slamming of a car door. Brown and McNeill (1966) have also shown that our retention of words contains a phonemic component, as indeed it must, since we can retrieve words purely on the basis of their phonemic structure, as when we generate rhymes or homophones.

The presence of phonemic coding effects in long-term memory, or in the LTS component of two-component tasks (Baddeley 1972), is not incompatible with a dichotomous view of memory. It does, however, suggest that we should beware of oversimplification.

SEMANTIC CODING AND RECENCY

Using a probe recognition task, Shulman (1970) obtained evidence for a recency effect, even though he was cueing with a semantically related item rather than an identical probe item. Raser (1972) has obtained similar results under conditions which make an interpretation in terms of phonemic recoding highly unlikely. The recency effects obtained are considerably less marked than those typically found in free recall, but at the very least these results suggest that the assumption that all recency effects reflect a phonemically coded STS trace is an oversimplification. We shall return to this point later in the chapter.

In general, the evidence for phonemic coding in the recency component of free recall is very sparse. Craik (1968*b*) and Shallice (1975) have both shown that phonemic intrusion errors tend to come from the most recent serial positions in a free-recall task, but Glanzer, Koppenaal, and Nelson (1972) failed to find evidence of either phonemic or semantic coding in the recency component of free recall. They studied the effect on the recency component of interpolating a small amount of material between presentation and recall. The material varied in its relationship to the last few items in the list, being either unrelated or resembling them phonemically or semantically. The characteristics of the interpolated material seemed to have no effect on the magnitude of the recency effect; unrelated words were just as disruptive as words that were similar in sound or meaning. On the basis of these results, Glanzer and his associates suggest that there is no relationship between STS and type of coding.

RECENCY IN LTM

A number of studies have indicated that recency effects may occur in free recall under conditions where the operation of STS is almost certainly eliminated (Baddeley and Hitch 1976; Bjork and Whitten 1974; Tzeng 1973). Tzeng required his subjects to count backward for 20 seconds before and after presentation of each word in a list, a procedure which presumably eliminated any STS component. Nevertheless, a substantial recency effect was observed on each recall trial; furthermore, the tendency for the last few items in a list to be well recalled was still present on a later, final, free-recall test, in which subjects were asked to recall as many words as possible from each of the several lists they had previously recalled.

It is, of course, possible that recency effects operating over long periods of time may be based on quite different factors from those observed in the standard free-recall paradigm, although there is at present no clear evidence that this is the case. All we can conclude at present is that the recency effect does not necessarily reflect the operation of a short-term store.

AMNESIA

Perhaps the most difficult piece of evidence to accommodate within a standard dichotomous theory of memory (Atkinson and Shiffrin 1968) comes from patients such as K.F. (Shallice and Warrington 1970) who appear to have grossly impaired short-term memory with no apparent decrement in long-term learning ability. This is not, of course, incompatible with all dichotomous models (indeed, Shallice and Warrington interpret their results in terms of two stores); it does, however, cast considerable doubt on the assumption that short-term memory functions as a working memory that plays a central role in other information-processing tasks, such as reasoning and learning.

It is probably true to say that none of the results just described presents an insuperable problem for a dichotomous view of memory. Taken together, however, the results imply that the situation is considerably more complex than might be suggested by a simple model having two separate and clearly distinct memory systems. The question therefore arises as to whether the dichotomous view of memory has outlived its usefulness. The remainder of this chapter will be devoted to two alternative views of the question, both of which could reasonably be described as elaborations of the two-store view of memory.

Levels-of-Processing Approach

It has frequently been suggested that perception or pattern recognition involves the analysis of stimuli at a series of levels or stages (Self-ridge and Neisser 1960; Sutherland 1968). Preliminary levels of analysis are concerned with the more basic physical characteristics of the stimulus, such as its brightness or loudness or the lines or angles involved in a pattern, while higher levels of processing are more concerned with matching the input with already stored information and abstracting the meaning from the stimulus. It has also been suggested (Morton 1970; Baddeley and Patterson 1971) that each level of processing is likely to be associated with some type of temporary information store, with deeper levels of processing requiring the integration of information over longer periods; integrating phonemes into a word is likely to involve a shorter time sample than integrating words into a sentence, and hence will require a less capacious or durable memory store. It would therefore seem reasonable to expect to find an association between depth of processing and duration of the associated memory trace; further evidence for this will be found in the next two chapters.

In its earlier form, this view tended to be associated with an approach to memory in terms of a hierarchy of separate but interrelated stores (Morton 1970; Baddeley and Patterson 1971). More recently, however, Craik and Lockhart (1972) have proposed a more flexible levels-of-processing view of memory, which explicitly attempts to avoid the multistore approach. Trace durability is assumed to be entirely dependent on level of processing. Rehearsal may maintain a memory trace but cannot strengthen it; only deeper processing leads to an increase in trace strength. However, Craik and Lockhart do assume a primary or short-term memory system which functions very much as a working memory. This is assumed to be a flexible central processor which can operate at any of several levels in any of several encoding dimensions. As in William James's original concept of *primary memory,* it is assumed to be closely associated with consciousness, and its limited capacity is linked with the limitation in attentional capacity. The depth at which the primary memory operates will be determined largely by the demands of the task, with semantic demands leading to processing at a greater depth than if the subject is merely required to repeat back unrelated items with little semantic content. The primary memory system is responsible for rehearsing, and it will rehearse items in "chunks" at the appropriate level of operation; thus, we may rehearse a sound, a letter, a word, an idea, or an image. Such rehearsal, however, will merely postpone the onset of forgetting, unless it is used for yet deeper processing. In one sense, then, the theoretical framework suggested by Craik and Lockhart is attractively simple. It involves a single central control mechanism, the primary memory or attentional system, and interprets learning entirely in terms of moving through ever-deeper levels of processing.

The levels-of-processing view has already proved empirically fruitful. Craik and Watkins (1973) tested the hypothesis that rote rehearsal does not strengthen the memory trace in an ingenious study requiring subjects to hold single words in storage for varying lengths of time. Subjects listened to a series of word lists and attempted to report after each list just the last word beginning with a particular letter. For example, given the letter *b* and the word sequence *cabbage, bag, rat, cupboard, blonde, table, bath, elephant,* the subject would begin by remembering *bag,* which he would then discard when *blonde* appeared. This in turn would be discarded when *bath* appeared, and this word would be the one he was required to recall. Note that the amount of time he is required to hold any given item can be manipulated by varying the number of unwanted items intervening between that and the next wanted item. At the end of the experiment, subjects were asked to recall as many of the words presented as possible. The results obtained showed no relationship between probability of recall and the amount of time a given word had been held, pending the arrival of the next critical word. Hence, the Craik and Lockhart suggestion that rehearsal per se does not lead to learning was supported.

A substantially similar conclusion was reached by Woodward, Bjork, and Jongeward (1973), using a slightly different approach to the same problem. However, they *did* observe a positive relationship between amount of rehearsal and probability of recognition. The discrepancy between results based on recall and recognition is an interesting one and clearly merits further investigation. Further evidence supporting the levels-of-processing view comes from studies by Craik and Tulving (1975), in which the type of processing of a given item is systematically manipulated. The deeper the level of processing required, as measured by time to complete processing, the better the subsequent recall, despite the absence of a learning instruction.

The levels-of-processing approach to memory has a number of attractive features. As Craik and Lockhart point out, multistore models are frequently taken far too literally as reflecting the operation of a series of rigidly separate boxes, each of which has the sole purpose of storing information. The Craik-Lockhart view places a very healthy emphasis on memory as an integral part of other forms of information processing, such as perception and pattern recognition. In a similar vein, the simple distinction between phonemic and semantic coding is also clearly inadequate to reflect the great complexity of coding processes that go on in human memory, and a levels-of-processing approach avoids this temptation to oversimplify. Finally, the association between primary memory and a limited-capacity attentional system, although not novel, is a point which has far too often been neglected in focusing too exclusively on the phonemic aspects of short-term memory.

While the Craik-Lockhart approach avoids many of the dangers of a too-rigid multistore approach to memory, it is, I believe, itself open to a number of problems. First, there is a good deal of evidence which does not fit particularly neatly into this framework. In particular, the evidence from neuropsychological studies appears to suggest the existence of a number of rather clearly defined storage systems. For example, the patient K.F. (Shallice and Warrington 1970) appears to have a very specific defect associated with an auditory-verbal store (Warrington and Shallice 1969). Comparable modality-specific memory defects are found for visual memory (Milner 1968; Yin 1969). While it could be argued that such patients are simply showing the effects of defective coding at the relevant level, one would expect this to be reflected in perceptual deficits, which does not appear to be the case. Similarly, amnesics with long-term memory deficits show little evidence of failure to process information at a sufficiently deep level; they can converse quite normally, though they cannot subsequently remember the topic of conversation.

Neuropsychological evidence becomes particularly crucial in view of the conceptual difficulty of testing this hypothesis using normal subjects. This arises from the difficulty of independently specifying the level of processing involved in a given task. While there would be considerable agreement in many cases as to which of two tasks involves the deeper processing, it is almost invariably the case that depth of processing is correlated with some other factor. For example, deeper processing is likely to take longer, hence confounding depth of processing and total time, which, as we saw in Chapter 2, is a very effective predictor of amount of learning. We can, of course, avoid this confounding by using material which differs in initial familiarity or meaningfulness; familiar or meaningful material will be presumably processed to a greater depth more rapidly. However, most theories of learning would predict that meaningful and familiar material would be better learned and better retained than unfamiliar, meaningless material, so this type of evidence is itself equivocal.

As Craik and Lockhart point out, the simplified dichotomous view of memory has difficulty in handling nonverbal memory; as we shall see in the next two chapters, there is abundant evidence for separate memory systems for different modalities, and any complete view of human memory must take these into account. However, Craik and Lockhart do not suggest any means by which one could compare the depth of processing involved in two different modalities or, indeed, the processing demands within the semantic domain. How should one decide whether a particular instance of associative coding is more or less deep than another instance of coding in terms of a visual image? * If one is content to use the levels-of-processing concept as a simple rule of thumb, such difficulties may perhaps be outweighed by its overall usefulness. As a scientific hypothesis, however, its long-term value is likely to be reduced by the difficulty in obtaining an independent measure of depth of processing.

To sum up: the levels-of-processing approach suggested by Craik and Lockhart is useful in providing the researcher with a rule of thumb or "neutral point" from which to explore the relationship between coding and memory, without needing to become too involved in the question of how many kinds of memory there are, a topic which has been growing somewhat stale in recent years. However, there remains some doubt, first, as to whether the general principles of an

---

* In actual practice, the many studies on depth of processing do not seem to have revealed more than those levels that would be assumed by a dichotomous view. Typically, subjects are shown to exhibit the poorest retention when words are processed as visual patterns or individual letters (e.g., by instructing the subject to detect certain letters). Retention is somewhat better with phonemic coding (e.g., finding a rhyme), and is best with semantic coding (e.g., judging a word's pleasantness). I know of no good evidence for deeper levels of processing within the semantic domain leading to better retention, and more recently Craik and Tulving (1975) have emphasized richness of coding at a given level, rather than depth as the main factor governing the probability of recalling semantically coded material. Such a view is also of course consistent with most alternatives to a levels-of-processing view.

association between depth of coding and durability of memory trace are strictly testable and, second, as to whether the application of this approach to specific problems, such as the nature of the serial position effect or an explanation of amnesia, will prove fruitful.

Working Memory

As we saw earlier, a division of memory into two clearly separate components, STS and LTS, is a useful hypothesis which has generated considerably greater understanding of the memory system than existed 10 years ago. However, it is almost certainly a gross oversimplification, and continued preoccupation with the question of whether a dichotomy adequately represents the memory system seems perhaps more likely to impede future progress than to enhance it. The attempt by Craik and Lockhart to reexamine and explain a wide range of phenomena by depth of coding represents one approach to this problem; a second alternative, which has a good deal in common with the Craik-Lockhart approach, is presented in a recent paper by Baddeley and Hitch (1974). This paper takes as its starting point the question of whether STS can indeed be shown to function as a working memory, as has frequently been claimed (Hunter 1964; Posner and Rossman 1965; Atkinson and Shiffrin 1971).

The simple question underlying the experiments carried out by Baddeley and Hitch was the following: If a separate STS exists, what function does it serve? There is, of course, no *logical* necessity for any part of human behavior to have functional or survival value. It is quite conceivable that STS could be a system which has no importance beyond that of keeping experimental psychologists busy. If this is the case, however, then I for one feel that I would rather busy myself in other ways. On the other hand, if STS does play an important general role in the processing of information, then understanding the nature of its role may tell us more about the system. In either case, the question "What use is STS?" would seem to be worth asking.

Despite the crucial role in human information processing that many theorists have assigned to STS, the concrete evidence that it plays such a role is remarkably sparse. A number of studies have shown that learning and recall do make demands on a subject's general processing capacity, as reflected by his performance on some secondary task such as card sorting (Murdock 1965), tracking performance (Martin 1970), or a reaction-time task (Johnston, Wagstaff, and Griffith 1972). However, evidence that impairment on these secondary tasks stems from their occupation of the subject's short-term working memory is simply not available. Indeed, if we are to interpret the recency effect in free recall as reflecting the subject's working memory, then it appears that neither card sorting (Murdock 1965; Baddeley, Scott, Drynan, and Smith 1969) nor mental arithmetic (Silverstein and Glanzer 1971) can be said to affect working memory, despite their clear influence on long-term memory. Furthermore, an attempt by V. Coltheart (1972) to show effects of acoustic similarity in a concept-formation task proved unsuccessful, whereas semantic similarity had a clear influence on performance. Even more damaging to a simple view of STS as a working memory are data from the patient K.F.; despite a digit span of only two items and grossly defective performance on the Brown-Peterson task, K.F. nevertheless showed no apparent decrement in comprehension or long-term learning, both of which might be assumed to make heavy demands on working memory. Baddeley and Hitch (1974) therefore attempted to collect direct evidence of working memory by studying the role of STS in each of three tasks—verbal reasoning, prose comprehension, and long-term learning—all of which would be supposed by most theorists to rely heavily on working memory.

VERBAL REASONING AND WORKING MEMORY

The task was one in which subjects were presented with a series of sentences, each purporting to describe the order of occurrence of two letters and each being followed by the two letters either in the order described by the sentence (in which case the subject should respond *true*) or in the reverse order (to which the subject should respond *false*). Thus, a subject might be presented with a sentence *A is not preceded by B—BA,* whereupon his response should be *false*. Sentence difficulty ranged from that of simple active sentences (e.g., *A precedes B—AB*) through more complex sentences, which might involve passives (*A is preceded by B—BA*), negatives (*B is not followed by A—BA*), or both (*A is not preceded by B—AB*). Besides being typical of a wide range of studies on reasoning (Wason and Johnson-Laird 1972), the test has also been shown to be sensitive to the subject's intelligence level and to be susceptible to both environmental and speed-load stress effects (Baddeley 1968c; Brown, Tickner, and Simmonds 1969).

In one set of experiments, subjects were given from one to six digits to hold in immediate memory while performing the reasoning task. It was argued that if STM did indeed serve as a working memory, then filling it almost to capacity by an additional digit-span task should drastically impair performance on any task demanding working memory. Preliminary experiments suggested that subjects could hold one or two items in immediate memory with no observable impairment in either speed or accuracy of reasoning. However, when the load was increased to six items, a clear impairment occurred. In order to explore the impairment further, subjects were required either to remember a six-digit number, which they continued to rehearse aloud during the solution of the visually presented reasoning task, or to count from one to six at a rapid rate. This task was intended to impair rote rehearsal while making minimal demands on STS (Peterson 1969), whereas rehearsing a six-digit number, which approached the memory span for many of the subjects tested, should make considerable demands on working memory.

Figure 8–1 shows the effect of these conditions on the time subjects needed in order to solve problems of varying degrees of complexity. The condition in which articulation was suppressed but memory load was low produced a small and marginally significant decrement in performance. The six-digit number, however, produced a much more substantial decrement, which furthermore interacted significantly with the difficulty of the task, being most dramatic in the case of the most difficult negative passive sentences. This pattern of results is consistent with the hypothesis that reasoning makes demands on a working memory system, and furthermore suggests that the effects are not simply attributable to the suppression of rehearsal. It is important to note, however, that despite the imposition of a near-span concurrent memory load, subjects were still able to perform the task relatively accurately; although some decrease in speed occurred, the decrement was far from catastrophic. This strongly suggests that the limits of memory span are not the limits of working memory—or, in other words, that working memory and memory span are by no means synonymous.

As we saw in Chapter 7, there is a good deal of evidence for a close association between phonemic coding and short-term memory. The second series of experiments therefore attempted to explore the role of phonemic coding in the verbal reasoning task just described.

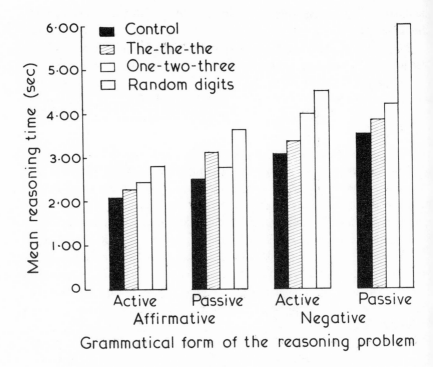

Figure 8–1   Effects of concurrent articulatory activity on reasoning time. Note that rehearsing a random series of six digits has the most decremental effect and that this effect is greater for more complex sentences. Source: A. D. Baddeley and G. Hitch, *Working memory*, in G. A. Bower (ed.), *The Psychology of Learning and Motivation* (New York: Academic Press, 1974), vol. 8, p. 56.

This was done by replacing the letters *A* and *B* in the sentence to be processed by letters which varied in their degree of both phonemic and visual similarity (visual similarity typically does not influence STM). Thus in a phonemically similar condition, the sentence *A follows B–BA* would be replaced by the sentence *F follows S–SF*. Four sets of letter pairs were used, as follows: low phonemic similarity, low visual similarity (*MC, VF*); high phonemic, low visual similarity (*FS, TD*); low phonemic, high visual similarity (*OQ, XY*); and high phonemic, high visual similarity (*BP, MN*). There proved to be a small but highly reliable effect of phonemic similarity, with sentences containing phonemically similar letters taking longer to process than those with dissimilar letters, whereas visual similarity did not affect performance. Once again, then, the pattern of results resembles what one might expect on the assumption that a phonemically based STS plays a role in reasoning. But again, the magnitude of the effect suggests that our manipulations are only peripherally influencing the working memory system. We shall return to this point later in the chapter.

COMPREHENSION

The concurrent memory load task was again used to study the role of STS, this time in the comprehension and retention of prose. In one study, subjects listened to passages taken from a test of reading ability and subsequently answered questions on the content of the passage. Questions were carefully designed to avoid using identical words, and hence to minimize verbatim recall and maximize reliance on semantic factors. During the presentation of the passage, subjects were required to watch a television monitor on which sequences of digits appeared. In the control condition, subjects simply copied each digit as it occurred; in the two experimental conditions, subjects were required to delay recall until they had accumulated either three or six digits, at which point the digits were to be recalled and written down. Hence, all the subjects were writing a comparable number of digits, but they differed as to whether they were required to store one, three, or six digits during the prose comprehension task. Out of 8 test questions, a mean of 5.9 were answered correctly when subjects were only holding one digit in store (the control condition), a mean of 5.6 when three digits had to be held, and a mean of 4.8 when the load increased to six digits. As in the case of the reasoning task, a small storage load apparently does not reliably impair performance, whereas a load of six items does, although again the effect is far from catastrophic.

A further experiment examined the role of acoustic similarity in sentence comprehension, this time using individual sentences; the subject was required to detect a change in word order which changed a meaningful and grammatical sentence to a much less acceptable, nongrammatical form. For example, the sentence *The unhappy crazy boy had a wicked father* might be changed to *The unhappy crazy had boy a wicked father;* the second sentence is not, of course, absolutely meaningless, but the difference between the two was sufficiently large to allow subjects to make a discrimination reliably and quickly. Performance on such sentences was compared with that on semantically comparable sentences comprising a large number of phonemically similar words (e.g., *The sad mad lad had a bad dad*). The results showed that although subjects took no longer to read the phonemically similar sentences out loud in a posttest, they nevertheless took longer to decide whether or not they were meaningful. Again the phonemic similarity effect was statistically reliable, but once again it was relatively small in magnitude.

The tasks studied could at best be regarded as giving a very crude and inadequate representation of prose comprehension, but within these limits they did present evidence consistent with results of the verbal reasoning test—namely, that performance is impaired by a concurrent load of six items but not by a load of three or less. The tests also suggest that phonemic coding may have a small but consistent effect on performance.

FREE RECALL

The third task studied was that of free-recall learning. This is particularly interesting because it allows the role of short-term memory in long-term learning to be investigated, while throwing light on the relationship between working memory and the recency effect in free recall. The recency effect has long been regarded as one of the most characteristic phenomena associated with short-term memory. In recent years, however, a number of somewhat puzzling discrepancies have arisen between the characteristics of the recency effect and those that one might wish to attribute to a short-term working memory. As mentioned earlier, such concurrent tasks as card sorting and mental arithmetic, which might be assumed to make heavy demands on working memory, were found by Murdock (1965) and Silverstein and Glanzer (1971) to leave recency unimpaired. Furthermore, the failure of Glanzer, Koppenaal, and Nelson (1972) to find any evidence for phonemic coding in the recency effect, coupled with the observation by Shulman (1971) of semantic coding effects, suggests that the association between short-term memory and phonemic coding does not apply to the recency portion of free recall. It therefore seemed worthwhile to test the clear prediction from current dichotomous theories of memory that filling the short-term memory span with digits to capacity should catastrophically reduce the recency effect, since both are assumed to rely on the same limited-capacity system.

Subjects simultaneously listened to a sequence of 15 unrelated words and watched a television screen on which digits appeared. As in the prose comprehension study, they were required to copy the

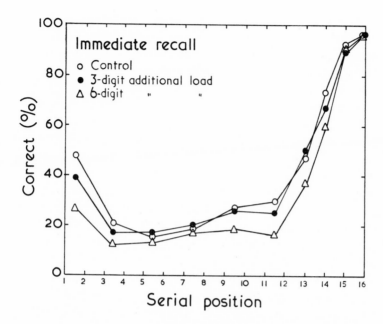

Figure 8–2   Effect of an additional short-term memory load on immediate and delayed free recall. A load of six items causes an impairment in overall performance but does not diminish the recency effect. Source: A. D. Baddeley and G. Hitch, Recency re-examined, in S. Dornic (ed.), *Attention and Performance VI* (forthcoming 1976).

digits down either singly or after having processed either three digits or six digits. The digit-processing task started before the words were presented, and subjects were instructed to abandon the task as soon as the recall signal was given. Performance with a three-digit load is shown in Figure 8–2. It is clear that the LTS or long-term component of the task was consistently affected by the six-digit load condition but showed no reliable impairment when subjects were holding only three digits. A subsequent study in which the words were presented visually and the digits aurally has given substantially similar results (Baddeley and Hitch 1976). These results are consistent with the pattern found for both reasoning and prose comprehension and again suggest that subjects can apparently hold up to three items without making substantial demands on general processing capacity. More surprising is the apparent lack of any reliable effect of digit load on the recency component. It appears to be the case that a subject can hold six items in his working memory without producing any appreciable decline in the recency effect. This result strongly suggests that the recency effect in free recall is quite unrelated to the memory system underlying digit span.

Considering the overall pattern of their experimental results, Baddeley and Hitch conclude that there does seem to be enough consistency to suggest a single working memory system operating in verbal reasoning, prose comprehension, and free-recall learning. All three tasks show a reliable degree of impairment when the subject is concurrently required to remember six digits, but little or no decrement when he is holding three items or less. Furthermore, in the two cases in which phonemic similarity was studied, reliable effects were found, as might be expected on the basis of earlier work on the memory span. However, the magnitude of the effects of both storage load and phonemic similarity suggests that working memory and memory span are by no means synonymous. Subjects were able to reason, comprehend, and learn very effectively even when holding a sequence of six digits, a memory load approaching the span of many subjects. This strongly suggests that the two tasks do overlap but that (1) a considerable amount of the working memory system is not available to the memory span, (2) two or three items can apparently be held in span without placing any substantial load on the working memory system.

In interpreting these results, Baddeley and Hitch suggest that they reflect a dual STM system comprising a working memory not unlike the central processor assumed by Craik and Lockhart, together with an articulatory rehearsal loop. Such a loop has, of course, been suggested by a number of workers, including Atkinson and Shiffrin (1968), Glanzer and Clark (1963), and Morton (1970), who suggests that such a loop may perform an important function as an output buffer in which speech responses may be stored pending their emission as speech.

Baddeley and Hitch suggest that this articulatory or verbal loop may function as a limited-capacity "slave" system, which can be used to supplement the central processor. The proposed working memory system can perhaps best be illustrated by considering its application to a basic experimental paradigm of verbal memory: the memory span.

MEMORY SPAN

It is suggested that the memory span depends on the interaction of the two subsystems. The verbal loop is able to store a limited amount of speechlike material in the appropriate serial order, but its capacity is limited to about three items. Provided this capacity is not exceeded, the material may be stored in a continuous rehearsal loop, which makes few demands on the central processing component of the system.

An indication of the capacity of the verbal loop has been obtained by Baddeley, Thomson, and Buchanan (1975), who demonstrated a clear relationship between word length and memory span. Their results are shown in Figure 8–3. A further experiment showed that the word-length effect disappears when articulation is suppressed by requiring the subject to count repeatedly up to six during presentation

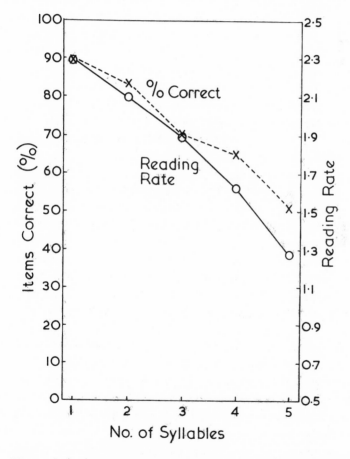

Figure 8–3 Memory span for words varying in number of syllables. Subjects attempted to recall sequences of five words. Source: A. D. Baddeley, N. Thomson, and M. Buchanan, Word length and the structure of short-term memory, *Journal of Verbal Learning and Verbal Behavior* 14 (1945): 583.

of the words, suggesting that the effect of word length is entirely attributable to the articulatory loop; when this loop is preempted by a counting task, subjects are forced to rely entirely on the central processor, which shows no apparent word-length effect. Studies by Murray (1968) and Estes (1973) have shown that the acoustic similarity effect is also eliminated if subjects are required to count during presentation of the material to be remembered.

Finally, Baddeley, Thomson, and Buchanan (1975) have shown that the crucial feature of the word-length effect is the time taken to articulate the word in question, not the number of syllables or phonemes. They found memory-span performance on words like *Friday* and *harpoon* was consistently poorer than performance with words like *bishop* and *wicket,* which were matched in number of syllables, number of phonemes, and frequency of occurrence in the language but take less time to say. This suggests that the system resembles a tape recorder, whose capacity is limited by time rather than by the amount of information or number of events. Since STM in general appears to be limited in number of items held rather than time (see Chapter 7), it seems unlikely that the central executive component of the system is also time-based.

Thus, there is a growing body of evidence to suggest that the apparent association between phonemic coding and STM may be largely, if not entirely, attributable to the utilization of the articulatory verbal loop. The loop appears to be responsible for both word-length and phonemic similarity effects and can apparently be preempted by requiring the subject to perform some redundant, irrelevant verbal activity, such as reciting the word *the* or counting. This consistently impairs memory performance, but its effects are far from dramatic, suggesting that the articulatory loop is by no means essential to the operation of working memory. The system does, however, provide a useful temporary store which has the additional advantage of making few demands on the central processor.

R. Conrad (1972) suggests the possibility that the ability to take advantage of this system may be an important prerequisite of learning to read. He claims that children first begin to remember pictured objects in terms of their names at about the time they become capable of learning to read, and he tentatively suggests that the two phenomena may be related. It can plausibly be argued that the child, attempting to translate a series of visual letters into speech sounds, might find it very useful to have a temporary store which will hold the sounds of those letters already decoded. So much the better if this can be achieved, as Baddeley and Hitch suggest, without placing too great a demand on the central processor, which is likely to be heavily overloaded by the process of visual-auditory translation. Such a view is, of course, still highly speculative, although it does have some support from an association between reading retardation and (1) the absence of a clear phonemic similarity effect with visually presented letters (Liberman et al 1976), (2) the occurrence of excessive order errors in memory-span tasks (Bakker 1972), and (3) the observed relationship between reduced digit span and dyslexia (Naidoo 1970). Furthermore, a recent study by Levy (1975), using normal adults, finds gross impairment in the retention of sentences read under an articulatory suppression condition. The role of articulation in reading would appear to merit further exploration.

To return to the memory span: it is assumed by Baddeley and Hitch that the central processor may increase the span beyond that of the verbal loop in two ways: first, by increasing the efficiency with which the rehearsal loop is employed and, second, by itself serving as an information store. It seems likely that the central processor enhances the value of the verbal loop by reduction coding—that is, by recoding material in a more compact form. For example, a series of letters may be grouped into a smaller number of speech sounds; thus, the letter sequence *F-I-E-L-D* might be "chunked" into a single word rather than five letter names. The central executive component of the working memory system is probably also useful in the process of retrieval from the verbal loop, not necessarily because retrieval in itself requires this system (although this may be the case), but rather because it allows contextual cues to come into play in interpreting the information retrieved from the verbal loop. Hence, the subject who is serving in an experiment on retention of digits will know that a deteriorated trace should be interpreted as *8* rather than *h*. It seems likely that the central processor itself has storage capability, since blocking the verbal loop by articulatory suppression leaves the subject able to perform both span and free-recall tasks, albeit less efficiently. Imposing a memory load approaching span has a far from catastrophic effect on reasoning or comprehension. This would seem to imply that some of the central executive system cannot be diverted to memory. However, such a conclusion cannot be drawn with confidence until it has been shown that subjects can still reason while holding a sequence of digits equal to their span.

The Baddeley-Hitch interpretation of the memory span therefore differs from that proposed by Craik and Lockhart primarily in emphasizing the distinction between the central processor and a separate articulatory rehearsal loop, and in attributing to the functioning of this loop the evidence for phonemic coding, articulatory suppression, and word-length effects in STM. A rather more dramatic source of difference is revealed in the treatment of the recency effect in free recall.

WORKING MEMORY AND THE RECENCY EFFECT

In this section we shall reconsider the recency effect in free recall in the light of recent experimental work. Three theoretical interpretations will be considered.

Recency and STS. The most commonly held view, described in the previous chapter, views recency effects in free recall as representing the output of a short-term or primary memory store. This view is incorporated in the Atkinson-Shiffrin model, which regards recency as one of several manifestations of STS, which is also assumed to be the memory store underlying memory span, the Brown-Peterson short-term forgetting effect, and various probe tasks. Perhaps the most active current proponent of a simple two-store view of memory is Glanzer (1972), who bases his conclusions almost exclusively on the free-recall paradigm. On the basis of this, he has concluded that STS is quite insensitive to coding effects (Glanzer, Koppenaal, and Nelson 1972), to the effects of a supplementary mental arithmetic task (Silverstein and Glanzer 1971), or to the length of the constituent units (Glanzer and Razel 1974). This view of memory can be criticized on two major counts: (1) for assuming that the recency effect in free recall is typical of short-term memory tasks and (2) for assuming that the recency effect itself reflects a separate short-term working memory store.

First, it is clear that a number of variables which have a dramatic effect on such tasks as memory span, the Brown-Peterson task, or the Waugh-Norman probe task have no influence on the recency effect in free recall. This shows up particularly clearly in those variables which might be assumed to reflect the operation of the articulatory rehearsal loop: namely, the acoustic similarity, word-length, and articulatory suppression effects. Such variables have been shown to affect a wide range of STM tasks and, furthermore, to influence reasoning, language comprehension, and learning. Of course, one might argue that the recency effect represents the output of the central executive system. If this were the case, however, recency would surely be influenced by such concurrent tasks as mental arithmetic or card sorting, which presumably make substantial demands on the central processor; yet no such effects occur. Indeed, perhaps the most striking feature of the recency effect is its insensitivity to variables other than delay or interpolation of material (Glanzer 1972). While there is considerable commonality between memory span and impairment on tasks which might reasonably be supposed to rely heavily on working memory, the recency effect in free recall shows no such overlap. If one wishes to maintain that working memory is synonymous with the recency effect in free recall, then one must assume that such a working memory is not involved in mental arithmetic, digit span, or card sorting (see Figure 8–4). Furthermore, some component which is involved in supplementary tasks of this sort does appear to influence reasoning, language comprehension, and learning. In short, if one is to assume that the recency effect in free recall represents the operation of a working memory system, then it seems likely that one must postulate a further working memory system which is independently responsible for the wide range of phenomena shown in Figure 8–4.

A second major difficulty for a simple two-store view of recency comes from the evidence for recency effects in long-term memory. Glanzer and Razel (1974) describe an intriguing experiment on free recall of proverbs which shows a dramatic recency effect; this is interpreted as evidence that the short-term store is capable of holding as many proverbs as it can hold unrelated words. A striking incidental feature of this experiment is the observation of a pronounced recency effect after a delay. Glanzer and Razel do not discuss this further, presumably attributing it to the use of a relatively short delay task, involving the repetition of only four words. However, an unpublished replication by Thomson and Baddeley showed a very marked recency effect even after a delay of 30 seconds during which the subject continuously copied digits, a task which typically completely eliminates the recency effect. Other long-term recency effects have been reported by Tzeng (in the experiment described on p. 164), Bjork and Whitten (1974), Dalezman (1974), and Baddeley and Hitch (1974). The latter study showed a marked recency effect in the incidental recall of anagram solutions, despite the fact that most solutions were followed by up to a minute of problem-solving activity, and the last item by over a minute's discussion of the problem-solving strategies used by the subject. It is difficult to see how these results can be interpreted in terms of a short-term store of limited capacity. At the very least, they suggest that recency should not be regarded as unequivocal evidence of short-term storage, and they imply that one must either find a

Task	Variable			
	Phonemic Similarity	Word Length	Presentation Rate	Additional Memory Load
Paired-Associate learning	+ [1]	?	+ [12]	+ [17]
Probed recall	+ [2]	+ [8]	0? [13]	+ [18]
Brown-Peterson STM task	+ [3]	?	?	?
Free recall (SM component)	+ [4]	0 [9]	+ [14]	+ [5]
Prose comprehension	+ [5]	+ [10]	+ [15]	+ [5]
Reasoning	+ [5]	?	?	+ [5]
Memory span	+ [6]	+ [11]	+ [16]	+ [17]
Recency in free recall	⊙[7] [7]	⊙[9] [7]	⊙[5] [5]	⊙[5] [5]

Figure 8–4   The influence of a range of variables on basic memory tasks. A plus sign means that the variable in question affects performance on the task; a large circle, that it does not. A question mark means that no clear evidence is available. Note the consistent pattern across all tasks other than the recency effect. Numbers refer to a single reference experiment in each case. 1. Baddeley (1970); 2. Kintsch and Buschke (1969); 3. Baddeley (1968b); 4. Baddeley and Warrington (1973); 5. Baddeley and Hitch (1974); 6. Conrad and Hull (1964); 7. Craik and Levy (1970); 8. Clifton and Tash (1973); 9. Craik (1968a); 10. Flesch (1948); 11. Baddeley, Thompson, and Buchanan (1975); 12. Bugelski (1962); 13. Waugh and Norman (1965); 14. Glanzer and Cunitz (1966); 15. Poulton (1958); 16. Laughery and Pinkus (1966); 17. Baddeley and Thomson (unpublished); 18. Sternberg, Knoll, and Nasto (1969).

separate explanation for these long-term recency effects or, preferably, produce an explanation which will account for recency in both long- and short-term memory situations.

Recency and phonemic coding. An alternative explanation put forward by Craik and Lockhart (1972) suggests that the recency effect reflects a coding strategy adopted by the subject. They hypothesize that subjects code earlier items in a relatively durable semantic code, while relying on a less durable phonemic code for the last few items. Since such items can be recalled almost immediately, they do not demand the more complex semantic processing that would be required for more delayed recall. There is no doubt that subjects can, and occasionally do, adopt such a strategy (Shallice 1975). However, it is highly unlikely that such strategy differences underlie all recency effects, since clear effects occur under incidental learning instructions (Baddeley and Hitch 1976) when the subject would have no reason for changing his strategy in processing later items, since he would not expect to have to recall the material. Similarly, pronounced recency effects occur in free-recall tasks in which the subject does not know on any given trial whether immediate or delayed recall will be required; under these conditions, the subject would surely be unwise to adopt the strategy suggested.

Furthermore, one might expect such a strategy to yield impaired recall of the last few items when recall is delayed. While such *negative recency effects* do occur under certain conditions (Craik 1970), they are not characteristic of the delayed free recall of individual lists. Negative recency effects appear to show up most clearly when items which have been immediately free-recalled are subsequently re-recalled. This suggests that it is the initial recall rather than the initial presentation which differentially affects the last few items.

There are two possible reasons why this may be so. First, if all items are encoded both semantically and phonemically, and if the phonemic code is less durable than the semantic, then the later items may be accessible on a phonemic basis, whereas earlier items will not be. If one further assumes that a retrieval constitutes in some sense a second learning trial, then the most recent items are initially encoded both semantically and phonemically and subsequently retrieved phonemically, whereas earlier items are both encoded and retrieved using the more durable semantic code. Evidence that the last few items are phonemically encoded comes from the study of error patterns in free recall; these indicate that phonemic intrusions come predominantly from items which are presented in later serial positions and recalled almost immediately (Craik 1968b; Shallice 1975).

A second possible interpretation of negative recency effects is based on the well-established observation that when an item is presented on two learning trials, the further apart the learning trials, the better the subsequent recall (Melton 1970). When late items are recalled immediately, the recall trial will serve as a massed training trial, which should produce poorer long-term retention than the more distributed training afforded by presenting an item early and recalling it relatively late.

Recency and retrieval strategy. A third approach is to regard the recency effect as the result of a retrieval strategy. Such a view was proposed by Tulving (1968) and was further elaborated by Baddeley and Hitch (1974) in accounting for the failure of a concurrent digit-span task to disrupt the recency effect in free recall. Tulving distinguishes between primary and secondary organization. Organization by order of input is one type of primary organization, and using this as a retrieval cue may produce both primacy and recency effects. The limited size of the recency effect, suggesting that recency is only an effective cue in the last few items, might reasonably be attributed to limitations on the discriminability of recency cues. The advantage of interpreting recency in terms of a retrieval strategy is that it can presumably be applied to any available store, or possibly to any subset of items within that store, provided the subset can be adequately categorized. Baddeley and Hitch suggest that when an interpolated activity is classed in the same category as the learned items, then interpolated events will be stored along the same dimension; hence, they will take over the recency cues from the items to be remembered.

Baddeley and Hitch go on to suggest that a similar type of recency retrieval strategy may be reflected in memory for any clearly specified class of events, such as football games, parties, or meals at expensive restaurants. Unfortunately, this type of information is difficult to check, since one tends not to have objective evidence of attendance at football games or parties. Baddeley and Hitch (1976) went on to test this hypothesis using rugby players, who were asked first to recall as many teams as possible against which they had played in that season; the players were subsequently given a list of games played and required to tick off those teams which they recognized as having actually been their opponents. Figure 8–5 shows the probability of recalling a given game, granted that the player recognized having played the game on looking at the list. Despite irregularities caused by particularly memorable games (the most marked of these being the occasion on which one of the teams tested won its first league game!), there is a very clear recency effect. Since most players tended to miss some games, it proved possible to analyze separately the effect of elapsed time and number of interpolated games on probability of recall. Number of interpolated games proved to be the determining factor, with elapsed time having no substantial effect on recall probability.

Memory for Rugby Games

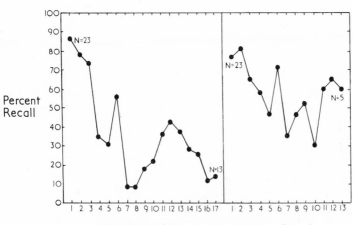

Number of intervening games played

Figure 8–5   A recency effect in long-term memory. Rugby players attempted to recall the names of teams they had played against and subsequently ticked off on a list those games they recognized having played in. The curves represent the probability of recalling an item which was subsequently recognized, as a function of the number of subsequent games for two separate clubs. The number of players contributing to a given point N diminishes with increasing number of interpolated games, since few players took part in every game. Source: A. D. Baddeley and G. Hitch, Recency re-examined, in S. Dornic (ed.), *Attention and Performance VI* (forthcoming 1976).

While recency does appear to be a very general phenomenon which can be interpreted in terms of a retrieval strategy, there remain a number of unsolved problems. Perhaps the most obvious of these is the question of why recency is not observed in a standard free-recall situation when the material interpolated is clearly different from the items to be remembered, as is usually the case. One tentative suggestion is as follows. The recency retrieval strategy is one which will be employed only if better retrieval strategies are not available. In general, semantic coding strategies will predominate in long-term learning and will suggest more complex organizational processes, and hence more complex secondary retrieval strategies. Recency effects tend to be minimal with categorized lists, and those cases in which recency effects typically are found in long-term memory all have in common a tendency for inter-item organization to be minimal. In the study by Tzeng (1973), subjects were required to count backward before and after each word, hence minimizing inter-item encoding opportunities. In the anagram study cited by Baddeley and Hitch (1974; 1976), subjects were not aware that they would have to recall the items subsequently, and since each item was unrelated to the others, there was no reason for the subject to attempt to organize them in any way. A similar generalization holds for games of rugby, since these are mainly "friendly" matches; there is no clear pattern of league positions, nor is there any geographical or regional significance. It may well be the case that in other, more closely or hierarchically organized sports, other retrieval strategies would be employed and the recency effect suppressed.

One might expect recency effects to occur particularly strongly in retrieval from parts of the memory system in which organization is minimal. If, as the evidence for intrusion errors suggests, the last few items in an acoustically presented free-recall list are held in some temporary phonemic form, then it seems plausible to assume that these items may be accessed on the basis of recency cues. Similarly, if it is assumed that in a dichotic listening situation the material on the unattended ear is stored in some relatively unorganized form, then the paradoxical results reported by Bryden (see p. 246) become interpretable. He observed that items on the unattended ear showed a marked recency effect in recall, regardless of whether they were recalled before or after the items on the attended ear. It is therefore suggested that the recency effect represents the operation of a retrieval strategy which is typically used in the absence of a more adequate strategy, such as might be provided by semantic inter-item associations. As such, it tends to be characteristic of peripheral stores, with relatively simple coding, or of more complex material which happens to have been encoded in such a way as to minimize inter-item organization.

This view of recency is, of course, highly speculative, and although it should be relatively easy to test, there is at present simply not enough evidence to evaluate it. One should also bear in mind that although it might appear more parsimonious to have a single explanation of recency effects in long- and short-term memory, they may in fact represent basically different phenomena. However, until the relationship between the two is clarified, it is unlikely that an adequate explanation of either can be produced.

An Overview

Between the late 1950s and the early 1970s, the dominant view of memory changed from that of a relatively undifferentiated unitary system to that of a system based on two distinct stores: an acoustically based, limited-capacity, short-term store, and a more durable, semantically based, long-term store of enormously greater capacity. This view is itself proving to be an oversimplification. In particular, the concept of coding has extended far beyond the initial simple dichotomy between acoustic and semantic encoding and has begun to play a more central theoretical role than such factors as rate of forgetting and storage capacity. This change is associated with an increasingly functional approach to memory; whereas the characteristic 1960s view of memory was that of a store that had the sole function of holding information which might or might not be used in other information-processing tasks, the tendency in the 1970s is to regard memory as an integral part of other information-processing tasks, such as perception, pattern recognition, comprehension, and reasoning. This is reflected both in a growing interest in working memory—that is, in the role of storage processes in other information-processing tasks—and in a growing awareness of the importance of coding. Coding is essentially the other side of the same coin, and it represents the mnemonic consequences of processing information in different ways.

A third reason for abandoning a simple dichotomous view of memory springs from the growing interest in nonverbal memory, studies of which have produced clear evidence for quite separate visual, auditory, and kinesthetic memory systems. Although we know considerably less about any of these than we know about verbal memory, it is already becoming clear that they do not represent simple unitary systems either. They appear to involve a hierarchy of stores (or at least levels of storage), with the durability of the particular storage system increasing with increasing depth of processing, a picture with very clear similarities to the organization of verbal memory.

CHAPTER

9

Visual Memory

AS WE SAW from the studies by Murdock and Walker (1969) and Margrain (1967) described in Chapter 7, memory that is specific to a single sense modality does not appear to be confined to a bank of brief sensory registers that feed into a modality-free, short-term memory system. The next two chapters will discuss sensory memory in more detail, particularly visual and auditory memory, the two modalities on which most studies of sensory and perceptual memory have concentrated.

The Persistence of Vision

If a brightly glowing cigarette is moved about in a dark room, it will appear to leave a trail of light behind; if conditions are appropriate, this trail will persist long enough for shapes and letters to be drawn in the air. The tendency for a visual trace to persist after the stimulus has moved was investigated as long ago as 1740 by Segner, who measured the duration of the effect by attaching a glowing ember to a rotating wheel. By rotating the wheel at a speed which just allows a complete circle to be drawn, and then measuring the time taken for a single revolution, the durability of the visual persistence can be measured; this was estimated by Segner to be approximately 100 msec (cited by Mollon 1970, p. 182).

In recent years, Haber and his associates have used a range of techniques to measure the duration of visual persistence. In one study, Haber and Standing (1969) presented a black outline circle on a white background, followed by a blank white field. The circle was presented repeatedly, always for 12.5 msec, while the duration of the intervening blank could be varied by the subject. His task was to set the blank interval at a point where the figure could just be seen to disappear between presentations. This was found to occur at a blank interval of about 250 msec, suggesting that the 12.5-msec stimulus was persisting for this amount of time. This increased to 440 msec, however, when the intervening field was left dark. Persistence duration was the same whether the blank was presented to the same eye as the figure or to the other eye, suggesting that the phenomenon was occurring at some point after information from the two eyes had been combined, and was hence not a purely retinal effect. In another study, Haber and Nathanson (1968) measured visual persistence by moving a narrow slit to and fro across a figure. At slow rates, only part of the figure is visible at any one time, but as the rate of oscillation increases, a point is reached at which the whole figure becomes visible, since a given part will be re-exposed before the effects of the previous exposure have faded. Both this and a third method, in which a click is set by the subject to coincide with the onset or apparent offset (cessation) of a flash of light (Haber and Standing 1970), gave the same result as the first study, that the visual persistence of a brief stimulus appears to last for about 0.25 second. An intriguing feature of Haber's results is the tendency for longer stimuli to show less persistence than short. It is as if the system were specifically designed to ensure that all stimuli were held for a standard length of time; might this be the time needed to complete a preliminary stage of processing? A similar phenomenon in auditory memory is described in Chapter 10.

Iconic Memory

We have so far discussed only the apparent duration of relatively simple stimuli, a topic that may seem somewhat remote from the study of memory. The continuity between this type of perceptual phenomenon and memory storage was first made apparent in a series of experiments by Sperling (1960). When an array of nine random letters is shown briefly to a subject, he will report a maximum of four or five items correctly. Sperling was concerned to discover whether this limit was set by the number that could be perceived or the number that could be remembered. If items are forgotten rapidly, then by the time the first few items have been recalled, the rest may have been forgotten. Sperling tackled this problem by sampling from the set of items and using performance on the small sample as an indicator of overall amount retained, just as an opinion pollster will base his conclusions about the attitude of an entire country on the results of an interview sample. In one experiment, 12 letters, arranged in three rows of four items each, were presented for 50 msec. In his sampling of partial-report condition, Sperling subsequently required the subject to report only one of the three rows. This was done by following the offset of the display with a tone; a high tone requested recall of the top row, a medium tone the middle row, and a low tone the bottom row. Since the subject does not know which row will be used until after the letter display has ended, performance on the rows sampled can be regarded as typical of the whole array, provided that rows are sampled equally often in an unpredictable pattern. The total number of letters being stored can thus be determined by multiplying the total for a single row by three. When tested immediately, subjects gave evidence of retaining about 9 of the 12 letters presented, but as the delay between the offset of the display and presentation of the cueing tone increased, performance declined; performance after a 1-second delay was little better than the four or five letters produced with the standard whole-report technique. Sperling attributes his results to a visual memory trace with a relatively large storage capacity and a duration of less than 1 second. Neisser (1967), who gives an excellent (though now somewhat dated) account of work in this area, has suggested the term *icon* for this very short-term visual trace.

Subsequent experiments have studied the rate of forgetting in more detail (Averbach and Coriell 1961; Averbach and Sperling 1961). In one such study, Averbach and Sperling (1961) presented 18 letters and subsequently cued the recall of a single letter, using a visually presented bar to indicate the location of the item to be reported. They presented the cue at various times, ranging from 0.5 second before to 5 seconds after the offset of the stimulus array, which was shown for 50 msec. In one set of conditions, the visual field before and after the stimulus was at the same level of illumination as the stimulus itself; in a second set, the pre-field and post-field were both dark, a condition assumed to favor the persistence of visual afterimages. The results are shown in Figure 9–1; with light pre- and post-fields, iconic storage appears to have a limit of about 0.5 second. This is extended to about 5 seconds with a bright stimulus and dark pre- and post-fields, a result which is interpreted as evidence that storage based on a retinal afterimage may occur over relatively long intervals. The two curves in Figure 9–1 are not necessarily based on the same underlying mechanism, however.

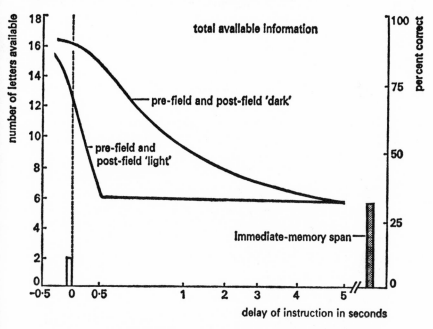

Figure 9–1   Information available to one observer from two kinds of stimulus presentation. The right ordinate is the average accuracy of partial reports; the left ordinate is the inferred store of available letters. Average immediate memory span is indicated on the right. Source: G. Sperling, A model for visual memory tasks, *Human Factors* 5 (1963): 21. Reprinted by permission of The Johns Hopkins University Press.

Averbach and Sperling specified the items to be reported on the basis of their spatial location. Subsequent work has shown that items can be cued on the basis of their shape (Turvey and Kravetz 1970) or size or color (Von Wright 1968). Nonphysical characteristics, however, cannot be used in this way; if the subject is asked to select digits from a mixture of digits and letters, he appears to be unable to do so, and his performance falls to the level obtained with the total-recall method (Sperling

1960). This suggests that the icon is represented in terms of physical but not associative dimensions.

If the iconic store has a duration of less than 0.5 second, it will only be useful if the information can be extracted from it very rapidly and fed into some more durable store. Sperling (1963) studied the rate of readout from the icon, using a modification of a technique employed by Baxt in studying the same problem in 1871. Baxt exposed an array of six or seven letters for 5 msec and followed the stimulus array with a flash of light at one of four intensities after a delay ranging from 0 to

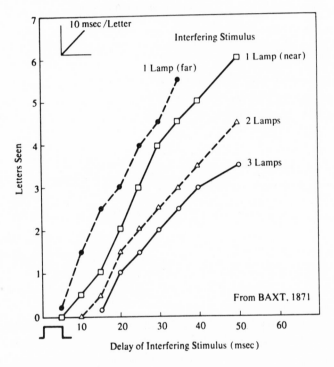

Figure 9–2 Number of letters seen, as a function of delay between the onset of a 5-msec lettered stimulus and a 120-msec blank interfering stimulus. The parameter is the intensity of the interfering stimulus. The time course of the lettered stimulus is indicated at the lower left. Source: G. Sperling, A model for visual memory tasks, *Human Factors* 5 (1963): 23; figure based on the protocols of N. Baxt, Über die Zeit welche nötig ist, damit ein Gesichtseindruck zum Bewusstsein kommt und über die Grösse der bewussten Wahrnehmung bei einem Gesichtsein-drucke von gegebener Dauer, *Pflügers Arch. ges. Physiol.* 4 (1871): 325–336. Reprinted by permission of The Johns Hopkins University Press.

50 msec. The results are shown in Figure 9–2. The shorter the interval between stimulus and light flash, the fewer the letters reported. Note that the relationship is linear, with a slope that is approximately the same for all four intensities, although there is a clear tendency for a more intense light to have a more drastic effect at all delays. This pattern of results suggests that letters are being read out from the iconic store at a constant rate (because of the linear relationship) of about 10 msec per letter. The flash appears to interfere with this process, with bright flashes exerting their effect more rapidly than dim ones. Sperling repeated this work, except that instead of erasing the stimulus with a flash of light, he used a pattern mask comprising a random array of letter fragments, since he found this to be a more effective mask than a light flash. The distinction between masking by light and masking by a figure or contour, which has come to be termed *metacontrast,* has subsequently become important. Nevertheless, Sperling's results were essentially the same as Baxt's in showing a linear function with a slope of 10 msec per letter, a slope which Sperling showed to be constant across a wide range of conditions.

Although these results imply a letter-scanning or readout rate of 100 letters a second, the subject obviously does not report them at this rate; indeed, there is often a delay of several seconds before he begins to report, which must mean that the readout from iconic memory is fed into a second, more durable store. Sperling concluded that this is an acoustic store, since he noticed that subjects were making acoustic confusions (e.g., *B* instead of *V*) in their reports. He assumed initially (Sperling 1963) that the transfer occurred via the same rehearsal system that is also responsible for subvocal rehearsal in such tasks as the digit span. Since there appears to be a maximum rehearsal rate of about ten items per second (Landauer 1962), there is clearly a mismatch between this and the visual scan, which is feeding in items at ten times this speed.

This problem is illustrated by the situation in which a letter sequence is exposed and then masked so as to allow less than a 100-msec total exposure. If readout is limited by the rehearsal system, subjects should report no more than the one letter that can be rehearsed in this time. In fact, subjects report about three letters. In order to avoid this problem, a later model (see Figure 9–3) assumes a further memory store between the visual scan and the phonemic rehearsal loop. Sperling (1967) terms this additional component the *recognition memory buffer.* Its job is to convert the visual image of a letter provided by the visual scan into an articulatory motor program which transfers the information via the rehearsal system into an acoustic store, either silently by subvocal rehearsal or, if the rehearsal is spoken, via the sound of the subject's own voice.* The discrepancy between the rate of input to the recognition memory buffer (100 letters per second) and its rate of output (10 per second) occurs because the buffer is capable of setting up rehearsal programs faster than it can execute them. Because of this mismatch between input and output rates, a buffer store is required; this will hold rehearsal programs that are waiting to be executed. It is assumed that the storage capacity of the buffer is limited, hence the limitation on

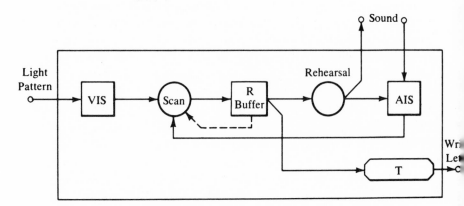

Figure 9–3   Sperling's recognition buffer model of memory. R = recognition buffer. Source: G. Sperling, Successive approximations to a model for short-term memory, *Acta Psychologica* 27 (1967): 290. Reprinted by permission.

number of items available, which restricts whole-report performance to about four items.

CHARACTERISTICS OF THE ICONIC STORE

A crucial feature of work on iconic memory has been the use of masking to interrupt processing. After the initial work of Sperling, disagreement arose as to the interpretation of the masking effect. The issue is discussed by Kahneman (1968) and can be briefly summarized in the following question: Does the mask actually stop further processing of the icon (the interruption hypothesis), or does it combine with the icon to form a composite figure in which processing is impaired but not prevented (the integration hypothesis)?

* Compare the role assigned to the articulatory rehearsal loop in the discussion of working memory in the previous chapter.

If the integration view is correct, then masking provides a much less clean tool for the analysis of iconic storage than was at first supposed. This issue has stimulated a great deal of research, much of it confusing and apparently contradictory. However, a recent and very elegant series of experiments by Turvey (1973) suggests a possible resolution of the problem. Turvey's paper contains no fewer than 18 experiments and a good deal of closely argued theory, so that in the space available we can do no more than outline the logic of Turvey's approach and his main conclusions. Turvey's starting point is the work carried out by Kinsbourne and Warrington (1962a; 1962b) at about the same time as that stemming from Sperling's original experiments. Their work was essentially independent of Sperling's and produced results that appeared to be inconsistent with his in two respects. While Sperling's results showed a linear increase in number of letters reported as a function of increasing interval between stimulus and mask, Kinsbourne and Warrington reported that three letters became available at approximately the same target-mask interval as one; if the subject can report one letter correctly, then typically he can report three. In addition, they discovered a simple relationship between the duration of the target and the duration of the interval between target and mask necessary to avoid masking. The relationship was multiplicative (target duration × interstimulus interval = a constant) not additive, as might be expected from Sperling's work.

Turvey appears to have been the first person to follow up this result. His procedure in general involved presenting a single target letter and masking with either random noise or a pattern mask comprising a patch of bars of the same thickness of stroke as the letters used (see Figure 9–4). Using the random noise pattern, Turvey first confirmed the multiplicative relationship reported by Kinsbourne and Warrington. He then

Random   Pattern   Example of
noise   mask   target

Figure 9–4   Examples of noise mask, pattern mask, and target used by Turvey. Source: M. T. Turvey, On peripheral and central processes in vision: inferences from an information-processing analysis of masking with patterned stimuli, *Psychological Review* 80 (1973): 4. Copyright 1973 by the American Psychological Association. Reprinted by permission.

went on to show that light *energy* rather than time is the crucial target variable; a 2-msec target exposure at 20 ft-lamberts gives the same result as an 8-msec exposure at 5 ft-lamberts. (The fact that the visual system treats light intensity and duration as interchangeable over periods up to 100 msec has been known for many years and is usually termed Bloch's law.) The next step was to discover whether the masking effect occurs when the target and noise mask are presented to different eyes, implying a process occurring after information from the two eyes has been combined, or is limited to the case where both target and mask are presented to the same eye, implying a relatively peripheral process. Turvey's results are clear: masking by a nonfigural noise field occurs only with monoptic presentation, implying a peripheral effect. This is one point at which Turvey's results differ from those of Kinsbourne and Warrington, for reasons which are not apparent.

A number of earlier studies have compared binocular and monocular masking. Broadly speaking, monocular effects have been found when a homogeneous light flash is used (e.g., Mowbray and Durr 1964), while binocular effects are confined to situations in which the mask contains contours (e.g., Schiller 1965). This is confirmed by Turvey in a study comparing the effects of random noise and pattern masks presented to either the same eye or the eye opposite to the target. While random noise effects are confined to monoptic presentation, pattern masking occurs with both monoptic and dichoptic presentation. This implies two separate masking processes: a peripheral effect, dependent on the amount of light energy in the target and mask, and a more central effect, which appears to depend on the presence of contours in the mask.

Turvey goes on to show that this dichoptic pattern-mask effect does not follow the multiplicative function discovered by Kinsbourne and Warrington; a target lasting 3 msec is just as effective as an equally bright target lasting 10 msec, and a dim target is as effective as a bright one. The crucial variable for the dichoptic pattern-mask effect proves to be the interval between the onset of the stimulus and the onset of the mask. Unlike the energy-based peripheral masking effect, the central pattern-mask effect is additive rather than multiplicative (target duration + interstimulus interval = a constant). One additional difference between the two types of masking is shown by using a forward masking paradigm, in which the mask comes before the target. In the case of a monoptic noise mask, forward masking is as great as backward masking, whereas with a dichoptic pattern mask, forward masking is virtually absent.

So far, the peripheral and central masking effects have been kept as separate as possible to simplify the situation; what happens when they operate simultaneously, as they presumably do under normal conditions? This is investigated by presenting the pattern mask to the same eye as the target, so that the mask is presumably capable of affecting the target at both the central and peripheral levels. The important determinant of peripheral masking is the relative energy of target and mask, whether this is determined by intensity or duration, whereas the central effect is influenced only by the length of delay separating target and mask onset. This being so, the duration of the mask should affect the peripheral system (a longer mask implies more light energy) but not the central system, for which only onset time is important. This is investigated in an experiment in which the duration of the target (three letters) is held constant, mask duration is varied from 2 to 500 msec, and the minimum interval at which masking is avoided is determined. One of the most interesting features of this experiment is the reports of the subjects. When the duration of the mask is less than 10 msec, subjects tend to report a single, rather messy figure comprising both the letters and the noise; they make errors that are equally likely at all serial positions. At mask durations exceeding 25 msec, subjects report a clear image which they say they do not have time to read. Errors show a clear serial-position effect, as if a readout process had started from the left and been interrupted before completion. Experienced subjects were consistently better than average at mask durations above 10 msec, but not in the case of briefer masks. A subsequent experiment showed that a change in the relative intensity of target and mask affected performance over the early part of the function (based on the peripheral effect) but not at mask durations beyond 25 msec, confirming that the two parts of the function represent different processes.

Turvey suggests that the peripheral energy-based masking effect is consistent with the integration hypothesis of masking, with target and mask combining to form a composite stimulus whose legibility depends on the intensity of the target relative to that of the mask. He suggests, however, that the interruption hypothesis provides a better account of the central pattern-mask effect. He cites Kolers's (1968) analogy of a clerk or shop assistant serving a customer; the clerk represents a central decision mechanism, and the customer to be served represents a visual signal which must be processed. If only one customer is present, the clerk will find out a good deal about his wants and interests. If a second customer arrives, however, this process may be curtailed, especially if the second customer is particularly demanding. Whereas the central pattern-mask effect is assumed to be due to the take-over of the decision or readout process by a subsequent "customer," the peripheral effect may be seen as a conflict between two customers in attempting to reach the clerk.

The analogy is well illustrated by two experiments in which the two processes are pitted against each other. In the first of these, Turvey shows that the effect of a pattern mask may be eliminated if it is followed by a noise mask presented to the same eye as the pattern. In this case, the second customer is being eliminated by a third, who is subsequently unable to take over the "clerk" because he does not have the appropriate characteristics (no contours = no service).

The second demonstration concerns a previously reported phenomenon that has caused a good deal of interest without being adequately explained—namely, the observation of a U-shaped relationship between the number of items reported and the interval separating pattern mask and target (Haber 1969, pp. 11–12). Why should a mask be less effective after short or long delays than after an intermediate delay? One possibility is that masking after short delays is likely to affect the customer before he reaches the clerk. Masking at this stage involves the peripheral integration of target and mask, and its severity has been shown to depend on the relative energy of the target and mask. If the target has greater energy than the mask, it will continue to be perceived, and since a composite of the two will arrive at the decision-making clerk as a single customer, no central masking will occur. At slightly longer delays, the target will already have reached the central processor before the mask appears. The arrival of the mask will thus take over the processor and terminate the processing of the target. As the delay becomes even longer, the amount of target processing completed before the arrival of the mask will increase; finally, at very long delays, the target will have been processed by the time the mask arrives.

Such a U-shaped function will not occur when the target is less bright than the mask. Once again, at short delays the target and mask will combine before reaching the processor, but a weak target will not be discriminable from the background noise of the mask. At longer delays the target will have reached the decision-making "clerk" before the mask arrives, so that their relative intensity will not be a relevant factor. This is tested by measuring the number of letters reported correctly as a function of the delay between target and mask onset at

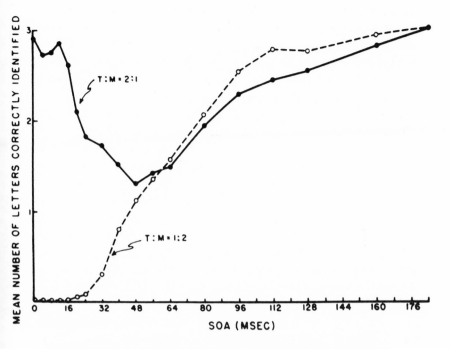

Figure 9–5 Mean number of correct identifications as a function of the interval between pattern and monoptic mask. The filled circles represent the condition in which the target was twice as bright as the mask, the unfilled circles the condition in which the target was half as bright as the mask. Source: M. T. Turvey, On peripheral and central processes in vision: inferences from an information-processing analysis of masking with patterned stimuli, *Psychological Review* 80 (1973): 40. Copyright 1973 by the American Psychological Association. Reprinted by permission.

two levels of relative target brightness. The results are shown in Figure 9–5. When the target is twice as bright as the mask, a U-shaped function occurs; when it is half as bright, the standard relationship between target detection and mask delay is found.

To summarize: Turvey's results suggest that two types of masking occur. One is peripheral, is sensitive to target and mask energy, and shows a multiplicative relationship between target duration and interstimulus interval. It is relatively insensitive to differences in practice, and it subjectively gives rise to a composite of the target and the mask. The other is central, depends on the figural nature of the mask rather than its energy, and shows an additive relationship between target duration and interstimulus interval. Performance is susceptible to improvement by practice, and masking subjectively appears as an interruption of the processing of a previously clear target.

How can these effects be fitted into what we already know of iconic memory? Turvey suggests that the content of iconic storage may, in one interpretation, be considered as "a description of a visual object or objects, suitable for subsequent operations of pattern recognition" (Turvey 1973, pp. 44–45). By "description," of course, is meant a representation in terms of certain critical physical features. The relevant features probably include location, size, and color (all of which can be used as retrieval cues with the partial report technique), but not associative features, such as whether an item is a digit or a letter. Turvey suggests that iconic memory consists of a series of peripheral visual systems conveying information from the retina to the cortex about the various features of the stimulus (e.g., size, location, color, etc.). The various systems work in parallel at differing processing rates, depending among other things on stimulus intensity. It is these systems that are affected by the peripheral masking effect. A more central system is using the information from the various peripheral systems to decide what is being signaled. It is this decision process that is interrupted by pattern masking. In the context of the present chapter, the importance of Turvey's work lies in the way in which he uses conceptually simple information-processing techniques to tease out details of the operation of two interacting processes. As such, it presents a very good example of the application of the information-processing approach to memory. Whether the approach can be applied with a similar degree of success to the more complex aspects of human memory remains to be seen.

RECOGNITION BUFFER

There seems to be some doubt about the characteristics of the recognition buffer in Sperling's model. In the 1967 version the buffer converts "the visual image of the letter provided by the scanner into a 'program of motor instructions' and stores these instructions" (Sperling, 1967, p. 28). In a later version (Sperling 1970) the conversion appears to be done by the scanner, leaving the very short-term iconic store as the only visual store in the system. This seems to imply that only material for which a verbal rehearsal program can be set up will be remembered, which is clearly false. It therefore seems necessary to assume a further visual memory store, which could occur either before

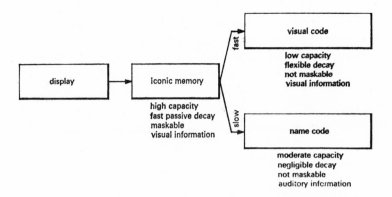

Figure 9–6   Coltheart's conceptualization of the iconic memory system. Note that he assumes a rapidly created visual code, together with a rather more slowly generated name code. Source: M. Coltheart, Visual information processing, in P. Dodwell (ed.), *New Horizons in Psychology: 2* (New York: Penguin, 1972), p. 75. Reprinted by permission.

the motor-rehearsal code store or, as M. Coltheart (1972) suggests, in parallel with it. Coltheart's model is shown in Figure 9–6. It has the interesting feature of allowing for the possibility that an item might conceivably be correctly reported without in fact being consciously "seen"—that is, without a visual code's being constructed. Such a view may at first sight seem illogical: surely a visual stimulus must be seen before it can be named?

The crux of the question is what is meant by being "seen." It is not logically necessary that visual information must be consciously available in order to be utilized, and Coltheart (1972) cites a number of studies which suggest that the meaning of a word may influence its perception independently of its visual characteristics. Two examples will suffice: Wickens, Shearer and Eggemeier (1971) showed subjects words that are characteristically rated as either "good" (e.g., *mother, rose*) or "bad" (e.g., *knife, poison*). The words were presented too briefly to be visible to the subject, who was then given a pair of words, one "good" and one "bad," neither of which had in fact been presented. When told to select the word that had been shown, subjects were consistently more likely to select the word that had the same evaluation as the stimulus. Hence, having been shown the word *poison,* subjects were likely to choose *knife* rather than *rose* as the word shown. It may be recalled that reading errors in certain dyslexic patients who can read concrete but not abstract words also suggest that meaning may be encoded in parallel with the phonological characteristics of a word (Marshall and Newcombe 1966).

The second illustration comes from an unpublished study at the University of Sussex by J. Pickering, who used a task in which subjects were shown a letter sequence and required to decide as soon as possible whether it formed an English word. Before each test sequence, Pickering presented a different letter sequence for a period of 30 msec, too short for most subjects to be aware that anything had preceded the stimulus. Nevertheless, the prior sequence had a marked effect on detection time, with words being detected faster if preceded by other words than if preceded by nonwords. Facilitation also occurred if wordlike sequences (e.g., *stup*) preceded words, indicating that letter structure was responsible, not semantic cues. Presumably, separate systems are used for analyzing individual letters or wordlike sequences. A presentation that is too brief to produce a conscious percept is nevertheless enough to cue one system or the other. If the appropriate system is cued, processing will be facilitated. Thus, it seems probable that Coltheart's model should, in fact, have more than two parallel systems.

Furthermore, it seems likely that the various systems are linked. Posner, Boies, Eichelman, and Taylor (1969), for instance, present evidence that subjects given the name of a letter may generate a visual code or image and use this to facilitate subsequent letter recognition. A position similar to this is suggested by Turvey (1973), who conceives of a network of decision-making processors operating in parallel on the contents of the iconic store. The cross-links in such a network allow the information from one processor to facilitate analysis in another. Workers in the field of artificial intelligence have coined the word *heterarchy* to describe a flexible, interrelated system of this type, as opposed to a *hierarchy,* a system such as Sperling's model in which processing involves passing the information through an orderly chain of stages, with each stage of analysis depending on the completion of the stage before.

The greater processing power of a heterarchical system is well illustrated by the program devised by Winograd (1972) for the analysis of language (see Chapter 13). Whereas earlier conceptualizations of language analysis tended to consider each sentence first syntactically and then semantically, finally using reasoning to resolve any remaining inconsistencies, Winograd's program allows all three to operate simultaneously and to interact, thereby enormously reducing the amount of fruitless information processing required.

A further implication of a heterarchical model like the one suggested by Turvey's paper is that the concept of a scanner begins to seem less appropriate. One dictionary defines the word *scan* as to "turn the eyes or attention successively to each part," which implies a serial process. While a serial readout initially seemed the obvious interpretation of the results obtained by Baxt (1871), Sperling (1960), and Averbach and Coriell (1961), the evidence now seems to point to a parallel processing readout, in which several items undergo processing at the same time (Sperling 1970; Coltheart 1972). This does not mean that the processing of all items will necessarily be at the same speed; indeed, there is good evidence that this is not the case. When a row of letters is presented, the letters at both ends will be processed more rapidly than those in the center, and they may thus evade the effects of masking by being processed before the arrival of the mask (Merikle, Coltheart, and Lowe 1971).

It should be clear by now that the analogy of a shop assistant or clerk serving one or more customers is far too simple. It is misleading for at least three reasons. First, it implies a situation in which goods go from the clerk to the customer, whereas the flow of information in iconic storage is in the opposite direction. Second, it suggests a single-channel serial process, whereas the evidence suggests that information about a range of physical characteristics across the whole visual field is simultaneously being transferred. Third, it neglects the crucial fact that in normal perception neither the separate features of a single stimulus nor the characteristics of successive stimuli are independent. In this respect, the pattern-mask paradigm itself is atypical in presenting successive stimuli that are quite unrelated.

A more appropriate analogy is that of a military operations room during a battle. Information is fed in by radio from observers at various points, each with his own job and his own location; some are concerned with the amount of enemy tank activity, others with road movements, a third group with rail activity, a fourth with enemy artillery, and so on. The staff of the operations room records this information on a central display, which is interpreted by a senior officer; he draws conclusions about enemy troop deployment and tactics and passes them on to the operations room of the general who is in charge of strategy. To minimize the distortion that arises when an individual observer tries to make interpretations on insufficient data, the field observer's job is rigidly prescribed. He simply reports the number of relevant objects (e.g., tanks or trains) sighted within a fixed time period and signals this for a specified length of time. The interpretation is left to the operations room officer and to his superior. The system can be "jammed" by arranging for large numbers of sightings of tanks or troops (real or simulated) that are not related to the actual strategy of the attack. The analogy here is to the random noise masking of iconic memory, in which a target stimulus is swamped by a mass of irrelevant signals.

The operations room display is analogous to the iconic memory store, with information about the features characterizing a given location being represented for a limited period of time. Pattern masking is represented by the enemy's feint or change in troop deployment, which results in a sudden, rapid change in the information arriving at the military operations room. Under these circumstances, the officer immediately abandons his previous hypotheses about enemy tactics and attempts a fresh appraisal. Once abandoned, the previous pattern on the display cannot be recovered, and the officer's information about the prior situation will be limited to the analyses and decisions already made and passed on to the general in charge of strategy. Since such information is continuously being passed on, however, the information will be recoverable, provided the officer had enough time to perform the initial analysis, a process that occurs much faster than the general's staff can turn the information into decisions about enemy strategy. Note that although the system is hierarchic in the sense of involving a chain of information-processing stages, the stages themselves and the various parallel operations within a stage all interact to produce a heterarchy rather than a rigid hierarchy. The process is continuous; both the general and the officer may ask for specific information to test particular strategic or tactical hypotheses, and in both cases their assessment of the situation is based on integrating information flowing from a range of separate but not independent sources. Like the customer-clerk analogy, the military operations room comparison is likely to prove misleading in some respects, but meanwhile it does appear to do more justice to the complexity of the iconic memory system.

Short-Term Visual Memory

We have suggested that the contents of the iconic store are not items such as letters but the basic visual data from which a pattern recognition system can create items. We have further suggested that the visual patterns created are held in a second, more durable visual store, which for the sake of convenience we shall refer to as *short-term visual memory*, or visual STM. What evidence is there for such a store? Posner and Konick (1966) studied the ability to remember the location of a point on a line over intervals ranging from 0–30 seconds. They found virtually no forgetting when the subject was left free to "rehearse," but forgetting did occur when he was required to process digits during the delay; the more demanding the processing, the greater the forgetting. Dale (1973) has studied memory for the location of a dot in a field 1 foot square. The field was illuminated from beneath, with the dot presented as a shadow on a sheet of paper laid over the field. After the requisite exposure time, the subject must turn away and begin to process visually presented digits. After the appropriate delay, he is then required to mark the remembered location of the dot on the sheet of paper. Figure 9–7 shows the results of an experiment in which the duration of the stimulus was varied. Forgetting clearly occurs in a very systematic way.

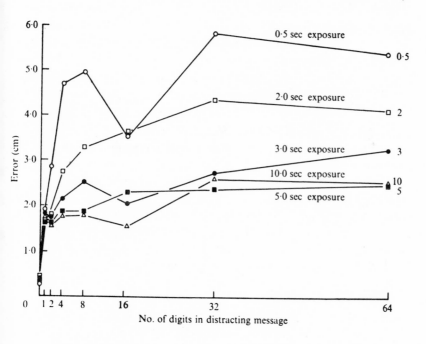

Figure 9–7 Short-term memory for the location of a dot in a 1-foot-square field as a function of exposure time. Subjects processed visually presented digits at a rate of one per second during the retention interval. Source: H. C. A. Dale, Short-term memory for visual information, *British Journal of Psychology* 64 (1973): 5. Reprinted by permission.

The time course is very different from that observed with iconic memory, which would in any case have been masked in this situation by the visually presented interpolated digits.

It might be argued, however, that a system which handles the retention of something as basic as the location of a single dot may be quite different from the visual STM system that we have suggested may be holding the letters read out from iconic memory. A rather closer analogue was discovered by Posner and Keele (1967) in an ingenious experiment in which reaction-time techniques were used to study the retention of a single letter. Subjects were shown a letter (e.g., *A*) followed by a second letter after a delay ranging from 0 to 2 seconds. The subject was required to decide whether the second letter had the same name as the first letter or was different. In half the cases where the same name letter was used, it was also visually identical (i.e., both uppercase, *A–A,* or both lowercase, *a–a*); on the remaining positive trials, the two letters were visually different (*A–a* or *a–A*), while on negative trials, different letters were presented (*A–B* or *A–b*). After short delays, the physically identical letters (*A–A*) gave rise to faster responses than the physically different ones (*A–a*), implying that the subject was remembering and using the physical characteristics of the letter. After about 1.5 seconds the effect disappeared, suggesting that the subject was changing from a match based on visual coding to one based on a name code.

This interpretation is supported by a recent study by Wilkins and Stewart (1974), which is based on the assumption that visual processing depends primarily on the right hemisphere of the brain, while language is represented principally in the left hemisphere (Milner 1971). Wilkins and Stewart performed a Posner letter-matching study, with the second letter occurring after 50 msec or 1 second. The first letter appeared in the center of the visual field, and the comparison letter was then presented either to the left half of the retina (which projects onto the right hemisphere of the brain) or to the right half (which projects onto the left hemisphere). After the short 50-msec delay, accuracy was higher for letters routed to the right or visual hemisphere, whereas after a delay of 1 second, letters were processed more accurately when input was via the language-processing left hemisphere.

Posner and Keele (1967) interpreted their letter-matching data as suggesting a visual trace with a decay time of about 1.5 seconds. Posner (1969) and his collaborators have subsequently shown that the memory involved differs from iconic storage (1) in not being susceptible to pattern masking, (2) in having a smaller storage capacity (about two or three letters), and (3) in being susceptible to disruption by a concurrent information-processing task, a factor which Doost and Turvey (1971) have shown to be relatively unimportant in iconic memory. Thus, there is little doubt that a visual memory system which differs from iconic memory is involved.

Does the system also differ from that shown for retention of a single location by Posner and Konick (1966) and by Dale (1973)? This might seem likely if rate of forgetting is used as a criterion, since forgetting in the letter-matching study is an order of magnitude faster than that shown for the dot experiments. There are, however, several very basic differences between the two situations. The dot experiments involve very simple stimuli, tested by recall and scored in terms of mean error, whereas the letter-matching studies use complex forms, a recognition test, and a reaction-time measure. Moreover, there is a logical problem in using the letter-matching experiments to estimate the rate of forgetting of the visual code. In the interval between presentation and test, two things are happening: the visual code is being forgotten, and the name code is being generated. The 1.5-second time constant observed presumably represents the point at which it becomes more efficient to use a name code than a visual code. Once the subject has opted for the name code, his RT will be unaffected by the visual code, although it may conceivably be present in degraded form for an indefinite period.

A study by Phillips and Baddeley (1971) attempted to avoid this problem by applying the reaction-time technique to recognition memory for patterns that were too complex to allow the development of an adequate name code in the time available. The patterns comprised a 5×5 matrix of squares, any one of which had a 50-percent chance of being filled. They were presented for 0.5 second and were followed by a pattern mask to eliminate iconic storage effects. After a delay ranging from 0.3 to 9 seconds, a second matrix pattern was presented. The second pattern was either identical or had one of the 25 squares changed, and the subject's task was to decide as quickly as possible whether the two patterns were the same or different. Both RT and errors showed forgetting, leveling out at 9 seconds rather than 1.5, as in the letter-matching test. It appears that the 1.5-second time constant is due to the development of the name code, and hence does not represent a basic feature of visual memory.

Is it, in fact, reasonable to expect a single invariant rate of forgetting for visual memory? Dale's (1973) results make this seem unlikely, since he found that exposure duration determined forgetting rate. A subsequent series of experiments by Phillips (1974) shows that degree of complexity is also an important factor. He used the procedure just described to study the retention of patterns comprising 4×4, 6×6, or 8×8 matrices presented for 1 second. Examples of these, together with forgetting curves, are shown in Figure 9–8. Note that retention of the most complex 8×8 pattern is approaching the 50-percent chance level within 3 seconds, while 4×4 patterns are still well retained after 9 seconds. In this particular experiment the

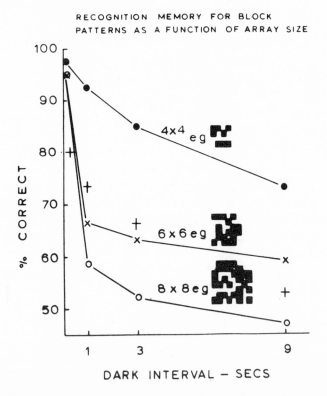

RECOGNITION MEMORY FOR BLOCK
PATTERNS AS A FUNCTION OF ARRAY SIZE

DARK INTERVAL – SECS

Figure 9–8   Recognition memory for random patterns as a function of complexity. Examples of the three types of pattern used are shown in the figure. Each pattern was followed by either an identical pattern or one which had a single square changed. Source: W. A. Phillips, On the distinction between sensory storage and short-term visual memory, *Perception and Psychophysics* 16 (1974): 284. Reprinted by permission.

interval between presentation and test was left dark, so that the result would reflect both iconic memory and visual STM. Phillips suggests that this is why the complex 64-square pattern is initially as well retained as the simple 16-square pattern. Phillips goes on to demonstrate that the virtually perfect performance shown by both simple and complex patterns after very short delays does indeed reflect a different process. He compares retention over the first 600 msec when the target and test stimulus are in exactly the same place (as in the previous experiment) with retention when the whole test stimulus is simply moved one square to the right. The results are shown in Figure 9–9, from which it is clear that performance on immediate test is unaffected by pattern complexity only when the two patterns are in the same location. Under these conditions, a change is perceived by the

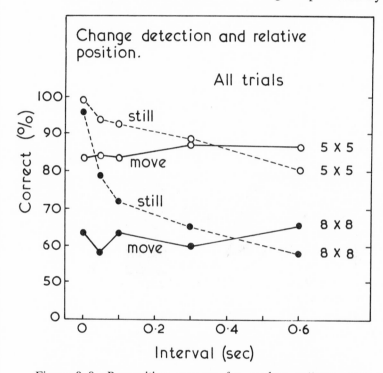

Figure 9–9 Recognition memory for random patterns comprising 25 or 64 squares. In the "still" condition, the recognition pattern appeared in the same location as the original stimulus; in the "move" condition, the pattern was displaced one square to the right. Note that the early part of the curve is not affected by pattern complexity over short delays in the "still" condition, suggesting the existence of a system which can handle large amounts of information, provided location is not changed. After 0.5 second the effect of movement has disappeared, leaving a clear effect of pattern complexity. Source: W. A. Phillips, On the distinction between sensory storage and short-term visual memory, *Perception and Psychophysics* 16 (1974): 285. Reprinted by permission.

subject as a flicker in the part of the pattern that has changed. Further experiments (Phillips and Singer 1974; Singer and Phillips 1974) have shown that the functioning of this brief initial store can be tied in very neatly with neurophysiological evidence based on the visual system of cats.

The studies just described have avoided the complicating effects of naming on visual memory by using stimuli that were too complex to be described verbally in the time available. An alternative approach to the problem is to interfere selectively with verbal memory. This approach was used by Kroll, Parks, Parkinson, Bieber, and Johnson (1970), who used a shadowing task—the repetition of a stream of spoken letters—to fill the delay between the presentation and test of a single letter which the subject was trying to remember. The target letter was presented as one of the letters to be shadowed, but it was differentiated by being either spoken in a different voice (male rather than female) or presented visually. There was a marked superiority for retention of the visually presented letter even after 25 seconds, thus supporting the subjects' contention that they remembered visually presented letters as an image but tried to rehearse acoustically presented items subvocally. A subsequent study (Salzberg, Parks, Kroll, and Parkinson 1971) manipulated the degree of acoustic similarity between the letter to be remembered and the shadowed letters. As predicted, visually presented letters were not affected, while acoustically presented letters showed impaired retention, provided the similar letters appeared within 4 seconds of the presentation of the target letter. A third study (Parks, Kroll, Salzberg, and Parkinson 1972) used the Posner and Keele (1967) letter-name matching task but filled the delay between presentation of the two letters with a shadowing task, to discourage the formation of name codes. As in the Posner studies, they found that physically identical letters (A–A) were classified as the same faster than physically different letters (A–a), but instead of vanishing after 1.5 seconds, as in Posner and Keele's study, the effect was still present after 8 seconds. They conclude that subjects can continue to maintain the visual code, provided there is an incentive to do so. A slightly different interpretation would be to suggest that shadowing prevents the formation of the verbal code, which would otherwise take precedence over the visual code.

More direct evidence of optional visual and verbal strategies was produced by Tversky (1969) in a study in which subjects were taught nonsense names for a series of schematic faces. They were then shown a single item (a name or face) followed by a second item which they were required to classify as either the "same" (when either physically identical or appropriately named) or "different" (when a mismatch occurred between a face and a name, or when two different names or faces were presented). The probability of the second item being a name or a face was used to manipulate the subjects' strategy; it was assumed that if the second item was nearly always a face, a subject might try to hold information about the first item in a visual code. This proved to be the case. When a face was highly probable, face matches were faster, and when a name was probable, name matches were faster, regardless of whether the first item of the pair was a name or a face. Tversky's results thus imply that subjects can decide which coding system to use and, if necessary, can generate and hold a visual code from the appropriate name.

It is clearly the case, then, that visual memory extends over periods considerably beyond the duration of the icon. The visual image or code appears to be at least partly under the subject's control, since he can generate visual codes from verbal stimuli and can maintain a visual code for up to 25 seconds under suitable conditions. When such "rehearsal" is prevented either by the complexity of the stimulus (Phillips and Baddeley 1971) or by an interpolated task (Posner and Konick 1966), forgetting occurs over a matter of seconds, suggesting that the system might reasonably be termed short-term visual memory. The next section is concerned with the evidence for a more durable visual memory system.

Long-Term Visual Memory

Convincing evidence that visual memory may extend considerably beyond a few seconds comes from Rock and Engelstein (1959), who studied memory for a single meaningless shape over periods extending up to a month. While subjects' ability to reproduce the figure by drawing declined sharply, they were able to select the shape in question from a range of similar shapes almost perfectly even after four weeks. We shall return to the discrepancy between recall and recognition later, meanwhile concentrating on recognition memory.

PICTURE RECOGNITION

Shepard (1967) compared recognition memory for pictures, words, and sentences, using a technique whereby the subject looked through a sequence of 600 items at his own rate and was then given 68 pairs of items, one item of each pair coming from the set studied, the other a new item. Subjects were extremely good at detecting the old item, making 88 percent correct decisions on sentences, 90 percent on words, and 98 percent on pictures. A similar result was obtained by Nickerson (1965). He presented 600 pictures of miscellaneous scenes and events and required the subjects to decide for each picture whether it was new or had been seen earlier in the series. Overall detection rate was 95 percent, ranging from 97 percent with 40 pictures between presentation and recognition to 87 percent with 200 interpolated pictures. Subjects were retested on 200 new and 200 old pictures at intervals ranging from a day to a year. Performance declined from 92 percent to 63 percent.

A third study found recognition memory for pictures even more dramatic than Shepard's and Nickerson's results suggest. Using the Shepard procedure and presenting 2,560 color slides for 10 seconds each, Standing, Conezio, and Haber (1970) showed that recognition was still above 90 percent after several days. Neither speeding up presentation to a rate of 1 second per slide nor showing the test slides with a left-right reversal had any marked effect on recognition performance.

Why should pictorial memory be so good? Goldstein and Chance (1971) suggest two factors. First, the various pictures differ on many features across a range of dimensions. If only a fraction of these features are stored, the Shepard two-choice discrimination technique will enable the subject to respond correctly, since a single familiar feature will be enough to discriminate the new picture from the old. Second, subjects may use verbal descriptions to supplement their visual memory. In order to minimize these two factors, Goldstein and Chance used material varying on far fewer dimensions than the miscellaneous photographs employed previously, and they tested retention with a more stringent recognition task. As material they used photographs of women's faces, magnified snow crystals, and inkblots. Only 14 stimuli were presented in each case, at a rate of 2–3 seconds per stimulus, with a 5–8-second interstimulus interval. Recall was tested either immediately or 48 hours later by showing subjects the 14 old stimuli mixed with 70 new ones, at a rate of 5 seconds per item. Subjects were instructed to be cautious and to keep their responses down to 14. Despite the more stringent recognition test, subjects detected 71 percent of the faces, 46 percent of the blots, and 33 percent of the snow crystals, all considerably above the chance detection rate of 14 percent, and virtually no forgetting occurred between the immediate and 48-hour tests. However, subjects were clearly not performing so impressively as in the studies using complex pictures, suggesting that partial learning and the multidimensional nature of the material may have played a part in the very high levels of recognition memory previously observed. Even so, given patterns as complex, abstract, and similar as snow crystals, even a 33-percent detection rate after 2 days is a remarkable achievement, while the recognition of 71 percent of the female faces glimpsed for only a few seconds is perhaps even more impressive. It is possible, however, that faces present a rather special case.

MEMORY FOR FACES

Warrington and Taylor (1973) compared recognition memory span for faces with span for surnames. They found, somewhat surprisingly, that perfect recognition occurred only if presentation was limited to a single face, whereas subjects could recognize lists of three or four surnames without error. On the other hand, faces showed no forgetting over a 30-second interval, whereas the surnames showed the usual decrement found when verbal material is tested using the Brown-Peterson technique. A study by Milner (1968), in which subjects studied a block of 12 photographs of faces for 45 seconds, found that the performance of normal subjects on a subsequent recognition test actually improved over a 90-second unfilled delay. This reminiscence effect was confirmed by Wallace (1970), although only with female subjects. He found that a reminiscence effect could be produced in male subjects by accompanying presentation of the pictures with loud white noise, suggesting an arousal interpretation of the reminiscence effect (see Chapter 2). Presumably, the female subjects in his previous experiments found the male experimenter more arousing than did the males; it would be interesting to replicate this study with a suitably arousing female experimenter!

It has occasionally been suggested that there may be a separate memory system specifically concerned with facial memory. Such an interpretation is suggested by Bodamer (1947) in discussing a case of prosopagnosia, a rare neurological condition in which the patient is unable to recognize previously familiar faces. In an attempt to test for a specific defect in memory for faces, Yin (1970) presented neurological patients suffering from localized lesions with a visual memory test. He had previously shown (Yin 1969) that the recognition of faces is impaired much more by upside-down presentation than were pictures of buildings that were selected so as to give the same recognition rate as faces, when both were presented in a normal orientation. This suggests that some important feature for facial recognition is lost when the face is inverted. If ability to use this feature is lost in certain neurological cases, this might be expected to produce a specific memory defect for faces, accompanied by the absence of a gross decrement when inverted faces are used. Patients were shown 40 photographs, comprising 10 normal and 10 inverted faces, plus 10 architecturally similar houses in the normal orientation and 10 inverted houses. Performance by patients with right or left posterior lesions and by control patients is shown in Figure 9–10. Right pos-

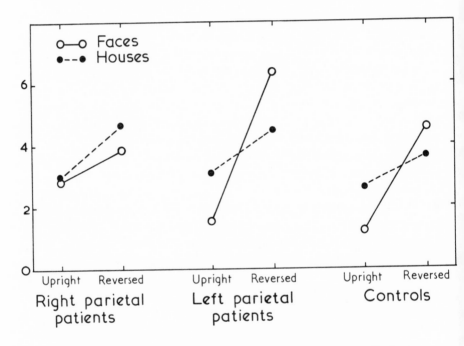

Figure 9–10   Evidence for a specific memory for faces. Patients with posterior right parietal lesions (left panel) are bad at recognizing faces but are not unduly impaired when the stimuli are inverted. Other patients and normal controls perform substantially better on properly oriented faces but show a dramatic impairment in facial recognition when the stimuli are inverted. Pictures of architecturally similar houses do not show this effect. Source: Data taken from R. K. Yin, Face recognition by brain-injured patients: dissociable ability? *Neuropsychologia* 8 (1970): 395–402.

terior lesion cases were worse at recognizing faces in their correct orientation than either of the other groups but were significantly *better* on inverted faces. In the case of houses, performance in the correct orientation was worse than for faces but was much less impaired by inversion. Note that the group which is relatively resistant to the effects of facial inversion shows the biggest inversion effect with nonfacial pictures.

Yin's evidence can be interpreted as supporting the idea that facial memory may be different from other types of visual memory in some way. Furthermore, it suggests that the factor causing such a dramatic impairment in facial memory following inversion may be crucial. Yin points out that it is very difficult to perceive any emotional or personality characteristics in inverted faces and suggests that patients with right posterior lesions may be particularly bad at perceiving such "social" or "semantic" factors. They therefore rely on the more physical and structural features of faces, which are less memorable but also less distorted by inversion. It should be possible to test this using a paradigm in which subjects classify normal or inverted faces on either "semantic" features (e.g., the pleasantness of the person) or structural features (e.g., head shape) and subsequently attempt to recognize the faces. In the correct orientation, the "semantic" group should be better, while the reverse should be true when the faces are inverted. Recent studies by Bower and Karlin (1974) and by Warrington and Ackroyd (1975) lend some support to this view. They found that instructing subjects to estimate such personal characteristics as the honesty or pleasantness of the person depicted enhanced subsequent recognition memory, presumably because subjects were induced to process the photographs at a deeper or more semantic level.

VERBAL FACTORS IN VISUAL MEMORY

While it seems unlikely that verbalization was an important factor in most of the studies so far discussed, there is evidence that verbal coding may play a significant part in remembering visual material. Carmichael, Hogan, and Walter (1932) presented a series of 12 ambiguous forms, together with labels suggesting one of two interpretations. For example, two circles linked by a bar might be labeled either *eyeglasses* or *dumbbells*. When subsequently required to reproduce the forms, subjects tended to distort their drawings in the direction of the appropriate label. A subsequent study by Prentice (1954), however, showed that the effect was not present with recognition testing, suggesting that the labels did not affect storage of the visual trace but instead produced distortion at retrieval. This view is consistent with the results of Hanawalt and Demarest (1939), who showed that labeling distortions can be produced when unlabeled figures are learned and subsequently cued by means of a label (e.g., *Draw the figure that looked like eyeglasses*).

Bahrick and Boucher (1968) found that instructions to use verbalization in learning a series of pictures impaired subsequent retention. They tested subjects both by requiring free recall of the names of the objects pictured and by requiring recognition of a picture of an object, such as a cup, from a set of eight similar cups. Somewhat surprisingly, there was no significant correlation between the probabilities of a given item being correct on the two measures, suggesting that whether a subject can recall that a picture of a cup has been shown is quite unrelated to his ability to remember the details of the cup.

Further evidence for a discontinuity between the recall and recognition of visual forms comes from a study by Cohen and Granstrom (1970). In their first experiment, irregular geometric visual forms were tested by recognition or reproduction after a 20-second interval, left either blank or filled by a backward counting task. Each subject was then shown the various figures again and required to describe each one. The adequacy of the description was measured in terms of how many of the other recognition distractor figures would also fit the description; the fewer the figures, the better the description. Each subject's performance on the memory task he had completed was then correlated with his score on the description task. There was a positive correlation between descriptive skill and recall performance whether the interval was filled or left blank, but there was no relationship between descriptive ability and recognition performance, suggesting a verbal component in recall that was absent from recognition. Two further experiments used the same patterns and required either reproduction or recognition after a 7-second delay. During the delay, subjects had to memorize either three faces or three names, which were tested after the geometric figures. If recall of the figures involves a verbal component, then it should be more impaired by the verbal name memory task than should recognition of the figures, which should be more affected by the subsequent facial memory task. This proved to be the case in both experiments.

It appears then that the *recall* of visual material is relatively poor, shows rapid forgetting (Rock and Engelstein 1959), and tends to rely on verbal coding, whereas visual *recognition* shows relatively little forgetting after the first few seconds and is not apparently affected by verbal factors. This suggests that visual LTS stores information efficiently but presents a greater retrieval problem than verbal LTS, which consequently tends to be used as a retrieval aid, albeit a somewhat inaccurate one. The distorting effect of a verbal label or cue on the recall of a visual scene is, of course, a factor of considerable practical importance in the case of testimony given by witnesses in a court of law. Some of the early work on this question is discussed by Hunter (1964, pp. 169–175), who concludes that recall of incidents by witnesses is rarely accurate and tends to be biased in the direction of the subject's expectations. Information obtained by intensive questioning of the subject is likely to be even less accurate, presumably because the subject is induced to try to provide information which he is too uncertain to produce spontaneously. It is in this sort of situation that the subject's recall is most likely to be influenced by leading questions (e.g., *Did you hear the defendant beating his wife?*— when it is not known whether the defendant has in fact beaten his wife). A recent study by Loftus and Palmer (1974) illustrates this point. They showed subjects a film of a collision between two cars. Subjects were then asked either *About how fast were the cars going when they hit each other?* or *About how fast were the cars going when they smashed into each other?* Subjects interrogated using the term *smashed* reliably gave a higher estimate of the speed (10.46 mph) than did those for whom *hit* was used (8.00 mph). Furthermore, when questioned a week later about the presence of broken glass, such subjects were more likely to report (wrongly) that glass was broken.

The most extreme view of the role of language in visual memory is represented by the *linguistic relativity hypothesis,* which stems from the work of the linguist Benjamin Lee Whorf. Whorf (1956) argues that language is not simply a way of expressing our view of the world; rather, language itself determines this view:

> We dissect nature along lines laid down by our native language. The categories and types that we isolate from the world of phenomena we do not find there because they stare every observer in the face; on the contrary, the world is presented in a kaleidoscopic flux of impressions which has to be organized in our minds—and this means largely by the linguistic system in our minds (Whorf 1956, p. 213).

From this it follows that people who speak a different language will perceive and remember the world in different ways. Whorf supports this contention with examples of the difficulty of translating statements in various Indian languages into English. For example, *It is a dripping spring* is represented in Apache by a phrase meaning *As water, or springs, whiteness moves downward.*

It follows from the Whorfian hypothesis that the subject's capacity for making and remembering perceptual distinctions will depend on the ability of his language system to encode such distinctions. It is often pointed out, for example, that Eskimo languages have a large number of adjectives describing different types of snow, and it would seem likely that Eskimos would be considerably better at remembering the condition of snow than would a European city dweller. However, such a result would not be crucial, since one does not need to subscribe to the Whorfian hypothesis to agree that experience in making discriminations is likely to carry over to remembering the material discriminated. Similarly, the demonstration that the speakers of a language having relatively few color terms are poor at recalling colors does not in itself provide a particularly convincing test of the Whorfian hypothesis. It is not sufficient to argue that verbal labeling is useful; the hypothesis suggests that such labeling is a principal determinant of perception and memory.

Evidence which seemed to support the linguistic relativity hypothesis was produced by Brown and Lenneberg (1954), who observed a close relationship between the accuracy with which a color could be recognized in a memory study and the codability of that color (as measured by the speed of naming), the degree of agreement across subjects as to the appropriate name, and the length of name. However, it is possible to argue that both the codability of the color and its memorability stem from its perceptual characteristics—in other words, that perception determines language and memory, the exact opposite to the Whorfian view. The issue has recently been reopened in an elegant series of experiments by Eleanor Rosch Heider (1971; 1972). She first demonstrated that certain colors appeared to be "focal." Such colors were selected as good examples of the eight basic color names: *red, yellow, green, blue, pink, orange, brown,* and *purple.* She found that both English-speaking students and students speaking a range of foreign languages from Hungarian to Tagalog all showed very substantial agreement on which colors were focal. She then studied the codability of the focal colors and of the colors which she termed *internominal;* these were chosen from the center of areas in which no color had been designated as the best example of a basic color name by speakers of any language. Requiring speakers of 23 different languages to name both types of colors, she observed a very clear tendency for focal colors to be described in fewer words and more rapidly than internominal colors.

Having established a set of focal colors which were readily codable, she then carried out a crucial experiment involving two groups of subjects, an English-speaking group of American subjects and a group of speakers of Dani. The Dani are a Stone Age people living in Dutch New Guinea who speak a language containing only two color terms. Even these two terms do not represent hue but roughly correspond to *dark* and *light*. If the Whorfian hypothesis is correct, then the Dani should not find focal colors any easier to recognize than internominal colors, since the Dani language is incapable of reflecting such a distinction. On the other hand, if the distinction is basically perceptual, and hence not dependent on linguistic factors, the Dani should also find focal colors easier to remember than internominal colors. Heider's results showed that although the overall level of performance of the Dani subjects was lower in all conditions, they exhibited just as great an advantage for focal colors as the American subjects did. Finally, a fourth experiment showed that Dani subjects found focal colors easier to associate with verbal labels in a long-term memory experiment lasting for several days. Heider's results therefore suggest very strongly that, at least for the case of color, perceptual characteristics are primary; perception determines what is retained, even in the absence of the appropriate linguistic distinctions.

The tendency for memory to be regarded as basically a verbal phenomenon is one which has also been challenged in recent years in the verbal-learning laboratory itself with the reawakening of interest in visual imagery.

Visual Imagery

EIDETIC IMAGERY

A frequent figure in memory folklore is the person with a "photographic memory." Do such people exist? There certainly does seem to be evidence that some subjects have visual imagery which is considerably more detailed and more persistent than the norm. In some cases at least, this is attributed to *eidetic imagery,* a persisting image of a visual scene which the subject sees as "outside his head" and is able to "read off" by moving his eyes, as if scanning the original scene.

The most dramatic claim for eidetic imagery comes from a study by Stromeyer and Psotka (1970), who presented their subject with a pattern of quasi-random dots on one day to one eye; on the following day, they presented to the other eye a similar pattern, which, when fused stereoscopically with the first pattern, caused a square to appear to stand out from the background (Julesz 1964). According to Stromeyer and Psotka, their subject was able to retain the first stimulus in sufficient detail to fuse with the second stimulus, even though it was viewed 24 hours later. Unfortunately, the subject in question does not appear to have been studied subsequently, and I know of no evidence from other subjects to indicate eidetic imagery with anything approaching this storage capacity or durability.

An extensive study by Leask, Haber, and Haber (1969) probably gives a more representative picture of the nature and extent of eidetic imagery. The study examined some 500 schoolchildren, of whom about 7 percent were classified as eidetic. This contrasts with work from the nineteenth and early twentieth centuries, which typically reports between 30 and 90 percent of children as showing evidence of eidetic imagery (Klüver 1932). As Leask et al. point out, however, the methodology used in these earlier studies tends to be of somewhat doubtful validity, and it is often far from clear that the subjects were not reporting either visual afterimages or vivid but noneidetic visual imagery. Similar problems were raised by Feldman's (1968) attempts to study the frequency of eidetic imagery in various African societies. She reports very variable and inconsistent results, which in some cases at least appear to have been due to the problem of deciding whether a given subject was genuinely eidetic. How can one decide?

Leask et al. used the following procedure: subjects were first given practice at looking at afterimages, describing their nature, and saying when and how they faded. They were then shown two black silhouettes —one depicting a family scene, the other an Indian hunter—and two colored illustrations taken from children's books, all displayed on an easel. In each case the subject was encouraged to look at the picture and move his eyes around it for 30 seconds. The picture was then removed, and the subject was encouraged to continue to look at the easel and say whether he could still see anything. If he responded "yes," he was encouraged to describe the picture; the relationship between where he was looking and his description was noted. He was asked from time to time whether he could still *see* it or was simply remembering it, and he was asked to say when the image faded. Haber (1969, p. 39), in a *Scientific American* article based on the research, gives the following tape-recorded protocol:

> The subject, a 10-year-old boy, was seated before a blank easel from which a picture from *Alice in Wonderland* had just been removed.
> EXPERIMENTER: Do you see something there?
> SUBJECT: I see the tree, gray tree with three limbs. I see the cat with stripes around its tail.
> EXPERIMENTER: Can you count those stripes?
> SUBJECT: Yes (pause). There's about 16.
> EXPERIMENTER: You're counting what? Black, white or both?
> SUBJECT: Both.
> EXPERIMENTER: Tell me what else you see.
> SUBJECT: And I can see the flowers on the bottom. There's about three stems, but you can see two pairs of flowers. One on the right has green leaves, red flower on bottom with yellow on top. And I can see the girl with a green dress. She's got blonde hair and a red hair band and there are some leaves in the upper left-hand corner where the tree is.
> EXPERIMENTER: Can you tell me about the roots of the tree?
> SUBJECT: Well, there's two of them going down here (points) and there's one that cuts off on the left-hand side of the picture.
> EXPERIMENTER: What is the cat doing with its paws?
> SUBJECT: Well, one of them he's holding out and the other one is on the tree.
> EXPERIMENTER: What color is the sky?
> SUBJECT: Can't tell.
> EXPERIMENTER: Can't tell at all?
> SUBJECT: No. I can see the yellowish ground, though.
> EXPERIMENTER: Tell me if any of the parts go away, or change at all as I'm talking to you. What color is the girl's dress?
> SUBJECT: Green. It has some white on it.
> EXPERIMENTER: How about her legs and feet?
> (The subject looks away from the easel and then back again.)
> EXPERIMENTER: Is the image gone?
> SUBJECT: Yes, except for the tree.
> EXPERIMENTER: Tell me when it goes away.
> SUBJECT: (pause) It went away.

Eidetic children typically report their images as occurring in front of their eyes, whereas they refer to memory images as being in their heads. Haber argues strongly for eidetic imagery being visual in nature and different from a normal memory image. He cites the following evidence for this view:

(1) Eidetic children remember parts of a picture which they do not claim to be able to see; in short, they themselves make a distinction between remembering and seeing an image.

(2) They report that the attempt to label the image interferes with its formation.

(3) The pattern by which images fade is described in remarkably similar ways by all eidetic children, suggesting a genuine phenomenon rather than an invention by the child.

(4) When asked to move their image from one surface to another, almost all children spontaneously report that it falls off the edge of the surface, and hence cannot be transferred in the same way as an afterimage can.

Children who are good eidetic imagers do not appear to have any other particular distinguishing characteristics. The information capacity of their images does not appear to be particularly large, nor do they appear to use their imagery in order to help them remember. Indeed, the two activities of imaging and remembering appear to be mutually conflicting, so that whenever an aspect of a picture is remembered and described, the eidetic image of that aspect tends to fade. Eidetic imagery does not appear to serve any particularly useful function; perhaps for this reason, it tends to be reported relatively rarely among adults. Indeed, Siipola and Hayden (1965) cite evidence for a higher incidence of eidetic imagery among retardates and suggest that such imagery represents a more primitive form of memory than that used by normal human adults. Whether or not this is the case, it seems to represent an intriguing but relatively unimportant byway on the road to understanding normal human memory.

ANALYSIS OF VISUAL IMAGERY

The first systematic study of visual imagery was made by Sir Francis Galton (1883), who circulated an imagery questionnaire to 100 people, many of them distinguished scientists or men of letters. He asked each of them to call to mind his breakfast table that morning and answer a series of questions about the images that appeared in his "mind's eye." The most striking feature of the results was the range of responses. Some people claimed that their visual images were as clear as the initial percept, while others had difficulty in even believing in the existence of visual imagery.

Unfortunately, however, although enormous differences occur in rated vividness of imagery, this appears to be unrelated to performance on visual memory tasks. In unpublished experiments of my own on visual imagery as a mnemonic, I have never found any relationship between a subject's rated vividness of imagery and the benefit gained from the imagery mnemonic. Similarly, in a visual memory task,

Sheehan and Neisser (1969) found no significant correlation between rated imagery and performance. Bartlett (1932) observed that his subjects tended to fall into two imagery categories: *visualizers,* who claimed that their recall was based on visual imagery, and *verbalizers,* who claimed to rely on words rather than images. Although visualizers tended to be very confident about their recall and verbalizers to be very diffident, the actual performance of the two types did not appear to differ.

Visual memory does tend to be correlated with performance on tests of spatial visualization. These typically involve manipulating and rotating patterns or objects. For example, a subject may be required to count the number of faces on a three-dimensional solid which is drawn in two dimensions, a task that involves visualizing the obscured portion of the solid on the basis of what is visible. A study by Shepard and Metzler (1971) investigated such mental spatial manipulation using drawings of the type shown in Figure 9–11. The subjects were shown two drawings of rotated solids and had to decide as quickly as possible whether the two represented the same object. The results are also shown in Figure 9–11. The judgment time increased linearly with angular difference between the two figures. Subjects claimed that they rotated one of the figures mentally until one end corresponded with the other. If the other end also corresponded, they responded "the same"; if not, "different." Figure 9–12 indicates that such "mental rotation" occurred at a rate of about 60° per second, whether in the plane of the picture or in depth.

Tests of spatial visualization have been found to predict memory performance, although the effects found are not very strong (Di Vesta and Ross 1971); such tests also predict time required to generate both images and verbal associations to stimulus words (Ernest and Paivio 1971). Di Vesta, Ingersoll, and Sunshine (1971) used factor analysis to study a range of tests of visual imagery and verbal ability. They found a clear separation between verbal ability and an imagery factor derived from tests requiring the subject to hold a percept in memory, to rotate it, or view it from many perspectives, and to restructure or reorganize it. Subjective ratings of vividness of imagery and of ability to control imagery were unrelated to spatial visualization and correlated most highly with the social desirability scale, a measure of the extent to which a subject is dependent on the recognition and approval of others!

As one whose visual imagery is subjectively quite vivid, I still find it surprising (social desirability notwithstanding) that such large dif-

223

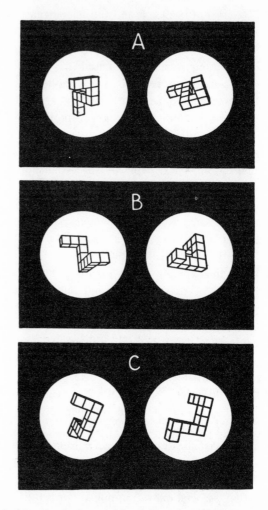

Figure 9–11 Examples of perspective line drawings presented to their subjects by Shepard and Metzler (1971): (a) a "same" pair of drawings, which differ by an 80° rotation in the picture plane; (b) a "same" pair, differing by an 80° rotation in depth; and (c) a "different" pair, which cannot be brought into congruence by *any* rotation. Source: R. N. Shepard and J. Metzler, Mental rotation of three-dimensional objects, *Science* 171 (1971): 702. Copyright 1971 by the American Association for the Advancement of Science.

ferences in rated vividness of imagery should be accompanied by no apparent behavioral consequences. This may be because visual imagery is an entirely internalized event, for which there is no obvious way in which two people can agree on an equivalent scale of vividness. As

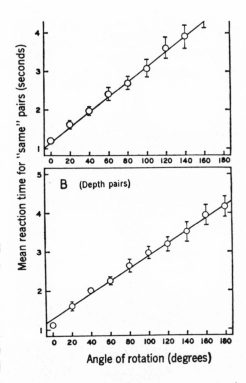

Figure 9–12 Mean reaction times to two perspective line drawings portraying objects of the same three-dimensional shape. Times are plotted as a function of angular difference in portrayed orientation: (a) for pairs differing by a rotation in the picture plane only; and (b) for pairs differing by a rotation in depth. Source: R. N. Shepard and J. Metzler, Mental rotation of three-dimensional objects, *Science* 171 (1971): 702. Copyright 1971 by the American Association for the Advancement of Science.

Mandler * has pointed out, if someone who claims to have no visual imagery is asked, for example, to describe the Taj Mahal, he tends to break off in mid-description with the comment "Yes, I *do* have visual imagery!" He often tends to draw the shape of the building in the air with his hands while describing it, which suggests that there may also be a kinesthetic imagery component. Subjective imagery may, however, be analogous to a visual display on a computer, grossly different from a printed or punched tape output from the same operation but containing exactly the same information. Thus, what determines the efficiency of visual memory is presumably the informa-

* George Mandler, 1971; personal communication.

tion stored, not the way in which it is subjectively displayed during output.

EVIDENCE FOR SEPARATE VISUAL AND VERBAL SYSTEMS

The most intuitively obvious evidence for nonverbal imagery in LTM comes from our ability to remember things that we would find great difficulty in describing at all adequately in words: a scenic view, the face of a friend, the sound of a piano, the taste of a cheese. Rather more formal evidence of a distinction between verbal description and recall is provided by Horowitz, Lampel, and Takanishi (1969), who compared children's description and recall of integrated scenes, such as a doll sitting on a chair and holding a flag, with non-integrated combinations (a doll, a chair, and a flag). Although children describe both situations as a simple list of items, they are much better at remembering the integrated sets.

A further body of evidence for separate visual imagery and verbal systems comes from the work of Paivio and his associates. He has shown that a rating of the probability that a word will evoke an image is by far the best predictor of how easily a word will be learned (Paivio 1969). Rated imageability differs from most predictors of ease of verbal learning, such as association value and familiarity, in having its major effect on the stimulus rather than the response in a paired-associate task. Sentences that comprise concrete or imageable words are also easier to remember than abstract sentences but are not understood any more rapidly; nor is it any easier to generate a sentence from a concrete word than from an abstract word (Yuille and Paivio 1967). In short, concreteness aids memory but is by no means essential for either generating or understanding language. A sentence such as *The theory has predictive value* may be hard to image, but it is not necessarily hard to understand.

A final source of evidence for separate visual and verbal memory systems comes from neuropsychology. There is abundant evidence from patients with unilateral damage to the temporal lobes that damage to the left hemisphere impairs verbal memory, while right temporal damage affects memory for visual material, such as designs and faces (Milner 1971). There is also a tendency for verbal material to be better recalled when presented to the right ear, which connects with the left hemisphere; such nonverbal tasks as tune recognition (Kimura 1967) or the interpretation of a speaker's emotional characteristics— for example, whether he is angry, sad, afraid, and so forth—are

226

better with the left ear (Haggard 1971). Finally, Baddeley and Warrington (1973), studying the defective long-term memory of amnesic patients, found that such patients were able to take advantage in free recall of clustering based on either acoustic similarity (e.g., *cat, can, man, mat*) or taxonomic category (e.g., *dog, zebra, horse, lion*) but failed to gain any advantage when groups of words were linked to form a visualizable picture (e.g., *the IRISHMAN gave a PENNY to the MONKEY playing a VIOLIN;* words to be recalled are in uppercase), whereas normal subjects gained an advantage from all three coding strategies. The amnesic patients' ability to utilize both phonological cues and category membership suggests that the linguistic component of their semantic memory is still functional, a view that was reinforced by their demonstration of an unimpaired capacity for generating words on the basis of either sound (e.g., words rhyming with *rug*) or taxonomic category (e.g., boys' names). Their inability to take advantage of the visual imagery mnemonic, however, suggests that they are impaired either in utilizing the imagery system or in taking normal advantage of the constructive component of semantic coding. Jones (1974) also found that amnesic patients with bilateral temporal lobe damage gained no advantage from instruction in using a visual imagery mnemonic, despite reporting success in generating the appropriate images during learning. However, imagery instructions are helpful to patients having a verbal memory deficit attributable to left hemispheric damage, which suggests that imagery principally depends on the right cerebral hemisphere.

To summarize: both Bower (1972) and Paivio (1971*b*) have suggested that the semantic system may function at two levels, one linguistic, the other based on sensory imagery. The two are closely connected and, in a sense, appear to have a common semantic "grammar," a set of rules whereby things are interrelated and organized. To use Bartlett's term, they involve similar schemata, the similarity presumably resulting from the fact that they are shaped by the same external world of experience. We shall return later in the chapter to the question of whether they are best regarded as separate systems or as two aspects of the same system.

SUPPRESSION OF VISUAL IMAGERY

It has proved much harder to explain why imagery provides such an effective aid to learning than to demonstrate its usefulness. As we mentioned earlier, attempts to use individual differences in either rated vividness of imagery or performance on spatial visualization tasks have not provided a particularly fruitful approach to understanding the processes underlying the use of imagery in memory. The attempt to find physiological correlates of imagery has proved even less productive; there surely must be physiological concomitants of imaging, but attempts to isolate them, using either eye movements or EEG measures, have proved very disappointing (Paivio 1971c).

Probably the most promising approach to the analysis of visual imagery has come from the imagery suppression studies of Lee Brooks (1967; 1968). In one of these studies, Brooks (1968) presented his subjects with the block letter F. A subject was required to look at the letter and then to turn away and hold it in his "mind's eye." He was instructed to start at the bottom left-hand corner and, moving in a clockwise direction, to classify each corner, saying "yes" if it was either a top or bottom corner or "no" if it was not; in this case the appropriate responses would be *Yes, Yes, Yes, No, No, No, No, No, No, Yes*. The subject responded either by speaking or by pointing to a series of printed *Y*'s and *N*'s which were irregularly located on a sheet of paper in front of him. Performance was consistently more rapid with a verbal than with a pointing response, an effect which Brooks attributes to the conflict between the visual image F which was being processed and the visual or spatial component involved in the pointing response.

Such a conclusion was supported by a second condition, in which the subject was required to hold in memory a sentence such as *A bird in the hand is not in the bush*. In this case he was required to classify each successive word as either a noun or a non-noun, and once again he responded either verbally or by pointing. In contrast to the imagery task, subjects found it consistently easier to respond to the verbal task by pointing rather than by speaking; presumably in this case, the verbal demands of the sentence retention task interfered with the verbal response. A similar example of interference between a visual image and visual processing is reported by Segal and Fusella (1969), who required their subjects to form images during a visual or auditory detection task. They found that a weak tone was less likely to be heard if the subject was imagining a sound such as a telephone ringing, while a faint light was less likely to be reported when the subject was imaging a visual scene, presumably in both cases because of overlap between the processing of the internally generated image and the externally presented signal.

In recent years, a number of attempts have been made to use the suppression technique to study the role of imagery in verbal memory. For example, Atwood (1971) reported that a visual processing task interfered more with the retention of highly imageable phrases (e.g., *Nudist devouring bird*) than it did with more abstract phrases (e.g., *The intellect of Einstein was a miracle*). He reported a converse effect for an auditory processing task, with the abstract material showing greater disruption than the concrete. Unfortunately, however, despite some support (Janssen 1976), several attempts to replicate this result by Bower, Munoz, and Arnold (1972), by Brooks (cited by Paivio 1971c, p. 374), by Neisser,* and by Quinn † have proved unsuccessful.

A study by Baddeley, Grant, Wight, and Thomson (1974) attempted to explore this discrepancy in more detail. As an interfering task, they used pursuit tracking, with the subject being required to follow with a stylus a spot of light moving along a circular path. They first demonstrated that this task caused dramatic impairment in performance on the visual imagery tasks previously explored by Brooks. Having established that the pursuit rotor was capable of interfering with visual imagery performance, Baddeley et al. then presented subjects with a paired-associate task in which they attempted to learn noun-adjective pairs that were either high in concreteness and imageability (e.g., *strawberry-ripe; bullet-grey; table-square*) or abstract and difficult to image (e.g., *gratitude-infinite; mood-cheerful; idea-original*). All subjects learned both types of material either at the same time as they performed the pursuit tracking or with no secondary task. Tracking had a small but statistically reliable effect on performance, but there was absolutely no difference in its effect on the two types of material. Concrete material was dramatically easier to retain than abstract material, but was no more affected by the visuo-spatial tracking task.

These results suggest that the imagery system involved in the spatial manipulation tasks devised by Brooks differs in an important way from the imagery system implied by subjective ratings of the imageability or concreteness of a word. The first of these was dramatically affected by the visual tracking task, while the second appeared to be completely immune to such disruption. In the past, it has been suggested that these two phenomena are aspects of a single system; imageable words were assumed to be easy to remember because they facilitated the formation of images by the subject, so that anything

* Ulric Neisser 1973; personal communication.
† J. Gerard Quinn 1972; personal communication.

which interfered with the subject's capacity for forming and manipulating images should disrupt the effect of rated imageability (Paivio 1971c). Since no interaction between the imagery level of the material and the disrupting task occurred, such a view runs into difficulties.

Baddeley et al. present an alternative view which requires a distinction between the *control process* of imagery, which represents an activity of the subject and may thus be disrupted by a concurrent visuo-spatial task, and the concreteness of the material. This represents the characteristics of the material that are already encoded in the subject's semantic memory store. As such, concreteness depends on the way in which the material has already been registered and thus is not dependent on the current activities of the subject. Hence, concreteness represents the characteristics of the material, whereas imagery represents an optional strategy which the subject may use in processing the material. On the basis of this distinction, Baddeley et al. predict that a concurrent pursuit tracking task will disrupt the use of a visual imagery mnemonic. This is because the mnemonic requires that the subject actively manipulate the visual characteristics of the verbal material. It is not sufficient to rely on existing semantic coding; codes must be made to interact in a visual or spatial way.

This prediction was explored in a series of as yet unpublished experiments by Baddeley and Lieberman. In the first of these, they showed that when subjects were induced to use the "one-is-a-bun" peg-word mnemonic (see p. 353), a concurrent pursuit tracking task did interfere with performance relative to a second condition in which subjects were induced to use a rote learning strategy. However, the magnitude of the decrement was far less dramatic than had been observed in the previous study, using the Brooks visualization tasks. One possible interpretation of this discrepancy was suggested by the possible distinction that may be drawn between a *visual* task (reflecting *what* is represented) and a *spatial* task (reflecting *where* it is represented). While the peg-word mnemonic clearly has a considerable visual component, it is far less dependent on locational or spatial coding than the Brooks tasks. Similarly, it might be argued that the pursuit rotor involves not only visual processing but also a very heavy spatial component.

In an attempt to separate these two factors, Baddeley and Lieberman reverted to using the Brooks tasks, which they had previously found to be dramatically disrupted by pursuit tracking. On this occasion, however, they compared the disrupting effect of two other tasks: one involved visual but not spatial processing, while the second involved just the opposite. The first task required the subject to judge the brightness of a stimulus. A projector presented a series of blank slides containing either two or three thicknesses of tracing paper. The subject was required to press a key whenever the brighter of the two stimuli appeared, but not to respond whenever the dimmer stimulus was presented. Hence, this condition involved a visual but not a spatial task. In the second condition, the subject was blindfolded and seated in front of a swinging pendulum. The pendulum emitted a tone and contained a photocell. Given a flashlight, the subject was instructed to attempt to keep the beam of the flashlight on the swinging pendulum. Whenever he was on target, the photocell caused the tone to change frequency, providing auditory feedback. Thus, the subject was presented with a task which was clearly spatial but involved no visual stimulus. If the crucial element of disruption comes from the visual component, then the brightness discrimination should cause impairment, whereas if the spatial element is crucial, the reverse should be the case, with the auditory tracking causing impairment. The results were fortunately very clear. The auditory tracking caused far greater impairment on the Brooks spatial task than on the equivalent verbal task, while for the brightness judgment no such difference occurred. In short, it appears that, for the Brooks tasks at least, disruption is spatial rather than visual.

A similar conclusion was reached independently by Byrne (1974), using a technique that required the subject to point to an array of Yes and No responses; when the pattern of pointing is consistent with the visual array being recalled (e.g., both following a clockwise circular path), performance is unimpaired, whereas an incompatible pointing response causes a dramatic drop in performance. A third line of evidence in favor of the spatial rather than purely visual nature of imagery comes from a study by Neisser and Kerr (1973); this showed that subjects gained virtually as much advantage from an image such as *dagger inside box* or *daffodil inside Napoleon's pocket*, in which one item would be visually obscured by the other, as in the case where both were visible.

On the basis of the spatial-visual distinction, Baddeley and Lieberman suggested that a location mnemonic, in which the spatial component was crucial, should show particularly clear disruption effects. They tested this by requiring subjects to learn a sequence of ten items either by rote or by utilizing a location mnemonic in which subjects were to imagine themselves walking through the university campus and leaving each of the ten items at one of ten previously designated locations. The results were clear-cut, showing (1) that the location mnemonic was helpful when performed alone and (2) that it was drastically disrupted by a concurrent pursuit tracking task.

The results so far suggest that it is possible to interfere with the control process involved in forming, manipulating, and utilizing images, though not with the more basic semantic characteristics which cause subjects to rate a word as being concrete or imageable. The evidence also indicates that the control process is spatial rather than visual in nature, at least for the tasks and disruptions so far studied. It is, of course, possible that subsequent research will demonstrate a means of producing pictorial rather than spatial disruption; until this has been demonstrated, we can conclude that the imagery system is spatial but not that it is visual.

IMAGERY AND THE STRUCTURE OF LTS

How is the spatial imagery system we have just discussed related to long-term memory? One interpretation presented by Paivio (1971c; 1975) asserts that LTS is divided into two separate but interrelated systems: one represents visual information and is responsible for the effects of imagery, while the other is linguistic in nature. The case for two separate systems is stated particularly clearly in a recent paper by Paivio (1974), which describes a series of experiments using the technique devised by Moyer (1973), in which subjects were required to judge which of two verbally specified animals was the larger. Moyer observed that the mean time to make this judgment was closely related to the similarity in size of the animals concerned. Thus, it takes subjects longer to decide whether a leopard is bigger than a rabbit than it does to decide whether a buffalo is bigger than a rabbit, just as if the subject were visually comparing self-generated images or scale models of the animals in question. However, other interpretations were possible, and Paivio's study attempted to investigate them.

Paivio showed that subjects made size judgments more rapidly about items if they were represented as pictures rather than as words. This was not simply attributable to the relative discriminability of the material, since the opposite occurred when subjects were required to make judgments of relative pronounceability, with verbal representations being judged more rapidly than pictorial stimuli. Further evidence that size judgments involve visual or spatial processing came from another study in which the physical size of the actual stimulus items to be compared was systematically varied. This allowed Paivio to compare congruent judgments, in which the drawing of the larger of the two animals was physically larger (e.g., a large picture of a zebra and a small picture of a cat) or incongruent ones (small zebra picture, large cat picture). He found that an incongruent stimulus pair slowed down the judgment, while congruent pairs speeded it up, implying, by analogy with the previously described studies by Brooks, that the visual processing system was in some sense implicated in the size judgment. When the same items were represented as words in large or small print, no such effect of congruency occurred, suggesting that the comparison process overlaps with the process involved in perceiving pictures of objects but not words. Paivio's results certainly suggest that the task is carried out in a visuo-spatial system, but does this necessarily imply separate storage systems for imagery and linguistic information? Could these results not, for instance, be interpreted along the lines suggested by Baddeley, Grant, Wight, and Thomson (1974)? They propose both a visuo-spatial control process, which can be disrupted by a concurrent spatial task, and a separate semantic store. As Anderson and Bower (1973) suggest, this may represent information in an abstract code which is neither visual nor linguistic.

A recent paper by Potter and Faulconer (1975) presents evidence favoring such a view. Their study started from the well-established observation that it takes more time to name an object represented by a picture than it takes to read that name, a result which might appear to fit particularly neatly into Paivio's two-system view. Since a linguistic response is required, a stimulus within the linguistic domain will be more effective than a stimulus in the visual domain. However, this is not strong evidence, since most theorists would agree that more processing is likely to be involved in retrieving the name of a pictured object than in a simple reading response, which does not necessarily involve any semantic processing at all.

A more interesting case occurs with the decision as to whether an instance belongs to a particular category or not. The knowledge that a dog is an animal or that a hammer is a tool is generally regarded as part of the hierarchical linguistic structure. If this is so, then requiring a subject to decide whether a pictured object, such as a *hammer*, is a member of the category *tools* should be particularly slow, since the subject will presumably first need to name the item and then search the hierarchical linguistic system to decide about its superordinate category name. On the other hand, if both linguistic and visual information is stored within the same abstract system, no switch would be necessary, and one would not necessarily expect the subject to take any longer to decide that a *picture* of a hammer is a member of the class *tools* than that the *word* "hammer" is in the relevant category. Potter and Faulconer therefore presented their subjects with a series of category names; after each one the subject was shown either a picture or the name of an item and was required to decide as quickly as possible whether the item in question belonged to the category. They found that subjects were in fact somewhat faster at categorizing pictures than words and did both these tasks more rapidly than they were able to name a picture. They consider and reject a number of alternative explanations for their results, and they conclude that their experiment supports the hypothesis of a single abstract semantic memory system which contains both linguistic and pictorial information and which can be accessed equally well by words or pictures.

We shall return to the question of semantic memory in Chapters 13 and 14. Meanwhile, the available evidence suggests a separate visuo-spatial processing system, possibly a subsystem of working memory, which may be disrupted by concurrent visuo-spatial activity but does not necessitate the assumption of a visual LTS system that is separate from a more abstract semantic memory.

As I hope the preceding chapter has illustrated, visual memory is an enormously broad field, ranging in scale from traces which survive only a few milliseconds (and which can best be discussed in terms of purely perceptual processes) to basic issues involving the structure of semantic memory. With the exception of iconic memory, the field was unduly neglected in the 1950s and 1960s, but this has been changing in recent years, and I would anticipate considerable future development.

CHAPTER

10

Auditory, Kinesthetic, Tactile, and Olfactory Memory

I N THE PREVIOUS CHAPTER we discussed visual memory, the most adequately explored area of sensory memory. The evidence suggested a fairly clear division into three major levels, each broadly associated with a stage of visual processing. They range from iconic memory, which is limited to basic visual dimensions; through short-term visual memory, in which the visual input has been categorized into items such as letters or geometrical shapes; to long-term visual memory, in which the visual stimulus may be encoded much more richly in terms of meaningful objects or, in the case of faces, people. A similar distinction can be drawn with auditory memory, although there is still very little agreement on which experiments fit into which stage or, indeed, on how many stages are involved.

Auditory Memory

The clearest and most cogent recent discussion of the stages of auditory memory is provided by Massaro (1972), in a paper which has the additional virtue of emphasizing the fact that sensory memory forms an integral part of the process of perception, something which can easily be lost sight of in an approach that concentrates exclusively on memory. We shall broadly follow Massaro in classifying auditory memory into three stages analogous to the stages in visual memory. It should, however, be noted that the distinctions are much more controversial than in visual memory, simply because the necessary crucial experiments have not yet been done.

Although we shall be emphasizing the similarities between auditory and visual memory, it is important to bear in mind the very basic differences between hearing and vision. The most fundamental of these is that the *spatial component,* which is so important in visual perception, is either absent from auditory perception or has to be coded in terms of time or intensity; an example of this is *sound localization,* whereby differences in the times at which signals arrive at the two ears are used as a cue to the location of the sound source.

An issue that concerns a number of the studies to be discussed is the question of whether there is a separate auditory memory system for speech sounds. There is considerable evidence suggesting that the left hemisphere of the brain is specialized for speech processing, whereas the right hemisphere is used for perceiving non-speech sounds. Thus, when two conflicting sounds are presented simultaneously to the two ears, the right ear (connecting with the left cerebral hemisphere) shows an advantage for perceiving digits, words, and consonants and for recognition of a speaker's voice, while the left ear is better at perceiving environmental sounds, clicks, pitch patterns, and melodies (Milner 1971). However, recent evidence suggests that the distinction is not so clear-cut as was originally believed. Haggard (1971) found a left ear advantage for detection of the emotional tone of a speaker's voice, and Studdert-Kennedy and Shankweiler (1970) showed that the right ear advantage in the perception of consonants does not apply to vowels. Moreover, patients in whom the links between the two halves of the brain have been cut to control epileptic seizures show evidence of understanding at least concrete words with the right hemisphere, although only the left appears to be capable of initiating speech (Gazzaniga and Sperry 1967). More direct evidence for a distinction between memory for speech and non-speech sounds comes from a number of the memory studies to be discussed subsequently. However, in no case is it really clear that the results imply a sharp dichotomy. Given the choice between a unitary system and a dichotomy, the unitary view has the advantage of parsimony, and for that reason we shall proceed on the assumption that speech is remembered in terms of the same memory system as non-speech sounds, meanwhile bearing in mind that a dichotomy is a real possibility.

Before examining the evidence, we must face one final problem: lack of agreement about the stages of auditory memory is reflected in the absence of a generally accepted set of terms. Neisser (1967) suggested the term *echoic memory* for the auditory equivalent of iconic memory. Unfortunately, however, it now seems likely that the examples he cites are based on the auditory equivalent of the visual short-term memory system reflected in the Posner letter-matching task, so that the implied equivalence of iconic and echoic memory may be misleading. We shall therefore, with some reluctance, discard the term echoic memory, referring to the equivalent of iconic memory as *preperceptual auditory memory* (Massaro 1972) and to the memory systems associated with the later stages of information processing as *short-term auditory memory* and *long-term auditory memory*.

PREPERCEPTUAL AUDITORY MEMORY

Evidence exists for a system closely analogous to iconic memory. Like iconic memory, it is subject to masking at two levels, one probably reflecting a disruption of the input to the system, the other probably based on a blocking of the readout process. When a brief tone is rapidly followed by a second, louder tone, the detection of the first tone will be impaired. The probability of detection decreases as the interval between tones becomes shorter or the relative intensity of the second tone becomes greater. A study by Elliot (1967) followed a 10-msec target tone with a 100-msec period of masking noise. Masking decreased as the interval between tone and noise increased, and was virtually absent at intervals greater than 100 msec. This suggests that the processing of the initial tone is complete within 100 msec, and hence cannot be disrupted by the noise mask. Later studies have also found a 100-msec limit to the period over which masking of this type can occur. Deatherage and Evans (1969) found a 100-msec masking limit and, in addition, showed that this limit was reduced when the intensity of the masking stimulus decreased.

These results alone would not necessarily imply a memory store; it is conceivable that the masking noise, being louder, is transmitted along the auditory pathway more rapidly, and hence overtakes the target in transmission. An overtake hypothesis cannot, however, account for the occurrence of *forward masking,* in which detection of a target is impaired by an earlier and louder noise burst. The overtake hypothesis would predict that the louder masking noise would travel faster than the target and should therefore have left the auditory pathway before the target arrives at the cortex. Since there is no doubt that such forward noise masking does occur (Homick, Elfner, and Bothe 1969; Robinson and Pollack 1971), the masking data can be regarded as evidence for the existence of a brief preperceptual auditory store.

What are the temporal characteristics of the preperceptual auditory store? One of the very few experiments giving an indication of the decay characteristics of the preperceptual memory trace is a study by Plomp (1964). A 200-msec burst of noise was followed, after a silent interval of variable duration, by a second noise burst, which was used to give an indirect measure of the fading trace of the first stimulus. When the trace of the first stimulus is strong, the second stimulus needs to be relatively loud to be discriminated above it; hence, at 2.5 msec the second noise burst has to have a loudness of 65 db to reach a 75-percent detection criterion, whereas after 80 msec a 15-db noise is sufficient, suggesting a massive drop in trace strength within 80 msec. A series of experiments by Efron (1970a; 1970b; 1970c) also tried to measure the duration of an auditory sensation, in this case by requiring the subject to adjust the onset of a light to correspond with the apparent offset of a tone. Efron found an apparent duration of approximately 130 msec, a duration which was relatively independent of stimulus duration, so that a 30-msec tone and a 100-msec tone would both appear to last for 130 msec. As Haber (1971) has pointed out, a similar effect occurs in iconic memory, with stimuli tending to produce a 250-msec iconic trace regardless of their brevity. In both cases, this duration is presumably linked to the time necessary for stimulus processing and is a device whereby very brief stimuli are held in store long enough to be analyzed and hence perceived. The apparent *duration* of a tone has also been shown to be reduced when it is followed by a second, masking tone (Gol'dburt 1961). Von Békésy (1971) has suggested that this may be an important determinant of the acoustics of concert halls, since the apparent loudness and duration of a note may be reduced as a result of masking by its own echo.

So far there appears to be a clear analogy with iconic memory: the auditory image appears to be prolonged for rather more than 100 msec, regardless of stimulus duration. It is subject to disruption by noise presented either before or after the target stimulus, but only if the mask is presented to the same ear (Deatherage and Evans 1969);

similarly, Turvey (1973) observed of visual "noise" that a flash of light will only disrupt the icon if it is presented to the same eye as the target stimulus. The masking effect seems to be based on an integration of target and mask, not on the interruption of one by the other; as such, the effect depends on the relative intensities of the target and the mask.

Is there also an analogue to pattern masking? Massaro (1970) has performed a series of experiments which appear to provide a very close parallel. His situation differs from the auditory masking experiments so far described in that it requires the subject do more than detect the presence or absence of a signal; instead, the subject is required to discriminate between two 20-msec tones. On each trial, one of these is presented and then followed, after a varying interval, by a masking tone of the same intensity as the target tone. The subject's task is to say whether the higher or lower of the two tones was presented. Figure 10–1 shows the probability of correct discrimination as a function of the interval between tone and mask for three subjects tested. All three curves tend to reach asymptote by about 250 msec, a result which Massaro interprets as evidence for an auditory image lasting about 250 msec. However, such an interpretation is open to question.

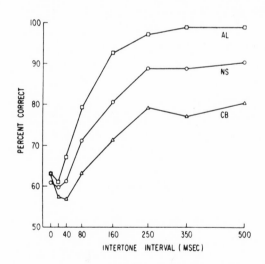

Figure 10–1   Percentage of correct identifications of a test tone for three subjects (AL, NS, and CB) as a function of the silent interval separating the tone from a masking tone. Source: D. W. Massaro, Preperceptual auditory images, *Journal of Experimental Psychology* 85 (1970): 413. Copyright 1970 by the American Psychological Association. Reprinted by permission.

Massaro's results clearly do imply storage of information, but there is no direct evidence that an image is involved. The studies by Efron in which subjects were specifically instructed to indicate the apparent duration of the auditory image give values considerably lower than the 250 msec observed by Massaro. Given Massaro's assumption that the simpler the decision required, the longer the useful life of an image and the greater its apparent duration (1970, p. 416), exactly the opposite would be expected: Efron's duration judgment *should* be possible for longer than Massaro's pitch judgment, and hence should produce a longer estimate of duration. What little evidence there is does not seem to support Massaro's claim that his results reflect the operation of an auditory image.

A second, more far-reaching problem is raised by the contention that "since recognition performance levels off at about 250 msec, the image probably decayed within this period" (Massaro 1972, p. 129). An equally reasonable interpretation is that all the necessary information has been extracted from the trace after 250 msec, in which case performance would not be affected by either the subsequent persistence or disruption of the trace. A good deal of evidence is cited by Massaro (1972) for an auditory perceptual processing time ranging from 125 to 300 msec, depending on the familiarity of the material. Vowels tend to take about 125–200 msec to process and, when used in a masking study (ibid.), give masking functions which asymptote in this range. In this case Massaro cites the masking data as evidence of processing time, not as evidence that vowels produce a less durable trace than tones. Further support for the view that Massaro's findings reflect processing time and processing interference rather than image-decay time comes from the work of Leshowitz and Cudahy (1973), Cudahy and Leshowitz (1974), and Loeb and Holding (1975). They have pointed out that Massaro employed naïve subjects and that frequency discrimination tasks are typically subject to long-term practice effects. They have shown, in a series of experiments including a replication of Massaro (1970), that subjects improve dramatically with practice and in the limit show no masking for intervals greater than about 50 msec. The fact that subjects can learn to disregard the mask leads them to conclude that it does not interfere with the signal at a sensory level but rather that it disrupts the processing of the signal.

In conclusion, Massaro's discrimination masking technique does appear to provide convincing evidence for a trace lasting for *at least* 250 msec. He does not, however, appear to be justified in claiming that performance is based on an auditory image, or that his technique provides evidence of the decay time of the trace. Since there appears to be little evidence from other sources of an auditory store with a duration of 250 msec, we shall assume that Massaro's studies reflect the process of transferring information into a more durable short-term auditory memory store, with the asymptote indicating the point at which the transfer ceases. In some cases, particularly where the asymptote is low, this *may* reflect the point at which the trace becomes unusable. In the currently available studies, however, it seems more likely that transfer stops because it is no longer necessary.

SHORT-TERM AUDITORY MEMORY

How durable is short-term auditory memory? An extensive series of experiments by Wickelgren (1969) concerned itself with this question, among others. Recognition memory for pitch was studied using a delayed comparison task in which a tone was presented and followed by a second tone after a delay ranging from 0 to 180 seconds. Subjects were required to judge whether the two tones were the same or different or, in other experiments, whether the second tone was higher, lower, or equal in pitch to the first. Wickelgren analyzes his data in terms of a trace strength model based on signal detection theory and concludes that the memory trace for pitch comprises two components: a short-term component, which decays exponentially to zero with a time constant of 3 to 9 seconds; and an intermediate-term trace, lasting for 40 seconds or more.

In another study, Wickelgren (1968) tested H.M., the amnesic patient described extensively by Milner (1966), and found that the short-term component of his pitch memory was quite normal, while the intermediate-term component appeared to be absent. Warrington and Baddeley (1974) have obtained a similar result in an experiment with amnesic patients on short-term memory for the visual location of a dot. In other cases, in which the visual or auditory memory tasks used do not show rapid forgetting in normal subjects (and hence presumably reflect secondary or long-term memory), amnesic patients show a marked impairment (Prisko 1963; Sidman, Stoddard, and Mohr 1968; Warrington and Taylor 1973). Taken as a whole, these results suggest that the sensory memory system of amnesic patients shows the same dichotomous pattern as their verbal memory, with normal STS but impaired LTS.

Wickelgren's conclusions about auditory memory are therefore broadly consistent with information on other types of memory. How representative are they of other studies of auditory STM? Attempts to explore the duration of auditory STM are faced with the problem of separating memory of the auditory stimulus itself from verbal STM based on a transformation of the acoustic stimulus into an articulatory (hence easily rehearsable) form. Three basic techniques have been used to avoid this problem. In the partial-report technique, the subject is presented with information simultaneously from several sources. Since he cannot recode and rehearse more than one source in the time available, a partial-report advantage will only occur if the subject delays recoding until the partial-report cue is presented. The second technique, based originally on studies of selective attention, involves presenting two simultaneous messages, requiring the subject to shadow or repeat one of these (thus fully occupying the verbal system), and then testing retention of the unattended material. The third compares the retention of verbal material presented aurally, when both auditory and verbal memory contribute to performance, with its retention after visual presentation, when the auditory memory component is absent. These three techniques will be considered in turn.

Partial-report technique. A number of studies using Sperling's work on iconic memory as a model have used the partial-report procedure to estimate the rate of forgetting of auditory information. Moray, Bates, and Barnett (1965) in their "experiments on the four-eared man" showed that auditory poststimulus cuing was feasible. They presented auditory stimuli from four separate directions simultaneously and showed that a partial-report technique, whereby one of the four locations was cued, led to better performance than the whole-report technique, in which subjects tried to recall material from all four locations. Unfortunately, they used only a single delay, so that no information about rate of forgetting is given.

A subsequent study by M. Treisman and Rostron (1972) used three locations and presented two successive 100-msec tones at each. After a delay of 0, 400, 800, or 1,600 msec, a test tone was presented by a fourth loudspeaker. The subject was required to judge whether the test tone had occurred in either the initial set of three tones or in the second set of three. Treisman and Rostron estimated that an average of 3.4 of the 6 tones were available on immediate test and 2.1 after their longest delay, 1.6 seconds. Rate of forgetting was virtually linear over the range studied, and since performance was not approaching asymptote, it provides no reliable evidence as to the duration of the auditory memory trace.

Rather better evidence on this point is provided by Darwin, Turvey, and Crowder (1972) in an experiment involving the auditory presentation of three items (digits or consonants) simultaneously, one at each of three locations. Subjects were cued visually for recall from one of the locations after a delay of 0, 1, 2, or 4 seconds, and this was compared with a whole-report condition in which recall of all locations was required.

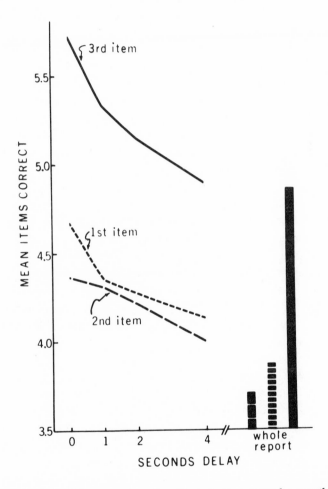

Figure 10–2   Mean number of auditory items reported correctly as a function of the delay between presentation and cue. The items were presented from three separate sources simultaneously. The bar on the right indicates the percentage of correct recall when the subject was asked to report all three items. Source: C. J. Darwin, M. T. Turvey, and R. G. Crowder, An auditory analogue of the Sperling partial report procedure: evidence for brief auditory storage, *Cognitive Psychology* 3 (1972): 259. Reprinted by permission.

The results are shown in Figure 10–2. This shows a forgetting curve which has still not reached asymptote after 4 seconds but is clearly likely to do so within the range of 3–9 seconds suggested by Wickelgren's study. There are clear serial position effects, with the last item presented being much better recalled whether tested by the partial- or whole-report techniques.

A similar rate of forgetting was found in an earlier study by Pollack (1959) in which a word from a pool of 31 potential targets was presented in noise and subsequently tested by presenting a recognition set of two alternatives. Narrowing down the alternatives led to a higher detection rate; the advantage diminished with delay and was virtually absent after 5 seconds. By this time the subjects appeared to have recoded the auditory stimulus into a verbal description and were presumably no longer relying on the deteriorating auditory trace.

Selective attention and auditory STM. Experiments on selective attention by Cherry (1953) included one condition in which the subject was instructed to shadow (attend to and repeat) a passage of prose presented to one ear while ignoring the message on the other ear. When the two messages were identical, subjects noticed the identity, provided the lag between the two was not too great. This result was confirmed by Anne Treisman (1964), who found that the identity was noted at a longer delay when the shadowed message was leading (4.3 seconds) than when it was lagging (1.3 seconds). This result is frequently cited as evidence for differential durability of attended and nonattended information. This apparent difference may be due to a variety of factors, however, including the following: (1) the attended message receives deeper processing; (2) the attended message is repeated and therefore is heard twice and spoken once by the subject; and (3) the events that prompt the subject into making a spontaneous comparison between the two messages differ in the two cases. Furthermore, since Treisman found that the identity was noticed just as readily when one message was in a male voice and the other in a female voice, it seems likely that the comparison is not based on a simple auditory memory trace.

A more direct method of measuring the retention of an unattended auditory stimulus was used by Erikson and Johnson (1964). They presented occasional faint tones to subjects reading prose. At varying delays following the tone, a reading lamp was switched off; this was a signal for the subject to report whether he had heard a tone within the preceding 20 seconds. Detection rate, based on "certain" judgments, dropped from about 47 percent on immediate test to 25 percent after 10.5 seconds, with a false alarm rate of about 20 percent. While this result may possibly reflect the duration of a genuine auditory short-term trace, it is open to the objection that subjects are quite capable of performing an auditory detection task while engaged in simultaneous visual activity (McGrath 1963) and may have registered the occurrence of a tone in some more durable nonacoustic store on at least some of the occasions.

In an attempt to avoid this problem, Norman (1969) required his subjects to shadow prose presented to the attended ear, a task which has been shown to lead to virtually no long-term retention of material presented to the nonattended ear (Cherry 1953). Norman studied the short-term retention of unattended material by presenting two-digit numbers to the nonattended channel. He found evidence of retention after a few seconds, but none after 20 seconds of interpolated shadowing. However, the digits were presented on an otherwise unoccupied channel, and since subjects were able to detect their onset, it is possible that they may again have been boosting their performance by rapidly switching attention to the nonattended channel.

Glucksberg and Cowan (1970) attempted to avoid this problem by embedding the unattended memory material (digits) in a stream of prose. Hence, subjects were shadowing the prose presented to one ear while ignoring that presented to the other, except when the occurrence of a green light signaled them to report whether a digit had ap-

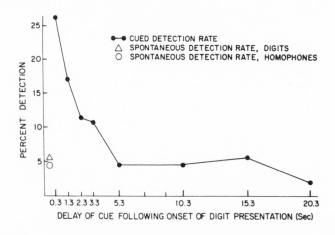

Figure 10–3   Probability of reporting a digit presented on the nonattended ear as a function of the delay between digit and cue. Source: S. Glucksberg and G. N. Cowan, Memory for non-attended auditory material, *Cognitive Psychology* 1 (1970): 153. Reprinted by permission.

peared on the unattended channel. Performance as a function of the interval between digit and test is shown in Figure 10–3, which suggests a trace duration of about 5 seconds. However, although Figure 10–3 suggests a gradually fading trace, retention seemed subjectively to be more of an all-or-none phenomenon. Subjects virtually always reported either a specific digit or nothing, never that they had heard a digit but could not remember what it was. Furthermore, subjects all reported that there had been no delay between the digit and the green light, suggesting the absence of either direct time tags or of trace strength cues which could be used as time tags. Both these features could be taken to suggest that forgetting is by displacement rather than trace decay, a conclusion that finds further indirect support from a recent study by Bryden (1971).

Bryden used the dichotic memory task developed by Broadbent (1958), in which pairs of digits are presented simultaneously, one to each ear, after which the subject is required to recall as many of the presented digits as possible. Typically, when presentation rate exceeds one pair per second, subjects report all the digits from one ear before reporting any from the other, generally producing better performance on the ear reported first. Bryden instructed his subjects to attend to and rehearse the digits presented to one ear; he further instructed one group to recall these items first and the unattended items second, while another group was to recall them in the opposite order. Bryden's results are shown in Figure 10–4. They contain two striking features: first, the serial position curve for the unattended ear shows a marked recency effect, while that for the attended ear is relatively flat; and second, order of report has a much more dramatic effect on the retention of attended items. The flat serial position curve for attended items is not too surprising, since the various rehearsal strategies used may well have overridden any temporal or ordinal presentation cues. Furthermore, the disruption of rehearsal by the need to recall the unattended material would be expected to impair the retention of attended material (Brown 1958; Peterson and Peterson 1959).

Performance on the unattended items is much more intriguing, however. The dramatic recency effect presents clear evidence of forgetting, while the relatively small effect of delaying recall while the attended message is reported suggests that neither time nor interference from subsequent recall is responsible for this forgetting. Again, the simplest interpretation might seem to be the assumption of a short-term auditory store of limited capacity in which forgetting is based on displacement by subsequent auditory items. Note, however, that the sound of the subject's

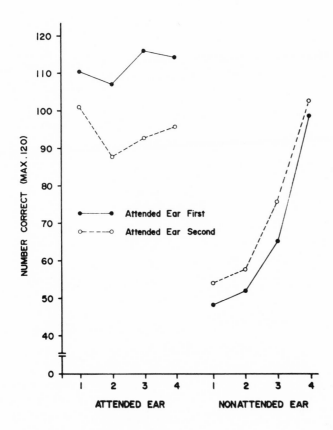

Figure 10–4   Retention of dichotically presented material as a function of attention and report instructions. Note that order of report has a much larger effect on the attended ear, but recency has a much stronger effect on the nonattended ear. Source: M. P. Bryden, Attentional strategies and short-term memory in dichotic listening, *Cognitive Psychology* 2 (1971): 103. Reprinted by permission.

own voice in recalling the attended items does not appear to displace items from this short-term auditory store, a point we shall return to in the next section. An alternative hypothesis is suggested by the attempts to account for recency effects in LTM discussed in Chapter 8 (p. 181), where it was suggested that recency effects reflect a retrieval strategy based on ordinal cues—in other words, last in, first out. It was further suggested that this is a relatively primitive strategy, typically used when other retrieval cues are not available. The short-term auditory trace of an unattended message might seem to present the type of impoverished

247

retrieval situation in which ordinal cues might provide the best available retrieval strategy.

Auditory and visual presentation. It has been known for at least half a century that the auditory presentation of a sequence of items leads to better recall than does visual presentation, at least over the last items (Von Sybel 1909). Figure 10–5 shows the results of a study by Conrad and Hull (1968) in which subjects recalled sequences of six digits pre-

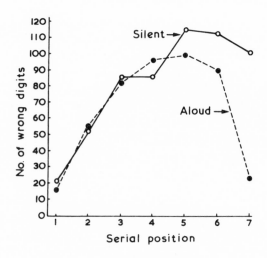

Figure 10–5   Effect of presentation mode on serial position of errors. Subjects either read the items silently or pronounced them aloud. Source: R. Conrad and A. J. Hull, Input modality and the serial position curve in short-term memory, *Psychonomic Science* 10 (1968): 136. Reprinted by permission.

sented visually and accompanied by the instruction to read them either silently or aloud. Vocalization clearly enhances performance on later items. This advantage comes from hearing the items rather than articulating them; it disappears when the sound of a subject's voice is masked by loud noise (Murray 1965) and is clearly present when visual and auditory presentations are compared and no articulation is required (Murdock 1967).

This enhanced recency effect is usually attributed to a short-term sensory store. Crowder and Morton (1969) have termed it *precategorical acoustic storage* (PAS) and have investigated it in some detail, using the *suffix effect.* This is a phenomenon first observed by Conrad (1960), who noted that recall of a spoken digit sequence was impaired when followed by an irrelevant additional item which the subject was free to ignore. Thus the spoken sequence 7961348 would be recalled better than the sequence 7961348-0, even though the zero was merely a recall signal that was present on every trial. Crowder and Morton (1969) showed that this effect occurs primarily when acoustic presentation is followed by an acoustic suffix (although Hitch [1975] subsequently showed an analogous but much smaller effect when visually presented digits are followed by a visual suffix). The nature of the suffix is critical, with no impairment found when the suffix is visual or is not speechlike.

Figure 10–6 shows the results of a study in which a spoken digit sequence was followed by either a spoken zero, a doorbell buzzer, or nothing. Only the spoken suffix disrupts recall. Given that the suffix is spoken, however, its semantic content is unimportant. Digit recall is no more disrupted by the word *zero* than it is by the reverse sound *rosy* or by a neutral vocalization designed to convey as few articulatory features as possible (Crowder and Raeburn 1970). It is this insensitivity to semantic factors that has induced Crowder and Morton to refer to the

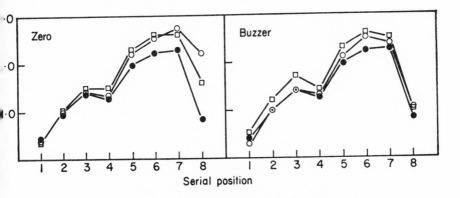

Figure 10–6   Effect of an auditory suffix on the retention of spoken digits. In the left panel, two suffix conditions with a speech sound delivered at different delays are compared with no-suffix control data. Identical conditions are represented in the right panel, except that a buzzer is substituted for the speech suffix (the control data are the same in each panel). A spoken suffix, zero, disrupts retention of the last few items, the effect being greater for a suffix presented after a 0.5-second delay (unfilled circles) than after a 2-second delay (unfilled squares). A buzzer of comparable intensity has no effect at either delay. Source: R. G. Crowder, Waiting for the stimulus suffix-decay, delay, rhythm and readout in immediate memory, *Quarterly Journal of Experimental Psychology* 23 (1971): 330.

store as "precategorical." The suffix effect is not always an all-or-none phenomenon, however; it occurs to a reduced extent when the suffix is presented in a different voice from the digits—for example, male versus female—or in a different location (Crowder 1973; Morton, Crowder, and Prussin 1971).

Crowder (1971*b*) has recently observed that the advantage of auditory over visual presentation does not apply to all speech sounds. When subjects were required to recall sequences of sounds selected from a set which differed only in the initial consonant (*bah, dah, gah*), no auditory advantage occurred and no suffix effect was found, whereas both occurred for material with differing vowel sounds (*bee, bih, boo*). His initial conclusion was that the acoustic store can hold vowels but not consonants; from this somewhat startling statement he went on to argue that the auditory memory store is unlike a tape recorder, since it does not simply represent the acoustic input but appears to handle consonants and vowels differentially. Darwin and Baddeley (1974) suggested an alternative explanation in terms of discriminability. They compared the acoustic store with a rather low-fidelity tape recorder. The information stored in the short-term system is enough to allow simple discriminations, such as those involved in Crowder's vowels, but not his more difficult consonant discriminations. They went on to show that syllables based on more discriminable consonants (*ash, am, ag*) do produce both an auditory advantage and a suffix effect, while the suffix effect shown by vowels decreases as they are made less discriminable (see Figure 10–7).

Further experiments tested an additional hypothesis suggested by Crowder that vowels show clearer acoustic storage effects because they represent a steady-state sound, whereas consonants are based on a rapidly changing sound pattern. Demonstration of a clear suffix effect for diphthongs (e.g., *day, dhow, dour*), which have a continuously changing sound pattern, allowed Darwin and Baddeley to reject this interpretation and again pointed to acoustic similarity as the basic variable, with easily discriminable sounds giving the clearest evidence of an auditory store.

Does this imply that the simple tape recorder analogy is therefore accurate? Probably not, since Watkins (1972) has shown that the extent of the advantage for a list of words presented aurally is not affected by the number of syllables in the words. This suggests that the system is storing words rather than syllables or phonemes, a result which suggests that a good deal of processing has already occurred before the material enters the auditory memory store. It seems wise to regard both

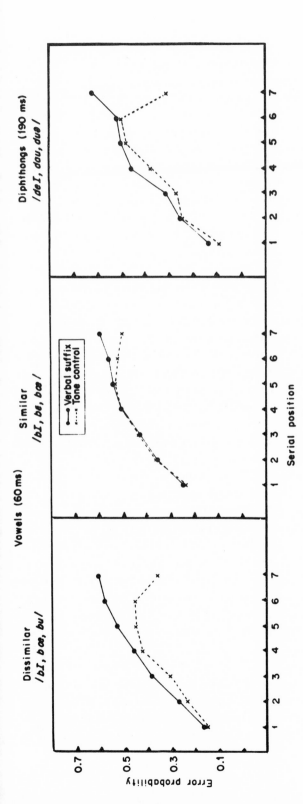

Figure 10–7 Mean error probabilities as a function of serial position for lists of seven syllables read silently or aloud. The modality effect is reflected in the tendency for the last item to be better recalled when spoken aloud. Note that the effect depends on the acoustic similarity of the material. Source: C. J. Darwin and A. D. Baddeley, Acoustic memory and the perception of speech, *Cognitive Psychology* 6 (1974): 51.

the tape recorder analogy and Crowder and Morton's claim that the system is precategorical as simple working hypotheses about a system that is probably quite complex.

It is clear from the evidence we have examined that a short-term auditory memory system must exist. Some such system is reflected in the work on tonal memory by Wickelgren (1969) and D. Deutsch (1970), the partial-report studies of Darwin, Turvey, and Crowder (1972), and the suffix-effect studies of Crowder and Morton (1969), all of which indicate some form of acoustic storage. Do they represent a single system? There appears at present to be no evidence that compels one to assume a multiple system. Whether a unitary view will continue to be tenable when we begin to understand the more detailed functioning of auditory STS remains to be seen.

LONG-TERM AUDITORY MEMORY

Auditory LTM clearly exists; without it we could surely not recognize the voice of a friend on the telephone, recall the opening bars of Beethoven's Fifth Symphony, or recognize a bang as the slamming of a car door. However, despite its obvious existence, we know remarkably little about it. Probably the only area of substantial research into auditory LTM has been that stemming from the applied military problem of training sonar operators. For many years, acoustic sonar devices have been used to detect and identify approaching submarines; consequently, something is known about training people to make auditory discriminations, a task which clearly involves auditory LTM (e.g., Corcoran, Carpenter, Webster, and Woodhead 1968). Nevertheless, interest has typically been in training techniques rather than in memory per se, and there appears to have been little or no development of our theoretical understanding of auditory LTM.

Work on memory for meaningful sounds is equally sparse. Phillipchalk and Rowe (1971) have compared the serial and free recall of environmental sounds (e.g., a dripping tap, a crowing cock) with the recall of their verbal equivalents. They found no difference in free-recall performance but poorer serial retention of the environmental sounds. An analogous result is obtained when the serial and free recall of pictures is compared with verbal recall (Paivio and Csapo 1969). Both results are interpreted by Paivio (1971c) as evidence for the peculiar appropriateness of verbal material for serial rehearsal and recall. Unfortunately, however, environmental sounds and pictures were recalled verbally in both these studies. This highlights the problem of verbal labeling with such material. To what extent is the subject remembering the sound or picture, and to what extent is he remembering a verbal label? The fact that sounds and pictures do not behave in the same way as the equivalent words suggests that the effect is probably not in this case due to verbal labeling, although one could argue that the process of naming during either input or recall may have disrupted serial memory more than free recall. It is difficult to avoid such problems when using easily labeled sounds, and hence there would clearly be an advantage to studying less easily namable sounds, such as unfamiliar voices, melodies, or birdcalls, and then testing by recognition.

Long-term auditory memory is clearly an area of considerable potential interest. How well do we recognize people by their voices? One's intuitive feeling is very well indeed! If so, does this imply a special innate capacity for remembering voices, and can this fact be used to design other auditory recognition tasks, such as those involved in the design of mobility aids for the blind?

Memory for music. The psychology of music presents another area in which auditory memory is an important factor. A number of investigators have studied the retention of individual tones; in addition to the previously described study by Wickelgren (1969), D. Deutsch (1972*a*; 1972*b*; 1973) has shown that the probability of forgetting a tone is increased if similar tones are interpolated between presentation and test. Long-term retention of individual tones is very poor (Bachem 1954), except in the case of subjects who have absolute pitch, the ability to identify and name an isolated note. Bachem found that such subjects were no better than normal subjects at remembering tones over intervals of 1 minute or less. At longer intervals, however, performance of normal subjects declined to near chance, while the absolute pitch subjects continued to be able to recognize a note to within the nearest semitone. As Siegel (1974) suggests, this is probably because subjects with absolute pitch label the stimulus, and remember the label, which they then check against the recognition tone. Attempts to train subjects to have absolute pitch have met with limited success (Cuddy 1968), although Brady (1970) did manage to train himself to be accurate to within two semitones after two months of practicing half-an-hour a day.

Most studies of tonal memory have examined recognition rather than recall, but Berg (1975) had his subjects sing their response, and scored it by matching against a pitch pipe. The method is somewhat laborious, and depends on using subjects with experience in singing. He tested the memory span of seven such subjects and found a mean span of about 5 notes, and a range of spans from 4 to 7 notes. Recognition memory for sequences of tones has been studied by Dowling (1971; 1972) and by Dowling and Fujitani (1971), who stressed the importance of contour, the rise and fall of successive notes. They showed that subjects are quite good at recognizing a sequence of tones provided its contour is unchanged, even though it has been transposed to another octave, and even though the absolute intervals between successive tones have been modified. They point out that it is extremely common in Western music for successive themes to be similar in contour, but different in interval, and cite examples ranging from "Three Blind Mice" to Bach fugues. In a second experiment, Dowling and Fujitani studied the ability of subjects to recognize familiar tunes under various distortions, and noted that the recognition rate fell from 99 percent to 66 percent correct when the absolute intervals between successive notes were varied, even though contour was maintained. This suggests that subjects do retain information about absolute interval as well as contour in long-term musical memory. A similar conclusion was reached by White (1960), who also had his subjects recognize familiar tunes, such as "Auld Lang Syne," under varying distortions. White's subjects were correct 94 percent of the time when the tune was unmodified; this dropped to about 80 percent when the overall pitch was changed, and to about 50 percent when the contour was maintained but the intervals between successive notes were transformed in a nonlinear way, suggesting that pitch, contour, and absolute interval are all represented in the long-term trace of familiar tunes. It is clear that research on the role of memory in music has hardly yet begun. It seems likely that "semantic" factors, based on the subject's familiarity with the relevant musical conventions, will be important. Someone with an interest primarily in rock music is less likely to remember the theme of an unfamiliar eighteenth-century fugue than a Bach enthusiast, and both would be likely to have difficulty in remembering a piece of Arabic music. How close a parallel can be drawn between the role of such factors in music and that of semantic factors in verbal memory, however, remains to be seen.

To summarize: there appears to be adequate evidence of auditory memory functioning at a series of levels, ranging from the micro-memory systems involved in perception up to those involved in recognizing the voice of a friend one has not encountered for many years. Although our knowledge of auditory memory is still very patchy, however, it is considerably better than our knowledge about the memory systems for kinesthesia, touch, and smell, which we shall be discussing in the rest of this chapter.

Motor Memory

The most striking characteristic of motor memory is its apparent durability. Having once learned to ride a bicycle, swim, or skate, one never seems to forget. If this is indeed the case, it makes no sense to discuss either short- or long-term forgetting, since neither presumably occurs.

In answering the question of whether motor forgetting ever occurs, we must first make a distinction between *continuous skills* and *discrete skills*. Continuous skills involve continuous responses to a varying stimulus; the tracking activity involved in steering a car or flying a plane is typical of this type of skill, as is the skill of balancing on a moving bicycle. Discrete skills involve specific responses to specific stimuli; typing and manually changing gear on a car are examples of discrete motor skills.

RETENTION OF CONTINUOUS SKILLS

As everyday observation suggests, continuous tasks are remarkably resistant to forgetting. Bilodeau and Bilodeau (1961) reviewed a range of continuous tracking studies, none of which showed substantial forgetting. The classic experiment in this area is probably that of Fleishman and Parker (1962), who studied the learning and retention of a very difficult three-dimensional tracking skill, somewhat analogous to that of flying a plane on the attack phase of a radar intercept mission. Figure 10–8 shows the learning of the task, which involved 357 separate 1-minute trials spread over a 6-week period, together with its retention after 9, 14, or 24 months. It is clear that even after 2 years very little forgetting occurs. Such forgetting as does occur is largely limited to the first recall trial. Hammerton (1963) has confirmed this latter observation and has shown that the small decrement on the first recall trial is reduced even further when the skill is overlearned.

In general, then, the retention of continuous motor skills is remarkably high, with forgetting being largely confined to the first test trial after the delay.

RETENTION OF DISCRETE SKILLS

In the case of discrete skills, such as typing, forgetting clearly does occur, as Figure 2–5 (p. 28) showed. Comparable forgetting curves have been obtained by Neumann and Ammons (1957), and by Ammons,

255

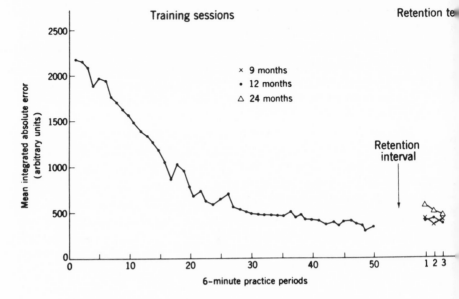

Figure 10–8   Retention of a well-learned tracking skill. The difficult three-dimensional compensatory tracking task, analogous to the skill of flying an airplane, is well retained even after the longest interval of 24 months. This is characteristic of continuous motor skills. Source: E. A. Fleishman and R. F. Parker, Jr., Factors in the retention and relearning of perceptual motor skill, *Journal of Experimental Psychology* 64 (1962): 218. Copyright 1962 by the American Psychological Association. Reprinted by permission.

Farr, Bloch, Neumann, Dey, Marion, and Ammons (1958), to name but a few. In discussing the discrepancy between retention of continuous and discrete motor skills, Adams (1967, p. 237) suggests that it may be the subjects' tendency to use verbal mediators in discrete tasks which leads to their vulnerability to forgetting. As he points out, however, the attempt by Trumbo, Ulrich, and Noble (1965) to test this hypothesis produced negative results. Subsequent work on short-term motor memory (described below) makes a purely verbal interpretation of motor forgetting even less plausible.

SHORT-TERM MOTOR MEMORY

In his book *The New Psychology,* Scripture (1905) described an experiment on the memory of arm movements in which the subject, with

256

eyes closed, runs his finger along the top edge of a horizontal meter rule until it meets a stop. The stop is then removed, and after a delay of 0, 10, or 20 seconds he tries to repeat the movement as exactly as possible. Scripture observed a systematic decrease in accuracy over time, which he attributed to the progressive deterioration of the memory trace.

Some 60 years later, Adams and Dijkstra (1966) confirmed this finding in a much more extensive study using a virtually identical technique. They further examined the effect of repeating the learning trial, and they found that this both increased the accuracy of immediate recall and reduced the rate of forgetting (see Figure 10–9), a result not unlike that found by Hellyer (1962) for verbal memory. Here, however, the similarity with verbal STM ends. Keppel and Underwood (1962) showed that forgetting in the analogous verbal STM task depends crucially on interference from prior items, with the first item to be tested showing very little forgetting. In the case of motor STM, how-

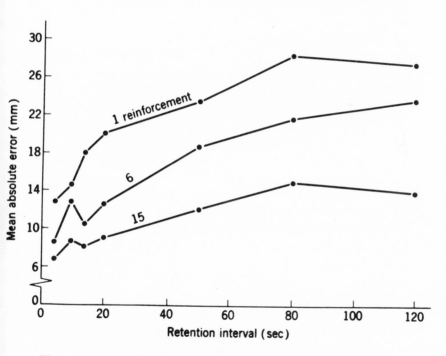

Figure 10–9   Short-term retention of a simple linear motor response as a function of time and number of reinforced repetitions of the response. Source: J. A. Adams and S. Dijkstra, Short-term memory for motor responses, *Journal of Experimental Psychology* 71 (1966): 317. Copyright 1966 by the American Psychological Association.

257

ever, Montague and Hillix (1968) found no evidence of PI. Posner (1967) directly compared the retention of kinesthetic information from the angular movement of a hidden lever with the retention of the equivalent movement when visually guided. He found that kinesthetic STM showed spontaneous forgetting that was little affected by interpolated activity; this contrasted with forgetting in visual STM, which occurred only when the retention interval was filled by a digit-classification task.

Is motor STM therefore completely insensitive to activity during the retention interval? Williams, Beaver, Spence, and Rundell (1969) explored this question further, again using a lever-positioning response. They compared the retention of digits with motor STM and, like Posner and Rossman (1965), found a clear decrease in verbal retention as the interpolated task became more demanding; like Posner (1967), they found no such effect on motor STM, despite the fact that the intervening task involved the motor act of writing. However, when the subject was required to manipulate the lever during the interval, motor retention *was* impaired. Kantowitz (1972) studied this phenomenon using the horizontal arm movement technique pioneered by Scripture. He too found that interpolated motor activity impaired retention over a 20-second interval, but he was unable to find any effect of either the difficulty of the interpolated motor task or of its similarity to the movement to be recalled. However, before concluding firmly that these factors do not affect motor STM, it would be wise to repeat this study using the lever-positioning technique, which is probably somewhat less variable than the horizontal task.*

There appears, therefore, to be general agreement that motor STM may be impaired by interpolated motor activity. Whether such activity *necessarily* impairs retention is less certain, since Williams et al. (1969) found no effect from an information-processing task which involved the motor activity of writing.

The simple generalization that motor STM is unaffected by interpolated information processing which is not motor in nature has also been questioned by recent results. Using the lever-positioning task, Posner and Keele (1969) and Stelmach and Wilson (1970) have observed that digit processing does impair the retention of short movements (e.g., 25–35°), whereas long movements (115–125°) are unaffected. An even greater divergence from earlier findings was reported by Keele

---

* It is perhaps worth noting in this connection that Adams and Dijkstra's forgetting curve (Figure 10–9) is based on 105 subjects, a previous study based on 42 subjects having given a very "noisy" curve. Using lever positioning, Posner and Konick (1966) obtained a reasonably smooth curve from 12 subjects.

and Ells (1972), who suggested that the discrepant results for long and short movements might reflect their reliance on different cues. Subjects were asked to reproduce a rotary movement after 0 seconds or 7 seconds, during which they either rested or classified digits as odd or even and high or low. The movement was either active, in which case the subject moved the lever, or passive, in which case he gripped the lever while the experimenter moved it. Normal cues were disrupted in two ways. First, on half the active trials a pulley system ensured that the resistance of the lever varied during the movement, whereas on recall it was always constant. Second, in half the cases the recall movement started in the same place as the original movement, so that the subject could rely on remembering either the extent of the movement or the location of the endpoint; on the rest of the trials, however, the starting point on the recall trial varied, so that in order to respond correctly the subject had to remember the extent of the movement, not just the location of the endpoint of the initial movement. The results resemble those of visual memory studies more than earlier motor memory studies in showing virtually no forgetting when the delay was unfilled, together with a substantial decrement for all lengths of movement when the interval was filled with the digit-processing task. This pattern was substantially the same, regardless of whether the tension of the lever and the starting point at recall were constant or varied. Before discussing this result, we shall describe a further series of discrepant results obtained with a somewhat dissimilar technique.

Pepper and Herman (1970) and Herman and Bailey (1970) required their subjects to push or pull a static knob with a predetermined degree of force and then reproduce that force after a delay. The force exerted was displayed as a movable trace on the face of an oscilloscope, which provided visual feedback during the acquisition response but was not visible during recall. Using this procedure, Pepper and Herman tested the retention of a force over unfilled intervals of 4, 8, 12, 30, and 60 seconds and found no evidence of forgetting, a result completely at odds with those of most earlier studies. A second experiment produced an even more unexpected result: performance was found to improve over the 30-second interval studied. This study also observed a reliable decrement in performance when the retention interval contained a counting task. Yet another surprising result appeared when several repetitions were given of the force to be remembered. In contrast to Adams and Dijkstra's observation that additional trials enhance recall, Pepper and Herman found an impairment when the number of repetitions was increased. Pepper and Herman point out that their subjects tend to overshoot, whereas earlier studies typically report errors of undershooting. As might be expected from adaptation-level theory (Helson 1964), interpolating a larger force tends to exaggerate this tendency, whereas a smaller interpolated force tends to minimize it, with the effect being greater as the interpolated force is presented closer to recall (Herman and Bailey 1970).

Pepper and Herman explain their results in terms of a model involving a spontaneously decaying motor trace which may be influenced by the subsequent level of muscle tension. Such interference is seen most clearly in the adaptation-level effects just described, but it may also occur when a secondary task like counting causes an incidental change in muscle tension. There would probably be considerable agreement on the existence of a motor memory trace which, since it is not easily rehearsed, tends to decay spontaneously even during an unfilled delay. There is also good evidence for adaptation-level effects, not only from Herman and Bailey's study but also from a study on recalling a horizontal arm movement (Craft and Hinrichs 1971). Thus, it is probably necessary to assume the two components proposed by Pepper and Herman; whether they will prove sufficient to explain the very complex pattern of results in this area is much less certain. However, Pepper and Herman's suggested model does seem readily testable, particularly if a task is selected in which both spontaneous undershooting and overshooting conditions occur.

Nevertheless, an alternative explanation of the discrepancies observed might be suggested. All of those situations in which a nonmotor mental load left retention unimpaired allowed the subject to use the distance moved as a major cue. Situations in which mental load did impair retention tended either to eliminate movement (as with Pepper and Herman's and Herman and Bailey's use of a knob fixed to a strain gauge) or to make movement an irrelevant cue (as with the Keele and Ells study). It is conceivable that in these situations the subject attempts to rely on visuo-spatial imagery; * if this is the case, then it is perhaps not surprising that these results resemble those of visual STM in showing disruption by interpolated mental activity. This point could be tested relatively easily by comparing the effects of interpolated visual and motor activity during the retention interval.

In conclusion, although there is clear evidence of short-term forgetting, attempts to explore the short-term motor memory system in greater

* Note that the Herman studies used a visual cue during acquisition.

detail have proved disappointing. It is, however, generally true that for-getting occurs without interpolated activity and is frequently unaffected by interpolated mental activity. Both these results suggest that covert rehearsal is not a major factor, at least in the simple task of remember-ing the extent of a movement.

LONG-TERM MOTOR MEMORY

As we noted earlier, there appears to be good evidence for the forgetting of discrete motor skills, such as typing, but little evidence of forgetting of continuous skills. Why should this be?

Unfortunately, we know virtually nothing about the principles under-lying either of these phenomena. One can speculate, of course. An inter-ference theorist might wish to argue that a continuous skill comprises a chain of S–R connections which occur together only when that skill is being performed. Since the relevant sequence of stimuli does not occur at any time other than when the skill is being practiced, it does not be-come associated with any conflicting alternative responses and is thus free from interference. Discrete skills, on the other hand, comprise stimuli and responses that are not linked into a continuous isolated se-quence but may be used in different combinations for other purposes at other times. For example, the auditory stimulus of a letter A may evoke quite different responses in a subject, depending on whether he is typing or writing, and a similar keying response may be used in both typing and using an adding machine.

However, the few attempts to apply the concepts of interference theory to the long-term retention of motor skills have so far proved dis-couraging. Lewis (1947) succeeded in demonstrating RI effects in a perceptual motor task requiring a control movement in response to a light. Interpolated learning, in which an antagonistic response was re-quired to the same stimulus light, did impair retention of the initial re-sponse, but subsequent attempts to demonstrate the standard inter-ference phenomena found in the verbal-learning laboratory proved unsuccessful. Thus, Lewis, McAllister, and Adams (1951) found that amount of interference *increased* with the degree of original learning, in clear contrast to the verbal memory situation, in which well-learned material is least susceptible to RI. An attempt to study PI in long-term motor memory by Duncan and Underwood (1953) showed no reliable interference effects on the retention of a task involving moving a lever in response to a series of colored lights. In the 20 years since these studies were published, remarkably little attention has been paid to the puzzling problem of long-term motor memory, which despite its obvious practical importance remains relatively unexplored.

Tactile Memory

Bliss, Hewitt, Crane, Mansfield, and Townsend (1966) studied tactile memory using a device which delivered brief pulses of air to the underside of each of a subject's 24 finger joints. They found that subjects typically had a span of four or five stimuli, although one subject who was able to group the stimuli was able to remember seven or eight. Using a delayed sampling technique based on that used by Sperling (1960) for visual memory, Bliss et al. looked for a comparable very short-term tactile memory trace. On the whole, their results were disappointing. There was some evidence for an advantage from the partial-report technique, which the authors interpret as evidence for a tactile trace lasting for about 0.8 second, but effects of delay tended to be too small and variable to allow any firm conclusions.

Evidence for tactile STM with a somewhat longer duration comes from a study by Gilson and Baddeley (1969) using a method based on the Peterson technique. Blindfolded subjects, touched on the underside of their forearms, attempted to point to the location touched after intervals ranging from 0 to 60 seconds, during which they either counted backward or rested. Forgetting occurred over the first 45 seconds in both cases but was more extensive under the counting condition, suggesting that some form of rehearsal was possible but was not sufficient to prevent forgetting. Sullivan and Turvey (1972) obtained somewhat similar results and also noted that no build-up of PI was found with this task. In this respect, tactile memory differs from the equivalent verbal task (Keppel and Underwood 1962) and resembles kinesthetic (Montague and Hillix 1968) and visual STM (Warrington and Baddeley 1974).

A little work has also been done on tactile LTM. Hill (1974) has studied the recognition of letters presented by touch. Milner and Taylor (1972) have used a tactile memory task in studying patients in whom the commissure linking the two cerebral hemispheres has been cut to control major epileptic seizures. Patients were required to match irregular wire patterns either immediately or after delays of up to 2 minutes.

When the task was performed by the left hand (and hence the right cerebral hemisphere), most patients could do the task even after a considerable delay, whereas they were unable to perform even the immediate task with the right hand, suggesting that the task depends heavily on the predominantly spatial right hemisphere. In a similar vein, Hermelin and O'Connor (1971) have noted that blind subjects appear to be more efficient at reading Braille with the left hand (and hence the right hemisphere) than with the right hand. It seems likely, however, that both these tasks may have a much greater spatial or haptic component than the tactile STM tasks described earlier, in which the subject's role in perception is much more passive and static.

Olfactory Memory

It is commonly believed that smells, like skills, are never forgotten. Smells also appear to be extremely good retrieval cues for apparently forgotten events; in Victor Hugo's words, "Nothing awakens a reminiscence like an odor." However, although this characteristic feature of smells has continued to intrigue novelists over the years, it had not been studied scientifically until two recent papers by Engen.

The first of these (Engen, Kuisma, and Eimas 1973) studied STM for odors. Subjects smelled a cotton swab impregnated with one of a set of 100 different smells and, after an interval ranging from 3 to 30 seconds, judged whether a second swab had the same or a different smell. Performance was well above chance and showed no tendency to decline over the 30-second interval. A second group of subjects attempted to remember five different odors before being given a sixth swab, which they were required to judge as the same or different from any of the five odors presented. Level of performance was slightly lower, but there was still no evidence of forgetting over the 30-second delay.

In a subsequent study, Engen and Ross (1973) investigated LTM for odors. Their first experiment involved presenting the subject with 48 different odors. Retention was tested by presenting 21 pairs of smells, each comprising one of the 48 "old" smells and one "new" smell. Subjects correctly recognized an average of 67 percent of the smells and showed no evidence of forgetting over the 30-day retention period studied. A second study showed a somewhat higher detection rate when subjects had a smaller set of smells to "learn," with 77 percent correct retention of 20 smells versus 67 percent retention of 48 smells. When each "old" smell was paired with a similar "new" distractor (e.g., onion with garlic), performance fell from 77 to 64 percent correct but was still well above chance. Subjects tended to give higher preference ratings to familiar smells but were no better at recognizing them, suggesting that verbal labeling was not a major factor in these studies.

To summarize: although the level of immediate recognition of smells is considerably poorer than for equivalent visual or auditory tasks, there is no evidence of forgetting, at least over a 3-month interval. There is no suggestion of a dichotomy between STM and LTM, and there is probably nothing equivalent to rehearsal.

CHAPTER

11

Organization and Retrieval
from Long-Term Memory

T HE LAST TWO CHAPTERS have been concerned with modality-specific memory and have explored the retention of material by the various sensory and perceptual systems. In everyday life, however, pure and isolated modality-specific memory is the exception rather than the rule, at least in the case of long-term memory. When I recall a dinner I attended last night, for example, my memory is not purely visual or auditory or olfactory; rather, it is an amalgam of all these, together with a strong semantic overlay. Indeed, if I wished to recall it in a year's time, I suspect that much the most efficient cue would be a semantic cue, such as the name of the colloquium speaker who was being entertained at the dinner. Our knowledge of the world is derived from all our sense modalities; we hear about visual events and read about auditory events, and we organize all this information in ways which typically make the original sensory modality a relatively unimportant feature of our subsequent recall. Much more important is the way in which the information is organized and the implications of this for subsequent retrieval.

The remaining chapters of the book will be concerned with this problem. We shall begin in the present chapter with the early work of the

Gestalt psychologists, who were the first group to attempt a systematic study of organization in memory. Their approach stems from a primary interest in perception and reflects an attempt to generalize the organizational principles they observed in the realm of perception to the problem of human memory. The next section will go beyond the perceptual analogy to study the evidence for semantic organization in verbal memory; this will be followed by a discussion of why organization should enhance memory, which in turn will lead to a consideration of theories of retrieval.

Gestalt Psychology and the Perceptual Analogy

Until the 1940s the main opposition to the S–R associationist view of memory came from Gestalt psychology. Associationism saw conditioning as fundamental to the understanding of behavior and attempted to explain complex behavior as a combination of basic S–R bonds, whereas Gestalt psychology took perception as its model. Gestalt psychologists were particularly impressed by the fact that groups of items tend to be perceived as patterns; the observer appears to use such factors as similarity, proximity, and continuity to organize a cluster of items into a unified whole. Two examples of such organization are shown in Figures 11–1a and 11–1b. Note that in both cases the relationship among the items is just as important as the items themselves, hence the Gestalt slogan that "the whole is greater than the sum of its parts." The Gestalt psychologists claimed that behavior and experience could not be characterized in terms of simple atomic units, since the units interacted to produce an overall pattern.

The most direct influence on memory of the Gestalt view of perception was in the study of memory for form. It was predicted that the trace of a remembered shape would change over time so as to become progressively simpler and more symmetrical—in other words, to become a better gestalt. As mentioned earlier (see Chapter 4), this hypothesis proved amazingly difficult to test and ceased to be a live issue (Riley 1962; Baddeley 1968c).

VON RESTORFF EFFECT

A more fruitful development from the perceptual approach to memory was the demonstration by Von Restorff (1933) that an isolated

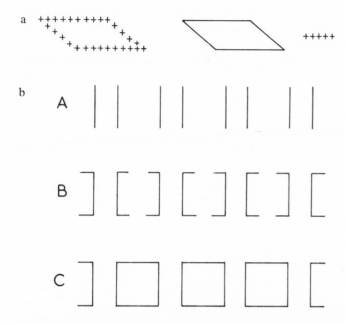

Figures 11–1a and 11–1b   Two illustrations of Gestalt principles in perception. Figure 11–1a illustrates the tenet that "the
whole is greater than the sum of its parts"; a parallelogram made
up *of* crosses is not the same as a parallelogram *and* crosses.
Figure 11–1b shows three determinants of perceptual grouping.
In A, grouping is determined by proximity; in B, continuity
counterbalances the proximity factor and favors grouping of
less proximal lines; and in C, closure eliminates the possibility
of grouping adjacent parts of separate figures. Source: C. E.
Osgood, *Method and Theory in Experimental Psychology* (New
York: Oxford University Press, 1953), p. 213. Copyright 1953
by Oxford University Press, Inc. Reprinted by permission.

item in an otherwise homogeneous list will be better recalled than a
homogeneous item. Thus, a three-digit number will be better learned if
it is presented within a list of nonsense syllables than if it is surrounded
by other numbers. Von Restorff interpreted this in terms of the figure-
ground effect, the tendency for a visual pattern to be perceived as an
isolated form against a background. The isolated number forms a trace
which stands out from the background of syllables and which is thus less
likely to be assimilated into the background. However, although the isolation of an item leads to better learning, there is no evidence for the
slower rate of forgetting predicted by Gestalt theory (Saul and Osgood
1950; Green 1956).

An explanation in terms of reduced interference operating on the dissimilar isolated item has also been suggested. This was tested by New-man and Saltz (1958), who pointed out that the isolated item (1) should be less subject to both stimulus and response generalization, and hence should occur less frequently as an intrusion, and (2) should act as a particularly distinctive and effective stimulus, and hence should im-prove the overall level of learning by reducing the level of intra-list similarity. They tested this by embedding a nonsense "word" (e.g., *neglan*) in a list of high-frequency words to be learned by the serial anticipation method. The isolated item was better recalled than the equivalent word in a homogeneous control list, but contrary to the inter-ference theory predictions, it occurred more frequently as an intrusion and did not lead to better recall of either the following word or the list as a whole.

Green (1956; 1958) proposed an attentional interpretation of the Von Restorff effect, with the crucial factor being the surprise value of the isolated item rather than isolation per se. In his first experiment, Green (1956) demonstrated that when two isolated items are presented, only the first produces a substantial Von Restorff effect. A subsequent experiment (Green 1958) showed that the first novel item following a block of homogeneous items (as in Figure 11–2) is well retained regardless of whether it is isolated or the first item of a block.

SERIAL POSITION	CONTROL GROUP	CHANGE GROUP	ISOLATION GROUP
1	X	X	X
2	0	X	X
3	X	X	X
4	0 ←	0 ←	0 ←
5	X	0	X
6	0	0	X
7	X	0	X
8	0	0	0
9	X	0	0
10	0	X	0
11	X	X	0
12	0	X	0

Figure 11–2   Structure of the lists used by Green (1958) to study the role of change and isolation in the Von Restorff effect. The critical item is the fourth. Items were pairs of con-sonants or digits. Source: R. T. Green, Surprise, isolation and structural change as factors affecting recall of a temporal series, *British Journal of Psychology* 49 (1958): 24. Reprinted by per-mission.

Why should "surprise" lead to better learning? One possibility is that surprise leads to high arousal, which has in turn been shown to lead to better long-term retention (see Chapter 3). An unpublished experiment by Rosemary Drynan at the University of Sussex explored this possibility by recording level of arousal (measured by the galvanic skin response) during a free-recall task in which the crucial item was printed in a different color. There was a significant tendency for the isolated item to produce both a high GSR and better immediate recall, but a contingency test suggested that these two phenomena were not statistically related. In view of Kleinsmith and Kaplan's (1963) observation that high arousal favors *delayed* recall, it would be interesting to repeat this study with a longer delay; however, since the Von Restorff effect did occur and was not associated with level of GSR, arousal can at best offer only a partial explanation.

A second possibility is based on the concept of time-sharing. The subject has a limited amount of learning time, which he must distribute among the items to be recalled. Any item which attracts attention may obtain more than its "fair share" of processing time. This would lead to better retention, but since the total processing time is held constant, it will be at the expense of other items in the list; hence, the absence of an overall improvement in performance, a phenomenon observed by Newman and Saltz (1958) and others. This could be tested by leaving the subject free to control the amount of time he spends viewing each item, the prediction being that the surprise item will be viewed for longer and will be better retained but that, when learning is measured in terms of mean amount learned per unit time, the isolated item will show no better learning than a homogeneous control—in other words, that the total time hypothesis will hold. An alternative strategy would be to use the technique of requiring the subject to rehearse aloud, a technique that allows the experimenter to observe the number of times each item is rehearsed (Rundus and Atkinson 1970). The time-sharing interpretation of the Von Restorff effect would predict that the isolated item will get more than its fair share of rehearsal.

ZEIGARNIK EFFECT

A second influence of Gestalt psychology on memory comes from Kurt Lewin's attempt to apply Gestalt principles to the study of motivation. One of Lewin's students, Zeigarnik (1927), studied the effect of interrupting a task on its subsequent recall. Her subjects performed a range of 22 tasks, such as threading beads, learning a poem, and drawing a vase. She allowed subjects to complete half the tasks but prevented them from finishing the remainder, forcibly if necessary. When subsequently asked to list the tasks, Zeigarnik's subjects consistently recalled more interrupted tasks. It might be thought that the occasionally somewhat forceful manner of interruption made the tasks more memorable. Such an explanation would not, however, explain the occurrence of a Zeigarnik effect in the recall of anagram solutions (Baddeley 1963b), in which interruption simply involved telling the subject the solution to the anagram. Zeigarnik's explanation of the effect is that the interruption leads to an "unresolved tension" which tends to maintain the memory trace of the task in question. Consistent with this view is Ovsiankina's (1928) demonstration that the effect disappears if subjects are subsequently allowed to complete the unfinished tasks, hence presumably dissipating their "unresolved tensions."

Unfortunately, more recent work in this area has produced conflicting results, often failing to find a Zeigarnik effect. After a very detailed review of the literature and an extensive program of experiments, Van Bergen reached the conclusion that "the problem of the selective recall of uncompleted and completed tasks must be regarded as one of these 'questions which seem to lead nowhere' " (Van Bergen 1968, p. 267).

INSIGHT AND MEMORY

The third area in which Gestalt theory impinged on memory was in its attempt to apply perceptual principles to the study of problem solving and learning. Unlike the associationists, who stressed the quasi-random accumulation of S–R habits by trial and error, the Gestalt psychologists were concerned with *insightful* learning, in which the subject perceptually reorganizes the situation and quite suddenly "sees" the solution.

In the area of animal learning the controversy focused on whether insightful learning occurs. In concrete terms, the point at issue was whether rats learning a discrimination would learn gradually or would react consistently first to one cue, then another, until they hit the right "hypothesis," at which point their performance should suddenly change from a chance level to consistent correctness.

In the area of human behavior, the issue was concerned less with the occurrence of insightful behavior than with the claim that insightful learning led to better organized and hence more durable traces. A good many illustrations of this view were given in Katona's book *Organizing and Remembering,* published in 1940 and subsequently largely neglected. A typical experiment involved presenting subjects with the following set of numbers:

$$2\ 9\ 3\ 3\ 3\ 6\ 4\ 0\ 4\ 3\ 4\ 7$$

$$5\ 8\ 1\ 2\ 1\ 5\ 1\ 9\ 2\ 2\ 2\ 6$$

One group of subjects was allowed 3 minutes to memorize the set, while a second group spent 3 minutes attempting to discover an organizing principle within the sequence. Recall of the sequence was tested both immediately and after 3 weeks. On immediate test there was no difference between the groups, with 33 percent of the memorizers and 38 percent of the principle-seeking group recalling it perfectly. After 3 weeks, however, there was a very marked difference, with 23 percent of the principle-seekers still recalling perfectly, while none of the memorizers was successful. What is the principle? It involves starting at the beginning of the bottom row with digit 5 and successively adding 3 and 4 (i.e., *5 + 3 = 8 + 4 = 12 + 3 = 15,* etc.). Concerned with practical problems of education, Katona argued strongly that learning should be regarded as a process of discovery rather than the slow accumulation of associative bonds by rote learning. Nevertheless, he was swimming against the tide of the times, and his work appears to have had little influence on the subsequent study of memory.

In recent years, however, there has been a revival of interest in the more complex and cognitive aspects of memory. A good example of this is de Groot's (1965; 1966) studies of chess players. To the nonexpert, one of the most amazing features of a chess master is his ability to play several games of chess simultaneously while blindfolded, implying accurate memory of several complex and continually changing patterns of pieces. In his analysis of the characteristics of a chess master, de Groot (1965) claims that the great superiority of the master lies in his perceptual ability rather than his memory. At the level of master play, chess is a comparatively stereotyped game, since the range of defensively sound positions at any point is relatively limited. The master player apparently perceives the position as a relatively few major configurations, not as an array of 20 or 30 individual chess pieces; according to de Groot, it is this ability to reorganize the board perceptually that allows the chess master's apparently phenomenal memory.

De Groot (1966) studied this directly, using chess positions taken from games between chess masters. The positions were presented for successive 5-second periods. After each exposure, the subjects—five masters and five weak players—attempted to reproduce the position on a chessboard; correct pieces were left in place and incorrect pieces re-moved before the next exposure. The results are shown in Figure 11–3. It can be seen that after a single 5-second exposure, the masters were able to place over 90 percent of the pieces correctly, compared with about 40 percent for weak players, who took 5 trials to reach the initial level of the masters. One interpretation of this result is that the masters found the positions more predictable because of their greater familiarity with master play; hence, they could make up defects in their recall by intelligent guesswork. This was tested by omitting the

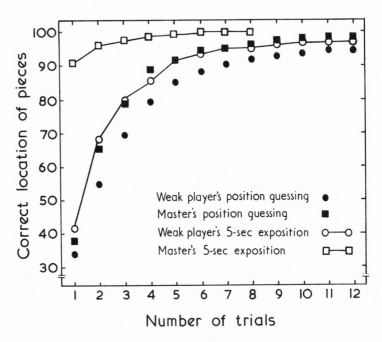

Figure 11–3   Cumulative percentage of correctly located chess pieces for master players and weak players. Note that the master players are almost entirely correct after a single 5-second presentation, while the weak players perform only slightly better than when required to guess the position of the pieces with feed-back but no visual exposure. Source: From *Thought and Choice in Chess*, by Adriaan D. de Groot (New York: Basic Books, 1965). © Mouton & Company, 1965, Basic Books, Inc., Pub-lishers.

exposure to the board, thus forcing subjects to reconstruct the position entirely on the basis of guesswork. As Figure 11–3 shows, the weak players were virtually as good at guessing as the masters; indeed, the weak players appear to be able to perform practically as well by sheer guessing as when they are actually shown the position. This result supports the subjects' introspective reports in suggesting that the superior retention shown by the masters was based on their greater ability to perceive the position as an organized whole.

Semantic Organization and Memory

Despite the publication of Katona's *Organizing and Remembering* in 1940, for the next 20 years the role of organization in memory was almost completely ignored. The field was dominated by associationism, which aimed to study human learning and memory in the simplest, most constrained laboratory setting. During this period the tendency of subjects to impose organization on the material to be learned was generally regarded as a source of unwanted variability, to be eliminated by using nonsense material presented at a rapid rate. Since the subject was usually required to pronounce each item as it appeared, he was generally kept so busy with individual items that he had little opportunity to organize the list as a whole. Despite this degree of constraint (or probably because of it!), it continued to prove difficult to obtain consistent results. Anyone who has worked with nonsense syllables will know that, despite the effort put into scaling their association value, familiarity, pronounceability, and so forth, the correlation between these measures and the learning of *individual* syllables is low (see Chapter 2), although the relationship can be made to appear impressively high by basing each point in the correlation on a large sample of syllables (e.g. Noble, Stockwell, and Pryer 1957). The probable reason for this lack of consistency is that subjects will use any strategy they can devise to give meaning to an item or pair. Most of the attempts to predict ease of learning assume only one such basis, be it mediating associations, ease of pronunciation, familiarity, or similarity to English. Given a flexible and ingenious subject, it is hardly surprising that no measure based on a single coding dimension has proved to be an accurate or reliable predictor of learning. Indeed, the best way of predicting the difficulty of a nonsense syllable pair is still to ask subjects (Prytulak 1971), presumably because subjects can base their judgments on the whole range of possible coding strategies, whereas most measures are limited to one coding dimension.

Since the mid 1960s, there has been a tremendous resurgence of interest in the role of organization in human memory. The change in intellectual climate probably began first with the reaction against nonsense syllable material in favor of words, and it was accelerated by the growth of interest in free recall. Since this technique allows subjects to recall the words presented in any order they wish, there is much more scope for organization than in the more traditional serial and paired-associate techniques, in which the experimenter attempts to exert maximal control over the subject's behavior.

In discussing the modern work on organization and memory, we shall begin by examining three sources of evidence for the importance of organization before going on to discuss some of the theoretical issues involved. The evidence suggests (1) that organized material is easy to learn, (2) that subjects will impose their own organization on random material, and (3) that the requirement to organize the material leads to good retention, even when the subject has not been told to learn it.

ORGANIZATION WITHIN THE STIMULUS MATERIAL

One exception to the lack of interest in organization in the 1950s is the work stemming from information theory. As early as 1950, Miller and Selfridge had shown that the more closely a string of words approaches the statistical structure of English, the more easily it will be learned. However, although information theory was applied to both traditional verbal-learning tasks (Baddeley 1964) and to free recall (Garner 1962), its influence was largely on short-term memory, and it is therefore discussed in that context (see Chapter 7).

In the more orthodox areas of verbal learning, the first studies of organizational factors in free recall were very much in the associationist tradition. It had been known for many years that if a subject is given a word and asked to produce the first word he thinks of, certain responses are much more frequent than others; for example, *knife* tends to evoke *fork, black-white, man-woman,* and so forth. Jenkins and Russell (1952) studied the free recall of a list of 48 words comprising 24 such pairs and found that highly associated words tended to be recalled together, despite the fact that the words had been presented in random order. In a subsequent study, Jenkins, Mink, and Russell (1958) systematically varied the strength of association between the word pairs by selecting the second word of each pair on the basis of the frequency with which it occurred as a free association to the first word. A different degree of associative strength was selected for each of four lists of

12 pairs. Their results showed that the higher the degree of association between the word pairs, the greater the probability of recall.

Deese (1959) extended this technique beyond the study of pairs of words by using lists of 15 words which were either all high-frequency, all low-frequency, or all zero-frequency associates of the same stimulus word. One such list used associates to the word *butterfly*: on the high associative frequency list were *moth, insect, wing, bird, fly, yellow, net, pretty, flower, bug, cocoon, color, stomach, blue, bees*; on the zero-frequency list were *book, tutor, government, study, early, velvet, winter, payroll, line, zebra, spray, arrow, help, arithmetic, typical*. Each of 18 lists was presented together with a list "name," which was either the original stimulus word (e.g., *butterfly*) or an irrelevant word (e.g., *deliberate*). As predicted, recall of high associative frequency lists (7.35 words correct) was higher than for low-frequency lists (6.08 words) or for zero-frequency lists (5.50 words). However, Deese observed that high-frequency lists were not only probable associates of the original stimulus word but also tended to be associatively related to each other; and when the average degree of inter-item associative strength was computed for each of the 18 lists, it was found to be highly correlated ($r = .88$) with number of words recalled. It was also related to erroneous responses; highly related lists produced fewer intrusions from outside the list ($r = .55$). Somewhat surprisingly, giving subjects the initial stimulus words as the list name led to slightly, though not significantly, poorer retention.

The effects shown by Deese could, of course, be due to either of two related variables: (1) the fact that the words in the list are direct associates of each other, or (2) the fact that they are related by sharing a common associate (e.g., *butterfly*). The first of these was further explored by Rothkopf and Coke (1961), who required the free recall of a list of 99 words which varied in the extent to which they were associatively interrelated. Although the list as a whole had no overall associative structure, the probability of recalling an individual word was a function of the number of other words in the list known to elicit it as associate. This reinforces the conclusion of Jenkins and Russell (1952) that inter-item associations will enhance recall.

The second factor, organization based on a shared common associate, has been studied most extensively with lists of items taken from the same taxonomic category. Bousfield (1953) studied the recall of a 60-item list comprising 15 animals, 15 names, 15 professions, and 15 vegetables, presented in scrambled order. Despite the random order of input, Bousfield's subjects tended to recall items in clusters; having recalled one animal, a subject was more likely next to recall another animal than to recall an item from another category, an effect which tends to increase during learning (Cohen 1963).

Categorization not only increases recall but also produces clustering, the effect being greater for exhaustive categories from which all possible instances are included—for example, *North, South, East, West*—than for nonexhaustive categories—for example, *lion, zebra, horse, camel* (Cohen 1966). Recall is also better for high-frequency associates to the category name (e.g., *lion, zebra, horse, camel*) than for items low in the associative norms (e.g., *elk, anteater, puma, lynx*) and when items from within a category are presented in blocks rather than in scrambled order (Cofer, Bruce, and Reicher 1966). Both exhaustive categories and high-frequency associates are likely to have strong inter-item associations, and the question arises as to whether the effect of category clustering can be explained entirely in terms of associations between items within the category.

Is categorization simply a convenient way of manipulating the associations between words, which Deese (1959) has shown to be important in free recall, or is it a separate phenomenon? Cofer (1966) discusses this and concludes that in the original studies of Bousfield and the later studies by Cohen, inter-item associations probably do account for most of the observed effect. However, he also discusses a study by one of his students, Marshall (1967), who explicitly investigated this question by comparing the free recall of categorized pairs of items (e.g., *wool-silk*) with noncategorized pairs of equal associative strength (e.g., *whistle-train*). Marshall found a reliably greater degree of clustering with categorized pairs. The effect on recall scores, however, is not discussed, apart from Cofer's statement that "word recall is somewhat better, also, for the categorized than the non-categorized items" (Cofer 1966, p. 191). Fortunately, Marshall does report mean recall scores, and it is possible to extract 11 independent groups in which categorized and noncategorized pairs were matched for associative strength. There is an overall difference in favor of categorized pairs (8.58 pairs out of 12, compared with 8.05), which holds for 9 of the 11 comparisons. When a Wilcoxon test is used, the difference proves to be highly significant ($T = 4$, $N = 11$, $p < .01$). The size of the effect (.53 pairs) is half that found between the highest and lowest degree of association studied by Marshall (1.06 pairs). It seems likely, then, that categorization does have an effect on both recall and clustering which is not attributable to direct associations among the words within the category.

We have so far shown that subjects are able to take advantage of organization provided by the experimenter and that this is reflected in both retention scores and clustering of responses during recall. The data presented do not, however, necessarily imply active organization by the subject and are quite consistent with an associationist view of memory. A passive associationist theory would have much more difficulty in accounting for the evidence discussed in the next section, which shows that subjects impose their own organization when presented with randomly selected lists of words.

SUBJECTIVE ORGANIZATION OF RANDOM MATERIAL

The tendency of subjects to cluster related responses at recall provides a useful index of subjective organization, but one which unfortunately requires (1) using material with preselected categories and (2) assuming that the subject is basing his organization on the categories selected by the experimenter.

Tulving (1962) proposed an alternative measure of subjective organization that does not depend on the experimenter's prior assumptions about the basis of organization and which is therefore applicable to multitrial free recall of noncategorized lists. He noticed that subjects learning lists of unrelated words tend to recall groups of words in the same order on repeated trials, and he derived from information theory a simple measure of consistency of output order. Tulving's measure of subjective organization (SO) essentially counts the frequency with which any two recalled items are reproduced as a pair in the same order on successive recall trials, expressing this as a proportion of the number of such repetitions expected by chance. This measure certainly underestimates the degree of organization, since it considers only pairs of words occurring in the same order, whereas words could still be regarded as part of the same subjective unit if they tended to be recalled together, even if the recall order within such a cluster varied from trial to trial. Nevertheless, SO appears to give broadly the same results as later and more complex measures.

The application of Tulving's measure is illustrated in Figure 11–4, which shows the results of an experiment in which subjects learned a list of 16 unrelated nouns, presented in a different order on each of 16 trials. Subjective organization is correlated with degree of learning; it appears to make little difference whether SO is estimated on blocks of two or three trials, and the lack of a substantial increase in SO for the "statistical subject" shows that the observed increase is not simply an inevitable result of the increase in number of items recalled over trials. Further

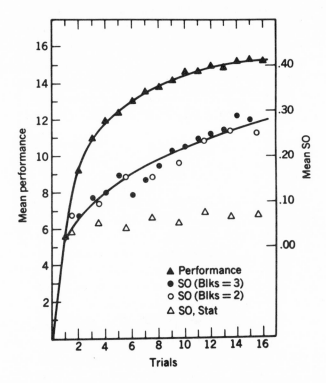

Figure 11-4   Free-recall learning performance and subjective organization as a function of trials. The upper curve represents the mean number of words correctly recalled; the middle curve represents the degree of subjective organization; and the un-filled triangles show the levels of subjective organization which would be expected by-chance, given that level of recall. Source: E. Tulving, Subjective organization in free recall of "unrelated" words, *Psychological Review* 69 (1962): 349. Copyright 1962 by the American Psychological Association. Reprinted by permission.

evidence for the relationship between SO and learning is provided by Earhard (1967), who found that fast learners show a higher degree of SO than slow learners. However, although there is typically a high correlation between SO and learning, this is not invariably the case (Carterette and Coleman 1963; Laurence 1966; Puff 1970).

Tulving (1966) contends that subjective organization is necessary for free-recall learning, and is not simply an incidental consequence of learning, as Carterette and Coleman (1963) have suggested. He reports

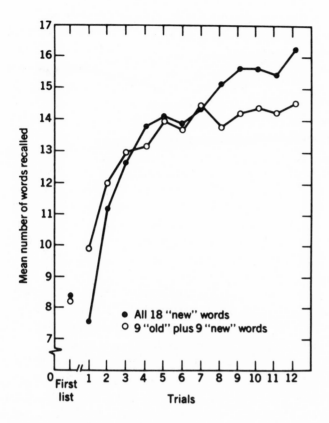

Figure 11–5 Rate of learning a list of 18 words for subjects who have previously learned either 9 of the 18 words (open circles) or 9 unrelated words (filled circles). Source: E. Tulving, Subjective organization and effects of repetition in multi-trial free-recall learning, *Journal of Verbal Learning and Verbal Behavior* 5 (1966): 197. Reprinted by permission.

two experiments which support his view. The first of these studied the recall of a list of 22 high-frequency nouns. Before learning the list, subjects were required to read through 22 pairs of items six times. One group read 22 names, each paired with a letter; for the other group, the 22 letters were paired with the 22 nouns that were to be learned. Subjects who had read the relevant nouns through six times learned no faster than subjects who read the irrelevant names, indicating that mere repetition does not assist the recall of high-frequency nouns.* In a sec-

---

* As Mechanic (1964) has shown, this is not the case for items, such as nonsense syllables, with which the subject is not already familiar.

ond experiment, subjects first learned a list of 9 words; they then went on to learn an 18-word list comprising either 9 old words and 9 new ones or else 18 new words. The results are shown in Figure 11–5. Although subjects who had previously learned half the list began learning at a higher level, their subsequent rate of learning and final level of performance were inferior to the control group, which learned an entirely new set of words. Tulving suggests that prior learning of part of the list led to poorer subsequent performance because the subjective units that were appropriate for learning the first list were carried over to the learning of the second list, for which they were no longer optimal. Novinski (1969) has repeated Tulving's findings and has shown a similar negative transfer effect when the procedure is reversed and learning of a whole list is followed by learning of part of the list. In this situation, the subjective units are presumably too extensive, making it difficult for subjects to differentiate between items which must still be recalled and those which appeared only on the first list.

Tulving's striking and counterintuitive results appeared to provide impressive evidence of the importance of subjective organization in free-recall learning. However, as Postman (1972) has pointed out, this evidence is indirect, and other interpretations are possible. For example, Roberts (1969) has shown in the part-to-whole transfer situation that subjects tend to devote a disproportionate amount of time to new items in learning the composite whole list, a strategy which might be expected to interfere with retention of the old items. Evidence in favor of such an interpretation comes from Novinski's (1969) observation that old items show the greatest impairment in such part-to-whole transfer experiments. Furthermore, Wood and Clark (1969) observed a much less dramatic part-to-whole negative transfer effect when subjects were informed of the nature of the two lists, while Slamecka, Moore, and Carey (1972) found that the negative transfer effect was replaced by positive transfer when subjects were urged to adopt a low criterion for emitting responses. This suggests that the negative transfer effect occurs because the subject recalls words, recognizes that they were in the first list, and assumes that they are therefore intrusions rather than correctly recalled items. The part-to-whole transfer effect is therefore not the unequivocal demonstration of organization that it first appeared to be. For this reason, it is necessary to look for more direct evidence of the importance of subjective organization in learning. The next section considers experiments in which the subject is induced to organize material in a particular way, and the effect of this organization on subsequent recall is then studied.

INSTRUCTIONS TO ORGANIZE

Mandler (1970) distinguishes three types of organization: seriation (organization on the basis of serial order), categorization, and relational imagery. While such a classification clearly oversimplifies the situation, it provides a useful framework within which to discuss organization.

Seriation. The value of sequential organization in memory has been appreciated since classical times, when it was combined with relational imagery and used by the early Greeks as the basis of mnemonic systems (Yates 1966). We clearly use seriation in remembering material like the names of the months of the year or the letters of the alphabet, and when we wish to recall the entire set, we generally do so serially. Earhard (1967) has shown that free-recall learning may be assisted if the relevant words can be ordered alphabetically on the basis of initial letter. Furthermore, Mandler and Dean (1969) have shown that subjects show a marked tendency to recall items in the order presented. When the list is presented in the same order on every trial, recall tends to be better than under the more usual free-recall procedure of randomized presentation, suggesting that subjects are able to take advantage of the serial organization (Mandler and Dean 1969; Jung and Skeebo 1967). Seriation probably helps recall because it provides a systematic retrieval strategy incorporating *all* the items presented. Other strategies tend to facilitate the search and retrieval process for some, but not all, items.

Categorization. Mandler (1967) has shown a very close relationship between the process of organizing unrelated words into subjective categories and that of remembering the words. In a typical experiment, the subject would be given a pack of 100 cards, on each of which a word was printed. He was then instructed to sort the words into conceptual categories; typically, the sorting would be repeated until he reached a consistent categorization (95-percent agreement between successive trials). He would then be required to recall as many of the words as possible. There were three major results.

First, for this task, instructions to categorize were as good as instructions to remember. Subjects were told to remember, categorize, or both; all did equally well. Subjects given an equal exposure to the words without instructions to categorize or remember (they were simply required to arrange them in seven columns) recalled significantly less.

Second, there was a very consistent relationship between amount recalled and degree of categorization, as indicated by the number of categories used in the sorting task. Mandler further showed that this relationship was still strong when the number of sorting trials was held constant and subjects were instructed as to how many categories were to be used.

Third, the larger the category size, the smaller the percentage of words recalled from the category. Figure 11–6 shows the relationship between recall probability and category size, which according to Mandler (1967, p. 359) shows that "the relative recall from categories decays rapidly after the 5 ± 2 level has been passed," suggesting that "the organization of lists involves the division of the items into categories of size 5 ± 2 and with hierarchies of subordinate and superordinate categories" (Mandler 1970, p. 111). The idea is an attractive one, but the only abrupt discontinuity discernible in Figure 11–6 occurs at 3 rather than 5 items. Figure 11–6 indicates that subjects clearly

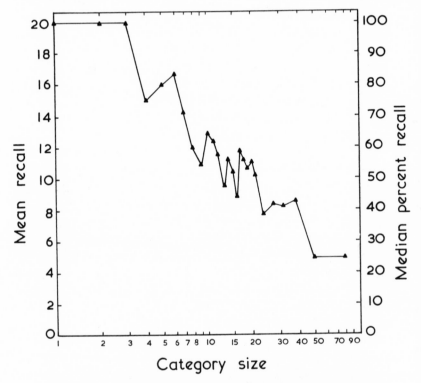

Category size

Figure 11–6   Median percentage recall as a function of category size. Source: Based on G. Mandler, Organization and memory, in K. W. Spence and J. T. Spence (eds.), *The Psychology of Learning and Motivation* (New York: Academic Press, 1967), vol. 1, p. 358. Reprinted by permission.

can recall considerably more than 7 items from a given category. Hence the case for a hierarchy of fivefold categories, though theoretically intriguing, is not particularly strong.

Relational imagery. In recent years, there has been an enormous growth of interest in the topic of visual imagery, which, having ceased to be regarded as respectable following the advent of behaviorism in the 1920s, crept back into the psychological laboratory with the development of the cognitive information-processing view of memory. Miller, Galanter, and Pribram (1960) drew attention to traditional mnemonic systems using visual imagery, and Paivio (1969) amassed overwhelming evidence that the rated imagery value of words was a far better predictor of verbal learning than any of the more standard measures, such as frequency or association value.

While there is by now a great deal of evidence for the importance of imagery (see Chapter 9), at this point we shall confine ourselves to two experiments. Bugelski, Kidd, and Segmen (1968) tested the mnemonic system described by Miller et al., in which subjects first learn a series of ten "peg-words," each rhyming with one of the digits from one to ten (*one-bun, two-shoe, three-tree, four-door, five-hive, six-sticks, seven-heaven, eight-gate, nine-wine, ten-hen*). Subjects were instructed to use the mnemonic in remembering ten-word lists by forming a composite visual image between each word to be learned and its corresponding peg-word; for example, if the first word was *dog,* the subject should imagine a *bun* (rhyming with *one*) being eaten by a *dog.* A list of ten words was then presented at a rate of 2, 4, or 8 seconds per word. Figure 11–7 shows the performance of the mnemonic group and that of control subjects who were not familiar with the mnemonic system. The visual imagery mnemonic clearly aids learning, but it is apparently not helpful with a rapid presentation rate, presumably because the subject does not have time to create the appropriate composite image.

This result suggests that visual imagery is a powerful mnemonic aid. Bower and Winzenz (1970) have shown, however, that instructions to visualize are not in fact essential. They found that instructions to construct a sentence linking the two words are almost as good as imagery instructions and lead to much better retention than merely reading a linking sentence, which in turn is better than rote repetition (see Table 11–1). Note also that recognition memory shows similar effects, although the range of scores is limited by a ceiling effect. Both these studies suggest that it is important that the subject integrate the stimulus and response into an organized whole. Both agree that visual

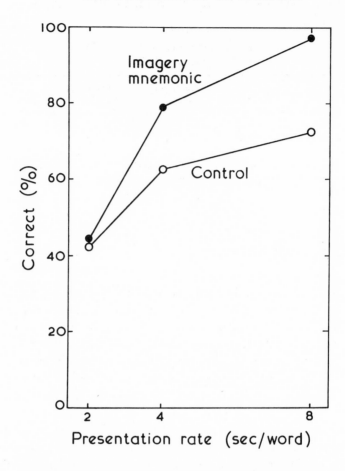

Figure 11–7 Percentage recall of items as a function of presentation rate for subjects with and without the aid of a peg-
word visual imagery mnemonic. Note that the mnemonic is not
useful at rapid presentation rates. Source: Based on B. R.
Bugelski, E. Kidd, and J. Segmen, Image as a mediator in one-
trial paired-associate learning, *Journal of Experimental Psychology* 76 (1968): 69–73.

imagery is an effective way of doing this, at least with concrete nouns.
The success of the linking-sentence technique suggests that visual
imagery may not be essential; on the other hand, it is possible that
visual imagery accompanied the generation of the sentence in many
cases. This, of course, bears on the intriguing question of the relationship between the visual and verbal memory systems, which was discussed in Chapter 9.

TABLE 11–1
*Average correct responses per list (max = 15) as a
function of study conditions.*

TEST TYPE	REPETITION	SENTENCE READING	SENTENCE GENERATION	IMAGERY
Recall	5.57	8.17	11.50	13.10
Recognition	12.03	13.10	14.80	14.67

Source: G. H. Bower and D. Winzenz, Comparison of associative learning strategies, *Psychonomic Science* 20 (1970): 120.

Organization and Retrieval

Mandler (1972) has claimed that all learning involves organization. While such a view probably constitutes an act of faith rather than an empirically testable hypothesis, it is certainly the case that organization plays a very important role in most learning. Why should this be?

One suggestion is that organization aids retrieval. Human memory is often likened to a vast library (e.g., Broadbent 1966). In order to be useful, the books in a library must be organized and shelved in a systematic way, otherwise finding the appropriate book becomes so slow as to make the library unusable. There is no advantage to having the book if it cannot be located when needed. It is often suggested that one of the major limits of human memory is set not by the ability to store information but by the ability to retrieve what has been stored. What is the evidence for such a view?

One of the most obvious indications that we know more than we can recall comes from experiments comparing recall and recognition memory. For example, Mandler, Pearlstone, and Koopmans (1969) found that the mean recall of 100 words presented five times was 38 percent. On the other hand, when required to recognize the 100 words mixed with 100 unrelated filler words, subjects had a score of 96 percent, with a mean false alarm rate of 7 percent, indicating that subjects had in some sense learned considerably more than the 38 words they could recall.

One interpretation of such a result is that recognition avoids the retrieval limitation. However, it can equally well be argued that recognition simply allows the subject to take advantage of partial learning. A single attribute of an item may be sufficient to allow its recognition but be quite inadequate for completely recalling or reconstructing the item. Furthermore, a direct comparison of recall and recognition is very difficult, since in order to test recognition performance, the "old" items which the subject is trying to remember must be mixed with "new" items; otherwise, the subject could score 100 percent by simply claiming to recognize every word shown to him. But performance will then depend on the size of the set of new filler or distractor items in which the old items are embedded; the greater the proportion of new distractors, then the lower the probability of an old item being recognized (Davis, Sutherland, and Judd 1961). This effect, in turn, is based on the fact that increasing the number of new items will increase the probability that the new items will contain items that are similar to the old (Dale and Baddeley 1962). It is in fact possible, by increasing the similarity between the old items and the new fillers, to reverse the usual relationship and produce poorer recognition than recall scores (Bahrick and Bahrick 1964; Bruce and Cofer 1967).

Phenomenologically, probably the most convincing evidence for a retrieval limitation is what Hart (1965) has termed the "feeling of knowing." Most people have experienced the frustration of trying unsuccessfully to recall something, often a name, with which they are very familiar. One usually knows that the information has been stored; indeed, it often seems to pop up unexpectedly shortly afterward. Hart investigated this phenomenon by questioning his subjects on topics of general information. When the subject could not answer a question, he was told to decide whether or not he really knew the answer. On a subsequent recognition test, items that had evoked a feeling of knowing were recognized correctly 76 percent of the time, compared with a 43 percent score on items-which the subject did not think he knew. In a similar vein, Brown and McNeill (1966) read out definitions of obscure English words and required their subjects to produce the word. They observed cases in which the subject reported that the word was "on the tip of his tongue," although it could not be produced. In such instances, the subject frequently knew how many syllables were in the word and at least some of the constituent speech sounds. For example, in trying recently to recall the name *Oxnard* (a small Southern California port), I knew that it had two syllables, of which the first contained the vowel *o,* and the second *a.* I immediately recognized it when it was suggested, with a feeling of complete certainty. As Aristotle pointed out (Dennis 1948), such partial recall of acoustic features appears to be particularly characteristic of the recall of proper names. However, although such experiences are subjectively very convincing, they too are open to the objection that they reflect inadequate learning rather than a retrieval limitation.

Such an objection is much harder to sustain in the case of a study by Tulving (1967) in which the standard free-recall procedure was modified by requiring three successive recall trials after each presentation of a list of words. He found that although subjects tended to recall about the same number of words on each successive test, only about 50 percent of these appeared in all three recalls. Thus, considering the three recall trials as a whole, subjects gave evidence of knowing considerably more than they could retrieve on any single trial. This phenomenon has been explored in more detail by Patterson (1972) using a 50-word list made up of categories comprising 4, 6, 8, 10, or 12 instances. She found that the larger the category, the lower the recall probability and the greater the tendency for different items to be recalled on successive trials. Patterson interprets her results in terms of a retrieval limitation set by the subjects' memory search routines. The larger the category, the more difficult is the problem of establishing a systematic search pattern. The more random the search pattern, the greater the trial-to-trial variability in item retrieval.

The most popular technique for studying retrieval limitation, however, is that of *cuing*—that is, providing information which the experimenter hopes will direct the subject's memory search. The classic example of this technique is provided in a study by Tulving and Pearlstone (1966) in which subjects learned categorized lists of 12 or 48 words, containing 1, 2, or 4 words per category (e.g., *FRUIT— apple, grapefruit, plum, cherry*). Half the subjects were cued by being given the relevant category names when asked to recall (e.g., *FRUIT*), and half were not. Subsequently, both groups gave a second recall with the category names present. On the first recall, cued subjects remembered substantially more words than uncued subjects. This, however, was entirely attributable to the tendency for uncued subjects to omit whole categories completely; on those categories which they did recall, their performance was no worse than that of the cued subjects. When the uncued subjects were subsequently provided with cues, their performance approached that of the cued group.

There is therefore good evidence to suggest that subjects often store more information than they are able to retrieve on any given trial; to use Tulving's (1968) distinction, items may be *available* (i.e., learned) but not *accessible* (i.e., retrievable). Any explanation of this clearly depends on one's conceptualization of the process of retrieval. Four approaches to retrieval will be considered in the next section.

Models of Retrieval

SAMPLE-AND-RECOGNIZE MODELS

Shiffrin (1970) has proposed a model of retrieval that assumes an "executive decision maker" which controls a recursive search process. This is applied to the search set, a subset of the information in long-term memory which is relevant to the retrieval demands of the situation. In the case of free-recall learning, this will be largely determined by time and context tags which delimit the list of words to be recalled. Information is assumed to be sampled at random from within the search set and examined by the executive decision maker which then decides whether to emit the response that has been retrieved or to reject it as an already emitted response. The process of sampling continues until some criterion is reached, whereupon the search process stops. This criterion may represent either the successful recall of the complete list or, more frequently, a given number of successive samples which have produced no "new" items. Clearly, such a model is an oversimplification, but with a few modifications it can in fact account for a remarkably large proportion of the available data.

One obvious question raised by the model is whether such a sampling involves replacement of the items recognized and emitted as responses. The most plausible assumption appears to be that of sampling with replacement, since the recall of an item tends to increase its probability of subsequent recall (a sampling-without-replacement hypothesis would suggest a decrease in recall probability). Further evidence comes from studies in which subjects have been required to generate items from a given semantic category. Bousfield and Sedgewick (1944) required subjects to produce as many items as they could from a specified category (e.g., birds), and plotted the rate of responding as a function of time. Figure 11–8 shows the characteristic negatively accelerated function typically obtained, with the first few items being produced very rapidly and subsequent items taking longer and longer to produce. The shape of the function is broadly consistent with the hypothesis that subjects sample at random and replace items; the greater the number of items they have emitted, the greater the probability that they will resample an item that has already been produced and, since they have been instructed not to repeat items, the greater the likely delay between responses. As Indow and Togano (1970) have pointed

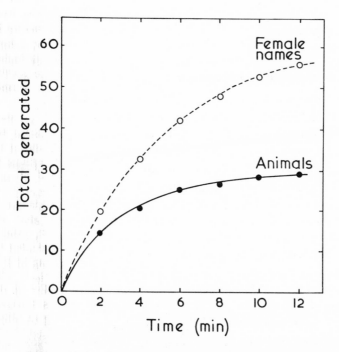

Figure 11–8   Cumulative curves showing the performance of a single subject required to generate items from each of two categories. Note that the rate at which new items are produced decreases, approaching an asymptote determined by the size of the category concerned. Source: T. Indow and K. Togano, On retrieving sequence from long-term memory, *Psychological Review* 77 (1970): 318. Copyright 1970 by the American Psychological Association. Reprinted by permission.

out, this basic sampling model is an oversimplification; nevertheless, it provides a remarkably good first approximation to the data obtained.

Shiffrin (1970) has elaborated this sampling model by building in further assumptions about response strength (with strong responses being more likely to be sampled than weak responses) and the size of a set of items sampled (with small sets leading to a higher probability of retrieval than large sets). This second point is consistent with the observation (Murdock 1962) that the probability of a given item being recalled in a free-recall experiment declines with the length of the list—or, in other words, with the size of the set of items from which the subject is sampling. In an ingenious experiment, Shiffrin (1970) demonstrated that it was list length per se that was the crucial factor, not the number of items intervening between the presentation of an item and its recall, as interference theory might predict. He did so by combining long and short lists in a study in which subjects were required to recall not the last list they had heard but the one before it. In the crucial condition, when a short list had been followed by a long list, Shiffrin showed that recall of the short list was considerably higher than when a long list was followed by a short list, despite the greater amount of RI which would have been expected in the former condition.

If the further plausible assumption is made that recalling an item tends to strengthen that item, then the model is able to account for some intriguing and apparently counterintuitive evidence produced by Brown (1968) and Slamecka (1968). Brown required two groups of subjects to recall as many of the 50 U.S. states as they could. In one of the two conditions, he had previously read out 25 of the possible 50. The subsequent recall performance showed that although this group had a higher total number of states recalled, they nevertheless recalled significantly *fewer* of the 25 states which had not been primed than the control group. This study has been repeated and extended by Tulving and Hastie (1972). A similar inhibitory effect of cuing in free recall was observed by Slamecka (1968), who presented subjects with a list of unrelated words and subsequently presented a sample of the words at recall. It was anticipated that these would act as retrieval cues and would enhance performance by facilitating the recall of other, nonrecalled items. Instead, overall performance was depressed; comparable inhibition effects have been observed by Slamecka (1969) and Wood (1969). The major exception to this conclusion, as Slamecka (1972) and Baddeley and Warrington (1973) have pointed out, occurs when categorized lists are used and when the items provided cue the subject into a category which would otherwise not be recalled.

As Rundus (1973) has noted, a sampling model can handle these negative cuing effects relatively easily, given the assumption of *stop rules*. A stop rule is a decision rule which determines when the reiterative retrieval process should cease; clearly, such rules must operate at some levels, since subjects do not go on attempting to recall indefinitely. In the Shiffrin model, the stop rule involves a decision about the probability of retrieving further correct items, which in turn is based on the number of retrievals which have been made without producing such new correct items. It is assumed that giving the subject a subset of the items to be recalled will increment the strength of these items and, in doing so, will increase the probability of their being sampled subsequently. Such items will thus tend to be both sampled and resampled disproportionately often, with the result that the stop rule, based on the number of such nonproductive resamples, will come into operation at a point when many of the weaker items have not yet been sampled.

Nevertheless, Shiffrin's model can be criticized for the implausibility of some of its basic assumptions. First, in assuming that temporal and contextual cues delineate the set of words presented in a list, which then constitutes the search set, the model appears to avoid the problem of retrieval, not solve it. If the subject really has delineated the full set of items after a single presentation, then one might expect him simply to keep on sampling until all items were recalled. Clearly, this does not occur, since single-trial free-recall performance is far from perfect, especially with long lists. For this reason, it is necessary for the model to make further strong assumptions about the stop rules involved.

These assumptions allow an ingenious account of the effect of list length on recall probability (Shiffrin 1970, pp. 389–390) and are plausible when (1) response time is limited, (2) the search process is particularly difficult or fatiguing, or (3) rapid responding is important. However, none of these conditions is typical of single-trial free recall. Subjects in free-recall studies typically stop responding well before the end of the 1-minute period generally allowed for recall. It is rarely the case that any stress is placed on speed of response, and if subjects' comments are to be believed, single-trial free recall is a less stressful, fatiguing task than digit-span or paired-associate learning. Finally, if recall scores are reduced because subjects stop searching too soon, one might expect that instructions to continue responding would improve performance substantially. Keppel and Mallory (1969) found that instructions to adopt a laxer criterion led to more responses, but these were almost entirely intrusions rather than additional correct items. Slamecka, Moore, and Carey (1972) similarly found no significant effect of criterion level on normal free-recall learning, although criterion did, of course, affect the Tulving part-to-whole transfer effect (see p. 280).

One way around the more implausible assumptions of the sampling model is to dispense with the concept of sampling a delimited set of items and to assume a response-generation process prior to the recognition stage.

GENERATE-AND-RECOGNIZE MODELS

It has often been suggested (e.g., Dale 1967; Kintsch 1968; Bower, Clark, Lesgold, and Winzenz 1969) that recall involves a process of generating plausible responses and subsequently "editing" these and emitting responses which are recognized as correct. Dale (1967) showed that those English county names which were most likely to be generated by subjects attempting to enumerate all English counties were better recalled than less frequent county names. This difference did not occur when memory was tested by recognition, suggesting that the frequency effect was influencing the generation of responses rather than their recognition. Similarly, Bower et al. (1969) showed that a hierarchically organized list which could be generated on the basis of a few relatively simple rules was particularly easy to learn. While it is easy to see how such generating rules can be applied in the case of categorized material, it is less obvious how sets of unrelated words are generated. One might plausibly argue that the process of learning involves the subject in setting up a series of subrules linking the items to be learned into a coherent retrieval plan. Although this is intuitively plausible, however, once again it tends to assume the very process that it is trying to explain. Similarly, the question of how the subject recognizes a response as correct and suitable for emission presents problems, particularly in view of what has been termed the *encoding specificity hypothesis.*

THE ENCODING SPECIFICITY HYPOTHESIS

The encoding specificity hypothesis was originally formulated by Tulving and Osler (1968) to account for the results of a study designed to explore further the role of retrieval cues, which Tulving and Pearlstone (1966) had shown to have a powerful influence on recall. Instead of the category names used in the previous study, they used weak associates of the words to be remembered; thus the cues for *MUTTON* were *fat* and *leg,* and those for *CITY* were *dirty* and *village.* Their basic condition involved presenting the word to be remembered in capital letters together with the cue or cues in lowercase. Subjects were told that the lowercase word might help them remember and were asked to see how the word and cue were related. Tulving and Osler's results showed that even a weak associate will aid recall if presented during both the learning and recall phase but that an associate had no such effect when presented only at recall. Nor was there any advantage in cuing if different cues were presented at learning and recall. Finally, they found no advantage to presenting two cues rather than one. They conclude from this that "specific retrieval cues facilitate recall if and only if the information about them and about their relation to the to-be-remembered word is stored at the same time as the information about the membership of the to-be-remembered word in a given list" (Tulving and Osler 1968, p. 593). This view, which they termed the encoding specificity hypothesis, therefore suggests that a retrieval cue serves as a kind of mnemonic "handle" which, if attached to a word during learning, will facilitate retrieval when presented at recall. It is not helpful to present such a "handle" unless it has been attached during learning; nor is it helpful to attach one handle and then present a different handle at recall.

Before we go on to discuss this hypothesis further, it is perhaps worth pointing out the distinction between the clear and testable hypothesis summarized in the above quotation and the position subsequently adopted by Tulving (1974), which he describes as the *encoding specificity principle:*

> the properties of the memory trace of a word event are determined by specific encoding operations performed on the input stimuli, and . . . it is these properties, rather than the properties of the word in semantic memory, that determine the effectiveness of any given stimulus as a retrieval cue for the event. The principle suggests that if a stimulus in the retrieval environment renders possible or facilitates recall of the target word T, the retrieval information was appropriate to or compatible with the information contained in the episodic trace of T. Conversely, if a particular stimulus is ineffective in retrieving a particular trace, the conclusion follows that the appropriate relation was lacking (Tulving 1974, pp. 778–779).

Note that the "principle" is not an experimentally testable hypothesis; it assumes a particular relationship between encoding during storage and subsequent retrieval, and it proposes to use this assumed relationship to explore the way in which items are encoded. While the assumption is a plausible one and its proposed use is interesting and potentially fruitful, the apparent promotion of encoding specificity from a hypothesis to a principle should not be taken at face value. It represents a move away from a clear and testable hypothesis (which, it can be argued, was shown to be incorrect) to a general, untestable, pre-theoretical assumption, which may or may not prove useful in further exploring the nature of retrieval.

The present discussion will be confined to the testable hypothesis rather than the untestable "principle." It will focus on a series of experiments by Tulving and Thomson (1973) which produced results that are claimed to be inconsistent with existing sample-and-recognize or generate-and-recognize models. Tulving and Thomson claim that all such models subscribe to two basic assumptions, and they then proceed to describe a series of experiments which gave results that are incompatible with these assumptions. The first assumption is that each word has a single representation in memory corresponding to its dictionary meaning or meanings; encoding or using the word in any of a range of situations is assumed to activate its internal representation, a process which can be regarded as analogous to attaching a marker or tag. The second assumption is that access to long-term memory is automatic; whenever a word is presented, it has immediate and unimpaired access to its representation in memory. Consequently, when an item is presented for subsequent recognition, its location in long-term memory is accessed directly, and the presence or absence of the appropriate tag will become immediately apparent.

The basic experimental paradigm employed by Tulving and Thomson involves presenting subjects with a target word (e.g., *COLD*) accompanied by a retrieval cue which is a weak associate of the target (e.g., *ground*). In a later part of the experiment, the subject is induced to generate the target word (*COLD*) by requiring him to produce a series of free associations to a strongly associated word (e.g., *hot*). Subjects are then asked to look down their generated associations and mark any items which occurred in the previously presented list. Subjects generated about 80 percent of the 12 target words from the original learned list but were able to recognize only 18 percent of these as words they had previously tried to remember. Since subjects given the appropriate retrieval cues were able to recall a much higher proportion of items presented (59 percent) than they were able to recognize, a simple generate-and-recognize model of retrieval clearly runs into difficulties. Since the model assumes that the process of recall itself involves a recognition stage, it should not be possible to recall items which cannot be recognized. In view of the magnitude of the effect and its apparent reliability, it clearly presents an interesting theoretical challenge. We shall consider three potential lines of explanation.

The first approach might be to attempt to defend a generation-recognition model as follows. All statements about the relative ease or difficulty of a recognition response will depend on the number and type of distractor items against which the "old" items must be recognized. Davis, Sutherland, and Judd (1961) showed that the advantage of recognition over recall could be eliminated if the size of the sample from which an item must be recognized was increased sufficiently, and Dale and Baddeley (1962; 1966) pointed out that this phenomenon was itself dependent on the tendency for large sets of distractors to contain items which were highly similar to the items to be recognized. Underwood (1965) has shown that high associates (such as would be produced in the free-association condition) are particularly difficult to discriminate from correct items in tasks involving the free recall of unrelated words. Recognition is likely to be further impaired by the fact that such words have just been generated by the subject, and hence would presumably have occurrence tags of some sort. In other words, a subject would have a more difficult task than that of simply remembering whether the word had occurred recently in that experimental context, as is presumably normally the case in word-recognition studies. He would have to make the finer discrimination of whether the word had been both presented by the experimenter and generated by himself or had been generated only by himself.

Tulving and Thomson did go some way toward covering this last point in experiment 2 of their paper, which presented one subgroup with the associates generated by their fellow subjects. This is clearly an improved design, since the distractors produced would not then have the additional "strength" acquired during the generation process. Under these conditions, the hit rate increased from 18 to 25 percent, a difference which was not statistically significant. However, an equivalent recognition control in a subsequent study by Reder, Anderson, and Bjork (1974) produced a much more dramatic effect, with detection rate increasing from 38 percent, when subjects were recognizing items from sets generated by themselves, to 72 percent, when the distractors were generated by other subjects. There is, therefore, some evidence to suggest that the poor recognition of items which could be generated may be explicable at least partly in terms of what we already know about recognition memory.

A second criticism that has been leveled at the Tulving-Thomson paradigm is that its effects stem from confusing and misleading the subject. Santa and Lamwers (1974) argue that the initial lists learned give subjects a strong expectation that cues will be *remote* associates of the words to be remembered. As a result of this, subjects discount *high* associates when required to recognize items from among their own free-association responses. Santa and Lamwers went on to test this hypothesis in two studies modeled on the procedure adopted by Tulving and Thomson. Subjects were first given a number of practice lists in which low associates were consistently used as retrieval cues, followed by a crucial experimental list in which the retrieval cues presented during learning were replaced by high associates of the words to be remembered. Subjects who were not warned of this change performed no better than subjects given no cues whatsoever, while those warned that some of the cues were high associates of the words to be recalled performed just as well as they had on previous lists, when the same cues were presented during both learning and recall.

The third difficulty for the encoding specificity hypothesis is raised in a study by Reder, Anderson, and Bjork (1974), who showed that the encoding specificity effect occurred only in the case of high-frequency words. When subjects were required to learn lists of words which occur relatively rarely in the language, highly associated words proved to be very effective as retrieval cues, despite the fact that they were not presented during the learning phase. Reder et al. explain their results in terms of the tendency for high-frequency words to have many more different meanings than low-frequency words. Hence, a word like *water* will have a slightly different meaning when presented in the context of *drinking* than in the context of *lake*. They point out that *Webster's Seventh New Collegiate Dictionary* lists eight main senses of the noun *water,* 16 subsenses, and 19 sub-subsenses. In contrast, low-frequency words such as *hippopotamus* or *aspirin* tend to have very few meanings. If one assumes that what is learned in a verbal memory experiment is one meaning of a word, then it is hardly surprising that with high-frequency words the meaning learned may differ from that subsequently cued by a strong associate; since low-frequency words tend to have only one meaning, a strong cue *will* tend to direct the retrieval search to the appropriate semantic unit.

THE SEMANTIC SEARCH HYPOTHESIS

Let us return to the original Tulving and Osler (1968) study, in which it was shown that when the retrieval cue was changed from that presented during learning, subsequent recall was impaired. This result is completely consistent with the encoding specificity hypothesis. This may, however, not be the most fruitful interpretation. The hypothesis assumes that the unit of learning is the word, and that this "is always 'learned' when it is first presented . . . in the sense that the probability of its recall increases from a value near zero immediately prior to the presentation to unity immediately after" (Tulving 1968,

p. 7). Such a view confuses recall from primary memory, which possibly does operate at the level of the word, with recall from secondary memory, which operates primarily at a semantic level. Bearing this distinction in mind, we can explore an alternative interpretation of the retrieval cue phenomenon.

Let us suppose that a retrieval cue acts as a hint about what part of the memory store should be searched. In the case of an obvious hint, such as a category name, it is not necessary to specify the cue during learning (Fox, Blick, and Bilodeau 1964), a result which Tulving has to explain in terms of spontaneous category naming on the part of the subject during learning. In the Tulving and Osler study, the subject integrated the word and its cue to form a semantic unit. As we saw from the previously described study by Bower and Winzenz (1970), this produced a very strongly integrated unit which was evoked when either of the constituent items was presented. Needless to say, the semantic unit formed from one pair (e.g., *CITY-dirty*) is unlikely to be the same as that formed by the other pair (e.g., *CITY-village*); consequently, for a subject who has learned *CITY-dirty,* the cue *village* is unlikely to direct him to the relevant semantic unit.

The clearest evidence that subjects learn at the level of semantics rather than words comes from a study by Light and Carter-Sobell (1970) using polysemous words—that is, words having more than one distinct meaning, such as *JAM* (strawberry jam and traffic jam). Subjects were presented with a list of such words, each accompanied by an adjective which clearly directed the subject to one of the two meanings. They were then given a recognition test in which the word was presented alone, with the same adjective, or with an adjective suggesting the other meaning. When the adjective was omitted, recognition dropped from 64 to 43 percent; when the "wrong" adjective was supplied, recall dropped to. 27 percent. A subsequent experiment included a further condition in which the adjective accompanying learning differed from that in the recognition test but suggested the same interpretation of the noun (e.g., *strawberry JAM* and *apricot JAM*). Recognition in this condition was 45 percent, compared with 73 percent for the same adjective and 29 percent for the "wrong" adjective. Thus, a cue may facilitate recall even though it was not present at input, provided it directs the subject to the appropriate location in semantic memory. As Light and Carter-Sobell point out, they made no attempt to make their consistent adjectives synonymous, but it does seem likely that the same dictionary meaning was accessed by both cues in the semantically congruent condition. However, the fact that semantically congruent cues proved worse than identical cues in both this study and in a subsequent study by Marcel and Steel (1973) suggests that it is not sufficient to have the input and retrieval cues access the same dictionary meaning.

This point is made particularly clearly in a paper by Barclay, Bransford, Franks, McCarrell, and Nitsch (1974) which points out that while a word presented in isolation may tend to have a relatively small number of dictionary meanings, its range of meanings may increase substantially when it is presented in the context of another word or sentence. They give the instance of the word *piano*, which would tend to have quite different aspects of its meaning emphasized by *The man lifted the piano* than by *The man tuned the piano*. In the first case, the weight of the piano is the essential feature; in the second, the sound of the instrument is emphasized. They use the term *semantic flexibility* to describe the capacity of a single word to support a range of different semantic emphases, and they describe a series of experiments which explore the role of this concept in verbal memory.

In the first of these experiments, they presented subjects with a series of sentences, each of which was selected from a pair of sentences referring to the same noun; for example, *The secretary put the paper clips in the envelope* or *The secretary licked the envelope*. Subjects were then given a retrieval cue that was either appropriate or inappropriate to the sentence they had heard (e.g., *something that can hold small objects* or *something with glue*). Subjects given semantically appropriate cues recalled a mean of 4.7 out of a possible 10 target items, whereas those given inappropriate cues recalled only 1.6. The second experiment showed that even when the same verb was employed in the two alternative sentences (e.g., *The man lifted the piano* versus *The man lifted the infant*), an appropriate cue (*something heavy* versus *something cuddly*) led to substantially better recall. In a final experiment, subjects were required to recall the whole sentence, and appropriate cues were compared with inappropriate cues and with cueing by the object of the sentence. For a sentence such as *The man lifted the piano,* the cue *something heavy* was reliably more effective than either an inappropriate cue (*something tuneful*) or the word *piano* itself.

These results suggest that the unit that is learned is not that of a single meaning but of one aspect of the meaning of the word. Another way of expressing this is that the subject encodes the information to be remembered in terms of an area of *semantic space*, not in some specific location representing the dictionary definitions of the words in the sequence. Subjects do not learn words; they learn semantic interpretations based on the words presented. As we shall see in the next two chapters, this point becomes even clearer when one considers the learning of passages of prose rather than isolated words or phrases.

CHAPTER

12

Memory for Prose: Similarity, Redundancy, and Syntax

WE HAVE SO FAR been concerned almost exclusively with memory for isolated visual or auditory items. However, as Bartlett pointed out, most of the memory that we experience in everyday life is not of this kind; it is concerned with sequences of events which typically form part of an organized whole. As such, a sentence or a passage of prose seems more likely than a list of unrelated words to provide an analogue to memory in everyday life.

The classic work on the retention of prose is, of course, that of Bartlett, described in Chapter 1. For 30 years following the publication of *Remembering*, there was relatively little development in our understanding of memory for prose; in recent years, however, with the trend away from the artificiality of the classical verbal-learning tradition, there has been a considerable growth of interest in the topic of memory for prose, approached initially from the viewpoint of interference and information theory and, more recently, through the rapid growth in the area of psycholinguistics. These approaches will be considered in turn.

Interference Theory

There have been sporadic attempts to apply the principles of interference theory to the retention of prose. Coleman (1962) used the
repeated-reproduction technique in an attempt to demonstrate extra-
experimental interference effects in the recall of word sequences. He
presented the following jumble of words, each written on a separate
card, to the first of a chain of subjects:

> *about was good-looking way and treating made of that a him the
> quiet youngster nice he manners a them girls wild go with*

The cards were then shuffled and the subject's task was to try to
remember this sequence and arrange the cards in the appropriate
order. The second subject did likewise and passed the cards on to a
third subject, who in turn passed them on to the fourth, and so on. By
the sixteenth recall, the word order had become:

> *he was a youngster nice quiet with manners good-looking and a
> way of treating them that made the girls go wild about him*

Coleman interprets this in terms of the extra-experimental interference hypothesis. However, in view of the almost complete failure
of this hypothesis under more rigid tests (see Chapter 5), this result is
probably better explained in terms of Bartlett's concept of "effort
after meaning."

Several studies have attempted to demonstrate RI effects in the retention of prose, but these have rarely proved very successful. An
exception is the work of Slamecka (1960; 1961), who found both PI
and RI effects with sentences. However, he used extremely abstract
material, a typical sentence being *Communicators can exercise latitude in specifying meaning however they choose provided that such
definitions conform somewhat closely to regular usage.* He also presented his sequences a word at a time, paced at a rate of 3 seconds
per word, and tested by the method of serial anticipation. Under
these conditions, it is doubtful if the material was in fact meaningful
to the subjects.

When conditions are less constrained, it appears to be difficult to
show interference effects. Ausubel, Robbins, and Blake (1957) had
their subjects read a passage on Buddhism followed by what they term
"a multiple choice Buddhism achievement test." The next day, half
the subjects read a second passage on Christianity. When tested eight
days later, these subjects remembered just as much about Buddhism

as the group given no interpolated passage. Is there, perhaps, no basic conflict between Buddhism and Christianity? Later studies tried to take this question into account by using an interpolated passage on Zen Buddhism that was judged to be "similar but conflicting" (Ausubel, Stager, and Gaite 1968). Again no interference was found, leading the authors to conclude that the retention of meaningful discourse involves different principles from rote learning.

This conclusion has been challenged by Anderson and Myrow (1971), who cite a number of studies which have found "at least some retroactive inhibition." They describe two experiments in which items within the second passage differed as to whether they were consistent, neutral, or inconsistent with facts in the initial passage. Their two experiments ran into a number of technical problems, and they conflict as to whether overall performance is enhanced or degraded by a similar interpolated passage. However, both their studies suggest that performance is better on points of agreement between the two passages than on points of conflict.

A rather more dramatic effect has been obtained by Crouse (1971) in a study which required subjects to learn a biographical passage comprising a large number of facts about a fictitious poet, John Payton. For example, the passage began with the following two sentences: *Payton was born in Liverpool at the end of October 1810. When he was only five years of age his father, who was a servant, was killed by a robber.* The passage went on in this vein, until finally concluding: *Soon after this, however, he began to suffer hemorrhages in the lungs, and after much misery, he died in Geneva on April 12th, 1859.* Having studied and recalled a passage of this sort, subjects went on to learn two further passages of a similar nature, each based on the same biographical framework but containing different detailed "facts." One, for example, concerned a fictitious poet, Samuel Hughes: *Hughes was born in Paddington at the end of October, 1805. When he was only nine years of age, his father, who was a weaver, was killed in a swimming accident.* It finally concluded: *Soon after this, however, he began to suffer hemorrhages in the lungs, and after much misery, he died in Paris on March 18th, 1846.* One control group learned two unrelated passages, one about an island and the other about a library, while a second control group rested for a comparable interval. Subjects were then tested on the initial passage by being asked for individual pieces of information (e.g., *Where was John Payton born? How did his father die?*). Clear interference effects were found, with subjects given interpolated biographical passages recalling only 54 percent as much as subjects given the unrelated passages, who did not differ from subjects who had rested during the delay interval. This result has been replicated and extended by Anderson and Bower (1973), who observed a drop in cued recall from a mean of 10.77 items correct to a mean of 8.00 items, and in free recall from 10.46 to 7.54, out of a maximum of 22 items. There is, therefore, no doubt that the phenomenon of interference can be demonstrated with prose material, provided one is prepared to go to sufficient lengths. Note, however, that there was no difference between the two control groups studied by Crouse, implying that learning two interpolated passages that were not conceptually similar produced no interference at all. Furthermore, even with passages that were artificially constructed to increase similarity to the highest possible degree, the size of the interference effect observed by Anderson and Bower was far from dramatic. If it is necessary to go to these lengths to produce an interference effect at all in prose, then it seems unlikely that interference theory can provide a very promising approach to understanding how we normally remember meaningful material.

Remembering and Abstracting

A number of writers have commented on the analogy between remembering a passage and producing a précis or abstract of it. Gomulicki (1956) had his subjects read and recall passages of prose, which he then scored in terms of the number of "ideas" correctly reproduced. He found that subjects tended to remember what they regarded as the most important features of the passage and produced recall protocols which were remarkably similar to summaries of the passage produced by other subjects. Gomulicki argued that the process of recall was essentially equivalent to one of abstraction, and he suggested that the process went on during the input stage, not during the storage or retrieval of the information.

It follows from this view that if distortions occur during learning rather than storage, then they should not necessarily increase over time, as Bartlett's view would suggest. Such a conclusion is consistent with the results of a more recent study by Johnson (1970) in which three independent groups of subjects were asked to eliminate the less-important subunits of a story until only three-quarters, half, or one-quarter of the original number of words remained. Separate groups of subjects then learned the complete story and were required to recall it after intervals ranging from 15 minutes to 63 days. Figure 12–1 shows the mean percentage of linguistic subunits recalled at each delay as a function of judged importance. As in Gomulicki's study, there is a clear tendency for the more important items to be better recalled at all delays, but there is no evidence that unimportant items are subsequently forgotten more rapidly.

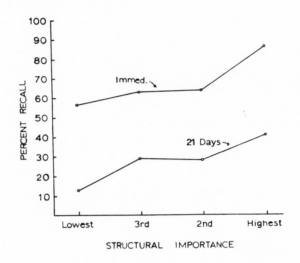

Figure 12–1   Immediate and delayed recall of the linguistic subunits of a passage as a function of the rated structural importance of the units. Note that those components rated most important are best recalled both immediately and after a 21-day delay. Source: R. E. Johnson, Recall of prose as a function of the structural importance of the linguistic units, *Journal of Verbal Learning and Verbal Behavior* 9 (1970): 16. Reprinted by permission.

Dawes (1966) attempted to quantify the distortions to be expected from Bartlett's work, but although he found clear evidence of distortion, the tendency to distortion was just as great after a short as after a long delay. A possible interpretation of this discrepancy comes from a study by Gauld and Stephenson (1967), who suggest that many of the distortions observed by Bartlett may occur because subjects know they have forgotten certain aspects of the passage but attempt to produce a coherent performance by extrapolating from what they do remember. Gauld and Stephenson showed that subjects instructed to recall only what they are sure of make considerably fewer Bartlettian intrusion errors; furthermore, subjects who were independently assessed in an interview as being conscientious tended to produce fewer errors. The standard Bartlett procedure of requiring the same subject to recall the same passage after varying delays may be particularly susceptible to this type of distortion, in view of Kay's (1955) demonstration that subjects tend to remember their own recall efforts rather than the material presented by the experimenter. Kay presented subjects with a passage which he required them to recall a week later; following their recall he read the passage again, after which there was a further week's delay before the next test. In this way, subjects were given a total of seven presentations and seven tests. Subjects characteristically went on making the same errors, despite the fact that each recall was followed by what should have been a correction. It seems likely then that the distortions observed by Bartlett are due at least in part to his use of a repeated-recall procedure and that when only a single recall is required, the process of remembering has a great deal in common with that of abstracting or summarizing. It follows from this conclusion that passages which are easy to summarize should also be easy to remember, and the next section will be concerned with the relationship between abstractability and recall.

Factors Governing Abstractability

If the process of remembering meaningful material is indeed analogous to that of abstraction, factors which make a passage easy to summarize should also make it easy to recall.

REDUNDANCY

The concept of redundancy as used in information theory is based on the ratio of the actual amount of information conveyed by a sequence of events to the maximum possible. Hence, the English language may be said to be redundant because (1) individual letters and words do not occur with equal frequency, and (2) the order in which they occur is constrained (e.g., Q is always followed by U, the is usually followed by a noun, etc.). In principle, a redundant message can always be recoded into a shorter, less redundant message. As might be expected on the abstraction hypothesis, redundant sequences are better recalled than nonredundant sequences of the same length. Miller

(1958) generated sequences using the letters S, N, X, and G either selected at random or according to a set of probabilistic rules whereby certain combinations were more likely than others. These redundant strings were learned much more rapidly than the random strings.

PREDICTABILITY

Whereas redundancy refers to the statistical constraints within a set of material (Garner 1962), predictability concerns the relationship between the structure of the material and the subjects' expectations. Hence, a novel in Polish is probably just as redundant as an English novel, but to an English subject would be much less predictable. With a very simple situation, such as that used by Miller (1958), it is probably fair to assume that with practice a subject's expectations will approach the objective probabilities. With more complex material, however, the discrepancy between subjective and objective probabilities is more of a problem, and it becomes much more satisfactory to use the subject's natural language, in which he has had years to learn the relevant probabilities.

Miller and Selfridge (1950) studied the role of predictability in learning word sequences using statistical approximations to English. These ranged from zero-order approximations, in which words were drawn from a dictionary at random, through first-order approximations, in which words were selected by their frequency in natural language, to second-, third-, fourth-, fifth-, sixth-, and seventh-order approximations and text. A second-order approximation is one in which the sequential dependencies between adjacent *pairs* of words approximate those of English. It is produced by giving subjects a single word and asking them to incorporate it into a sentence (e.g., given the word *dog*, a subject might produce *The dog bit the man*). The next word (i.e., *bit*) is then given to another subject with the same instruction, and he produces another sentence (e.g., *A bit of cake fell on the floor*), whereupon his next word (*of*) is given to the next subject. The second-order passage then comprises the sequence of words generated, one by each subject (in this case, *dog bit of . . .* , etc.). In a third-order approximation, the subject is given two words of context each time (e.g., *dog bit*); in a fourth-order, three words (e.g., *dog bit the*); and so forth. The higher the order of approximation, the greater the constraint and the more closely the sequence resembles normal English. Below are some examples generated in 1969 by University of Sussex psychology students:

First Order

Pomegranates mouthful handle man superhero perhaps hippopotamus amazing sex stored fircones plausible happy twinkle underestimated sun boggling joint beard mauve axolotl lewd freak-out exhausted

Second Order

would that although children like groovy scene one for goldilocks bears like werewolf virgins ten tickles hairy nostrils flapping voluptuously trailing walruses tusks emancipated suffragettes suffer little bogs oozing cataclysmic climax came cunningly consummated

Third Order

was growing beyond hope and glory hallelujah to unnerve destroy people is groovy mind-blowing freak-out unfortunately ending hysterically bubbling bath giggling hysterically underneath sparsely populated wasteland escalating into doom irretrievably obnoxious and placated

Fifth Order

by their example incalculable risks degradation for Xerxes while grovelling horribly amid decaying garbage was heaped disgustingly sideways beside bulging perverted earthworms lay mouldering silently in acid putrified thoughts Henriette fainted through excitement

For experimental use, however, the somewhat more prosaic efforts of naïve subjects are probably to be preferred. Miller and Selfridge (1950) and Morton (1964b) provide sources of such material.

Miller and Selfridge presented their subjects with test sequences of 10, 20, 30, or 50 words of zero, first, second, third, fourth, fifth, and seventh orders of approximation to English for immediate free recall. Recall scores increased with approximation to English up to the fourth order, but no difference was found between fourth, fifth, and seventh orders and text. Subsequent studies have shown that this leveling off does not occur if subjects are asked to recall the order in which the words were presented rather than just the words themselves. Under these conditions, text is recalled significantly better than the highest order of approximation (Marks and Jack 1952; Coleman 1963). In an experiment based on the Miller and Selfridge study, Tulving and Patkau (1962) scored recall in terms of both words and "adopted chunks," which consisted of a sequence of items recalled in the order in which they were presented. Hence, if a subject was shown items *ABCDEFGH* and recalled *HCDEFAB*, he would have recalled seven items but only three adopted chunks, *H, CDEF,* and *AB.* Tulving and Patkau found that although number of words recalled increased with order of approximation to English, number of recalled chunks remained constant.

A similar effect is found with letter sequences. As sequences increase in order of approximation to English word structure, from zero (e.g., *ubxwylt*) to first (e.g., *uhlmhor*), second (e.g., *tictoor*), third (e.g., *asterom*), and English words, mean recall probability increases (Baddeley 1971). It seems that the subject is recoding into larger chunks involving speech sounds based on combinations of letters, rather than individual letter names (i.e., *bed* will be pronounced as a single syllable, not as three letters). Consequently, recall is highly correlated with the predictability of the sequence ($r = .66$), a measure of how closely it approximates to English. It is not, however, influenced by acoustic similarity among the letter names comprising the sequence ($r = .05$), a variable which Conrad, Freeman, and Hull (1965) have shown to be important in the case of random consonant sequences. In a study analogous to that of Tulving and Patkau (1962), McNulty (1966) has shown that an increase in order of approximation to English words results in more letters being recalled but does not affect the number of adopted chunks remembered.

We have so far confined our attention to material in which degree of predictability was artificially manipulated. However, natural text also differs in its degree of predictability, and this in turn affects retention. Rubinstein and Aborn (1958) sampled a range of texts varying from children's stories to philosophical writings. They assessed the predictability of each sample using the cloze technique, in which the passage is presented with a given proportion of words omitted (e.g., every fifth word) and subjects are asked to guess the missing words. The more predictable the passage, the greater the probability of a correct guess. As might be expected, subjects guessed the children's stories more accurately than the philosophy, indicating that the stories were more predictable. The complete passages were then given to a separate group of subjects, with instructions to memorize them. Subsequent recall showed a high correlation ($r = .73$) between the predictability of a passage and the amount recalled.

The Role of Syntax

Returning to our orders of approximation to English, it is clear that the lower orders differ from text in a number of ways, one of the most obvious being that they are very ungrammatical (Coleman 1963). As Lewis Carroll demonstrated in such nonsense verse as *'Twas brillig and the slithy toves / Did gyre and gimble in the wabe,* it is possible to make nonsense both memorable and, in a curious way, meaningful by adding appropriate connecting words and grammatical tags.

Epstein (1961) studied this phenomenon and confirmed that sequences of nonsense syllables containing appropriate connecting words and bound morphemes (grammatical tags) were easier to learn than sequences without such grammatical aids. Thus subjects found it easier to recall *The yigs wur vumly rixing hum in jegest miv* than *The yig wur vum rix hum in jeg miv.* He found a similar effect with real words: grammatically correct nonsense such as *Cruel tables sang falling circles to empty bitter pencils* was easier to learn than a random sequence such as *Sang tables bitter empty cruel to circles pencils falling.* Epstein later observed that the effect disappeared when the items were presented one at a time on a memory drum instead of simultaneously on a card, suggesting that the subject needed to see the whole sequence to detect and make use of the grammatical cues (Epstein 1962). Further evidence that serial, word-by-word presentation of prose disrupts the normal processing and impairs recall comes from a study by Kulhavy, Dyer, and Caterino (1975). It may be recalled that it was under just such constrained conditions that Slamecka (1960; 1961) was able to obtain RI and PI effects in prose learning. O'Connell, Turner, and Onuska (1968) found that facilitation of learning by grammatical tags did not occur when the sequences were presented orally, and hence sequentially, in a monotone. The effect reappeared when the sequences were read with the appropriate intonation, presumably because the intonation pattern drew attention to the syntactic structure. Epstein's results have stimulated a considerable body of further work, not all of which has been successful in replicating the phenomenon, and a recent review by O'Connell (1970) concludes that the Epstein phenomenon is considerably more complex and less robust than the original studies might suggest.

Another approach to the role of syntax in memory was made by Marks and Miller (1964) using real words combined in each of four ways (examples follow).

(1) Normal sentences: *Noisy parties wake sleeping neighbors.*
(2) Anomalous sentences, which are made by combining the appropriate parts of speech from each of several sentences and which are grammatical, though intended not to be meaningful: *Noisy flashes emit careful floods.*
(3) Anagram strings comprising words from the sentences in scrambled order: *Neighbors sleeping noisy wake parties.*

(4)   Word lists compiled from the anomalous sentences and presented in random order: *Floods careful noisy emit flashes.*

Subjects listened to five sequences from one of the four conditions and then tried to reproduce them. The normal sentences proved to be much easier than either the anagram strings or the anomalous sentences, which in turn were easier than the random word lists.

This result was interpreted by Marks and Miller in terms of "a differentiation between semantic and syntactic factors and a facilitatory effect of both on learning" (1964, p. 4). However, such a view seems defensible only if it is claimed that semantic factors apply only to individual words, whereas syntax applies to the sentence as a whole. This seems to be a narrow and somewhat curious view of semantics, implying that the meaning of a sentence is the sum of the meanings of the constituent words. If this were so, the sentence *Fred killed the spider* would be semantically the same as *The spider killed Fred;* or to use an example from the experiment, *Fatal accidents deter careful drivers* would be semantically equivalent to *Deter drivers accidents fatal careful.* Equally implausible is the assumption that the semantically anomalous sentences are semantically equivalent to the random word lists. A sequence such as *Respectable cigarettes save greasy battles* or *Gallant detergents fight accurate fumes* would appear to be much easier to interpret semantically than *Cigarettes respectable battles greasy save* or *Accurate gallant fight fumes detergents.* In short, syntactic and semantic factors appear to be completely confounded in the anomalous sentences, thus invalidating any conclusions about the role of grammar as distinct from that of meaning. This is not because syntax is irrelevant but because a change in syntax inevitably modifies the meaning of a sentence.

INFLUENCE OF CHOMSKY

One of the major influences on the psychology of the 1960s was Noam Chomsky, whose revolutionary views on language had an influence far beyond the traditional bounds of linguistics. This was partly due to Chomsky's view of linguistics as cognitive psychology, since he holds that a theory of language is a theory about the functioning of the most characteristic aspect of the human mind. I shall not attempt to discuss Chomsky's work apart from the absolute minimum needed to understand its influence on memory; a very good review of Chomsky's work is given in Lyons (1970).

Chomsky was first concerned to show the inadequacy of either a simple S–R associative theory or a model based on the observed sequential dependencies among words, as suggested by an information theory approach. Neither of these can handle the fact that language is essentially "creative," in that we are continually understanding and producing sentences which we have never before encountered.* His second aim was to show that it was possible to describe all languages in terms of the operation of a few relatively simple grammatical rules. These rules allow any sentence to be transformed from its *surface structure*, which is determined by the specific words and grammatical constructions used, to its underlying *deep structure*. The difference between surface and deep structure is illustrated by the ambiguous sentence *They are flying planes*. This single surface structure can represent either of two deep structures, one of which could be paraphrased as *They are planes that are flying* (*They* being the planes), the other as *They are making planes fly* (*They* being the fliers). It is assumed that simple active declarative sentences (e.g., *Fred killed the spider*) are closer to the deep structure and hence require fewer transformations than negatives (*Fred did not kill the spider*) or passives (*The spider was killed by Fred*). These, in turn, require fewer transformations than negative passives (*The spider was not killed by Fred*).

Chomsky was concerned to produce a model that could generate any grammatically permissible sentence and no ungrammatical sentences in the language in question. Such a model represents a formal description of the language which does not necessarily describe the way in which people actually use the language; to use Chomsky's own terminology, it is concerned with linguistic *competence* rather than *performance*. However, it clearly does provide some interesting hypotheses as to how language may in fact be used, and a number of studies have attempted to investigate this by studying memory for sentences of various types.

SYNTACTIC MARKER MODEL

An ingenious study by Savin and Perchonok (1965) tested Miller's (1962) hypothesis that sentences may be stored in terms of their kernel, or deep structure, together with a code representing the neces-

---

* Even young children learning to talk produce sentences which they have almost certainly never heard. One morning, for example, one of my own children at the stage of experimenting with words followed a series of rather banal observations on the items on the breakfast table with the casual remark that "You don't put marmalade on cowboys."

sary transformations. Hence, the sentence *Hasn't the girl worn the jewel?* would be stored as *The girl has worn the jewel,* plus the coded information that the sentence involves a negative and a question. Such a view gained some support from a study by Mehler (1963), who observed that simple active declarative sentences which approximate most closely to the kernel were learned most rapidly, and that errors in recalling more complex sentences showed a "drift towards the kernel," as would be expected if subjects were forgetting some of the grammatical markers. Savin and Perchonok were interested in the hypothesis that grammatical markers impair sentence retention because they occupy space in a limited-capacity memory. They tested this hypothesis by presenting sentences of varying grammatical complexity, followed by a sequence of unrelated words; the subject was told to remember the sentence and as many of the unrelated words as possible. It was argued that the more complex the sentence, the greater the number of syntactic markers required and the smaller the amount of memory space left over for remembering the unrelated words. Savin and Perchonok studied a range of sentence types and produced 17 predictions as to the relative difficulty of the various types, all of which were supported by their data.

Unfortunately, however, this result has not proved to be very robust. Matthews (1968) failed to replicate it, and Glucksberg and Danks (1969) found a much weaker effect than that observed by Savin and Perchonok. They also noted that Johnson (1966) had observed that when sentences were learned as responses in a paired-associate task, the more grammatically complex the sentence, the longer the recall latency. When Glucksberg and Danks looked at recall latency, they found a very clear relationship between the delay in recalling the unrelated words and the number of words recalled. They concluded that their results could be interpreted most easily in terms of forgetting during the retention interval, the length of the interval being approximately related to the transformational complexity of the sentence. Such a conclusion is also consistent with the results of Epstein (1969), who found the Savin-Perchonok effect when the sentence was recalled before the unrelated words (as in the original study), but not when the words were recalled first. This suggests that the effect results from recalling the sentence, not from storing it, as the syntactic marker model maintains.

Studies using more conventional techniques show a similar pattern of results, with early studies appearing to support the syntactic marker hypothesis but subsequently proving to be methodologically unsound.

Consider the case of passive sentences, which Mehler (1963) found to be considerably harder to learn than active sentences. The passives used in the earlier studies tended to be longer and less "natural" than actives; however, Schlesinger (1966) showed that even when these factors were controlled, subjects were still twice as likely to recall a passive sentence as an active sentence as they were to do the converse. However, Jesperson (1924) pointed out that the vast majority of passives used in English (70–90 percent) are *truncated* (e.g., *girls' ears were customarily pierced in infancy*); that is, the subject, an unspecified "somebody," who did the piercing, is omitted. It appears, then, that passives are typically used in a situation where the subject of the kernel sentence is either obvious, unknown, or less important than the object. When this is not the case, we tend to use the active; hence, a nontruncated passive is likely to be recalled in its more "natural" active form. Slobin (1968) has shown that while only 23 percent of full passives are in fact recalled as passives, 75 percent of truncated passives are appropriately recalled, suggesting that the syntactic effects observed are in turn dependent on the underlying semantics, in this case the nature of the subject of the sentence.

MEASURES OF SENTENCE COMPLEXITY

An alternative approach to the role of syntax in memory was suggested by a computer program for syntactic analysis devised by Yngve (1960), in which a greater memory load is imposed by a left-branching phrase (e.g., *John's friend's wife's father's gardener's daughter's cat*) than by an equivalent right-branching phrase (*the cat belonging to the daughter of the gardener of the father of the wife of the friend of John*). The extent of left recursiveness in a sentence can be computed fairly simply (see Neisser 1967, p. 273) to give what is known as the sentence's *Yngve depth*. Martin and Roberts (1966) analyzed a range of sentence types and concluded that when length and sentence complexity are controlled, Yngve depth is an important determinant of recall probability, while other grammatical factors have only a marginal effect. However, a later study by Perfetti (1969) found no relationship between Yngve depth and sentence recall. In a subsequent study, Perfetti and Goodman (1971) compared 20 sentences of extreme Yngve depth (mean depth = 7) with 20 semantically equivalent versions of less mean depth (mean depth = 3). Ten of the sentences were better recalled in the deep form, and ten worse recalled. The authors conclude that Yngve grammar is not likely to advance our knowledge of psycholinguistic processes and suggest that there is more to be gained by attention to the meaning of sentences.

Martin and Roberts's study has also been criticized by Rohrmann (1968), who points out that in order to equate sentences for length and complexity, Martin and Roberts inserted additional adjectives and adverbs into some of their simple sentences. In doing so, they grossly complicated the deep structure of the sentences. Rohrmann suggests that the probability of recalling a sentence may depend on the transformational complexity of its deep structure. In order to test this, he compares the recall of subject nominalization, like *growling lions*, with object nominalizations, such as *raising flowers*. While the two are equivalent in surface structure, object nominalizations have a more complex deep structure, since they imply a subject (i.e., someone who raises the flowers), whereas subject nominalizations have no comparable deleted object. Rohrmann tested his structural complexity hypothesis by presenting subjects with equal numbers of subject and object nominalizations for immediate free recall. As predicted, he found better recall of the simpler subject nominalizations.

However, this in turn has been criticized by Paivio (1971a), who observed that Rohrmann's subject nominalizations tended to be more concrete and easy to visualize than his object nominalizations. When the effects of imagery were controlled, Paivio found no evidence for the deep structure hypothesis. A similar conclusion was reached independently by Wearing (1971) and has been extended by Richardson (1975).

Before leaving the topic of syntax, we should consider one further type of sentence which, though grammatical, is very difficult to remember or even understand—namely, the self-embedded sentence. This is discussed by Miller (1962), who gives as an illustration a rephrasing of the right-embedded sentence *This is the cow with the crumpled horn that tossed the dog that worried the cat that killed the rat that ate the malt that lay in the house that Jack built.* From this he builds up a self-embedded version of the same sentence:

The rat ate the malt
The rat that the cat killed ate the malt
The rat that the cat that the dog worried killed ate the malt
The rat that the cat that the dog that the cow tossed worried killed ate the malt, etc.

Miller goes on to describe an experiment on the recall of complex self-embedded sentences. He points out the subject initially responds in a monotone, as if repeating back a sequence of unrelated phrases. After several presentations, however, there tends to be an "Aha!" experience, and from then on the subject tries to produce normal sentence intonation. Miller concludes that the "Aha!" experience occurs when the subject perceives the syntactic structure of the sentence. This seems unlikely, in view of the fact that the subject was repeatedly presented with self-embedded sentences and hence must surely have learned the syntactic structure involved. It seems much more likely that the "Aha!" experience represents a realization of the *meaning* of the sentence.

As Miller (1962, p. 755) points out, "self embedding by its very nature places heavier demands on the temporary storage capacity of any device that attempts to cope with it." It surely does so because the various semantic constituents (the rat eating the malt, the cat killing the rat, etc.) are split and widely separated. Hence, the subject is unable to transfer material from a temporary working memory store into a more durable semantic form as he goes along. With normal speech, this process of semantic recoding appears to be so rapid that it places little strain on STS. This is well illustrated by K.F., the patient with defective STS studied by Shallice and Warrington (1970). He normally had no difficulty in understanding conversation. His performance did break down, however, in a task where comprehension was tested by nonredundant instructions about manipulating colored forms (Warrington and Shallice 1972). He could handle short instructions (e.g., *Touch a red circle*) but was unable to cope with longer sequences (e.g., *Touch the small red circle with the large green square*), presumably because the high information content led to relatively slow semantic encoding. In a normal person this would not matter, since the instruction can be held in working memory until processing is complete, but with defective STS this is not possible and performance breaks down. One might also predict that K.F. would have even greater difficulty than normal subjects in handling self-embedded sentences.

SYNTAX AND THE RECALL OF PROSE

As we have seen, there is little evidence for a major effect of syntax independent of semantics on memory for sentences. In the case of connected discourse, syntax seems even less important. We described earlier a study by Sachs (1967a) showing that recognition memory for the syntactic features of a sentence is very poor unless tested almost immediately, whereas semantic recognition memory showed little forgetting over the intervals studied. An incidental learning study by Wanner (1968) showed an even more rapid loss of syntactic information. Wanner used an ingenious procedure whereby the subject was presented with the instructions for an experiment and was then unexpectedly given a recognition test on the instructions themselves.

Similar results were obtained by Johnson-Laird and Stevenson (1970), who found in a recognition memory study that subjects confused sentences of the form *John liked the painting and he bought it from the Duchess* with sentences having the same meaning but quite different syntactic structure (*The painting pleased John and the Duchess sold it to him*). Even when instructed to retain material, subjects forget the syntactic detail very quickly. Using a running memory span procedure, Jarvella has concluded that verbatim recall is limited to the last clause presented (Jarvella 1970; Jarvella and Herman 1972).

In summary, it appears that the great surge of interest in the role of syntax in human memory following Chomsky's development of transformational grammar has led to a very simple conclusion—namely, that the importance of syntax in long-term memory is very much less than that of semantic factors. These will be considered in the next chapter.

CHAPTER

13

Semantic Memory

Some Basic Assumptions

A RECURRENT THEME throughout this book, and particularly over the previous chapter, has been the pervasive importance of semantic factors in long-term memory. What is meant by the term *semantic memory?* Tulving distinguishes between *semantic memory,* which he defines as "a system for receiving, retaining and transmitting information about meaning of words, concepts and classification of concepts," and what he terms *episodic memory,* which is concerned with "memory for personal experiences and their temporal relations" (Tulving 1972, pp. 401–402). An example of semantic memory might be knowing the chemical symbol for salt, while episodic memory would be exemplified by remembering a personally experienced event, such as meeting a retired sea captain while on holiday. There clearly *are* differences between these two situations, but it is questionable whether a distinction based on anything as subjective and phenomenological as personal reference is either viable or appropriate. Since all memory is surely based ultimately on personal experience, it is hard to see what is gained by assuming different memory stores depending on whether the personal reference is or is not recalled.*

An alternative way of conceptualizing the difference between remembering personal incidents and recalling information is in terms of the degree of abstraction involved. As the previous chapter suggested, long-term memory has a strong abstractive component; we tend to minimize memory load by stripping away inessential details and encoding new material in terms of existing schemata, keeping only enough to allow us to reconstruct the event if recall is required. Our memory of the chemical formula for salt differs from a single personal experience in being based on a large number of personal experiences, most of which happened many years ago when we first began to learn chemistry; they are linked only by the common abstracted core— namely, the piece of information that the chemical formula for salt is NaCl. It is, however, not only the case that semantic memory is built from personal experience by a process of abstraction; it is also the case that what appears to be a direct record of personal experience is itself a reconstruction based on an abstraction. The evidence for this has already been discussed in connection with the work of Bartlett and is illustrated even more clearly by work on legal testimony, which has shown repeatedly that witnesses tend to recall what they would expect to have happened rather than what actually occurred (Hunter 1957). Hence, although Tulving's distinction between episodic and semantic memory may provide a useful reminder of the range of semantic memory, it remains very doubtful whether this reflects a clear dichotomy between separate storage systems, as Tulving suggests. We shall therefore continue to use the term *semantic memory* to refer to both personal and general knowledge of the world. In doing so, we are assuming that the semantic memory system is, in effect, a model of the world, inside the subject's head, or in Bartlett's terms a set of interrelated schemata.

---

* This is well illustrated by the work of Byrne (1976), who asked housewives to produce menus for meals under certain constraints (e.g., an inexpensive three-course lunch) and recorded their ongoing description of the process. Both general principles (semantic memory?) and recall of specific meals (episodic memory?) were inextricably interwoven. He concluded that for this type of task, the semantic-episodic distinction was not very fruitful.

Semantic Factors in Sentence Memory

As we saw in the previous chapter, attempts to explain the retention of prose material in terms of its syntax proved ultimately disappointing. What appeared to be demonstrations of the importance of syntax for memory were subsequently shown either to be artifactual or to depend primarily on semantic rather than purely syntactic factors. Unfortunately, there exists no theory of semantics which could play a comparable role to that played by Chomsky's transformational grammar; consequently, the work we shall discuss in the present chapter reflects a relatively wide range of underlying views of semantics. We shall begin with the work of Clark, which assumes an approach to semantics derived from the semantic feature theory of Katz and Fodor (1963). This approach has something in common with the previously described work on syntax, since it concentrates heavily on the analysis of specific words in individual sentences.

SEMANTIC MARKING

Clark and Clark (1968) carried out a memory experiment in which subjects were presented with a number of sentences. Each sentence comprised a main and a subordinate clause and described the order in which two events occurred. Six possible forms of each sentence were prepared (e.g., *He tooted the horn before he swiped the cabbages,* or *Before he swiped the cabbages he tooted the horn*). Subjects subsequently tried to recall the sentences, and the form of the sequences recalled was compared with what would be expected if subjects remembered sentences in terms of syntactic features. In fact, the pattern of errors was inconsistent with the syntactic view, but the errors could be accounted for relatively simply by assuming that subjects have biases in favor of (1) reporting events in the order in which they occurred and (2) reporting main clauses before subordinate clauses. Clark and Clark report that both these tendencies occur in young children during the early stages of language development, and they suggest that their findings can readily be incorporated into a more general theory of memory for semantic distinctions.

The theory proposed is based on the concept of marked and unmarked semantic distinctions. A number of linguists have pointed out that many semantic features in English have two forms, a semantically

THE PSYCHOLOGY OF MEMORY

simple, unmarked form and a more complex marked form. For example, singular nouns are regarded as unmarked, whereas plural nouns are marked, typically by adding an *s* (Katz and Postal 1964; Greenberg 1966). Marking represents the deviation from some basic simple form; for example, the expression *not closed* could be regarded as a marked version of *open*. Clark and Clark suggest that in reading sentences, subjects extract and remember certain semantic distinctions; they subsequently may forget that a distinction was marked or, less often, unmarked. When attempting to recall the material, they generate sentences on the basis of the semantic features remembered, and since marked distinctions will tend to be lost, there will be a tendency for marked features to be recalled as unmarked. Clark and Clark maintain that a sentence in which the order of events described is inconsistent with the order in which they occurred (e.g., *He swiped the cabbages but first he tooted the horn*) involves the marking of the temporal order feature. Since markers tend to be lost through forgetting, it is more likely to be recalled as an unmarked sentence (e.g., *He tooted the horn and then he swiped the cabbages*).

The semantic marker approach to comprehension and memory has been explored most extensively in its application to comparative adjectives. The properties of many adjective pairs, such as *good* and *bad* or *long* and *short,* suggest that such pairs are not symmetrical but consist of one marked and one unmarked adjective. Unmarked adjectives can be used with neutral meaning (*How good is the news?*), whereas the opposite adjective indicates a strong expectation on the part of the speaker (*How bad is the news?*). Similarly, the neutral or unmarked adjective can often be used to refer to the dimension in question (e.g., *goodness, length*), whereas the opposite is typically not the case, presumably because of its non-neutral implications (e.g., *badness, shortness*). Clark and Card (1969) presented subjects with blocks of eight comparative sentences, each containing either a marked or unmarked adjective (e.g., *The pie is better than the cake* or *The cake is worse than the pie*). Subsequent sentence recall showed a clear tendency for marked adjectives to be recalled in their unmarked form. A number of subsequent studies have shown that unmarked adjectives are not only easier to remember but are also understood more rapidly (Clark 1969; Carpenter 1974), and that instructions employing unmarked adjectives are more efficient than those using marked adjectives (Wright and Barnard 1975).

Although the semantic feature approach to memory has been reasonably successful within the relatively limited range of memory situations to which it has been applied, it is essentially concerned with the mapping of semantics onto syntax. It has effectively pointed out that there are systematic rules whereby a particular adjective or order of report is chosen; such rules tend to be observed in generating word sequences representing a given semantic event, and sentences which do not conform to these conventions will tend to be regenerated in a more conventional form, unless the fact that the sequence deviates from the norm is itself stored. Knowledge of these underlying semantic conventions is, of course, both interesting and useful in predicting memory performance, but it does not appear to be the central factor in the retention of meaningful information. Clark's approach tends to conceptualize sentences as isolated linguistic objects, a view which is criticized by Barclay, Bransford, and Franks, who advocate what they call an *assimilation theory,* a view of sentence comprehension and memory which stresses the subject's active role in integrating with his existing knowledge the information from the sentence presented, a view not unlike that suggested by Bartlett and reviewed in Chapter 1.

ASSIMILATION THEORY

Unlike semantic feature theory, which assumes that the comprehension and retention of a sentence involves interpreting it by extracting the relevant semantic features and subsequently storing them, assimilation theory regards comprehension as a constructive process. It holds that the subject's already existing knowledge of the world is used, together with the information in the sentence presented, in creating a semantic structure which may go beyond the information actually specified. It is this latter point which distinguishes the assimilationist view most clearly from semantic feature theory, and it is this aspect of assimilation theory which is stressed most strongly by its adherents.

In the first of a series of papers, Bransford and Franks (1971) studied the ability of subjects to recognize previously presented sentences describing a complex event. Subjects first heard a series of sentences such as *The ants were in the kitchen; The ants ate the sweet jelly; The ants in the kitchen ate the jelly which was on the table;* and *The jelly was sweet.* When subsequently asked to recognize a series of sentences, some of which had in fact occurred and some of which had not, subjects tended to respond on the basis of how much of the overall sequence of events was conveyed by a given sentence. Hence, they were more likely to recognize (falsely) a sentence involving all the semantic information presented (e.g., *The ants in the kitchen ate the sweet jelly which was on the table*) than a shorter sequence (*The jelly was sweet*) which had in fact occurred. Bransford and Franks suggest that their subjects had encoded the incoming sentences in terms of a semantic structure which went beyond any of the individual sentences.

A similar point was made by Barclay (1973), who required his subjects to remember sequences of sentences describing the location of an array of five animals standing in a row. Some subjects were advised to use visual imagery, whereas others were induced to treat each sentence as an independent semantic unit. In the visual imagery group, subjects who had heard sentences such as *The bear is to the left of the moose* and *The cow is to the right of the bear* subsequently "recognized" sentences which they had not in fact previously heard (e.g., *The cow is to the right of the moose*), provided the sentences were consistent with the array described. Subjects induced to treat the sentences as independent objects performed very poorly but did not show this tendency. Bransford, Barclay, and Franks (1972) compared the retention of sentences of the following two types:

(1) *Three turtles rested beside a floating log, and a fish swam beneath them.*
(2) *Three turtles rested on a floating log, and a fish swam beneath them.*

Subjects presented with the second sentence tended to recognize falsely a sentence such as *Three turtles rested on a floating log, and a fish swam beneath it;* subjects who had originally been presented with sentence 1 showed no such tendency. Once again, Bransford, Barclay, and Franks suggest that the subject remembers a semantic construction incorporating the information presented in the sentences, but not the sentences themselves.

The type of experiment just described appeared to argue strongly for the view that subjects go beyond the information literally specified in the sentences they are required to remember, encoding the information in terms of what Bartlett would have called schemata. This, of course, does not mean that the concept of a semantic feature is of no value in explaining the results of memory studies, but it does suggest that the concept is insufficient. The subject's existing knowledge of the world clearly plays a crucial role in interpreting and remembering meaningful material. Unfortunately, how such information is stored and how it is employed in remembering new material are not at present specified by assimilation theory. One obvious possibility is that subjects use visual images to encode the information presented. In some of Barclay's experiments, subjects were explicitly instructed to do so, while the type of material used in the other experiments described would also lend itself to this form of coding. However, Franks and Bransford (1972) have shown that similar effects occur in remembering abstract material, such as *The emotional appeal for support elicited unselfish sympathy.* In short, Bransford, Barclay, and Franks have pointed very clearly to the need to know more about the way in which our knowledge of the world is stored. Attempts to tackle this important and difficult issue will be considered in the next section.

Models of Semantic Memory

After some ingenious initial work by Cattell (1887), the attempt to investigate semantic memory directly was neglected for the next 80 years (with the exception, of course, of Bartlett's work). One of the first modern attempts to reinvestigate it was Oldfield and Wingfield's (1965) experiments on naming objects and pictures. They observed that both the speed and accuracy of naming increased with the familiarity of the name (and presumably also the object itself), as measured by its frequency of occurrence in the Thorndike-Lorge (1944) word count. It seems likely that naming is analogous to the process of retrieving words from memory in order to talk. As would be predicted on this view, Oldfield (1966) found that aphasic patients who have difficulty in speaking fluently show an exaggerated form of the normal function, as Figure 13–1 shows.

Oldfield points out that normals show the kind of "tongue-tied" retrieval blocking typical of aphasics, if the stimuli to be named are presented rapidly enough to overload the retrieval mechanism. Oldfield explains his frequency effect in terms of the size of the set of items to be searched, arguing that there are more low-frequency items than high-frequency ones. This interpretation seems to require the assumption that the subject first decides on the frequency or familiarity and then uses this to access the appropriate part of his memory store, an implausible assumption which proved inconsistent with subsequent evidence (Bartram 1973).

The suggestion that the size of the set of items to be searched determines performance was revived in a somewhat different form by Landauer and Freedman (1968). They measured the time taken to

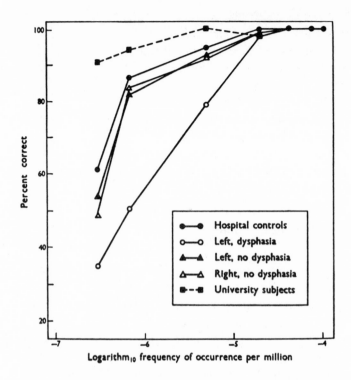

Figure 13–1   Probability of correctly naming a picture as a function of the frequency of occurrence of the name in the language. Note that the association between name frequency and probability of a correct response occurs for all groups but is particularly clear in the dysphasic patient group. Source: F. Newcombe, R. C. Oldfield, and A. Wingfield, Object naming by dysphasic patients, *Nature* 207 (1965): 1218. Reprinted by permission.

decide whether a given word (e.g., *dalmatian*) was a member of a previously specified category (e.g., *dogs*). They manipulated category size by ensuring that the smaller of two categories was a subset of the larger (e.g., *dogs* and *animals*), observing that it took longer for subjects to decide that a *dalmatian* is an *animal* than that it is a *dog*. The category-size effect also occurred in the case of negative instances; thus, it took longer to decide that a *chair* is not an *animal* than that it is not a *dog*. By analogy with Sternberg's (1966) high-speed exhaustive scan in STM (see Chapter 7), they suggest that subjects scanned the relevant semantic category. They assume, however, that the search was self-terminating (unlike Sternberg's STM model), with the subject responding "yes" as soon as he detected a match between the stimulus word (*dalmatian*) and an item in the set being scanned (*dogs*). In the case of negative stimuli, subjects must always scan the whole set before concluding that they should respond "no"; as this model would predict, size of set has a greater effect on RT to negative instances.

A problem for this model, however, is presented by the observation that processing time depends on the nature of negative as well as positive instances. Hence, it takes longer to decide that a *potato* is not a *tree* than that a *witness* is not (Collins and Quillian 1970; Wilkins 1971). A model which simply scans the relevant category for the presence of the target word and responds "no" if it is not found should not be sensitive to the nature of the negative instance. That it *is* sensitive suggests that some form of semantic *comparison* is an important component of the task.

An approach to semantics which is already influencing the study of memory is that based on computer simulation. Several programs are currently under development which aim at computer "comprehension" of natural English text and, at the same time, hope to serve as psychological models of human semantic processing (Quillian 1968; 1969; Winograd 1972; Rumelhart, Lindsay, and Norman 1972; Anderson and Bower 1973).

QUILLIAN'S MODEL

The first of these to stimulate testable psychological predictions was Quillian's program, the Teachable Language Comprehender (Quillian 1969). This program "comprehends" text by relating each assertion in the text to a large semantic memory network representing facts already known about the world. Any parts of the network that are successfully related to the assertion in the text are copied. These copies are then integrated to form a new structure, which is in the same form as the rest of the memory network. It is the formation of this new structure, relating the text to the already existing network, that is the essence of comprehension. Since the structure is in the same form as the semantic network, it can be added directly to the existing semantic memory. Note that although this was not designed primarily as a psychological theory, it does have one of the major features of semantic memory discussed earlier: namely, that it envisages comprehension as a constructive process. Creating a semantic structure requires the integration of the presented material with the multidimensional model of the world that constitutes the existing semantic memory; this structure itself then becomes part of the memory system.

Quillian's memory network comprises *units* and *properties*. A unit represents the memory's concept of some object, event, or assertion—that is, anything which can be represented in English by a word, phrase, or longer piece of text (e.g., *DOG, JOE SMITH,* or *THE U.S. CONSTITUTION*). Note that although we shall normally refer to units as if they were single words, the unit is stored as a semantic entity, not as a word. To emphasize this point, capital letters are used to represent units. Words are represented in the system by a *dictionary* in which each word is linked to one or more units.

A property represents some descriptive feature of a unit, such as would be represented in English by a verb phrase, a relative clause, or some kind of adverbial or adjectival modifier. Thus the unit *CANARY* might be linked with a number of properties, such as *is yellow, can sing, is kept as a pet,* and so forth. In addition, each property has a quantifier or value. Thus, the characteristic *is yellow* can be broken into the property *color,* which has the value *yellow.*

Finally, each unit has one obligatory feature: it must be linked to its superset, which in turn is a unit. Hence, *CANARY* would be linked to *BIRD,* and *BIRD* in turn to *ANIMAL.* New units can be constructed by modifying the properties of already existing units, which then become the superset of the new unit. For example, the unit *JOE–SMITH* can be modified to produce a new subset unit, *JOE–SMITH–AS–A–BOY,* by attaching the appropriate properties to the *JOE–SMITH* unit.

In order to comprehend text, the memory is searched for properties related to that text. All *candidate units* are scanned simultaneously until an overall meaning emerges which allows selection among the units. This initial semantic scan thus produces hypotheses about the text's meaning, and these are then checked syntactically. Note that the role of syntax is to facilitate semantic processing,' as appears to be the case in human memory. Any syntactically permissible relationship produced is then checked to see if its meaning is consistent with what has already been "comprehended." If it is, it is recopied, and the copy is encoded as part of the meaning of the text.

The brief outline just given inevitably oversimplifies the model, but it provides us with enough background to understand the experiments by Collins and Quillian that attempt to test its psychological validity. These are best explained in terms of Figure 13–2, which represents

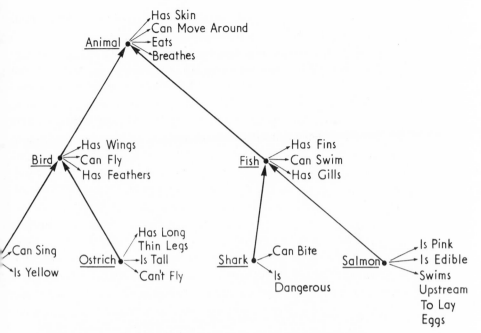

Figure 13–2 Illustration of hypothetical memory structure for a three-level hierarchy, as conceptualized by Collins and Quillian. Source: Based on A. M. Collins and M. R. Quillian, Retrieval time from semantic memory, *Journal of Verbal Learning and Verbal Behavior* 8 (1969): 241. Reprinted by permission.

units and their properties from a three-level hierarchy in the memory structure of Quillian's model. Note that each property is stored at the highest level unit to which it applies. Hence *can fly* is stored with *BIRD* rather than with each individual instance, thereby reducing the amount of storage space required. In the case of an exception like *OSTRICH*, the fact that it *can't fly* is stored with the unit itself. Comprehension of a statement involves finding a syntactically permissible path through the network. In the case of the sentence *A canary has skin*, this path would comprise the sequence *A canary is a bird, A bird is an animal, An animal has skin.*

The model was tested by presenting subjects with a series of sentences and measuring the time (RT) taken to decide whether they were true or false. The following assumptions were made:

(1) It takes time to move from a unit to a property or from a unit to its superset.
(2) Where one step depends on completion of another, the two RTs are added.

(3)   Retrieval proceeds from a given unit in all directions simultaneously.
(4)   The average time for a step does not depend on the level of the hierarchy involved.

In short, RT should depend, first, on the number of levels of the hierarchy that must be traversed and, second, on whether or not a property must be retrieved.

Two types of sentences were produced, involving each of three degrees of movement through the hierarchy. One type involved super-set relationships requiring a path through either two levels of the hierarchy (e.g., *A canary is an animal*), one level (*A canary is a bird*), or zero levels (*A canary is a canary*). The second type involved properties that were assumed to be stored either two levels above in the hierarchy (*A canary has skin*), one level above (*A canary can fly*), or at the same level as the unit concerned (*A canary is yellow*). An equal number of clearly false sentences were produced from both superset sentences (*A canary is a fish*) and property sentences (*A canary has gills*). The results are shown in Figure 13–3.

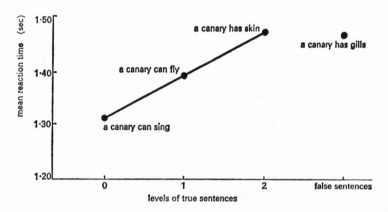

Figure 13–3   Average time to process a sentence as a function of the number of hierarchical levels in Quillian's model of semantic memory. Source: Based on A. M. Collins and M. R. Quillian, Retrieval time from semantic memory, *Journal of Verbal Learning and Verbal Behavior* 8 (1969): 244. Reprinted by permission.

As predicted, RT increases linearly with the number of levels of the hierarchy that must be traversed, the only exception being sentences like *A canary is a canary,* which are faster than might be expected. This is not really surprising, since no semantic processing is necessary; such sentences can be verified on the basis of a simple pattern match which Posner and Mitchell (1967) have shown to be particularly rapid. Apart from this, the data are consistent in suggesting that it takes about 75 msec to move from a unit to its superset and about 225 msec to retrieve a property from a unit.

In a subsequent experiment, Collins and Quillian (1970) made the additional assumption that if the same path in the hierarchy is used in two successive sentences, RT on the second sentence should be faster because a common path has been primed by the first sentence. For example, if verification of the sentence *A canary can fly* involves two stages, *A canary is a bird* and *A bird can fly,* then it should facilitate a sentence like *A canary has a beak,* which has a stage in common with it (i.e., *A canary is a bird*). Less facilitation should be found with a sentence like *A canary is yellow,* which does not share a common path in the hierarchy. This was tested and found to be the case. In addition, there was considerable facilitation on all adjacent sentences in which the same noun was used, suggesting that location of the unit corresponding to the noun comprises a major component of this task.

So far we have considered only true sentences, but how do subjects decide that a sentence is false? The model does not specify this, although it can be used to generate a number of testable hypotheses. The simplest of these would be to assume that a subject responds "false" when he can find no permissible path between the components of a sentence. This would imply that the nature of the negative instance should be unimportant, so long as no legitimate path exists. However, as Schaeffer and Wallace (1969) and Wilkins (1971) showed, it takes longer to decide that a *pine* is not a flower than that a *chair* is not a flower, suggesting that some sort of discrimination takes place, even though no permissible path exists. The more features a negative instance has in common with the category, the longer it will take to reject. This is consistent with the introspection of Collins and Quillian's (1972) subjects, who report that they consider several possible interpretations of a sentence before they reject it as false.

Collins and Quillian attempted to explore the question of negative decisions by considering two further hypotheses. The first is Schaeffer and Wallace's (1970) suggestion that the greater the degree of semantic overlap between the two components of the sentence, the longer it will take to respond "false." In order to test this, they produced two types of negative sentences, incorrect but semantically compatible (e.g., *An encyclopedia is short*) and semantically anomalous (e.g., *A collie has a sparkplug*). On the semantic overlap hypothesis, anomalous sentences should be rejected faster, since the two units are selected so as to be completely unrelated. The second hypothesis assumes that a negative response is slowed down when an extraneous path linking the two units of the sentence occurs and must be checked, the additional checking leading to a longer RT. An example would be the sentence *Madrid is Mexican,* where the association of both *MADRID* and *MEXICO* with *SPANISH* provides a possible link which must be checked before responding.

The two hypotheses were tested in a study containing four types of negative sentences: anomalous sentences with an extraneous path (e.g., *An almond has a fortune,* where the path is via *ALMOND COOKIES* and *FORTUNE COOKIES,* both served in U.S. Chinese restaurants); anomalous sentences with no extraneous path (e.g., *A pecan has a castle*); and compatible sentences with an extraneous path (e.g., *Madrid is Mexican*), and without one (e.g., *An encyclopedia is short*). Results showed significantly slower responding to sentences with an extraneous path, but no effect of anomaly. Collins and Quillian conclude that the nature of the negative is important only if it allows an extraneous inadmissible path between the two units.

At least one other interpretation is possible, however. Conceptually, the task can be divided into two phases: (1) producing an acceptable semantic interpretation of the sentence and (2) deciding whether this is in fact true—that is, whether it corresponds with the outside world. The first of these phases is likely to be slowed down by semantic anomaly, the second by semantic similarity. It takes a long time to comprehend the meaning of *A pecan has a castle,* but once interpreted, it can easily be rejected; RT to such sentences will depend on whether the time lost in comprehension is less than the time saved at the semantic comparison stage. The presence of an extraneous path may slow down either the comprehension stage, as in the example *A newspaper is red* (where the subject may confuse *red* with its homophone *read*), or the comparison stage, as in the Madrid example (where the adjective *Mexican* would be regarded by most subjects as semantically similar to the correct adjective, *Spanish*).

This interpretation is consistent with the introspective comments of Collins and Quillian's subjects, who claim that they always decide on an interpretation and can subsequently say why they decided a given sentence was false. This often involves imagery, as in the case of a subject who reported rejecting the sentence *A limousine has a rudder* because "I looked at the back of a limousine and didn't find any rudder." Responses are not always based on imagery, however; associative coding appears to have led one subject to reject falsely the statement *Gin is wet,* presumably because of the association *dry gin.* Evidence of a similarity effect in the absence of a direct extraneous path was indeed found in a subsequent experiment (Collins and Quillian 1972, exp. 3). Sentences like *A St. Bernard is a cat* were rejected relatively slowly, presumably because of the semantic relatedness of *cat* and *dog.*

By this stage the decision rules governing whether a sentence will be classified as true or false have become very complicated. In what they term the *conditional stopping hypothesis,* Collins and Quillian (1972) suggest that the subject chooses among at least five possible actions, some of which are themselves only vaguely specified (e.g., projecting the path in imagery to evaluate its truth value).

Thus, to cope with negative instances, the model has become considerably more complex. There are reasons to believe that it may need to become still more complex if it is to account for a number of subsequent results.

Category-size effect. A number of studies (Landauer and Freedman 1968; Landauer and Meyer 1972; Wilkins 1971) have observed that it takes longer to classify an item as belonging to a large category than to a small category. Collins and Quillian (1970) have argued that this is a function of the fact that large categories tend to have more hierarchical levels, but Landauer and Meyer (1972) argue strongly against such a view. A particularly difficult problem for the Collins-Quillian view is raised by Meyer and Ellis's (1970) demonstration of a category-size effect in the case of nonwords. Thus, it takes a subject longer to decide that a *mafer* is not an animal than it takes him to decide that it is not a type of dog. It is not easy to see how it can be argued that the link involves more levels of the hierarchy in the larger category, since no link presumably exists between nonwords and category names.

Associative frequency effects. A number of studies have shown that the strength of the preexisting associative links between the items being processed is a powerful determinant of reaction time. Wilkins (1971) showed that subjects can verify a dominant or salient member of a category consistently more rapidly than they can in the case of a less salient item. It takes less time to decide that a *robin* is a bird than that a *chicken* is. A related observation is that of Carol Conrad (1972), who showed that the properties typically assigned by Collins and Quillian to the lower items in a hierarchy (e.g., *can sing* in the case of *CANARY*) tended to be more salient features of the item in

331

question than the features used with higher-level items (e.g., *A canary has skin*). Furthermore, features which were frequently produced by subjects required to define an item were verified more rapidly than less frequently produced features. When this aspect of associative frequency was controlled, Conrad found that the hierarchical effect observed by Collins and Quillian remained for sentences involving class inclusion (*A canary is a bird* was still faster than *A canary is an animal*), but the effect disappeared in the case of semantic features.

This suggests, for example, that it is not necessary in deciding whether the sentence *A shark can move* is true to confirm that a shark is a member of the class *FISH*, which is a subcategory of the class *ANIMALS*, which have the characteristic that they move. It seems much more probable that the fact that sharks move is stored as part of the information about sharks; it seems counterintuitive that the method of deducing the characteristics of items from the characteristics of their supersets should be the only, or possibly even the normal way of operating. Hence, it seems likely that a subject who has responded "yes" to both *A shark can move* and *A snail can move* will have derived considerably more information than is implied by a simple hierarchical search; he has probably also processed information regarding the difference in the type and speed of movement involved.

A third problem for the simple hierarchical model of sentence verification comes from a study by Rips, Shoben, and Smith (1973), who showed that subjects took longer to decide whether items were members of the class *MAMMAL* than to decide whether they were *ANIMALS*, despite the fact that *MAMMAL* is a subset of the class *ANIMALS*. This probably reflects the fact that subjects are less familiar with the concept of a mammal than they are with the concept of an animal. At an intuitive level this result is not perhaps surprising, but it does present problems for a simple hierarchical model. One response to this problem is, of course, to turn the criticism on its head and argue that all the situations described are ones in which a greater number of intervening nodes occur for the less frequent items. However, while it is possible in principle to elaborate the semantic network in a post hoc manner on these lines, unless some means of specifying independently the number of intervening nodes is prescribed, the model ceases to be testable; as such, it would seem likely to become theoretically sterile.

A number of alternative semantic-processing models have been suggested in order to circumvent these difficulties; they include category search models (Landauer and Freedman 1968) and models which emphasize the comparison stage of the verification task rather than item retrieval (Schaeffer and Wallace 1970; Meyer 1970). On the whole, such models tend to be rather less ambitious than that of Quillian, and their proponents are prepared to accept that subjects are capable of employing a range of strategies in order to comply with the experimenter's demands. This is probably a realistic, if less clear-cut, view of the situation.

One component which tends to be neglected in Quillian's model is the process of accessing the individual units. In my own case, for example, the unit *CANARY* is probably considerably more accessible than the unit *PECAN,* and this will presumably tend to make the processing of sentences about pecans slower than sentences about canaries.* The next component involves comprehending the sentence or, in terms of Quillian's model, finding an acceptable path between the units. Finally, there is the question of comparing this path or structure with "reality" and deciding whether or not it is true. A sentence like *A dagger is explosive* is quite meaningful, since one can conceive of a world in which daggers would be in the habit of exploding, although this happens not to be true of the present world. Unless these stages can be separated empirically, it is not easy to see how a single clear and unambiguous interpretation of any given result can be provided. In the absence of such specification, it seems unlikely that the technique can continue to be fruitful.

WINOGRAD'S PROGRAM

An approach which avoids many of the problems of Quillian's model is embodied in Winograd's (1972) program for conversing with a computer in normal English. It does so by limiting itself to a very narrow, circumscribed world comprising blocks of various shapes, sizes, and colors which it can manipulate and answer questions about. It includes three subprograms: one for syntactic analysis, one for semantics, and a third for reasoning. The three operate simultaneously, which makes this program much more powerful than earlier models in which the various processes were performed successively. Another

---

* As Clark (1973) has pointed out, most studies in the field of semantic memory commit what he calls the *language-as-a-fixed-effect-fallacy* by failing to test whether performance differences apply across the sample of material, as well as the sample of subjects. Consequently, although we may be confident that the effects reported are not due to a few atypical subjects, they may be the result of one or two atypical items. Following Clark's paper, it is now standard practice to take both factors into account.

feature of the program is the absence of a clear distinction between the *data base* of information fed into the program (the computer's knowledge of its world) and the *executive routines,* which in most programs act as a separate component with a monitoring and controlling function (the computer's operating instructions). Winograd's program seems to be remarkably successful in "understanding" and "conversing" about its world. Like Bransford and Franks's subjects, it is not limited to repeating information previously provided. It can draw inferences and conclusions about that information, give "reasons" for its answers, and ask for further information in a very human way. This is best illustrated by an example.

The language-understanding system carries out actions and answers questions about a simple scene containing a table, a hand, a box, and several blocks and pyramids. The italic lines in lowercase were typed in by a person, and the uppercase lines are the computer's responses. Other lines are comments describing some of the features being exhibited.

(1) *pick up a big red block.*
OK.
The system answers "OK" when it carries out a command. In order to pick up the red block, it had to clear it off by finding a space for a green one and moving the green one away.

(2) *grasp the pyramid.*
I DON'T UNDERSTAND WHICH PYRAMID YOU MEAN.
There are three pyramids in the scene, so the program does nothing.

(3) *find a block which is taller than the one you are holding and put it into the box.*
The system has to figure out what is meant by "one" and "it," as well as using deduction to decide which block it is holding.
BY "IT," I ASSUME YOU MEAN THE BLOCK WHICH IS TALLER THAN THE ONE I AM HOLDING.
Printed out to keep us informed.
OK.
The hand has to set down the red block to pick up the taller blue one.

(4) *what does the box contain?*
THE BLUE PYRAMID AND THE BLUE BLOCK.

(5) *what is the pyramid supported by?*
Earlier, the system responded to *the pyramid* by saying I DON'T UNDERSTAND WHICH PYRAMID YOU MEAN. Now it assumes that we mean the one just mentioned.
THE BOX.

(6) *how many blocks are not in the box?*

Negatives such as "not" and "no" are handled whether they appear in clauses or noun groups (such as "no boxes").
FOUR OF THEM.

(7) *is at least one of them narrower than the one which I told you to pick up?*
The phrase "at least one of them" must be analyzed to refer back to the previous question, and *the one which . . .* must also refer to blocks. Noun groups can have complicated numbers, such as "at least one," "more than three," "exactly seven," etc. The memory of past events is used to deduce which block is *the one which I told you to pick up.* Notice the complicated syntactic structure in which *the one* is actually the object of a clause embedded two levels deeper.
YES, THE RED CUBE.

(8) *is it supported?*
Passives can be used without a "by . . ." phrase.
YES, BY THE TABLE.

(9) *can the table pick up blocks?*
NO.
The semantic rules make this a nonsensical question which therefore must be false.

(10) *can a pyramid be supported by a block?*
YES.
The deductive system finds an actual example, so it knows this is possible.

(11) *can a pyramid support a pyramid?*
I DON'T KNOW.
The question makes sense, but there is no example in the scene, so there is no way to tell without being able to examine the robot's programs.

(12) *stack up two pyramids.*
I CAN'T.
The robot tries and fails (Winograd 1972, pp. 8–10).

There is no doubt that Winograd's program is an impressive achievement. Note, however, that he makes the problem tractable by deliberately limiting the semantic world that is handled. While this is sensible strategy, it does leave open the question of whether the enormously greater richness and complexity of human semantic memory may not demand a qualitatively different approach from that used by Winograd.

RUMELHART-LINDSAY-NORMAN MODEL

A program which has features in common with Winograd's but which directly attempts to simulate human memory is the Rumelhart, Lindsay and Norman (1972) process model of long-term memory. It has obvious similarities with Quillian's model but is considerably more complex. Whereas Quillian's memory system has essentially two components—units and properties—with a single, associative-type link, the Rumelhart-Lindsay-Norman process model has two types of units or *nodes,* three types of information, and a whole range of relationships. It is considerably more linguistically oriented than Quillian's model, drawing particularly on the case grammar of Fillmore (1968); unlike Quillian's, it has as its prime object the development of a psychological theory.

Rumelhart et al. begin by emphasizing the fact that in everyday life, long-term recall has as much in common with problem solving as with standard laboratory list learning. This point is well illustrated by a protocol discussed by Norman (1970a).

> *Question: Where were you living in March of 1954?*
>
> "Well, I know I lived in ah Philadelphia in 1954 because I didn't move out of Philadelphia until 1961. And in, 19___ let's see, my parents moved into their house in 1950 or '51 because they got a 20-year mortgage and I know from a recent phone conversation that that's almost all paid. So we must have been living in um . . ."
>
> Eventually, the subject went on to recall the street address of the house, the school he went to, and other details. But he started out by bracketing the date with some known facts. First he got to the likely city, then he confirmed that by recalling when he moved out (to go to college). Then he selected the likely house by confirming the date he had moved into the house. Finally, he went to work trying to remember the house itself and the details around it.
>
> (Norman 1970a, p. 301)

Rumelhart et al. set themselves the ambitious task of producing a clearly specified memory model that is capable of this degree of flexibility. Their model comprises a *data base,* which represents information stored, and a number of *interpretive processes,* which represent the means of putting new material into the system and of manipulating and retrieving the information that is already there.

As in the case of the Quillian model, the basic element of the data base is the node, which represents a cluster of information in the memory. Nodes are of two types: *primary,* when they refer to general concepts, and *secondary,* when they refer to specific instances of a general concept. Hence, the general concept of a snake would be represented by a primary node, while the particular snake that is said to have killed Cleopatra would be represented by a secondary node.

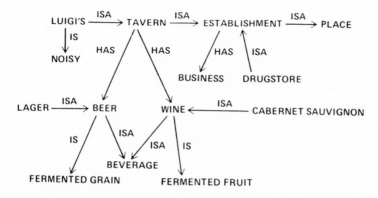

Figure 13–4 Representation of conceptual information in the system of Rumelhart, Lindsay, and Norman. Source: D. E. Rumelhart, P. H. Lindsay, and D. A. Norman, A process model for long-term memory, in E. Tulving and W. Donaldson (eds.), *Organization and Memory* (New York: Academic Press, 1972), p. 204. Reprinted by permission.

Three classes of information are distinguished: *concepts, events,* and *episodes.* A *concept* refers to a particular idea (e.g., *SNAKE*). An *event* is action-based and involves the actors, objects, and general scenario; the snake biting Cleopatra would be an example of an event. An *episode* comprises a series of events; hence, Cleopatra's holding the snake to her bosom, being bitten, and dying would be an episode. A concept is represented in the memory system by three major relations: (1) the class to which it belongs; (2) its defining characteristics; and (3) examples of the concept. Rumelhart et al. represent the class relationship by an arrow labeled *isa,* a compound word constructed from *is* and *a;* an example would be *JOHN isa MAN.* The property relationship is represented by an arrow labeled either *is* or *has,* as in *A MAN has HANDS* or *JOHN is TALL.* An example is represented by simply using the class or *isa* relationship in the reverse direction. Figure 13–4 represents the encoding of information about a tavern called "Luigi's" using this notation.

In order to encode an event or episode, the relevant concepts must be linked by relationships of a different kind. Following the case grammar of Fillmore (1968), Rumelhart et al. distinguish between an *action,* represented by a node with a circle around it, and various subsidiary features of the action, such as the *agent* (who is responsible for the action), the *instrument* (by which the action is per-

337

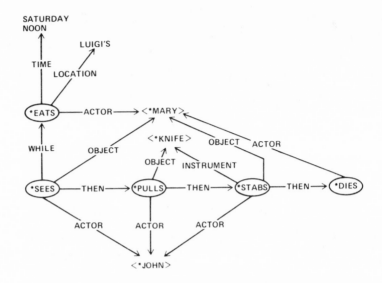

Figure 13–5   Representation of the episode *John murders Mary at Luigi's* in Rumelhart, Lindsay, and Norman's semantic memory system. Source: D. E. Rumelhart, P. H. Lindsay, and D. A. Norman, A process model for long-term memory, in E. Tulving and W. Donaldson (eds.), *Organization and Memory* (New York: Academic Press, 1972), p. 209. Reprinted by permission.

formed), the *object* (which is affected by the action), the *recipient* (who receives the effect of the action), the *time* and *location* of the action, and several more. Figure 13–5 represents an episode that occurred at Luigi's tavern using this notation. Can you work out what happened?

We have so far concentrated on the question of how information is represented in the data base of the system. How is it manipulated and subsequently retrieved? The major reorganizational process discussed by Rumelhart et al. concerns the formation of general concepts and the subdividing of existing concepts. If, for example, the system has been given information about several different birds, all of which eat and have wings, the system will form the general proposition that all birds eat and have wings. When a new bird is introduced, the information that it eats and has wings will not be added to the node representing the new bird, since the information is already associated with the superordinate code representing the concept *BIRD*. Hence, there is a tendency for common features to migrate, thereby becoming attached to progressively more general nodes, so long as this continues to be consistent with the incoming information.* If a particular generalization ceases to be consistent with incoming information, an attempt will be made to subdivide the relevant concept. For instance, after the individual has encountered a range of birds which all have the property *can fly,* if the concept of a *PENGUIN* is introduced as a bird that cannot fly, the class of birds will be subdivided.

The process of retrieving information from the data base is analogous to working through a maze. Each concept represents a choice point with a number of labeled paths going in different directions, each leading to another choice point. This process can be illustrated in the free-recall learning of a categorized word list. It is suggested that a semantic retrieval network is built up by the subject as he compares each new item with all other items in short-term memory and attempts to integrate them into higher-level concepts. For the subject to recall the list, the retrieval network must be held in a short-term memory system and used to access the appropriate concept nodes in LTM. Hence, the general concept *ANIMAL* will be held in STS and used to access the particular instances which occurred in the list. If the category name is lost from STS, the instances within that category will not be recalled.

Unfortunately, it seems unlikely that the assumptions underlying the model's simulation of list learning are valid. Its emphasis on STS does not seem to be borne out by such evidence as is available. It may be recalled from Chapter 6 that patients with grossly defective STS have no difficulty in free-recall learning and show no apparent abnormalities of semantic memory. Contrary to the assumptions made in the model, Bruce and Crowley (1970) have shown that items from the same taxonomic category do not need to be in STS at the same time for clustering to occur, while the experiment by Karalyn Patterson described on p. 159 gives no support to the assumption that STS is necessarily used to hold the retrieval network.

However, the Rumelhart-Lindsay-Norman model is still at an early stage of development, and it is certainly too soon for anything other than a superficial evaluation. It makes a determined frontal attack on a very important problem. It is linguistically much more sophisticated than Quillian's model and offers a much more convincing representation of semantic information than Quillian's hierarchical organization; as such, it offers a language that allows one's intuitions about long-

* It may be recalled that this particular feature of cognitive economy was also characteristic of Quillian's model and has been challenged by Carol Conrad (1972).

term memory to be formulated in much more plausible terms than do more traditional approaches. This is illustrated very clearly in Lindsay and Norman's textbook (1972, chaps. 9–10), which gives a very lucid account of the model. However, the model is obviously intended to provide more than just a useful new terminology, and this raises the fundamental question of how one evaluates a system of such complexity.

The method favored by Rumelhart et al. is that of computer simulation. The system is represented as a computer program, and the performance of the program is compared with that of a real subject; if the two are indistinguishable then the program is assumed to be a good model, at least for the conditions studied. However, dealing with a system of the complexity of human semantic memory presents special problems. The largest computer in the world is almost certainly not nearly big enough to encode the contents of a normal adult's semantic memory, so that any test must be based on an incomplete simulation, and even this is likely to make very great computing demands. Furthermore, if the system falls short of complete simulation, the decision has to be taken as to whether this represents a genuine failure of the model or simply reflects the limitations of the particular computer system used. Initially, this will probably be a fairly simple decision, but as the model grows in complexity, as it obviously must if it is to reflect the range and flexibility of processing of a sophisticated human subject, this decision is likely to become increasingly difficult.

A further problem is that of relating the system to experimental investigation. A system that is highly flexible will accommodate to any new empirical evidence without itself going beyond the evidence. Nevertheless, such a model would have two major drawbacks. First, the model's very flexibility would make it difficult to use predictively, so that it would not stimulate fruitful experimentation. Second, it is in principle possible to produce a range of models, all based on different assumptions but all producing the same behavior. If one has two or more models of semantic memory, all producing a reasonable analogue of human memory but based on different principles, how does one choose between them?

In view of the complexity of human semantic memory, however, I suspect we shall be spared that particular dilemma for many years to come. In the meantime, the attempt at simulation should at least draw our attention to the enormous elegance, flexibility, and power of the human memory system.

HUMAN ASSOCIATIVE MEMORY (HAM)

The previous sentence was written in 1971; in 1972, Anderson and Bower published results of a study testing a model very similar in structure to that of the Rumelhart-Lindsay-Norman model; their work suggests that the view just expressed may be far too pessimistic. Their model of Human Associative Memory (HAM) is described in detail in the book of that name published in 1973. This book not only presents a detailed computer-based model but also offers a wealth of empirical data that was used to test and guide its development. As its name implies, HAM is an associative model which assumes that the representation of a sentence in memory comprises a series of associations. As Figure 13–6 shows, HAM's representation of the semantic data base is similar to that of Rumelhart et al., with a particular word being linked to the relevant concept in long-term memory by a labeled association representing such relations as *isa* and *act*.

During the development of their model, Anderson and Bower were concerned with deciding whether clusters of items tend to be integrated as a single gestalt, an integrated whole which is greater than the sum of its parts, or constitute a collection of independent associations; the

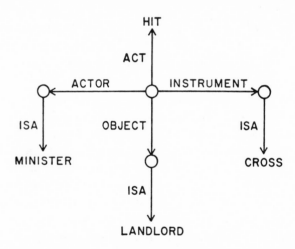

Figure 13–6   Associative structure for the sentence *The minister hit the landlord with a cross* according to Anderson and Bower's system, HAM. Source: J. R. Anderson and G. H. Bower, Configurational properties in sentence memory, *Journal of Verbal Learning and Verbal Behavior* 11 (1972): 602. Reprinted by permission.

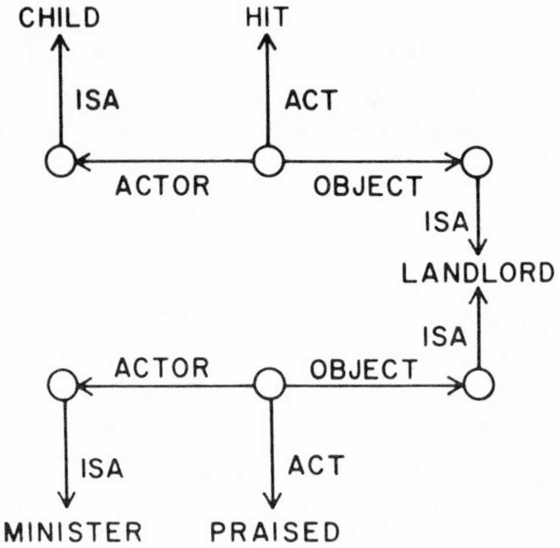

CHILD HIT

ISA ACT

ACTOR OBJECT

ISA

LANDLORD

ISA

ACTOR OBJECT

ISA ACT

MINISTER PRAISED

Figure 13–7 Representation within the HAM memory system of two sentences which share an object. Source: Based on J. R. Anderson and G. H. Bower, Configurational properties in sentence memory, *Journal of Verbal Learning and Verbal Behavior* 11 (1972): 596. Reprinted by permission.

latter assumption was built into their model, HAM. The ingenious method by which they tested this is illustrated in Figure 13–7, which shows the way in which two sentences having the same object might be represented in HAM's memory network.

Anderson and Bower presented a number of pairs of sentences with the same object, such as *The child hit the landlord* and *The minister praised the landlord,* always ensuring that the 2 presentations of similar sentences were separated by 16 other sentences. Subjects were then given various prompt-words from the sentence and required to recall the object, *landlord.* Such prompts might involve either the subject alone (*The child——the——*), the verb alone (*The——hit the——*), the subject and verb from the same sentence (*The child hit the——*), or a combination of the subject from one sentence and the verb from the other (*The child praised the——*). Note that in the latter case, combining the subject from one sentence and the verb from the other produces something which did not occur in either: a semantic structure which is different from any presented and would hence seem intuitively unlikely to be a good retrieval cue. However, a model which assumes, like HAM, that associations are independent would predict that this retrieval cue should be very effective, since the two associations activated both lead to the *LANDLORD* node. The results showed that the crossover condition led to the highest probability of recalling the object, .611, compared to .470 for the subject of the first sentence, .292 for the verb of the first sentence, and .579 for both subject and verb from the first sentence. This result appears to provide clear support for an interpretation based on independent associations, rather than one based on a gestalt or configurational approach to sentence memory. Anderson and Bower (1973) go on to apply their model to a wealth of empirical data, ranging from the classical phenomena of interference theory to the memory search paradigm of Sternberg (1966). However, their work on sentence memory in general, and the crossover result in particular, are central to their view of memory, and we shall therefore concentrate on them.

Anderson and Bower claim that their results are incompatible with a Gestalt view. Is this necessarily the case? At a purely methodological level, a Gestalt psychologist might argue that Anderson and Bower should not have specified to their subjects in advance the possibility that a crossover cue might occur. It is possible that subjects first attempt to recognize the crossover cue as a unit and that, if they fail to find it, they then consider the two components separately. In short, it is arguable that although subjects may normally treat sentences as integrated wholes, they are capable of considering the parts separately, if this seems necessary. Such a view would suggest that the crossover effect would be much less likely to be observed under conditions such as those typically used by Tulving and Thomson (1973), in which the detailed nature of the cues to be presented is not explained to the subject.

A much more basic criticism of HAM is made in a recent paper by Foss and Harwood (1975), who report two experiments which they claim are inconsistent with Anderson and Bower's model. The first of these involved an attempt to replicate the crossover effect just described. Subjects were required to rate the meaningfulness of 24 sentences and 28 "semi-sentences," such as *The experimenter ceased the entity* and *The wizard kept the nothing.* Subjects were told they would subsequently have to answer questions about the more highly meaningful items but were told not to try to memorize them by rote. The sentences were constructed in the same way as those used by Anderson and Bower; recall was subsequently tested with a similar range of prompts, and the nature of these prompts was explained to the subjects. The delay between a given sentence and its prompted recall was held constant at 38 items. Table 13–1 shows the mean probability of

TABLE 13–1

Mean probability of recalling the object of a sentence
as a function of cue type.

CUE	MEAN PROBABILITY OF RECALLING THE OBJECT OF THE SENTENCE	
	ANDERSON AND BOWER	FOSS AND HARWOOD
Subject 1	.470	.193
Verb 1	.292	.152
Subject 1 and verb 1	.579	.399
Subject 1 and verb 2 (crossover cue)	.611	.250
Predicted by HAM	.604	.314

Source: Data taken from J. R. Anderson and G. H. Bower, Configurational properties in sentence memory, *Journal of Verbal Learning and Verbal Behavior* 11 (1972): 594–605, and D. J. Foss and D. A. Harwood, Memory for sentences: implications for human associative memory, *Journal of Verbal Learning and Verbal Behavior* 14 (1975): 1–16.

recalling the object of the sentence, given the various cues for both the original Anderson and Bower study and the replication by Foss and Harwood. Note that in the replication the probabilities of recall are somewhat lower and the predicted superiority of the crossover cue does not occur.

Foss and Harwood's second experiment was concerned with the basic assumption underlying the class of associative models typified by HAM and by an associationist approach in general: namely, that the prompt effectiveness of a combination of cues may be predicted by adding the effectiveness of the constituent cues—or, in the language of Gestalt psychology, that the whole is no greater than the sum of its parts. In the context of the sentence memory experiment just described, this means that, given both the subject and the verb, the probability of recalling the object can never exceed the sum of the probabilities of recalling the object given the subject and the object given the verb. They point out that a ceiling effect must occur when these separate probabilities exceed 0.5, since a probability greater than unity is logically impossible. Thus, this hypothesis can only be tested when recall probabilities for individual cues are relatively low. For this reason, the data from Anderson and Bower's own subjects was incapable of refuting their model on this point, simply because many of their subjects were performing at a level which would produce a ceiling effect so far as this particular value is concerned.

Foss and Harwood therefore ran a second study, in which 24 sentences were again mixed in with 28 semi-sentences, and subjects were again required to rate items on their meaningfulness and to pay particular attention to the more meaningful items. The objects of the meaningful sentences were then cued using either the subject alone, the verb alone, or the combined subject and verb. (There was no crossover condition in this experiment.) Recall levels were sufficiently low to allow the proposed test of the hypothesis to be carried out, with the probability of object recall being .229 when the stimulus was used as a cue, .170 when the verb was used, and .469 when both subject and verb were presented. The results of individual subjects confirmed that the tendency for the *combined* cues to produce better recall than would be expected from summing the individual cues was characteristic of virtually all subjects, except those whose high level of performance led to ceiling effects. On the basis of these two experiments, Foss and Harwood argue for a gestalt or configurational interpretation of sentence memory, rather than the associative model incorporated in HAM.

Foss and Harwood's experiments probably represent only the opening shots in what is likely to become a major issue. But this issue is only a fragment of a very impressive body of empirical evidence and theoretical development, which clearly merits considerably more detailed discussion than we can provide at this point in time. One is tempted to agree with Anderson and Bower's own estimation of their achievement:

> HAM is the first of the network theories [compared to Quillian (1969); Rumelhart, Lindsay, and Norman (1972)] in which the *psychological meaning* of the networks has been carefully developed. It is not enough merely to construct an intuitively satisfying graph and assert that it represents certain information in memory. Such graphs acquire psychological meaning only after one has addressed himself to the necessary task of defining the functional properties of the networks—the mechanisms by which they are constructed, stored, searched, recognised, forgotten, used in reasoning, etc. HAM is distinguished from other models by the explications and detail with which these functional properties and their corresponding mechanisms have been developed and tested (Anderson and Bower 1973, p. 510).

Should I therefore revise my somewhat pessimistic views on the problems of evaluating computer simulations of semantic memory? There is little doubt that in the hands of Anderson and Bower, computer simulation has proved a fruitful technique, suggesting both new ideas and new ways of attacking old problems. However, one could argue that the process of simulation per se is not strictly necessary to Anderson and Bower's approach. For example, using mathematical techniques, Jones (1975) has attacked the question of the structure of knowledge in a very similar set of experiments to those just described. His approach makes far fewer assumptions and is concerned to investigate the structure of memory empirically. His results, based on memory for pictures and for sentences learned both with and without visual imagery, suggest that what the subject acquires are fragments comprising a cluster of features. Such fragments have the characteristic that any given feature will act as a cue for the cluster as a whole. What Jones terms the *fragmentation hypothesis* not only accounts for his own data and the main findings of Anderson and Bower, but also appears to be capable of explaining the deviations from Anderson and Bower's predictions which occur in their data.

The fragmentation hypothesis has not so far been applied as widely or tested as intensively as HAM has. One might also argue that its relatively atheoretical character makes it intrinsically less interesting than HAM; this clearly depends on how accurate Anderson and Bower have been in producing functional properties of their network which are at least broadly similar to the properties of human beings. If we really do construct our memory networks in the same way as HAM does, and if we search, recognize, forget, and reason in the same way, then there is no doubt that HAM is a major achievement.

CHAPTER

14

Supernormal Memory:
Mnemonics and Mnemonists

I N HIS CLASSIC WORK on memory, Ebbinghaus was careful to avoid using any aids to learning other than rote repetition. He explicitly rejected the use of mnemonic systems, and in this respect he has been imitated by the vast majority of psychologists studying memory, who have aimed to control the learning situation sufficiently rigidly to prevent subjects from using such aids. Although there has in recent years been an increase in work on mnemonic systems and the question of how memory performance can be improved, this aspect of memory has continued to interest the layman more than the psychologist. Murdock (1974), for example, suggests that we should wait until we have good theories of normal memory before we attempt to tackle the problem of how memory can exceed the norm, either by studying individual cases of people with good memories or by studying mnemonic systems which allow people with normal memories to improve their performance. My own view is that, far from being a distraction from the pursuit of understanding normal memory, such cases of supernormal memory provide not only clues as to the functioning of normal memory but also a way of testing the generality of our theories of memory.

I shall aim therefore in this final empirical chapter to discuss *supernormal memory,* a phenomenon which is not only interesting in its own right but which also throws light on the principles of memory discussed in the previous chapters. I shall first discuss the ways in which memory and performance can be improved by means of mnemonics, then describe a series of cases of individuals with apparently supernormal memories, and, finally, attempt to produce an account of the data in terms of the processes and principles of normal memory.

Mnemonics

Mnemonics represent schemes for helping to ensure the retention of material which would otherwise be forgotten. They range in complexity from the humble knot in the handkerchief up to the complex and even mystical systems devised in the Middle Ages (Yates 1966). Most systems form a combination of *reduction coding* and *elaboration coding* (Baddeley and Patterson 1971). Reduction coding involves stripping away irrelevant information so as to reduce the amount that needs to be stored. A case in point is the use of the acronym *ROYGBIV* to remember the order in which the colors of the spectrum appear (*red, orange, yellow, green, blue, indigo, violet*) by combining their initial letters. An elaboration code involves adding information beyond what is strictly necessary in order to make the material more memorable, either by adding further and possibly richer dimensions—for example, using visual imagery in order to enhance verbal recall—or by taking advantage of an already existing rich structure of meaning, such as that presented by language. An example of this might be the use of the sentence *Richard of York gains battles in vain* to recall the order of the spectral colors; the capitalized letters of the sentence give the initial letters of the spectral colors in the appropriate order. In the case of a reduction code, the everpresent danger is that of reducing the information to such an extent that it is no longer possible to reconstruct the original. In my own case, for example, I remembered having learned from an old friend that the following rhyme could allow one to reproduce the value of π to the first 20 decimal places:

Pie.
I wish I could remember Pi
Eureka cried the great inventor
Christmas Pudding Christmas Pie
Is the problem's very centre.

Unfortunately, despite remembering the rhyme, presumably via a combination of semantic, linguistic, and rhythmic cues, I could not remember how on earth one decoded it into the appropriate digits. I discovered on telephoning my friend that the rule is in fact very simple: one just counts the number of letters in each word and comes up with the answer 3.14158265358979323846.

A more common instance of failure to decode a reduction mnemonic, in my own case at least, is represented by the knotted-handkerchief mnemonic. I all too frequently discover on removing the handkerchief from my pocket that it has one, two, or even more knots, each apparently aimed at reminding me that I must remember something, but alas telling me no more. Curiously enough, despite the appearance of such a mnemonic on the cover of a popular text on memory, this type of mnemonic never appears to have been studied. And yet it does have intriguing implications for the nature of memory. We do in general have a remarkable ability to make and retrieve "mental notes" or instructions to do things. We use this faculty all the time, not only in such humble tasks as monitoring boiling kettles and cooking eggs but also in keeping track of what we are doing, where our destination is, and what we are intending to do. The remarkable thing is not that we occasionally forget to make a promised phone call or post a letter written the previous day but that we ever remember to do so! It is presumably not the case that we go on actively rehearsing the fact that we must post a letter from the previous night right through until the letter is actually posted, and yet we are remarkably good at retrieving the appropriate information at the right time. How are such mental notes stored? And how do we know when to retrieve them? The terms "forgetful" or "absentminded" tend to be applied to people who do not perform this task very well, and it would appear to be the case that such forgetfulness can be associated with advancing age and, probably, with the aftereffects of ECT or certain drugs. Indeed, from a practical point of view, this type of memory disturbance may present much more of a problem to the patient than inability to learn new material as tested in standard verbal-learning tasks. And yet we do not even have techniques for studying this important aspect of

349

memory. It is, of course, quite possible that standard verbal-learning tasks provide a convenient measure of a single system which underlies both, though the folklore which tends to associate both learning ability and absentmindedness with professors would seem to think otherwise! In any case, it would be nice to have some concrete evidence of what is involved in remembering to remember.

Two basic forms of elaboration coding tend to dominate mnemonic systems: the first utilizes semantic or verbal coding, the second visual imagery. We shall consider them in turn.

VERBAL MNEMONICS

Although most classical mnemonic systems involved imagery, this was not invariably the case. For example, a system devised by Peter Ramus in the sixteenth century proposed an organization of material on logical principles; information was represented in a hierarchical tree, with more abstract concepts dividing and branching into progressively more concrete instances. (Note the similarity to the hierarchical structure postulated in the various models of semantic memory described in the previous chapter.) As Yates (1966) points out, the conflict between the Ramist approach and rival systems which used imagery came to have a considerable religious significance. The Puritans in particular regarded images as wicked and liable to arouse "depraved carnal affections"! Imagery systems were also criticized for requiring the memorizer to remember a great deal of irrelevant information about the location representing the item, the elaborate image signifying it, and the links between location image and information.

However, as we saw earlier, the tendency for mnemonics to require the subject to elaborate the material to be remembered, hence requiring him to remember more than is strictly necessary, is characteristic of most systems. In some cases, though, attempts were made to ensure that the additional elaboration was also relevant to what was to be remembered. One example of this is presented by the Victorian schoolmaster Brayshaw, who published in 1849 his *Metrical Mnemonics*, intended to assist his pupils in remembering the dates of various historical events. The system, which is described by Hunter (1957), involves associating each of the digits 0 to 9 with one or more consonants. The consonants are then incorporated in a key word; this is fitted into one line of verse or doggerel, which also contains one or two outstanding facts about the person or event concerned.

The following two lines are taken from a lengthy "poem" incorporating what were presumably regarded as the salient facts of English history:

> By *men* near Hastings, William gains the Crown:
> A *rap* in Forest New brings Rufus down.

The first line refers to William the Conqueror's victory at the battle of Hastings, with the date of the battle being represented by the word *men*. The letters *m* and *n* are both associated in this system with the digit 6, hence reminding the schoolboy that the battle of Hastings occurred in 1066. The letters *r* and *p* in *rap* represent the digits 8 and 7, respectively, and hence the line reminds the pupil that William Rufus was killed in a hunting accident in the New Forest in 1087. The use of rhyme and rhythm help the sequence to be learned and subsequently recalled. With the decline in the fashion for the rote learning of dates, such systems have virtually disappeared, although as Figure 14–1 suggests, mnemonics may still have a role to play in education.

In contrast to visual imagery mnemonics, relatively little work has been done on linguistic mnemonic systems, although Bower has demonstrated the effectiveness both of hierarchical linguistic organization in free-recall learning (Bower, Clark, Lesgold, and Winzenz 1969) and of the use of rhyme in paired-associate learning (Bower 1970*a*). The very extensive body of work on the role of organization in memory (see Chapter 11) could be described as concerned with the factors underlying linguistic and associative mnemonics, but there has been little attention to verbal mnemonic systems as such, possibly because they are more complex and varied than the visual imagery mnemonics which will be considered next.

VISUAL IMAGERY MNEMONICS

As we saw in Chapter 9, there has in recent years been a revival of interest in mnemonic systems which employ visual imagery. A mnemonic system that was extensively used in classical times by orators who wished to memorize a lengthy speech is known as the "method of loci." This involves first memorizing a sequence of locations—for example, the various rooms and cupboards of one's own house. Each item to be remembered is then visualized in one of these locations. Hence, if I were trying to use this system to remember a shopping list comprising sugar, oranges, onions, tripe, and celery, I might visualize my front porch covered with piles of sugar, a layer of

S   for Sammy Snake   S   for Sammy Sn▮

This snake slithers and slides along making a soft hissing sound in words, like this 'ss▮
His name is Sammy Snake.

Sam sits hissing in the su▮

To Write This Letter:
Start at Sammy Snake's head and stroke him all the
way down to the tip of his tail. Sammy says it feels
good when you do that. (He does *not* like people to
draw him starting at his tail. That makes him very cross.)

h   for hairy hat man   H   for Hairy Hat Man
doing a Handstand
with His Hat on

The Hairy Hat Man hates hearing noise, so he never speaks above a whisper. This is why all you will
ever hear him say in words is "hhh . .". He is whispering "hhh . ." for "Hat Man". You may wonder
what he is doing going about with bare feet all of the time. Actually he never wears shoes because
they make too much noise. You see, he doesn't even want to hear the sound of his own footsteps.
(In a few words he makes no sound at all because he likes peace and quiet so much). Can you hear him
whispering "hhh . ." in these words?

He has a hundred hats.

The Hairy Hat Man always hurries along in the Reading Direction (this way ———→) like nearly everyone
else in Letter Land.

The Snake is Told 'Sh.' by the Hat Man

Sammy Snake is also one of the Hairy Hat Man's pets, and the Hat Man takes good care of
him. The only trouble is that Sammy Snake loves hissing. None of the other Letter People mind
his hissing-sound when he is beside them in a word, but the Hairy Hat Man hates noise. So when
Sammy Snake comes up behind *him* in a word the Hairy Hat Man turns back angrily and says
to him, 'sh.'! In fact, the Hat Man says 'sh.' to him so loudly that Sammy stops hissing right away
and tries to say 'sh' too.

This shop sells fresh fish.

Figure 14–1   A mnemonic system designed for teaching reading and writing. Source: L. Wendon, *The Pictogram System: Set
One,* Barton, Cambridge, England: Pictogram Supplies, 1972, pp.
17, 28, 38. Reprinted by permission.

oranges covering the floor of my hall, a string of onions hanging from the light in my sitting room, my staircase carpeted in tripe, the upstairs landing festooned with sticks of celery, and so forth. In order to recall the items, I simply imagine myself entering my house and visiting the various locations.

A related mnemonic is the use of number "pegs," in which numbers are each associated with a rhyming object (e.g., *one* with *bun, two* with *shoe, three* with *tree,* etc.). One then memorizes the items by visualizing their interactions with the relevant peg-word. Thus, if the first three items were *ship, glass,* and *pig,* you might visualize a bun with a ship sailing into it, a shoe inside a glass, and a pig up a tree. Recall can either proceed serially or be probed directly—for example by requesting the third item, in which case *three* is used to generate *tree,* which is found to contain *pig.* This method works extremely well provided the subject is allowed enough time to perform the initial encoding (Bugelski, Kidd, and Segmen 1968).

How do such mnemonics work? This question has been studied intensively by Bower (1970*b*; 1972), who determined six essential principles:

(1) Both the cues and items must be visualized.
(2) The images must be made to interact so as to form a single integrated image. When subjects are told to image the two items on opposite walls of a room, no facilitation occurs.
(3) The cues either must be easy for the subject to generate himself or must be provided by the experimenter during recall.
(4) More than one item may be associated with a given cue, provided the items are elaborated into a unitary image. If separate individual image combinations are produced using the same peg-word repeatedly, efficiency declines.
(5) Contrary to popular belief, there is no evidence that bizarre image combinations are more effective than obvious relationships.
(6) Semantic similarity among the encoding cues impairs performance.

Bower concludes that imagery mnemonics provide a retrieval plan which directs the subject to the appropriate storage location: the peg-word or locus "solves the search problem by providing the learner with a known bank of pigeon holes or file cabinets in which he stores the list items" (Bower 1970*b*, p. 502). As Bower (1972) acknowledges, however, this still does not explain why visual imagery should provide such a powerful link between the cue and the item.

Is this effect peculiar to visual imagery? As might be anticipated from the section on verbal mnemonics, there is a good deal of evidence that imagery *instructions* are not essential for enhanced learning. For example, Bower and Clark (1969) had subjects learn 12 serial lists of 10 nouns either by study and rehearsal or by linking them together to form a story. On immediate recall, lists were remembered virtually perfectly in both conditions, but when subsequently asked to recall all 12 stories the narrative group scored 93 percent correct, compared with 13 percent on list recall for the rote rehearsal group. In another study, Bower and Winzenz (1970) compared four paired-associate learning strategies: repetition, reading a sentence connecting the stimulus and response words, generating such a sentence, and linking the two words in a composite visual image. Sentence generation and imagery were comparable in efficiency, both being considerably more effective than either reading a linking sentence or rote repetition.

Bower interprets the better recall of words when linking sentences are generated by the subject, rather than merely read, in terms of the subject's greater "comprehension" of his own sentences (Bower 1972). In other words, a subject who is merely reading a sentence may do little or no semantic processing, whereas semantic processing is probably essential in generating a meaningful sentence. This was tested using an incidental learning procedure in which the incidental task involved either phonemic or semantic processing. To induce semantic processing, some subjects were asked to disambiguate sentences, while others were asked to generate plausible continuations of them. In the phonemic processing conditions, subjects looked for spelling errors or repeated each sentence three times. After processing 45 sentences, subjects were unexpectedly tested by being given the subject-noun of each sentence and required to recall the object-noun. Semantic processing produced 50 percent recall, compared with 20 percent for the phonemic tasks.

The evidence therefore suggests that semantic and imagery instructions both facilitate LTM. This could mean simply that subjects use imagery in all conditions, or it may reflect separate components of the semantic system. The latter view was proposed by both Bower (1972) and Paivio (1971b), both of whom have suggested that semantic memory contains separate but related linguistic and imagery systems. However, Bower has subsequently changed his position on this issue; most recently, he argues for a single semantic memory system which represents both visual and linguistic information in a modality-free abstract code (Anderson and Bower 1973). As we saw in the chapter on visual memory (see p. 232), the issue is still an open one. However, regardless of whether one assumes a dual system with separate imagery and language stores or a unitary abstract system, the question remains as to why the type of semantic coding used in either verbal or imagery mnemonics should aid retention more than other types of coding.

Semantic Coding: Why Is It Useful?

As Bartlett (1932) and Neisser (1967) have suggested, the understanding and remembering of meaningful material appears to be a constructive process, using the stimulus material together with an already existing semantic model of the world to create a meaningful structure. The process of recall involves reconstruction on the basis of what remains of this structure. Neisser (1967) speaks of the reconstructive process as analogous to the work of a paleontologist piecing together the fossilized bones of some long-extinct creature and from these scraps drawing conclusions about the appearance and habits of the original animal. A similar and perhaps closer analogy is that of an archaeologist who relies on the structures and objects created by a people to deduce their way of life. In the case of human memory, these structures are created during the process of comprehension, a process which involves integrating new material with existing structures. When subjects are required to process material semantically, they will tend to create a meaningful structure, from unrelated words if necessary, and this structure will tend to be remembered whether or not the subject is trying to learn it (Bower 1972).

Why should semantic processing leave such durable structures? One possible advantage to semantic processing lies in the fact that it is multidimensional. My semantic concept of a cat, for example, involves not only the word and its various verbal associates (*dog, mouse, cream,* etc.) but also what cats look like, sound like, the texture of their fur, what it feels like to pick a cat up or to be scratched by one. Multidimensional coding has two major advantages: (1) it allows greater discriminative capacity, and (2) it allows redundant coding.

DISCRIMINATIVE CAPACITY

The advantages of multidimensional coding are illustrated by some of the work on absolute judgments which has been stimulated by information theory. Experiments have found that if subjects are required to judge a series of stimuli and to assign each stimulus to an appropriate category, they are unable to cope with more than six or seven categories. Consider the case of tones differing in pitch. If more than seven different tones are presented, subjects will become confused and will assign different tones to the same category (Miller 1956). While this might appear to be a perceptual problem, the fact that the number of categories that can be used is the same whether the range of tones is wide (8,000 cps) or narrow (250 cps) suggests that perceptual discrimination is not the problem (Pollack 1952). When a two-choice comparative judgment task is used, subjects can discriminate hundreds of tones correctly, a fact which also indicates that the limitation is not one of sensory discrimination. It seems probable that the subject's limited capacity for making absolute judgments represents a memory limitation due to the difficulty of holding more than six or seven items "in mind" simultaneously, not a lack of sensitivity of the perceptual system. Even with an absolute judgment task, however, when the number of auditory dimensions was increased from 1 (pitch) to 6 (e.g., pitch, loudness, direction, duration, interruption ratio, and ratio of tone-on to tone-off time), Pollack and Ficks (1954) found that the number of stimuli correctly recognized rose from 6 in the unidimensional case to over 200 in the multidimensional task.

Another way of increasing the capacity for absolute judgments is to map the stimuli onto compatible preexisting names. Thus, Chapanis and Overbey (1971) showed that when subjects were required to use familiar and compatible names for different shades of colors (e.g., light bluish green) they were able to increase their discrimination from 9 to a mean of 33 out of a set of 36 colors. Many subjects were performing perfectly, and hence could almost certainly have discriminated many more colors had the set been larger. It is as if Chapanis and Overbey were circumventing the perceptual memory limitation by mapping the stimuli onto the subjects' already existing semantic schema for colors.

REDUNDANT CODING

Information that is coded along several dimensions is less likely to be forgotten than information coded unidimensionally, since the greater the number of dimensions, the greater the probability that at least one cue will survive to provide an available retrieval route (see Bower 1967). Jenkins (1967) found better learning in a picture-word paired-associate task when several different views of the object in the picture were used, rather than a single perspective. It also seems likely that high-imagery words are easy to learn at least partly because they are likely to have both a verbal and a visual code. In short, semantic coding may represent yet another example of the phenomenon of stimulus encoding variability discussed in Chapter 5 (see p. 91). The greater the number and range of encoded features, the greater the probability that one of these will be accessed, hence allowing the item to be retrieved.

I would like to suggest therefore that mnemonic systems reflect the same basic processes that underlie normal unaided memory. They reflect some of these processes particularly clearly (as in the case of visual imagery), and if we ignore them our view of human memory is likely to be impoverished and distorted.

Mnemonists

Mnemonic systems clearly represent the functioning of normal memory; hence, they seem likely to be explicable as the application of new strategies to normal basic memory processes. Will individuals with phenomenally good memories also be explicable in terms of normal processes, or will they require a qualitatively different set of concepts? As we have seen in previous chapters, amnesic patients, whose memory is grossly defective, can often throw light on the operation of normal memory. In this final section we shall consider the theoretical implications of a number of instances of people with abnormally good memory.

SUPERNORMAL VISUAL IMAGERY

In addition to the evidence for eidetic imagery, discussed in Chapter 9, there are a number of cases of subjects who appear to have extremely good visual memory which does not appear to rely on eidetic imagery. For instance, Gummerman and Gray (1971) report a case of a 19-year-old college student with remarkable ability to remember pictorial material. Having viewed a complex picture for 30 seconds, she can subsequently describe it accurately and in great detail. Her performance differs from the eidetic imagers described by Haber (1969) in a number of respects. First, she describes the image as "in her head" rather than "out there," and she does not need to move her eyes in order to scan the image, as is typically the case with an eidetic imager. She is equally able to recall with eyes open or closed and with a constant or varied fixation. She cannot perform tasks involving the superimposition of one image on another, and she is quite unable to perform the Stromeyer and Psotka (1970) task of superimposing binocular Julesz patterns. She also differs from a number of mnemonists whom we shall be discussing later in the chapter in her inability to use imagery to produce supernormal recall of nonpictorial material. Hence, her performance was not outstanding when she was required to remember 8×8 matrices filled with dots, digits, and geometric patterns. Her ability to reproduce complex random shapes was not particularly good, nor was her ability to recall verbal material presented visually. Finally, her retention of tachistoscopically presented letter arrays was within the normal range. Gummerman and Grey conclude that the imagery used by their subject does not appear to differ in quality from what many people experience, though it is of greater fidelity and duration.

As in the case of eidetic imagery, one is left with a certain feeling of disappointment by this study. The subject does indeed appear to have a remarkable ability to remember complex pictures, but attempts to pin down the nature of her supernormal ability or to examine its implications for normal memory apparently proved to be fruitless. Fortunately, however, there are at least two case reports of subjects with abnormally good visual memory where rather more progress has been made in exploring the mnemonic processes: the first of these concerns a study by Coltheart and Glick (1974) of a college student with a clear but limited visual mnemonic skill, while the second is the celebrated study by Luria of the Russian mnemonist S.

SUE D'ONIM (COLTHEART AND GLICK)

Coltheart and Glick first heard of their subject (whom they refer to as Sue d'Onim, subsequently abbreviated to O.) because of her ability to "talk backward." This skill involved pronouncing in reverse a word or a sequence of words spoken to her. For example, on hearing the spoken word *backwards* she could immediately reply *sdrawkcab*. This task had in the early years of the century been used as a visual imagery test, and it was found that even good visualizers had enormous difficulty in doing it. Anyone doubting this should try it for himself. Coltheart and Glick discovered that she could also repeat sentences backward, although once a sentence exceeded five or six words she began to experience difficulty. Discussion with her suggested that the problem arose because the ends of an excessively long sentence tended to disappear from her image. However, when she was advised to visualize longer sentences in the form of several short rows of words, the difficulty vanished, and she had no difficulty in handling sentences of up to nine words.

A number of experiments were carried out. In the first of these, O.'s ability to spell sentences backward was compared with that of six other students. Spelling rather than pronunciation was used because of the difficulty in deciding on the correct pronunciation of some words spelled backward (e.g., *hguor*). Six sentences were used, ranging in length from five to ten words. O. made only one error and performed the task considerably more rapidly than the best of the control subjects, all of whom made a substantial number of errors. O. was then tested on the Spatial Relations Test, which requires the mental rotation of perspective drawings. She was found to perform rather poorly on this task, a result which is consistent with her reported poor sense of direction and her difficulty in forming a mental map of the area in which she lives. She was very interested in ballet but apparently had great difficulty with choreographic exercises, which required her to imagine the location of several dancers simultaneously. When asked to take her image of a sentence and manipulate it in some way (e.g., rotate it, transform it into a different typeface or color), she reported an inability to do so. In short, she appears to have great difficulty in manipulating her visual images.

A further series of experiments explored her iconic memory (see Chapter 9). When shown a row of 8 letters for 100 msec, she was able to report a mean of 7.44 letters, whereas three control subjects reported 4.08, 4.98, and 5.21 letters. Coltheart and Glick went on to test whether this superiority lay in a greater rate of reading information into the iconic store, a greater resistance of information in the store to disruption, or an enhanced ability to transfer the contents of iconic memory into a verbal name code. They tackled this question by following the letters with a pattern mask after varying intervals (see p. 192 for a more detailed discussion of this technique). They observed substantial disruption when the mask followed the stimulus by only 25 msec, but within 50 msec performance was up to 6 letters correct out of 8, and by 100 msec it had reached asymptote. These results are interpreted, in terms of a model proposed by Coltheart (1972), as evidence (1) that O. can visually encode the material at about four times normal speed; (2) that she has a considerably higher than normal visual storage capacity; but (3) that her ability to translate the visual stimuli into a verbal code operates at a normal rate.

Whether or not one is prepared to accept the interpretation suggested by Coltheart's model, it is nevertheless clearly the case that O. performs at a remarkably high level on this test of iconic memory. Coltheart and Glick suggest on the basis of their experiments that the basic factor underlying her performance is her particularly durable visual images. They suggest that a normal subject has difficulty in reading visual images backward, not because he cannot form an image of a word but because the act of reading off the image tends to disrupt it. They suggest that it is the resistance of O.'s images to disruption which allows her to perform her "backward talking" so effectively. In the case of iconic memory, they suggest that the normal subject again experiences considerable impairment in performance because the act of reading off information from the iconic image disrupts it. However, while the extreme stability of the visual images helps O. in tasks where she is simply required to read off the image, it limits her ability to perform tasks in which the image must be manipulated in some way, hence her poor performance on tasks involving spatial visualization and the manipulation of images. Although there may be disagreement about the detailed interpretation of O.'s curious skill, the experiments performed do suggest that it is explicable within the framework of normal visual memory. A more exotic and possibly more revealing incidence of supernormal memory is described in Luria's account of a professional mnemonist whom he refers to as S.

S. (LURIA)

In his classic monograph *the Mind of a Mnemonist*, Luria, the distinguished Russian neuropsychologist, describes how in the mid-1920s, a man, S., appeared at his laboratory with a request to have his memory tested. He was a newspaper reporter and had been sent by his editor, who had noted his apparently remarkable memory capacity, something which the reporter himself took for granted. When presented with a sequence of words or numbers or letters, he was able to repeat them back without error, regardless of whether they were presented visually or aurally and whether he had to speak or write his answers. The sequence length was increased to 30, then 50, and then 70 without apparently presenting any problem to the subject. There appeared to be no limit to his immediate memory capacity. After 3 minutes of study, he learned a matrix of 50 digits perfectly, and he could recall them with apparent ease in any order, just as if reading them from a page. Even more remarkably, he appeared to show no forgetting. When the material was subsequently tested after days, weeks, months, or even years, retention was still perfect. His amazing skill was not confined to digits and words: he could remember events and scenes from long before and memorize any type of material, including scientific formulas and poems in languages he did not understand. How did he do it?

The most striking feature of S.'s account of the process whereby he memorized material stems from the remarkably intense synesthesia that characterized his mental life. Synesthesia, the tendency for one sense modality to evoke another, is far from uncommon but typically is very limited in extent; most people will tend to associate high-pitched sounds with bright colors and low-pitched sounds with darker, more somber colors. Similarly, it is far from uncommon for people to associate days of the week with different colors, particularly during childhood. S., however, showed this general phenomenon to a remarkable extent. For example, when presented with a tone with a pitch of 2,000 cps and an intensity of 113 db, S. said, "It looks something like fireworks tinged with a pink-red hue. The strip of color feels rough and unpleasant, and it has an ugly taste—rather like that of a briny pickle . . . you could hurt your hand on this" (Luria 1968, p. 23). Such experiences were not limited to pure tones. For example, he once commented to the psychologist Vygotsky, "What a crumbly yellow voice you have" (Luria 1968, p. 24). He had similar experiences with numbers, seeing them both in terms of shapes and colors: "One is a pointed number—which has nothing to do with the way it's written. It's because it's somehow firm and complete. Two is flatter, rectangular, whitish in color, sometimes almost a gray" (ibid., p. 26). He also saw in numbers apparent resemblances to people: "Take the number one. This is a proud well-built man; two is a high-spirited woman; three a gloomy person (why, I don't know); six a man with a swollen foot" (ibid., p. 31).

When S. was presented with material to be remembered, he encoded it in vivid visual terms, often using an imaginary location to distribute the images. For example, he would distribute the items to be remembered along a familiar street in Moscow; when he wished to recall them, he would simply walk along the street noting the items as he passed. When he made errors, these typically occurred because an item was "misperceived" rather than forgotten, usually because it was located in some dark corner or was rather small. For example, he forgot the word *egg* because he had imagined it placed against a white wall; it blended into the background and was not "noticed" during recall. The presence of an extraneous noise, such as a cough, during the presentation of the words to be remembered also tended to produce errors, in this case because the cough intruded into his image as a blur, splash, or puff of steam, which was liable to block off the image and make it difficult to "perceive" during recall.

Initially, S. used extremely rich and complex images, but subsequently, when he became a professional mnemonist, he developed a mnemonic system which utilized less detailed images, often relying on a symbolic rather than a sensory representation of the item to be remembered: "Earlier, if I'd been given the word *restaurant,* I'd have seen the entrance to the restaurant, people sitting inside, a Rumanian orchestra tuning up, and a lot else . . . now if I am given the word, I'd see something rather like a store and an entranceway with a bit of something white showing from inside—that's all, and I'd remember the word" (ibid., p. 42). He learned to avoid the problem of failing to "perceive" his images by always ensuring that they were large and well lit, if necessary by imagining a street lamp next to the object in question so as to provide the necessary illumination! Finally, since he was often presented with obscure or even meaningless words to remember, he spent long hours practicing the skill of breaking them up into components which he could then remember. He became extremely adept at this, and Luria describes a number of very dramatic demonstrations, including learning poetry written in Italian, a language with which he was unfamiliar, and mastering an extremely complex mathematical formula, which he remembered in terms of a complex anecdote. The first part ($N. \sqrt{d^2}$) was, for example, represented as follows: "Neiman (N) came out and jabbed at the ground with his cane (.). He looked up at a tall tree which resembled the square root sign ($\sqrt{}$), and thought to himself: 'No wonder the tree has withered and begun to expose its roots. After all, it was here when I built these two houses (d^2)' " (ibid., p. 49). The complete anecdotal sequence produced by S. was extremely bizarre and complex and would certainly overtax a normal subject's memory capacity. Nevertheless, it enabled S. to recall the formula perfectly, not only immediately but on a subsequent test 15 years later!

Did any type of material present problems for S? He himself reported that the most difficult task he had undertaken involved the recall of eight sequences of consonant-vowel nonsense syllables, all of which had the vowel *a* (e.g., *ma, va, na, sa, na, va*). These initially presented problems because their sound similarity produced highly similar synesthetic images, involving a thin grayish yellow line to represent the vowel and various lumps, splashes, and blurs of different colors to represent the consonants. S. solved the problem by producing composites of several syllables (*Mava Nasanava,* etc.), since these represented to him much more elaborate and distinguishable images and avoided the similarity problem.

Despite, or possibly because of, the richness of his imagery system, S. was very poor at utilizing other types of semantic encoding. For example, when presented with a list of words containing several birds, he was unable to recall the birds only; indeed, he had failed to notice that several instances of this category had been given. On another occasion, given the matrix

1234
2345
3456
4567

he took just as long to memorize it as if it had comprised entirely random digits. He subsequently commented that even if he were given the letters of the alphabet in order, he would be unlikely to notice this fact and would simply remember them as individual letters. The limitations of his mode of remembering also show up in his incapacity for remembering faces or voices. Because of the richness of his synesthesia, a different expression on a face or a different inflection in a person's voice completely changed its associated image and presented him with a stimulus which was continually varying in a most dramatic way.* His vivid imagery also interfered with his ability to comprehend passages of prose. Each word tended to be laden with vivid but often irrelevant detail: "Each word calls up images; they collide with one another, and the result is chaos. I can't make anything out of this. And then there's also your voice . . . another blur . . . then everything's muddled" (ibid., p. 65). Similar problems occurred when he was attempting to read. For instance, the phrase *the work got underway normally* evoked the following account: "As for *work,* I see that work is going on . . . there's a factory . . . But there's that word *normally.* What I see is a big, ruddy-cheeked woman, a *normal* woman . . . then the expression *get underway.* Who? What is all this? You have industry . . . that is a factory, and this normal woman—but how does

---

* This is an interesting further example of evidence supporting Martin's stimulus encoding variability hypothesis discussed in Chapter 5.

all this fit together? How much I have to get rid of just to get the simple idea of the thing!" (ibid., p. 128).

V.P. (HUNT AND LOVE)

Another mnemonist, V.P., has been studied recently by Hunt and Love (1972). Although V.P. is somewhat less dramatic in his mnemonic capacities than S. and rather less bizarre in his mental life, he does nevertheless have a remarkable memory. He was born in Latvia —in fact, not very far away from the birthplace of S. As a child he showed remarkable memory capacity and memorized 150 poems for a contest at the age of 10. Between the ages of 10 and 15 he lived in displaced persons camps in Germany and was educated at schools which did not have texts or teaching aids, a situation which required a particular stress on rote memorization. He subsequently emigrated to the United States, where he now works as a store clerk. An intelligence test suggested that he is intelligent but not exceptional (IQ 136); he is extremely good at languages, being bilingual in English and Latvian, fluent in German and Russian, and with a reading knowledge of virtually all modern European languages other than Greek and Hungarian. His major interest in life is chess, at which he is extremely good. In addition to being an excellent player, he gave exhibitions in which he played up to seven simultaneous chess games blindfolded.

Hunt and Love tested V.P.'s memory on a range of tasks, including a matrix of numbers similar to that used by Luria in testing S. V.P. was asked to remember a matrix consisting of six columns of eight random digits and was subsequently asked to recall them in various orders, either along rows or columns or diagonally. While he took rather longer than S. to study the matrix (6.5 as against 3 minutes), his subsequent recall was comparable both in accuracy and speed. Unlike S., he did not claim to rely on imagery, a claim which was supported in a study where a matrix was presented in which the numbers were irregularly spaced. This slowed down his performance when he was required actually to read out the digits but had no effect on the time to recall sequences, suggesting that he was not storing the particular visual array presented. When tested on a continuous paired-associates task in which CVC nonsense syllables were linked with two-digit numbers, his performance was perfect even over the longest lag, whereas a group of college students used as control subjects scored between 50 and 20 percent correct, depending on lag. When presented with Bartlett's story *The War of the Ghosts*, he reproduced the original story almost verbatim. Even after 6 weeks, recall was almost perfect, both results being dramatically better than those shown by control subjects. When presented with 30 nominalizations, half of which were easily visualized (e.g., *snarling tigers*) while half were more abstract (e.g., *rising honors*), his recall was considerably better than that shown by Paivio's (1971*a*) subjects but was by no means perfect; furthermore, as in Paivio's study, he showed better retention of the imageable items. His digit span on initial testing was not particularly striking (9 digits), but when offered the inducement of an additional $2 per digit for each digit exceeding his span, his performance improved dramatically, up to a total of 17 digits, a level of performance which far exceeded that of a control group who were also offered the monetary inducement.

After questioning about his mnemonic techniques, it became clear that V.P. differed markedly from S. When given Luria's book to read and asked for his comments, he remarked that he could think of no instances in which he had even experienced synesthesia, let alone used it as a mnemonic technique. Hunt and Love report less of V.P.'s own introspections about how he remembers than did Luria in his classic study. However, it appears to be the case that V.P. relies very heavily on linguistic or semantic associations. He is helped in this by his extremely wide knowledge of languages; because of this, even low-association-value consonant sequences tend to suggest a word in one language or another. It is not clear, however, how this would help him remember numbers or *The War of the Ghosts* verbatim. V.P. himself tends to regard his mnemonic skill as the result of his early upbringing in an Eastern European traditional Jewish culture which valued and encouraged rote memory. He regards cultural and personality factors as important, with good memorizers such as himself being rather passive individuals who are prepared to devote their energies to encoding the material presented to them without being too concerned with the purpose of remembering it.

AITKEN (HUNTER)

Before going on to discuss the implications of the mnemonists just described, we shall briefly consider a third case, that of a mathematician, the late Professor A. C. Aitken of the University of Edinburgh, who had great skill as a lightning calculator, together with a remarkable memory. Hunter (1962) gives an account which is devoted primarily to Aitken's calculative abilities but which also has interesting references to his mnemonic feats.* One example which Hunter describes in some detail is Aitken's recall of the first 1,000 decimal places of the value of π, which Aitken termed "a reprehensibly useless feat had it not been so easy." By arranging the digits in rows of 50, each row comprising 10 groups of 5, and then reading the digits over in a particular rhythm, he apparently found that he could very easily memorize them: "The learning was rather like learning a Bach fugue." Hunter tape-recorded Aitken's recall and describes it as follows:

> Sitting relaxed and still he speaks the first 500 digits without error or hesitation. He then pauses, almost literally for breath. The total time taken is 150 seconds. The rhythm and tempo of speech is obvious; about 5 digits per second separated by a pause of about half a second. The temporal regularity is almost mechanical—each successive block of 50 digits is spoken in exactly 15 seconds (Hunter 1962, p. 257).

The second 500 digits were spoken somewhat less regularly, and with rather more evidence of strain. Aitken himself attributed the hesitancy to the fact that some 21 years after he had originally memorized the sequence, he discovered that the version he had learned was erroneous and consequently had to relearn some 180 digits. He apparently found the previous learning to be troublesome, an interesting example of PI. He was also able to recite the sequence backward, but did this in a rather different way. Each successive group of 5 was visualized and "read off" from the image, a technique which he also used in memorizing strings of digits or number squares.

Although his published work concentrates on Aitken's calculative skills, Hunter also collected a good deal of as yet unpublished evidence of Aitken's remarkable memory capacity.† Aitken had been tested in 1933 by J. D. Sutherland, who had tested his retention of a list of 25 unrelated words which he had been allowed to read through twice, and of Bartlett's passage *The War of the Ghosts*. Some 27 years later, Hunter discussed the test with Aitken, who was able to recall the material, gradually building up the list a few words at a time until eventually he recalled a sequence of 25 words. Hunter was able to check the list of 25 unrelated words by referring to a paper read to the Scottish Branch of the British Psychological Society in 1937 by Sutherland. The list was exactly as Aitken had recalled it 27 years later; all 25 words were reproduced in the correct order. Aitken also

---

* I am grateful to Professor Ian Hunter for permission to quote from both his published and unpublished studies on Aitken.
† I. M. L. Hunter 1974; personal communication.

succeeded in recalling the Bartlett story, though in a shortened, slightly inaccurate version. On checking the records, however, Hunter discovered that Aitken had been presented with an edited version of the story. It was this that he recalled 27 years later, almost perfectly! On another occasion, Hunter decided to measure Aitken's digit span, and suggested he try to remember a sequence of twelve unrelated digits presented at a rate of one per second. Aitken succeeded in recalling most, but not all of the initial sequence, and complained that the presentation rate was far too slow, that it was "like learning to ride a bicycle slowly." He asked to have the digits read out at a rate of five per second; when this was done, he had no apparent difficulty in recalling sequences of 15 digits both forward and backward. Note that in this respect he differs from S. and V.P., both of whom tended to require a relatively slow presentation rate in order to allow recoding so as to make otherwise meaningless material meaningful. Aitken claimed that this was unnecessary, that he simply needed to relax and allow the material to impress itself on his memory. Hunter * suggests that although Aitken was not actively seeking associations, his knowledge of the properties of relationships among numbers was so rich that he made continuous use of mediating associations without consciously needing to seek them. For example, on hearing the year 1961 mentioned on one occasion, Aitken immediately recognized this as 37×53, and also $44^2 + 5^2$, as well as $40^2 + 19^2$. Clearly, numbers for Aitken were not the dry and formal nonsense material which they represent for most subjects.

To what extent are the mnemonists we have described explicable in terms of the concepts derived from normal memory? At a purely qualitative level, there are many similarities; the use of imagery made by S. and to a much lesser extent by Aitken mirrors a similar, though less dramatic, effect of imagery in enhancing normal memory. Aitken's use of rhythm again characterizes certain normal phenomena, such as the role of rhythm in memorizing verse. Similarly, the extensive use of natural language associations by V.P. parallels the utilization of such mnemonic aids in normal subjects, although with his extensive knowledge of languages and his well-practiced skill, V.P. is able to make much more effective use of such mediators than can a normal subject. Both V.P. and Aitken appear to be characteristic of the extreme of the normal population, rather than being qualitatively different. In both cases they happen to have spent long periods practicing their

* I. M. L. Hunter 1974; personal communication.

mnemonic skills in their youth, and V.P. at least suggests that the development of mnemonic skills is something which could be very much more widespread if it were regarded as culturally desirable. It is certainly the case, for example, that actors clearly master enormous amounts of verbal material during their professional lives, although I know of no objective study of this skill or of whether it generalizes to other material. It suggests, however, that rote memorization of considerable amounts of material is within the capacity of many people, given the incentive.

Luria's mnemonist S. appears to be a rather more extreme case. He is remarkable both in showing incredible memory skills and also in the degree of synesthesia he appears to experience. It seems probable that the two phenomena are related. It is possible, for example, that the fact that any input is coded along a whole range of sensory dimensions leads to a much more durable and accessible memory trace than is normally the case, where only one dimension or, in the case of semantic coding, two or three may typically be involved. Such multiple coding of individual items is probably also a prominent feature of V.P.'s mnemonic skills, although in this case the coding is of a less sensory nature. Aitken also tends to have this multiple coding of material, at least in the case of numbers, which are extremely rich in meaning for him, although he does not seem to search so actively for mediators as does S. or V.P. The two major factors underlying the performance of these mnemonists therefore seem to be (1) the role of imagery and (2) the presence of a rich network of meaningful associations. Both factors are also important in normal memory.

Conclusions

Considering the range of information just discussed on mnemonic systems and on individuals with remarkable memory skills, one is struck by two points. The first is that even the most bizarre instances tend to have parallels in normal memory; they appear to represent the extremes of the normal system, rather than something which is qualitatively different. The second is a realization of just how irrelevant and useless is the ability to remember large amounts of material verbatim, at least in present-day Western society. As Yates (1966) points out, before the advent of printing and of general literacy, the ability to remember large amounts of material was of very great importance. A culture which has a strong oral tradition will tend to value ability to memorize accurately. Mnemonic systems allowed the user to do exactly this; as such, they played an important role in the cultural life of the times. However, given cheap and easy methods of recording information accurately by writing, ability to remember in great detail became no longer valuable.

The general uselessness of their remarkable mnemonic skills is a point that crops up in all three of the mnemonists we have discussed in detail. S. was able to earn his living by giving displays of his talents but had previously apparently gained little advantage from them, other than being spared the trouble of taking notes in his previous job as a newspaper reporter. Similarly, V.P. described in some detail his feelings that his mnemonic abilities were of little value in modern American society and were essentially geared to an outdated European Jewish culture with a strong oral tradition. Aitken also regarded both his mnemonic and calculative skills as basically rather trivial, even though they were of some use in some of his mathematical work. He ceased to practice many of his calculative skills as soon as he gained access to calculating machines, which could do the work for him; however, he continued to exercise, and improve, certain aspects of mental calculation which were of value for his mathematical research. Similarly, although his fantastically good memory often proved useful on committees, whenever there was doubt as to what had been said at previous meetings, Aitken himself apparently took little pleasure in being used as a walking minute book.*

With one or two exceptions (in my own case, the knotted handkerchief), mnemonic systems are typically not particularly helpful in remembering the sort of information which one requires in everyday life. They are, of course, excellent for learning the strings of unrelated words which are so close to the hearts of experimental psychologists, but I must confess that if I need to remember a shopping list, I do not imagine strings of sausages festooned from my chandeliers and bunches of bananas sprouting from my wardrobe. I simply write it down.

---

* I. M. L. Hunter 1974; personal communication.

CHAPTER

15

Where Do We Go from Here?

WE BEGAN with a discussion of the two traditions in the study of memory. The first, originating with Ebbinghaus, tends to emphasize the need to limit and control the complexities of human memory in order to make the problem tractable. The second, represented by the approach adopted by Bartlett, prefers to accept the complexity of studying memory in more naturalistic situations rather than risking the exclusion of the subject's search for meaning, which it regards as central to the process of remembering. As we have seen, in the 1950s the Ebbinghaus approach was clearly dominant, as represented by functionalist and S–R associationist views of memory. In the 1960s the balance began to swing more in the direction of the Bartlett tradition, with the emphasis on less rigidly controlled techniques, such as free recall, and on increasingly complex information-processing interpretations of experimental results. It is probably true to say by the mid-1970s that the pendulum has swung very strongly toward the Bartlett rather than the Ebbinghaus approach. This is true both figuratively, in the emphases on richer experimental material and more complex and flexible theoretical interpretations, and also literally, in the sense that Bartlett's work is being cited very much more frequently than in the 1950s, and many of the experiments being performed and

370

the interpretations proposed are very close in spirit to Bartlett's own work of 40 years ago.

As someone who spent the first nine years of his research career in the Applied Psychology Unit at Cambridge, a unit which was founded by Bartlett, I am very happy at this state of affairs. There are probably fewer conceptual barriers between my own way of thinking and that of colleagues elsewhere than at any time since I entered psychology. This is clearly an advantage, particularly at a time such as this, when so much good work on memory is going on all over the world. And yet I am a little uneasy. For that reason, I was particularly intrigued to read a paper by Allen Newell, in a recent symposium on visual information processing (Chase 1973), who also appears to have some misgivings about the current state of cognitive psychology, misgivings which are echoed by two reviewers of the symposium volume, namely Ulrich Neisser (1974) and Alan Allport (1975). Since Newell, Neisser, and Allport are all very firmly in the information-processing tradition, their disquiet with this approach to psychology, at a time when it appears to be sweeping all before it, is particularly disconcerting. In this final chapter, I would like to use Newell's provocative paper as a starting point for a brief account of my own view of the current state of research on memory, a personal view of where we should be aiming.

Newell entitles his paper "You Can't Play Twenty Questions with Nature and Win," an implicit reference to the research technique advocated by Broadbent (1958) in his influential book *Perception and Communication*. Broadbent suggested that the optimal way of attempting to understand a psychological process was to adopt the split-half strategy. This strategy is shown most clearly in the game of Twenty Questions, where an object is selected and the contestant attempts to work out what that object is, using only yes/no questions. In this situation, as in many other search tasks, such as attempting to locate a fault in an electronic system or a car engine, the optimal strategy is to begin by asking general questions. Ideally, the first question should split the possible alternatives in half and decide which of the two halves contains the target. A second question should split this half again, and so forth and so on. Proceeding in this way, the twenty questions allow one to select one item correctly from 2^{20} (1,048,576) equally probable alternatives; as such, they represent a much more powerful search strategy than is normally adopted by the naïve searcher (Dale 1958).

In the research field, the method suggests that one should begin by asking very general questions and gradually narrow down the alternatives until only one explanation is feasible. Newell argues that although this may work very well for the game of Twenty Questions, it has not worked for psychology, where it has simply produced large numbers of dichotomies which are never resolved.

Newell's disquiet is summarized and echoed by Neisser as follows:

> An impressive number of talented people . . . are doing work of great ingenuity and sophistication . . . new discoveries emerge from their laboratories in a continuous stream. Nevertheless it is not clear that we are moving in the right direction, or indeed in any single direction at all (Neisser 1974, p. 402).

On what is this disquiet based?

Newell argues, first of all, that experimental psychology is phenomenon-driven, that it is currently principally concerned with generating and exploring relatively isolated phenomena. He cites some 60 such phenomena, ranging from Posner's letter/name matching test (see Chapter 9) to perceptual illusions. Although he concedes that the discovery of new phenomena is a sign of vigor, he goes on to argue that unless they are incorporated into some more systematic approach, we shall be no nearer to an understanding of human behavior in 50 years' time than we are now. We will have yet more phenomena, each accompanied by a range of experimental replications and extensions, but not accumulating in any systematic or meaningful way. It is this feeling that research in psychology is not *cumulative* that lies at the heart of Newell's dissatisfaction, which is echoed by Neisser and by Allport.

My own view is that we have made and are making substantial progress but that our current levels of aspiration are unrealistically high, with the result that some disillusion is inevitable. The trend over the last 15 years in the field of human memory has been in the direction of increasing awareness of the complexity of the problem. Consider, for example, the retention of connected prose. We have moved from the assumption that retention can be explained in terms of simple associations among the constituent words, through the rather more complex sequential relationships discussed by information theory, onto models of language based on transformational grammar, which in turn have proved not to be viable without the assumption of complex semantic factors. I suspect that with the problem of semantics we have come to the end of this particular line. It is a genuinely important problem, but possibly not at present a tractable one. Of course, the only way we will find this out is by attempting to tackle it, and even if we fail in this attempt, I have no doubt that we shall learn a great deal in the process. I myself would be pleasantly surprised if we do not experience a period of disillusion within the next few years. The more permissive conceptual language of information processing makes it relatively easy to pose interesting and potentially important problems, but given the enormous power and flexibility of the semantic memory system, producing adequate answers to the questions is likely to prove considerably more difficult.

I think that Newell is right in accusing us of being excessively phenomenon-driven. Fashions in experimental psychology still change with disconcerting rapidity, and we all like to be working on problems that are fashionable, for the very good reason that science is a social activity involving communication, collaboration, and competition. Unfortunately, however, when fashions change as rapidly as they appear to be changing in experimental psychology, it is always tempting to try to spot the next fashion and to switch problems in time to publish one or two papers skimming off the cream of new phenomena or suggesting an ingenious new interpretation, before moving on again to seek yet more phenomena. I believe that this is only possible in psychology because we are at an early stage of exploration; I suspect this would not be a possible strategy in chemistry or physics or biology, and I doubt if it will continue to be possible in psychology, provided we keep track of the phenomena we have discovered. I believe this may be the greatest danger of our preoccupation with the popular problems of the moment—that we lose track of what we have already accomplished and simply go round in circles, discovering and rediscovering the same phenomena.

But what have we accomplished so far? Is research in any area of psychology at present cumulative? I would like to suggest that work on human memory over the last 15 years has indeed been cumulative, though not in the sense of every additional paper's being a further brick in the "edifice of science." I doubt whether any science in fact cumulates in this simple additive sense. I do, however, believe that we know very considerably more about memory now than we did 15 years ago, even though, paradoxically, we are much more aware of our ignorance.

Consider, for example, the question of how many kinds of memory it is necessary to assume. This would appear to be an ideal candidate for Newell's strictures. A simple dichotomous question as to whether one has one or two systems, which appeared initially to yield a clear answer, has subsequently proved to be very much more complex. As the chapter on working memory suggests, neither a unitary nor a dichotomous system can handle the available evidence. My own current views on the nature of short-term memory probably bear as much resemblance to early models, such as that of Broadbent (1958), or to Neisser's concept of an active verbal memory (1967) as to the modal model of the early 1970s. The crucial difference, however, is in the evidence supporting the revised view. The concept of a verbal rehearsal loop, for example, is not a new one, but the evidence for its role in the effects of phonemic similarity, articulatory suppression, and word length *is* relatively new, as are the attempts to use these three phenomena in combination to explore the nature of the system. Similarly, the emphasis on STM as a working memory is not new, but the attempt to explore empirically its role in a wide range of information-processing tasks besides memory is relatively novel. I have used this particular instance simply because it is an area with which I myself am particularly familiar, but I would like to suggest that virtually every area of human memory study shows a similar cumulative advance over the last 10 years.

Take, for example, the area of visual memory, since this is closest to the area on which Newell was commenting. Had I tried to write a chapter on visual memory 10 years ago, I would have been largely limited to describing Sperling's work on iconic memory. Virtually nothing was known about short-term visual memory, memory for faces, long-term visual memory, or the role of verbal factors in visual recall. As I hope Chapter 9 illustrates, we do now know considerably more about visual memory, although it is probably true to say that we have only just scratched the surface of the problem. In short, I would like to suggest that we are indeed making genuine cumulative progress in the study of human memory, and that provided we are prepared to go on asking the basic questions (while recognizing that we are not likely to get neat and complete final answers), we shall continue to make progress.

But how can we be sure that we are going in the right direction, or indeed in any direction at all? My answer to this is the same as that offered by Neisser (1974): namely, that we must continue to check our concepts and results against our observations outside the laboratory. To use Egon Brunswik's (1956) term, we should be more concerned about the *ecological validity* of our concepts and phenomena. One way of deciding which of the wealth of newly discovered phenomena is worth pursuing is to ask oneself whether it is likely to survive outside the sheltered world of the psychological laboratory. To take a specific example, the dichotomous view of memory has proved extremely useful in conceptualizing and advancing research on amnesia (Baddeley 1975; Warrington and Weiskrantz 1973). At the same time, I believe our understanding of memory has benefited considerably from the influence of clinical data, which suggested that the dichotomous view of memory was correct as a first approximation but deviated from the modal model in certain crucial details (see Chapter 8).

To take another example, I for one find it reassuring that a concept as apparently esoteric as that of lexical marking (Clark and Clark 1968) crops up as an important factor in designing conversion tables that are easy for the public to use (Wright and Barnard 1975). Similarly, it is intriguing and gratifying to recognize the Craik and Lockhart (1972) levels-of-processing hypothesis casting light on problems of air traffic control. With computer assistance, the air traffic controller can be presented with solutions to various subproblems; he is, however, much more likely to forget the solution provided by the computer than he is to forget a solution he worked out for himself. The paradoxical result is that he is more likely to lose track of what is going on when he is assisted by the computer than in the more overloaded conditions of unassisted air traffic control.* In short, I would like to suggest that we know we are on the right track if our concepts are useful outside the context in which they were originally devised, and that we should actively seek out ecological validation.

There is growing evidence that cognitive psychologists are at last venturing outside their laboratories to identify problems. The recent growth of interest in such basic and important skills as reading (e.g., Meyer, Schvaneveldt, and Ruddy 1975), mental arithmetic (e.g., Sekuler, Rubin, and Armstrong 1971), and foreign-language learning (e.g., Atkinson and Raugh 1975) reflects a growing concern that experimental psychology should be useful as well as interesting. The fact that one can use the current concepts of cognitive psychology to attack these problems presents an encouraging contrast to the 1950s, when psychology was dominated by associationist concepts which were just too simplistic to be useful.

To give a personal example: less than a year ago I came across an aphasic patient who also had reading difficulties. I was intrigued to notice that, as in the case of the patient studied by Marshall and Newcombe (1966), he appeared to find concrete words much easier

---

* D. Hopkin 1975; personal communication.

than abstract words; he could read *inn* but not *in,* and *witch* but not *which.* This phenomenon should surely have implications for theories of reading, but the great mass of educational research on reading seemed to have no model that was sufficiently detailed to draw any clear conclusions; it was not even clear what questions should be asked. A good survey of the state of the art in 1971 is given in the symposium *Language by Ear and Eye* (Kavanagh and Mattingly 1972); a number of interesting speculative models are suggested, but not one is precise enough to be useful. However, the more recent work in this area (e.g., Coltheart, Davelaar, Jonasson, and Besner 1976; Marcel 1974; Meyer, Schvaneveldt, and Ruddy 1975) has produced more detailed models which are already suggesting new and intriguing methods for analysing dyslexia and relating it to both visual processing and verbal memory (e.g., Patterson and Marcel 1975; Shallice and Warrington 1975). These models will almost certainly prove too simple and sooner or later be discarded; but then, such models are a means to an end, aids to clearer conceptualization, not ends in themselves.

As another example, consider the question of intelligence. Mental testing probably represents both the most technically developed branch of applied psychology and the one which has had the greatest cultural impact. Yet its underlying concepts have scarcely developed beyond the static faculty psychology of the nineteenth century. In order to measure a person's intelligence, one presents him with a wide range of tasks, each assumed to measure the quantity of either the single faculty of "intelligence" or a cluster of such faculties, depending on one's theoretical bias. Many of the subtasks used have a major memory component. For example, the Wechsler Adult Intelligence Scale (Wechsler 1944) involves tests of (1) information, i.e., general knowledge (semantic memory?); (2) comprehension (semantic memory?); (3) mental arithmetic (working memory?); (4) similarities between various verbally presented items (semantic memory?); (5) digit span (STM?); (6) vocabulary (semantic memory?); (7) digit-symbol substitution (STM?); (8) picture completion, i.e., detecting the deficiencies in incomplete pictures (visual LTM?); (9) block design, i.e., reproducing an arrangement of colored blocks (visual working memory?); (10) picture arrangement, i.e., arranging a series of cartoon pictures in an appropriate sequence (semantic memory?); (11) object assembly, involving simple jigsaw puzzles (semantic visual memory?). This does not, of course, mean that the WAIS is simply a memory test, but it does suggest that intelligence, as measured by such tests, is very closely related to the functioning of the underlying memory systems.

An adequate approach to individual differences must surely be based firmly on an understanding of the underlying cognitive processes. Fortunately, after many years of neglect, there are signs that a number of cognitive psychologists are at last prepared to take seriously the question of individual differences (e.g., Hunt, Frost, and Lunneborg 1973). We clearly have a long way to go, but I see no reason why individual differences should not themselves provide a useful analytic tool. Just as the more extreme individual differences between amnesic and normal patients have allowed the experimenter to test models of memory, so individual differences within the "normal" range should provide new ways of testing hypotheses, as well as a deeper understanding of the richness and diversity which are so characteristic of human beings.

On balance, then, I remain a cautious optimist. We are not about to make a great leap forward, despite the welcome assistance of the digital computer, but we are finally daring to poke our noses outside the laboratory. Good applied work is difficult, and we are unlikely to revolutionize society by our next couple of experiments. But even if we are forced to abandon some of our pet theories, I am convinced that our techniques and ways of tackling problems will not have to suffer the same fate. You *can* play Twenty Questions with nature, and some of the time at least, you can win.

REFERENCES

Adams, J. A. (1955). A source of decrement in psychomotor performance. *Journal of Experimental Psychology* 49:390–394.

———. (1967). *Human Memory.* New York: McGraw-Hill.

Adams, J. A. and Dijkstra, S. (1966). Short-term memory for motor responses. *Journal of Experimental Psychology* 71:314–318.

Allport, D. A. (1975). The state of cognitive psychology. *Quarterly Journal of Experimental Psychology* 27:141–152.

Ammons, R. B., Farr, R. G., Bloch, E., Neumann, E., Dey, M., Marion, R., and Ammons C. H. (1958). Long-term retention of perceptual-motor skills. *Journal of Experimental Psychology* 55:318–328.

Anderson, J. R., and Bower, G. H. (1972). Configurational properties in sentence memory. *Journal of Verbal Learning and Verbal Behavior* 11:594–605.

———. (1973). *Human Associative Memory.* New York: Wiley, Halstead Press.

Anderson, R. C., and Myrow, D. L. (1971). Retroactive inhibition of meaningful discourse. *Journal of Educational Psychology Monograph* 62:81–94.

Anderson, R. C., and Watts, G. H. (1971). Response competition in the forgetting of paired associates. *Journal of Verbal Learning and Verbal Behavior* 10:29–34.

Archer, E. J. (1960). A re-evaluation of the meaningfulness of all possible CVC trigrams. *Psychological Monographs* 74; whole no. 497.

Atkinson, R. C., and Shiffrin, R. M. (1968). Human Memory: a proposed system and its control processes. In K. W. Spence and J. T. Spence (eds.), *The Psychology of Learning and Motivation: Advances in Research and Theory,* vol. 2. New York: Academic Press, pp. 89–195.

———. (1971). The control of short-term memory. *Scientific American* 225:82–90.

Atkinson, R. C., Holmgren, J. E., and Juola, J. F. (1969). Processing time as influenced by the number of elements in a visual display. *Perception and Psychophysics* 6:321–327.

Atkinson, R. C., and Raugh, M. R. (1975). An application of the mnemonic keyword method to the acquisition of a Russian vocabulary. *Journal of Experimental Psychology, Human Learning and Memory Section* 104:126–133.

Attneave, F. (1959). *Applications of Information Theory to Psychology.* New York: Holt, Rinehart and Winston.

Atwood, G. E. (1971). An experimental study of visual imagination and memory. *Cognitive Psychology* 2:290–299.

Ausubel, D., Robbins, L. C., and Blake, E. (1957). Retroactive inhibition and

REFERENCES

facilitation in the learning of school materials. *Journal of Educational Psychology* 48:334–343.

Ausubel, D., Stager, M., and Gaite, A. J. H. (1968). Retroactive facilitation in meaningful verbal learning. *Journal of Educational Psychology* 59:250–255.

Averbach, E., and Coriell, A. S. (1961). Short-term memory in vision. *Bell System Technical Journal* 40:309–328.

Averbach, E., and Sperling, G. (1961). Short-term storage of information in vision. In C. Cherry (ed.), *Information Theory: Proceedings of the Fourth London Symposium.* London: Butterworth.

Bachem, A. (1954). Time factors in relative and absolute pitch discrimination. *Journal of the Acoustical Society of America* 26:751–753.

Baddeley, A. D. (1963a). The coding of information. Unpublished Ph.D. thesis, University of Cambridge.

———. (1963b). A Zeigarnik-like effect in the recall of anagram solutions. *Quarterly Journal of Experimental Psychology* 15:63–64.

———. (1964). Language-habits, S-R compatibility, and verbal learning. *American Journal of Psychology* 77:463–468.

———. (1966a). The influence of acoustic and semantic similarity on long-term memory for word sequences. *Quarterly Journal of Experimental Psychology* 18:302–309.

———. (1966b). Short-term memory for word sequences as a function of acoustic, semantic and formal similarity. *Quarterly Journal of Experimental Psychology* 18:362–365.

———. (1968a). Delay and the digit probe. *Psychonomic Science* 12:147–148.

———. (1968b). How does acoustic similarity influence short-term memory? *Quarterly Journal of Experimental Psychology* 20:249–264.

———. (1968c). A three-minute reasoning test based on grammatical transformation. *Psychonomic Science* 10:341–342.

———. (1968d). Closure and response bias in short-term memory for form. *British Journal of Psychology* 59:139–145.

———. (1970). Effects of acoustic and semantic similarity on short-term paired-associate learning. *British Journal of Psychology* 61:335–343.

———. (1971). Language habits, acoustic confusability and immediate memory for redundant letter sequences. *Psychonomic Science* 22:120–121.

———. (1972a). Retrieval- rules and semantic coding in short-term memory. *Psychological Bulletin* 78:379–385.

———. (1972b). Selective attention and performance in dangerous environments. *British Journal of Psychology* 63:537–546.

———. (1975). Theories of amnesia. In A. Kennedy and A. Wilkes (eds.), *Studies in Long-Term Memory.* London: Wiley, pp. 327–343.

Baddeley, A. D., and Dale, H. C. A. (1966). The effect of semantic similarity on retroactive interference in long- and short-term memory. *Journal of Verbal Learning and Verbal Behavior* 5:417–420.

Baddeley, A. D., and Ecob, J. R. (1970). Simultaneous acoustic and semantic coding in short-term memory. *Nature* 227:288–289.

———. (1973). Reaction time and short-term memory: implications of repetition for the high-speed exhaustive scan hypothesis. *Quarterly Journal of Experimental Psychology* 25:229–240.

Baddeley, A. D., Ecob, J. R., and Scott, D. (1970). Retroactive interference effects in short-term memory. Paper presented at the annual meeting of the Psychonomic Society, San Antonio.

Baddeley, A. D., Grant, S., Wight, E., and Thomson, N. (1974). Imagery and visual working memory. In P. M. A. Rabbitt and S. Dornic (eds.), *Attention and Performance V*. London: Academic Press. pp. 205–217.

Baddeley, A. D., Hatter, J. E., Scott, D., and Snashall, A. (1970). Memory and time of day. *British Journal of Psychology* 22:605–609.

Baddeley, A. D., and Hitch, G. (1974). Working memory. In G. H. Bower (ed.), *The Psychology of Learning and Motivation*, vol. 8, pp. 47–90.

———. (1976). Recency re-examined. In S. Dornic (ed.), *Attention and Performance VI* (forthcoming).

Baddeley, A. D., and Levy, B. A. (1971). Semantic coding and memory. *Journal of Experimental Psychology* 89:132–136.

Baddeley, A. D., and Longman, D. J. A. (1966). The influence of length and frequency of training session on rate of learning to type. Unpublished manuscript, Medical Research Council Applied Psychology Unit, Cambridge.

Baddeley, A. D., and Patterson, K. (1971). The relationship between long-term and short-term memory. *British Medical Bulletin* 27:237–242.

Baddeley, A. D., and Scott, D. (1971). Short-term forgetting in the absence of proactive inhibition. *Quarterly Journal of Experimental Psychology* 23:275–283.

Baddeley, A. D., Scott D., Drynan, R., and Smith J. C. (1969). Short-term memory and the limited capacity hypothesis. *British Journal of Psychology* 60:51–55.

Baddeley, A. D., Thomson, N., and Buchanan, M. (1975). Word length and the structure of short-term memory. *Journal of Verbal Learning and Verbal Behavior* 14:575–589.

Baddeley, A. D., and Warrington, E. K. (1970). Amnesia and the distinction between long- and short-term memory. *Journal of Verbal Learning and Verbal Behavior* 9:176–189.

———. (1973). Memory coding and amnesia. *Neuropsychologia* 11:159–165.

Bahrick, H. P., and Bahrick, P. O. (1964). A re-examination of the inter-relations among measures of retention. *Quarterly Journal of Experimental Psychology* 16:318–324.

Bahrick, H. P., and Boucher, B. (1968). Retention of visual and verbal codes of the same stimuli. *Journal of Experimental Psychology* 78:417–422.

Bakker, D. J. (1972). *Temporal Order in Disturbed Reading*. Rotterdam: Rotterdam University Press.

Banks, W. P., and Atkinson, R. C. (1974). Accuracy and speed strategies in scanning active memory. *Memory and Cognition* 2:629–636.

Banks, W. P., and Fariello, G. R. (1974). Memory load and latency in recognition of pictures. *Memory and Cognition* 2:144–148.

Barclay, J. R. (1973). The role of comprehension in the remembering of sentences. *Cognitive Psychology* 4:229–254.

Barclay, J. R., Bransford, J. D., Franks, J. J., McCarrell, N. S., and Nitsch, K. (1974). Comprehension and semantic flexibility. *Journal of Verbal Learning and Verbal Behavior* 13:471–481.

Barondes, S. H. (1970). Some critical variables in studies of the effect of inhibitions of protein synthesis on memory. In W. L. Byrne (ed.), *Molecular Approaches to Learning and Memory*. New York: Academic Press, pp. 27–34.

Barnes, J. M., and Underwood, B. J. (1959). "Fate" of first-list associations in transfer theory. *Journal of Experimental Psychology* 58:97–105.

Bartlett, F. C. (1932). *Remembering*. Cambridge: Cambridge University Press.

Bartram, D. J. (1973). The effects of familiarity and practice on naming pictures of objects. *Memory and Cognition* 1:101–105.

Baxt, N. (1871). Über die Zeit welche nötig ist, damit ein Gesichteindruck zum Bewusstsein kommt und über die Grösse (Extension) der bewussten Wahrnehmung bei einem Gesichtseindrucke von gegebener Dauer. *Pflügers Arch. ges. Physiol.* 4:325–336.

Berg, P. A. (1975). Short-term memory for tone sequences. Unpublished Ph.D. thesis, University of London.

Berlyne, D. E., Borsa, D. M., Hamacher, J. H., and Koenig, I. D. V. (1966). Paired-associate learning and the timing of arousal. *Journal of Experimental Psychology* 72:1–6.

Bevan, W., Dukes, W. F., and Avant, L. L. (1966). The effect of variation in specific stimuli on memory for their superordinates. *American Journal of Psychology* 79:250–257.

Biederman, G. B. (1970). Forgetting of an operant response: physostigmine-produced increases in escape latency in rats as a function of time of injection. *Quarterly Journal of Experimental Psychology* 22:384–388.

Bilodeau, E. A., and Bilodeau, I. McD. (1961). Motor skills learning. *Annual Review of Psychology* 12:243–280.

Bjork, R. A., and Whitten, W. B. (1974). Recency-sensitive retrieval processes. *Cognitive Psychology* 6:173–189.

Blake, M. J. F. (1967). Time of day effects on performance in a range of tasks. *Psychonomic Science* 9:349–350.

Bliss, J. C., Hewitt, D. V., Crane, P. K., Mansfield, P. K., and Townsend, J. T. (1966). Information available in brief tactile presentations. *Perception and Psychophysics* 1:273–283.

Bloom, B. S. (1974). Time and learning. *American Psychologist* 29:682–688.

Bodamer, J. (1947). Die Prosop-Agnosie. *Arch. Psychiat. Nerven.* 179:6–54.

Bousfield, W. A. (1953). The occurrence of clustering in recall of randomly arranged associates. *Journal of General Psychology* 49:229–240.

Bousfield, W. A., and Sedgewick, C. H. (1944). An analysis of sequences of restricted associative responses. *Journal of General Psychology* 30:149–165.

Bower, G. H. (1967). A multi-component theory of the memory trace. In K. W. Spence and J. T. Spence (eds.), *The Psychology of Learning and Motivation: Advances in Research and Theory*, vol. 1. New York: Academic Press, pp. 299–325.

———. (1970a). Organizational factors in memory. *Cognitive Psychology* 1: 18–46.

———. (1970b). Analysis of a mnemonic device. *American Scientist* 58:496–510.

———. (1972). Mental imagery and associative learning. In L. W. Gregg (ed.), *Cognition in Learning and Memory*. New York: Wiley, pp. 51–88.

Bower, G. H., and Clark, M. C. (1969). Narrative stories as mediators for serial learning. *Psychonomic Science* 14:181–182.

Bower, G. H., Clark, M. C., Lesgold, A. M., and Winzenz, D. (1969). Hierarchical retrieval schemes in recall of categorized word lists. *Journal of Verbal Learning and Verbal Behavior* 8:323–343.

Bower, G. H., and Karlin, M. B. (1974). Depth of processing pictures of faces and recognition memory. *Journal of Experimental Psychology* 103:751–757.

Bower, G. H., Munoz, R., and Arnold, P. G. (1972). On distinguishing semantic and imaginal mnemonics. Unpublished manuscript, cited by Anderson and Bower (1973), p. 459.

Bower, G. H., and Winzenz, D. (1970). Comparison of associative learning strategies. *Psychonomic Science,* 20:119–120.

Bradley, B. P., and Morris, B. H. (1975). Emotional factors in forgetting. Unpublished Part II Research Project, University of Cambridge.

REFERENCES

Brady, P. (1970). Fixed scale mechanism of absolute pitch. *Journal of the Acoustical Society of America* 48:883–887.

Bransford, J. D., Barclay, J. R., and Franks, J. J. (1972). Sentence memory: a constructive versus interpretive approach. *Cognitive Psychology* 3:193–209.

Bransford, J. D., and Franks, J. J. (1971). The abstraction of linguistic ideas. *Cognitive Psychology* 2:331–350.

Braun, J. J., Patton, R. A., and Barnes, H. W. (1952). Effect of electroshock convulsions upon the learning performance of monkeys. I. Object-quality discrimination learning. *Journal of Comparative and Physiological Psychology* 45:231–238.

Brayshaw, T. (1849). *Metrical Mnemonics Applied to Geography, Astronomy and Chronology in Which the Most Important Facts in Geography and Astronomy and Dates in Ancient and Modern Chronology Are Expressed by Consonants Used for Numerals and Formed by the Aid of the Vowels into Significant Words.* London: Simpkin Marshall.

Briggs, G. E. (1954). Acquisition, extinction, and recovery functions in retroactive inhibition. *Journal of Experimental Psychology* 47:285–293.

———. (1974). On the predictor variable for choice reaction time. *Memory and Cognition* 2:575–580.

Broadbent, D. E. (1958). *Perception and Communication.* London and New York: Pergamon.

———. (1966). The well-ordered mind. *American Education Research Journal* 3:281–295.

Brooks, L. R. (1967). The suppression of visualization by reading. *Quarterly Journal of Experimental Psychology* 19:289–299.

———. (1968). Spatial and verbal components in the act of recall. *Canadian Journal of Psychology* 22:349–368.

Brown, J. (1956). Distortions in immediate memory. *Quarterly Journal of Experimental Psychology* 8:134–139.

———. (1958). Some tests of the decay theory of immediate memory. *Quarterly Journal of Experimental Psychology* 10:12–21.

———. (1959). Information, redundancy and decay of the memory trace. In *The Mechanisation of Thought Processes.* London: H.M.S.O.

———. (1968). Reciprocal facilitation and impairment of free recall. *Psychonomic Science* 10:41–42.

Brown, I. D., Tickner, A. H., and Simmonds, D. C. V. (1969). Interference between concurrent tasks of driving and telephoning. *Journal of Applied Psychology* 53:419–424.

Brown, R. W., and Lenneberg, E. H. (1954). A study in language and cognition. *Journal of Abnormal and Social Psychology* 49:454–462.

Brown, R., and McNeill, D. (1966). The "tip of the tongue" phenomenon. *Journal of Verbal Learning and Verbal Behavior* 5:325–337.

Bruce, D. R., and Crowley, J. J. (1970). Acoustic similarity effects on retrieval from secondary memory. *Journal of Verbal Learning and Verbal Behavior* 9:190–196.

Brunswik, E. (1956). *Perception and the Representative Design of Psychological Experiments.* Berkeley: University of California Press.

Bryden, M. P. (1971). Attentional strategies and short-term memory in dichotic listening. *Cognitive Psychology* 2:99–116.

Bugelski, B. R. (1962). Presentation time, total time, and mediation in paired-associate learning. *Journal of Experimental Psychology* 63:409–412.

Bugelski, B. R., and Cadwallader, T. C. (1956). A reappraisal of the transfer and retroaction surface. *Journal of Experimental Psychology* 52:360–365.

REFERENCES

Bugelski, B. R., Kidd, E., and Segmen, J. (1968). Image as a mediator in one-trial paired-associate learning. *Journal of Experimental Psychology* 76:69–73.

Butter, M. J. (1970). Differential recall of paired associates as a function of arousal and concreteness-imagery levels. *Journal of Experimental Psychology* 84:252–256.

Buttler, D. C., and Peterson, D. E. (1965). Learning during "extinction" with paired-associates. *Journal of Verbal Learning and Verbal Behavior* 4:103–106.

Byrne, B. (1974). Item concreteness vs spatial organization as predictors of visual imagery. *Memory and Cognition* 2:53–59.

Byrne, R. W. (1976). Memory in complex tasks. Unpublished Ph.D. thesis, University of Cambridge.

Carlson, J. B., and Duncan, C. P. (1955). A study of autonomous change in the memory trace by the method of recognition. *American Journal of Psychology* 68:280–284.

Carmichael, L., Hogan, H. P., and Walter, A. A. (1932). An experimental study of the effect of language on the reproduction of visually perceived form. *Journal of Experimental Psychology* 15:73–86.

Carpenter, P. A. (1974). On the comprehension, storage and retrieval of comparative sentences. *Journal of Verbal Learning and Verbal Behavior* 13:401–411.

Carterette, E. C., and Coleman, E. A. (1963). Organization in free recall. Paper presented at a meeting of the Psychonomic Society, Bryn Mawr, Pa.

Cattell, J. McK. (1887). Experiments on the association of ideas. *Mind* 12:68–74.

Ceraso, J. (1967). The recall of long and short stimulus lists. *American Journal of Psychology* 80:221–228.

Cermak, L. S. (1969). Repetition and encoding in short-term memory. *Journal of Experimental Psychology* 82:321–326.

———. (1970). Decay of interference as a function of the intertrial interval in short-term memory. *Journal of Experimental Psychology* 84:499–501.

Chapanis, A., and Overbey, C. M. (1971). Absolute judgments of colors using natural color names. *Perception and Psychophysics* 9:356–360.

Chase, W. G. (ed.) (1973). *Visual Information Processing*. New York: Academic Press.

Cherkin, A. (1972). Retrograde amnesia in the chick. *Physiology and Behavior* 8:949–955.

Cherry, E. C. (1953). Some experiments on the recognition of speech, with one and with two ears. *Journal of the Acoustical Society of America* 25:975–979.

Chomsky, N. (1965). *Aspects of the Theory of Syntax*. Cambridge: MIT Press.

Chorover, S. L., and Schiller, P. H. (1965). Short-term retrograde amnesia in rats. *Journal of Comparative and Physiological Psychology* 59:73–78.

Cieutat, V. J., Stockwell, F. E., and Noble, C. E. (1958). The interaction of ability and amount of practice with stimulus and response meaningfulness (*m, m'*) in paired-associate learning. *Journal of Experimental Psychology* 56:193–202.

Clark, H. H. (1969). Linguistic processes in deductive reasoning. *Psychological Review* 76:387–404.

———. (1973). The language-as-a-fixed-effect-fallacy: a critique of language statistics in psychological research. *Journal of Verbal Learning and Verbal Behavior* 12:335–359.

Clark, H. H., and Card, S. K. (1969). The role of semantics in remembering comparative sentences. *Journal of Experimental Psychology* 82:545–553.

Clark, H. H., and Clark, E. V. (1968). Semantic distinctions and memory for complex sentences. *Quarterly Journal of Experimental Psychology* 20:129–138.

REFERENCES

Clifton, C., Jr., and Birenbaum, S. (1970). Effects of serial position and delay of probe in a memory scan task. *Journal of Experimental Psychology* 86: 69–76.

Clifton, C., Jr., and Tash, J. (1973). Effect of syllabic word length on memory search rate. *Journal of Experimental Psychology* 99:231–235.

Cofer, C. N. (1966). Some evidence for coding processes derived from clustering in free recall. *Journal of Verbal Learning and Verbal Behavior* 5:188–192.

Cofer, C. N., Bruce, D., and Reicher, G. M. (1966). Clustering in free recall as a function of certain methodological variations. *Journal of Experimental Psychology* 71:858–866.

Cohen, B. H. (1963). Recall of categorized word lists. *Journal of Experimental Psychology* 66:227–234.

———. (1966). Some or none characteristics of coding behavior. *Journal of Verbal Learning and Verbal Behavior* 5:182–187.

Cohen, R. L., and Granstrom, K. (1970). Reproduction and recognition in short-term visual memory. *Quarterly Journal of Experimental Psychology* 22:450–457.

Coleman, E. B. (1962). Sequential interference demonstrated by serial reconstructions. *Journal of Experimental Psychology* 64:46–51.

———. (1963). Approximations to English. *American Journal of Psychology* 76:239–247.

———. (1964). Generalizing to a language population. *Psychological Reports* 14:219–226.

———. (1965). Learning of prose written in four grammatical transformations. *Journal of Applied Psychology* 49:332–341.

Collins, A. M., and Quillian, M. R. (1969). Retrieval time from semantic memory. *Journal of Verbal Learning and Verbal Behavior* 8:240–247.

———. (1970). Does category size affect categorization? *Journal of Verbal Learning and Verbal Behavior* 9:432–438.

———. (1972). Experiments on semantic memory and language comprehension. In L. W. Gregg (ed.), *Cognition in Learning and Memory.* New York: Wiley.

Coltheart, M. (1972). Visual information processing. In P. Dodwell (ed.), *New Horizons in Psychology: 2.* Harmondsworth, Middlesex: Penguin.

Coltheart, M., Davelaar, E., Jonasson, J. T., and Besner, D. (1976). Phonological coding and lexical access. In S. Dornic (ed.), *Attention and Performance VI.* Forthcoming.

Coltheart, M., and Glick, M. J. (1974). Visual imagery: a case study. *Quarterly Journal of Experimental Psychology* 26:438–453.

Coltheart, V. (1972). The effects of acoustic and semantic similarity on concept identification. *Quarterly Journal of Experimental Psychology* 24:55–65.

Conrad, C. (1972). Cognitive economy in semantic memory. *Journal of Experimental Psychology* 92:149–154.

Conrad, R. (1958). Accuracy of recall using keyset and telephone dial, and the effect of a prefix digit. *Journal of Applied Psychology* 42:285–288.

———. (1960). Very brief delays of immediate recall. *Quarterly Journal of Experimental Psychology* 12:45–47.

———. (1964). Acoustic confusion in immediate memory. *British Journal of Psychology* 55:75–84.

———. (1967). Interference or decay over short retention intervals. *Journal of Verbal Learning and Verbal Behavior* 6:49–54.

———. (1970). Short-term memory processes in the deaf. *British Journal of Psychology* 61:179–195.

REFERENCES

———. (1972). The developmental role of vocalizing in short-term memory. *Journal of Verbal Learning and Verbal Behavior* 11:521–533.

Conrad, R., Freeman, P. R., and Hull, A. J. (1965). Acoustic factors versus language factors in short-term memory. *Psychonomic Science* 3:57–58.

Conrad, R., and Hille, B. A. (1958). The decay theory of immediate memory and paced recall. *Canadian Journal of Psychology* 12:1–6.

Conrad, R., and Hull, A. J. (1964). Information, acoustic confusion and memory span. *British Journal of Psychology* 55:429–432.

———. (1968). Input modality and the serial position curve in short-term memory. *Psychonomic Science* 10:135–136.

Cooper, E. C., and Pantle, A. J. (1967). The total time hypothesis in verbal learning. *Psychological Bulletin* 68:221–234.

Corballis, M. C., Kirby, J., and Miller, A. (1972). Access to elements of a memorized list. *Journal of Experimental Psychology* 94:185–190.

Corcoran, D. W. J., Carpenter, A., Webster, J. C., and Woodhead, M. M. (1968). Comparison of training techniques for complex sound identification. *Journal of the Acoustical Society of America* 44:157–167.

———. (1971). *Pattern Recognition.* Harmondsworth, Middlesex: Penguin.

Corning, W. C., and Riccio, D. (1970). The planarian controversy. In W. L. Byrne (ed.), *Molecular Approaches to Learning and Memory.* New York: Academic Press, pp. 107–149.

Corteen, R. S. (1969). Skin conductance changes and word recall. *British Journal of Psychology* 60:80–84.

Craft, J. C., and Hinrichs, J. V. (1971). Short-term retention of simple motor responses: similarity of prior and succeeding responses. *Journal of Experimental Psychology* 87:297–302.

Craik, F. I. M. (1968a). Two components in free recall. *Journal of Verbal Learning and Verbal Behavior* 7:996–1004.

———. (1968b). Types of error in free recall. *Psychonomic Science* 10:353–354.

———. (1970). The fate of primary memory items in free recall. *Journal of Verbal Learning and Verbal Behavior* 9:143–148.

———. (1971). Primary memory. *British Medical Bulletin* 27:232–236.

Craik, F. I. M., and Levy, B. A. (1970). Semantic and acoustic information in primary memory. *Journal of Experimental Psychology* 86:77–82.

Craik, F. I. M., and Lockhart, R. S. (1972). Levels of processing: a framework for memory research. *Journal of Verbal Learning and Verbal Behavior* 11:671–684.

Craik, F. I. M., and Tulving, E. (1975). Depth of processing and the retention of words in episodic memory. *Journal of Experimental Psychology General* 104:268–294.

Craik, F. I. M., and Watkins, M. J. (1973). The role of rehearsal in short-term memory. *Journal of Verbal Learning and Verbal Behavior* 12:599–607.

Crönholm, B. (1969). Post-ECT amnesias in the pathology of memory. In A. Talland and N. Waugh (eds.), *The Pathology of Memory.* New York: Academic Press, pp. 81–89.

Crönholm, B., and Lagergren, A. (1959). Memory disturbances after electroconvulsive therapy. 3. An experimental study of retrograde amnesia after electro-shock treatment. *Acta Psychiatrica Neurologia Scandinavica* 34:283–310.

Crossman, E. R. F. W. (1961). Information and serial order in human immediate memory. In: C. Cherry (ed.), *Information Theory.* London: Butterworth, pp. 147–159.

386

REFERENCES

Crouse, J. H. (1971). Retroactive interference in reading prose materials. *Journal of Educational Psychology* 62:39–44.

Crowder, R. G. (1971*a*). Waiting for the stimulus suffix: decay, delay, rhythm, and readout in immediate memory. *Quarterly Journal of Experimental Psychology* 23:324–340.

———. (1971*b*). The sound of vowels and consonants in immediate memory. *Journal of Verbal Learning and Verbal Behavior* 10:587–596.

———. (1973). Representation of speech sounds in precategorical acoustic storage. *Journal of Experimental Psychology* 98:14–24.

Crowder, R. G., and Morton, J. (1969). Precategorical acoustic storage (PAS). *Perception and Psychophysics* 5:365–373.

Crowder, R. G., and Raeburn, V. P. (1970). The stimulus suffix effect with reversed speech. *Journal of Verbal Learning and Verbal Behavior* 9:342–345.

Crumbaugh, J. C. (1954). Temporal changes in the memory of visually perceived form. *American Journal of Psychology* 67:647–658.

Cudahy, E., and Leshowitz, B. (1974). Effects of contralateral interference tone on auditory recognition. *Perception and Psychophysics* 15:16–20.

Cuddy, L. L. (1968). Practice effects in the absolute judgment of pitch. *Journal of the Acoustical Society of America* 43:1069–1076.

Dale, H. C. A. (1958). Fault-finding in electronic equipment. *Ergonomics* 1: 356–385.

———. (1967). Familiarity and free recall. *Quarterly Journal of Experimental Psychology* 19:103–108.

———. (1973). Short-term memory for visual information. *British Journal of Psychology* 64:1–8.

Dale, H. C. A., and Baddeley, A. D. (1962). On the nature of alternatives used in testing recognition memory. *Nature* 196: 93–94.

———. (1966). Remembering a list of two-digit numbers. *Quarterly Journal of Experimental Psychology* 18:212–219.

———. (1969). Acoustic similarity in long-term paired-associate learning. *Psychonomic Science* 16:209–211.

Dalezman, J. J. (1974). Free recall and short-term memory: a symbiotic relationship or? Unpublished doctoral dissertation, Ohio State University.

Dallett, K. M. (1962). The transfer surface re-examined. *Journal of Verbal Learning and Verbal Behavior* 1:91–94.

Da Polito, F. J. (1966). Proactive effects with independent retrieval of competing responses. Unpublished doctoral dissertation, Indiana University.

Darley, C. F., Klatzky, R. L., and Atkinson, R. C. (1972). Effects of memory load on reaction time. *Journal of Experimental Psychology* 96:232–234.

Darwin, C. J., and Baddeley, A. D. (1974). Acoustic memory and the perception of speech. *Cognitive Psychology* 6:41–60.

Darwin, C. J., Turvey, M. T., and Crowder, R. G. (1972). An auditory analogue of the Sperling partial report procedure: evidence for brief auditory storage. *Cognitive Psychology* 3:255–267.

Davis, D. R., Sutherland, N. S., and Judd, B. (1961). Information content in recognition and recall. *Journal of Experimental Psychology* 61:422–428.

Dawes, R. M. (1966). Memory and distortion of meaningful written material. *British Journal of Psychology* 57:77–86.

Dawson, R. G., and McGaugh, J. L. (1973). Drug facilitation of learning and memory. In J. A. Deutsch (ed.), *The Physical Basis of Memory*. New York, Academic Press, pp. 77–111.

Deatherage, B. H., and Evans, T. R. (1969). Binaural masking: backward, forward and simultaneous effects. *Journal of the Acoustical Society of America* 46:362–371.

Deese, J. (1959). Influence of inter-item associative strength upon immediate free recall. *Psychological Reports* 5:305–312.

De Groot, A. D. (1965). *Thought and Choice in Chess.* New York: Basic Books.

———. (1966). Perception and memory versus thought: some old ideas and recent findings. In B. Kleinmuntz (ed.), *Problem Solving.* New York: Wiley.

Dement, W. C. (1960). The effect of dream deprivation. *Science* 131:1705–1707.

Dennis, W. (1948). *Readings in the History of Psychology.* New York: Appleton-Century-Crofts.

Deutsch, D. (1970). Tones and numbers: specificity of interference in short-term memory. *Science* 168:1605–1606.

———. (1972*a*). Mapping of interactions in the pitch memory store. *Science* 175:1020–1022.

———. (1972*b*). Effects of repetition of standard and comparison tones on recognition memory for pitch. *Journal of Experimental Psychology* 93: 156–162.

———. (1973). Interference in memory between tones adjacent on the musical scale. *Journal of Experimental Psychology* 100:228–231.

Deutsch, J. A. (1971). The cholinergic synapse and the site of memory. *Science* 174:788–794.

Deutsch, J. A., Hamburg, M. D., and Dahl, H. (1966). Anticholinesterase-induced amnesia and its temporal aspects. *Science* 151:211–223.

Deutsch, J. A., and Liebowitz, S. F. (1966). Amnesia or reversal of forgetting by anticholinesterase, depending simply on time of injection. *Science* 153: 1017–1018.

Di Vesta, F. J., Ingersoll, G., and Sunshine, P. (1971). A factor analysis of imagery tests. *Journal of Verbal Learning and Verbal Behavior* 10:471–479.

Di Vesta, F. J., and Ross, S. M. (1971). Imagery ability, abstractness, and word order as variables in recall of adjectives and nouns. *Journal of Verbal Learning and Verbal Behavior* 10:686–693.

Doost, R., and Turvey, M. T. (1971). Iconic memory and central processing capacity. *Perception and Psychophysics* 9:269–274.

Dowling, W. J. (1971). Recognition of inversions of melodies and melodic contours. *Perception and Psychophysics* 9:348–349.

———. (1972). Recognition of melodic transformations: inversion, retrograde and retrograde inversions. *Perception and Psychophysics* 12:417–421.

Dowling, W. J., and Fujitani, D. S. (1971). Contour, interval and pitch recognition in memory for melodies. *Journal of the Acoustical Society of America* 49:524–531.

Drachman, D. A., and Arbit, J. (1966). Memory and the hippocampal complex, II. *Archives of Neurology* 15:52–61.

Duncan, C. P., and Underwood, B. J. (1953). Retention of transfer in motor learning after 24 hours and after 14 months. *Journal of Experimental Psychology* 46:445–452.

Eagle, M., and Ortof, E. (1967). The effect of level of attention upon "phonetic" recognition errors. *Journal of Verbal Learning and Verbal Behavior* 6: 226–231.

Earhard, M. (1967). Subjective organization and list organization as determinants of free recall and serial recall memorization. *Journal of Verbal Learning and Verbal Behavior* 6:501–507.

Ebbinghaus, H. (1885). *Über das Gedächtnis.* Leipzig: Dunker. H. Ruyer and C. E. Bussenius (trans.), *Memory.* New York: Teachers College Press, 1913.

REFERENCES

Efron, R. (1970a). Effect of stimulus duration on perceptual onset and offset latencies. *Perception and Psychophysics* 8:231–234.

———. (1970b). The minimum duration of a perception. *Neuropsychologia* 8:57–63.

———. (1970c). The relation between the duration of a stimulus and the duration of a perception. *Neuropsychologia* 8:37–55.

Ekstrand, B. R. (1972). To sleep, perchance to dream (about why we forget). In C. P. Duncan, L. Sechrest, and A. W. Helton (eds.), *Human Memory: Festschrift in honor of Benton J. Underwood*. New York: Appleton-Century-Crofts, pp. 59–82.

Elliot, L. L. (1967). Development of auditory narrow-band frequency contours. *Journal of the Acoustical Society of America* 42:143–153.

Empson, J. A. C., and Clarke, P. R. F. (1970). Rapid eye movements and remembering. *Nature* 227:287–288.

Engen, T., Kuisma, J. E., and Eimas, P. D. (1973). Short-term memory of odors. *Journal of Experimental Psychology* 99:222–225.

Engen, T., and Ross, B. M. (1973). Long-term memory of odors with and without verbal descriptions. *Journal of Experimental Psychology* 100:221–227.

Epstein, W. (1961). The influence of syntactical structure on learning. *American Journal of Psychology* 74:80–85.

———. (1962). A further study of the influence of syntactical structure on learning. *American Journal of Psychology* 75:121–126.

———. (1969). Recall of word lists following learning of sentences and of anomalous and random strings. *Journal of Verbal Learning and Verbal Behavior* 8:20–25.

Erdelyi, M. H. (1970). Recovery of unavailable perceptual input. *Cognitive Psychology* 1:99–113.

Erikson, C. W., and Johnson, H. J. (1964). Storage and decay characteristics of non-attended auditory stimuli. *Journal of Experimental Psychology* 62:28–36.

Ernest, C. H., and Paivio, A. (1971). Imagery and sex differences in incidental recall. *British Journal of Psychology* 62:67–72.

Essman, W. B. (1970). Purine metabolites in memory consolidation. In W. L. Byrne (ed.), *Molecular Approaches to Learning and Memory*. New York: Academic Press, pp. 307–324.

Estes, W. K. (1973). Phonemic coding and rehearsal in short-term memory. *Journal of Verbal Learning and Verbal Behavior* 12:360–372.

Eysenck, H. J. (1964). *Experiments in Motivation*. London: Pergamon.

Eysenck, H. J., and Wilson, G. D. (eds.) (1973). *The Experimental Study of Freudian Theories*. London: Methuen.

Fechner, G. T. (1860). *Elemente der Psychophysik*. Leipzig: Von Breitkopf und Härtel.

Feldman, M. (1968). Eidetic imagery: a cross-cultural will-o'-the'wisp? *Journal of Psychology* 69:259–269.

Fillmore, C. J. (1968). The case for case. In E. Bach and R. T. Harms (eds.), *Universals in Linguistic Theory*. New York: Holt, Rinehart and Winston.

Fleishman, E. A., and Parker, R. F., Jr. (1962). Factors in the retention and relearning of perceptual motor skill. *Journal of Experimental Psychology* 64:215–226.

Flesch, R. F. (1948). A new readability yardstick. *Journal of Applied Psychology* 32:221–233.

Foss, D. J., and Harwood, D. A. (1975). Memory for sentences: implications for human associative memory. *Journal of Verbal Learning and Verbal Behavior* 14:1–16.

References

Fox, P. W., Blick, K. A., and Bilodeau, E. A. (1964). Stimulation and prediction of verbal recall and misrecall. *Journal of Experimental Psychology* 68:321–322.

Franks, J. J., and Bransford, J. D. (1972). The acquisition of abstract ideas. *Journal of Verbal Learning and Verbal Behavior* 11:311–315.

Freeman, P. R. (1973). *Tables of D prime and Beta.* Tracts for Computers XXX. London: Cambridge University Press.

French, J. W. (1942). The effect of temperature on the retention of a maze habit in fish. *Journal of Experimental Psychology* 31:79–87.

Freud, S. (1914). *Psychopathology of Everyday Life.* In A. A. Brill (ed.), *The Writings of Sigmund Freud.* New York: Modern Library, 1938.

Galton, F. (1883). *Inquiries into Human Faculty and Its Development.* London: Macmillan.

Gardiner, J. M., Craik, F. I. M., and Birtwisle, J. (1972). Retrieval cues and release from proactive inhibition. *Journal of Verbal Learning and Verbal Behavior* 11:778–783.

Garner, W. R. (1962). *Uncertainty and Structure as Psychological Concepts.* New York: Wiley.

Garskof, B. E., and Sandak, J. M. (1964). Unlearning in recognition memory. *Psychonomic Science* 1:197–198.

Gauld, A., and Stephenson, G. M. (1967). Some experiments relating to Bartlett's theory of remembering. *British Journal of Psychology* 58:39–49.

Gazzaniga, M. S., and Sperry, R. W. (1967). Language after section of the cerebral commissures. *Brain* 90:131–148.

Gibson, J. J. (1929). The reproduction of visually perceived forms. *Journal of Experimental Psychology* 12:1–39.

Gilson, E. Q., and Baddeley, A. D. (1969). Tactile short-term memory. *Quarterly Journal of Experimental Psychology* 21:180–184.

Glanzer, M. (1972). Storage mechanisms in recall. In G. H. Bower (ed.), *The Psychology of Learning and Motivation: Advances in Research and Theory,* vol. 5. New York: Academic Press.

Glanzer, M., and Clark, W. H. (1963). The verbal loop hypothesis: binary numbers. *Journal of Verbal Learning and Verbal Behavior* 2:301–309.

Glanzer, M., and Cunitz, A. R. (1966). Two storage mechanisms in free recall. *Journal of Verbal Learning and Verbal Behavior* 5:351–360.

Glanzer, M., Gianutsos, R., and Dubin, S. (1969). The removal of items from short-term storage. *Journal of Verbal Learning and Verbal Behavior* 8:435–447.

Glanzer, M., Koppenaal, L., and Nelson, R. (1972). Effects of relations between words on short-term storage and long-term storage. *Journal of Verbal Learning and Verbal Behavior* 11:403–416.

Glanzer, M., and Meinzer, A. (1967). The effects of intralist activity on free recall. *Journal of Verbal Learning and Verbal Behavior* 6:928–935.

Glanzer, M., and Razel, M. (1974). The size of the unit in short-term storage. *Journal of Verbal Learning and Verbal Behavior* 13:114–131.

Glaze, J. A. (1928). The association value of nonsense syllables. *Journal of Genetic Psychology* 35:255–269.

Glucksberg, S., and Cowan, G. N. (1970). Memory for non-attended auditory material. *Cognitive Psychology* 1:149–156.

Glucksberg, S., and Danks, J. H. (1969). Grammatical structure and recall: a function of the space in immediate memory or of recall delay? *Perception and Psychophysics* 6:113–117.

Glucksberg, S., and King, L. J. (1967). Motivated forgetting mediated by implicit verbal chaining. *Science* 158:517–519.

Godden, D. R., and Baddeley, A. D. (1975). Context-dependent memory in two natural environments: on land and underwater. *British Journal of Psychology* 66:325–332.

Gold, P. E., and King, R. A. (1974). Retrograde amnesia: storage failure versus retrieval failure. *Psychological Review* 81:465–469.

Gol'dburt, S. N. (1961). Investigation of the stability of auditory processes in micro-intervals of time (new findings on back masking). *Biofizika* 6:717–724. (English translation: *Biophysics* [1961] 6:809–817.)

Goldstein, A. G., and Chance, J. E. (1971). Recognition of complex visual stimuli. *Perception and Psychophysics* 9:237–241.

Gomulicki, B. R. (1956). Recall as an abstractive process. *Acta Psychologica* 12:77–94.

Goodwin, D. W., Othmer, E., Halikas, J. A., and Freemon, F. (1970). Loss of short-term memory as a predictor of alcoholic "blackout." *Nature* 227:201–202.

Goodwin, D. W., Powell, B., Bremer, D., Hoine, H., and Stern, J. (1969). Alcohol and recall: state dependent effects in man. *Science* 163:1358.

Green, D. M., and Swets, J. A. (1966). *Signal Detection Theory and Psychophysics*. New York: Wiley.

Green, R. T. (1956). Surprise as a factor in the von Restorff effect. *Journal of Experimental Psychology* 52:340–344.

———. (1958). Surprise, isolation and structural change as factors affecting recall of a temporal series. *British Journal of Psychology* 49:21–30.

Greenberg, J. H. (1966). *Language Universals*. Janua Linguarum. The Hague: Mouton.

Greenberg, R., and Underwood, B. J. (1950). Retention as a function of stage of practice. *Journal of Experimental Psychology* 40:452–457.

Greeno, J. G. (1969). *A Cognitive Interpretation of Negative Transfer and Forgetting of Paired-Associates*. Human Performance Center Memorandum, rep. no. 9. Ann Arbor: University of Michigan.

Greenough, W. T., and McGaugh, J. L. (1965). The effect of strychnine sulphate on learning as a function of time of administration. *Psychopharmacologia* 8:290–294.

Greenspoon, J., and Ranyard, R. (1957). Stimulus conditions and retroactive inhibition. *Journal of Experimental Psychology* 53:55–59.

Gummerman, K., and Gray, C. R. (1971). Recall of visually presented material: an unwonted case and bibliography for eidetic imagery. *Psychonomic Monograph Supplements* 3, no. 35.

Haber, R. N. (1969). Eidetic Images. *Scientific American* 220:36–44.

———. (1971). Where are the visions in visual perception? In S. J. Segal (ed.), *Imagery: Current Cognitive Approaches*. New York: Academic Press, pp. 36–48.

Haber, R. N., and Nathanson, L. S. (1968). Post-retinal storage? Park's camel as seen through the eye of a needle. *Perception and Psychophysics* 3:349–355.

Haber, R. N., and Standing, L. G. (1969). Direct measures of short-term visual storage. *Quarterly Journal of Experimental Psychology* 21:43–54.

———. (1970). Direct estimates of the apparent duration of a flash. *Canadian Journal of Psychology* 24:216–229.

Haggard, M. P. (1971). Encoding and the REA for speech signals. *Quarterly Journal of Experimental Psychology* 23:34–45.

Hamburg, M. D. (1967). Retrograde amnesia produced by intraperitoneal injection of physostigmine. *Science* 156:973–974.

Hamilton, C. E. (1950). The relationship between length of interval separating

391

two learning tasks and performance on the second task. *Journal of Experimental Psychology* 40:613–621.

Hamilton, P., Hockey, G., and Quinn, J. (1972). Information selection, arousal and memory. *British Journal of Psychology* 63:181–189.

Hammerton, M. (1963). Retention of learning in a difficult tracking task. *Journal of Experimental Psychology* 66:108–110.

Hanawalt, N. G. (1952). The method of comparison applied to the problem of memory change. *Journal of Experimental Psychology* 43:37–42.

Hanawalt, N. G., and Demarest, I. H. (1939). The effect of verbal suggestion in the recall period upon the reproduction of visually perceived forms. *Journal of Experimental Psychology* 25:159–174.

Hart, J. T. (1965). Memory and the feeling of knowing experience. *Journal of Educational Psychology* 56:208–216.

Hebb, D. O., and Foord, E. N. (1945). Errors of visual recognition and the nature of the trace. *Journal of Experimental Psychology* 35: 335–348.

Heider, E. R. (1971). "Focal" color areas and the development of color names. *Developmental Psychology* 4:447–455.

———. (1972). Universals in color naming and memory. *Journal of Experimental Psychology* 93:10–20.

Hellyer, S. (1962). Frequency of stimulus presentation and short-term decrement in recall. *Journal of Experimental Psychology* 64:650.

Helson, H. (1964). *Adaptation-level Theory: An Experimental and Systematic Approach to Behavior.* New York: Harper & Row.

Herman, L. M., and Bailey, D. R. (1970). Comparative effects of retroactive and proactive interference in motor short-term memory. *Journal of Experimental Psychology* 86:407–415.

Hermelin, B., and O'Connor, N. (1971). Functional asymmetry in the reading of Braille. *Neuropsychologia* 9:431–435.

Hill, J. W. (1974). Limited field of view in reading letters with the fingers. In F. A. Geldard (ed.), *Conference on Cutaneous Communication Systems.* Austin: Psychonomic Society, pp. 95–105.

Hine, B., and Paolino, R. M. (1970). Retrograde amnesia: production of skeletal but not cardiac response gradient by electro-convulsive shock. *Science* 169: 1224–1226.

Hintzman, D. L. (1974). Theoretical implications of the spacing effect. In R. L. Solso (ed.), *Theories in Cognitive Psychology: The Loyola Symposium.* Potomac, Md.: Earlbaum.

Hitch, G. J. (1969). A probe-recognition study of proactive interference in short-term forgetting. Unpublished manuscript, M.R.C. Applied Psychology Unit, Cambridge.

———. (1975). The role of attention in visual and auditory suffix effects. *Memory and Cognition* 3:501–505.

Hoagland, H. (1931). A study of the physiology of learning in ants. *Journal of Genetic Psychology* 5:21–41.

Hockey, G. R. J. (1973). Rate of presentation in running memory and direct manipulation of input processing strategies. *Quarterly Journal of Experimental Psychology* 25:104–111.

Hockey, G. R. J., Davies, S., and Gray, M. M. (1972). Forgetting as a function of sleep at different times of day. *Quarterly Journal of Experimental Psychology* 24:386–393.

Hockey, G. R. J., and Hamilton, P. (1970). Arousal and information selection in short-term memory. *Nature* 226:866–867.

REFERENCES

Holmes, D. S. (1972). Repression or interference? A further investigation. *Journal of Personality and Social Psychology* 22:163–170.

Homick, J. L., Elfner, L. F., and Bothe, G. G. (1969). Auditory temporal masking and the perception of order. *Journal of the Acoustical Society of America* 45:712–718.

Horowitz, L. M. (1962). Associative matching and intralist similarity. *Psychological Reports* 10:751–757.

Horowitz, L. M., Lampel, A. K., and Takanishi, R. N. (1969). The child's memory for unitized scenes. *Journal of Experimental Child Psychology* 8:375–388.

Hovland, C. I. (1938). Experimental studies in rote learning theory. III: Distribution of practice with varying speeds of syllable presentation. *Journal of Experimental Psychology* 23:172–190.

Hull, C. L. (1943). *Principals of Behavior.* New York: Appleton-Century-Crofts.

Hunt, E., Frost, N., and Lunneborg, C. (1973). Individual differences in cognition: a new approach to intelligence. In G. H. Bower (ed.), *The Psychology of Learning and Motivation,* vol. 7. New York: Academic Press, pp. 87–123.

Hunt, E., and Love, T. (1972). How good can memory be? In A. W. Melton and E. Martin (eds.), *Coding Processes in Human Memory.* Washington, D.C.: Winston/Wiley, pp. 237–260.

Hunter, I. M. L. (1957). *Memory: Facts and Fallacies.* Baltimore: Penguin.

———. (1962). An exceptional talent for calculative thinking. *British Journal of Psychology* 53:243–258.

———. (1964). *Memory.* Harmondsworth: Penguin.

Huppert, F., and Deutsch, J. A. (1969). Improvement in memory with time. *Quarterly Journal of Experimental Psychology* 21:267–271.

Hyde, T. S., and Jenkins, J. J. (1969). The differential effects of incidental tasks on the organization of recall of a list of highly associated words. *Journal of Experimental Psychology* 82:472–481.

Indow, T., and Togano, K. (1970). On retrieving sequence from long-term memory. *Psychological Review* 77:317–331.

Irion, A. L. (1959). Rote learning. In S. Koch (ed.), *Psychology: A Study of a Science.* New York: McGraw-Hill.

Irwin, F. W., and Seidenfeld, M. A. (1937). The application of the method of comparison to the problem of memory change. *Journal of Experimental Psychology* 21:363–381.

Jacobs, J. (1887). Experiments on "prehension." *Mind* 12:75–79.

James, H. (1958). Guessing, expectancy and autonomous change. *Quarterly Journal of Experimental Psychology* 10:107–110.

Janssen, W. H. (1976). Selective interference in paired-associate and free-recall learning: messing up the image. *Acta Psychologica* 40:35–48.

Jarvella, R. J. (1970). Effects of syntax on running memory span for connected discourse. *Psychonomic Science* 19:235–236.

———. (1971). Syntactic processing of connected speech. *Journal of Verbal Learning and Verbal Behavior* 10:409–416.

Jarvella, R. J., and Herman, S. J. (1972). Clause structure of sentences and speech processing. *Perception and Psychophysics* 11:381–384.

Jenkins, J. G., and Dallenbach, K. M. (1924). Obliviscence during sleep and waking. *American Journal of Psychology* 35:605–612.

Jenkins, J. J., Mink, W. D., and Russell, W. A. (1958). Associative clustering as a function of verbal association strength. *Psychological Reports* 4:127–136.

393

REFERENCES

Jenkins, J. J., and Russell, W. A. (1952). Associative clustering during recall. *Journal of Abnormal and Social Psychology* 47:818–821.

Jenkins, J. R. (1967). Effect of incidental cues and encoding strategies on paired-associate learning. Unpublished Ph.D. dissertation, University of Minnesota.

Jesperson, O. (1924). *The Philosophy of Grammar.* London: Holt.

Johnson, N. F. (1966). On the relationship between sentence structure and the latency in generating the sentence. *Journal of Verbal Learning and Verbal Behavior* 5:375–380.

Johnson, R. E. (1970). Recall of prose as a function of the structural importance of the linguistic units. *Journal of Verbal Learning and Verbal Behavior* 9: 12–20.

Johnson-Laird, P. N., and Stevenson, R. (1970). Memory for syntax. *Nature* 227:412.

Johnston, C. D., and Jenkins, J. J. (1971). Two more incidental tasks that differentially affect associative clustering in recall. *Journal of Experimental Psychology* 89:92–95.

Johnston, W. A., Wagstaff, R. R., and Griffith, D. (1972). Information processing analysis of verbal learning. *Journal of Experimental Psychology* 96:307–314.

Jones, G. V. (1975). Fragmentation in human memory. Unpublished Ph.D. thesis, University of Cambridge.

Jones, M. K. (1974). Imagery as a mnemonic aid after left temporal lobectomy: contrast between material-specific and generalized memory disorders. *Neuropsychologia* 12:21–30.

Julesz, B. (1964). Binocular depth perception without familiarity cues. *Science* 145:356–362.

Jung, C. G. (1906). *Experimental Researches.* In *Collected Works.* London: Routledge and Kegan Paul, 1972.

Jung, J. (1964). A cumulative method of paired-associate and serial learning. *Journal of Verbal Learning and Verbal Behavior* 3:290–299.

Jung, J. and Skeebo, S. (1967). Multi-trial free recall as a function of constant vs. varied input orders and list length. *Canadian Journal of Psychology* 21: 329–336.

Kahneman, D. (1968). Method, findings and theory in studies of visual masking. *Psychological Bulletin* 70:404–425.

Kantowitz, B. H. (1972). Interference in short-term motor memory: interpolated task difficulty, similarity or activity? *Journal of Experimental Psychology* 95: 264–274.

Karlin, L., and Brennan, G. (1957). Memory for visual figures by the method of identical stimuli. *American Journal of Psychology* 70:248–253.

Katona, G. (1940). *Organizing and Memorizing.* New York: Columbia University Press.

Katz, J. J., and Fodor, J. A. (1963). The structure of a semantic theory. *Language* 39:170–210.

Katz, J. J., and Postal, P. M. (1964). An integrated theory of linguistic descriptions. *Research Monograph no. 26.* Cambridge: MIT Press.

Kavanagh, J. F., and Mattingly, I. G. (1972). *Language by Ear and by Eye.* Cambridge: MIT Press.

Kay, H. (1955). Learning and retaining verbal material. *British Journal of Psychology* 46:81–100.

Keele, S. W., and Ells, J. G. (1972). Memory characteristics of kinesthetic information. *Journal of Motor Behavior* 4:127–134.

Keller, F. (1954). Cited in R. S. Woodworth and H. Schlosberg (eds.), *Experimental Psychology.* New York: Holt, p. 16.

REFERENCES

Keppel, G. (1968) Retroactive and proactive inhibition. In T. R. Dixon and D. L. Horton (eds.), *Verbal Behavior and General Behavior Theory*. Englewood Cliffs, N.J.: Prentice-Hall.

Keppel, G., and Mallory, W. A. (1969). Presentation rate and instructions to guess in free recall. *Journal of Experimental Psychology* 79:269–275.

Keppel, G., and Underwood, B. J. (1962). Proactive inhibition in short-term retention of single items. *Journal of Verbal Learning and Verbal Behavior* 1:153–161.

Keppel, G., Postman, L., and Zavortink, B. (1968). Studies of learning to learn. VIII: The Influence of massive amounts of training upon the learning and retention of paired-associate lists. *Journal of Verbal Learning and Verbal Behavior* 7:790–796.

Kimble, G. A. and Shattel, R. B. (1952). The relationship between two kinds of inhibition and the amount of practice. *Journal of Experimental Psychology* 44:355–359.

Kimura, D. (1967). Functional asymmetry of the brain in dichotic listening. *Cortex* 3:163–178.

Kinsbourne, M., and Warrington, E. K. (1962a). The effect of an after-coming random pattern on the perception of brief visual stimuli. *Quarterly Journal of Experimental Psychology* 14:223–234.

———. (1962b). Further studies on the masking of brief visual stimuli by a random pattern. *Quarterly Journal of Experimental Psychology* 14:235–245.

Kintsch, W. (1968). Recognition and free recall of organized lists. *Journal of Experimental Psychology* 78:481–487.

———. (1970). *Learning, Memory and Conceptual Process*. New York: Wiley.

Kintsch, W., and Buschke, H. (1969). Homophones and synonyms in short-term memory. *Journal of Experimental Psychology* 80:403–407.

Kleinsmith, L. J., and Kaplan, S. (1963). Paired associate learning as a function of arousal and interpolated interval. *Journal of Experimental Psychology* 65:190–193.

———. (1964). Interaction of arousal and recall interval in nonsense syllable paired-associate learning. *Journal of Experimental Psychology* 67:124–126.

Klüver, H. (1932). Eidetic phenomena. *Psychological Bulletin* 29:181–203.

Kolers, P. A. (1966). Interlingual facilitation of short-term memory. *Journal of Verbal Learning and Verbal Behavior* 5:314–319.

———. (1968). Some psychological aspects of pattern recognition. In P. A. Kolers and N. Eden (eds.), *Recognizing Patterns*. Cambridge: M.I.T. Press.

Kopp, R. Bohdanecky, Z., and Jarvik, M. E. (1967). Proactive effect of a single ECS on step-through performance on naive and punished mice. *Journal of Comparative and Physiological Psychology* 64:22–25.

Koppenaal, R. J. (1963). Time changes in the strength of A-B, A-C lists: spontaneous recovery? *Journal of Verbal Learning and Verbal Behavior* 2:310–319.

Koppenaal, R. J., Jagoda, E., and Cruce, J. A. F. (1967). Recovery from ECS-produced amnesia following a reminder. *Psychonomic Science* 9:293–294.

Kroll, N. E. A., Parks, T., Parkinson, S. R., Bieber, S. L., and Johnson, A. L. (1970). Short-term memory while shadowing: recall of visually and aurally presented letters. *Journal of Experimental Psychology* 85:220–224.

Krueger, L. E. (1970). The effect of stimulus probability on two-choice reaction time. *Journal of Experimental Psychology* 84:377–379.

Kubie, L. S. (1952). Problems and techniques of psychoanalytic validation and progress. In E. Pumpian-Mindlin (ed.), *Psychoanalysis as Science*. Stanford: Stanford University Press.

Kulhavy, R. W., Dyer, J. W., and Caterino, L. C. (1975). On connecting connected discourse: a comment on methodology. *Bulletin of the Psychonomic Society* 5:146–147.

Kumar, R., Stolerman, I. P., and Steinberg, H. (1970). Psychopharmacology. *Annual Review of Psychology* 21:595–628.

Landauer, T. K. (1962). Rate of implicit speech. *Perceptual and Motor Skills* 15:646.

Landauer T. K., and Freedman, J. L. (1968). Information retrieval from long-term memory. *Journal of Verbal Learning and Verbal Behavior* 7:291–295.

Landauer, T. K., and Meyer, D. E. (1972). Category size and semantic-memory retrieval. *Journal of Verbal Learning and Verbal Behavior* 11:539–549.

Laughery, K. R., and Pinkus, A. L. (1966). Short-term memory: effects of acoustic similarity presentation rate and presentation mode. *Psychonomic Science* 6:285–286.

Laurence, M. W. (1966). Age differences in performance and subjective organization in the free-recall learning of pictorial material. *Canadian Journal of Psychology* 20:388–399.

———. (1970). Role of homophones in transfer learning. *Journal of Experimental Psychology* 86:1–7.

Leask, J., Haber, R. N., and Haber, R. B. (1969). Eidetic imagery in children. II: Longitudinal and experimental results. *Psychonomic Monograph Supplements* 3:25–48.

Lehr, D. J., Frank, R. C., and Mattison, D. W. (1972). Retroactive inhibition, spontaneous recovery, and type of interpolated learning. *Journal of Experimental Psychology* 92:232–236.

Leshowitz, B., and Cudahy, E. (1973). Frequency discrimination in the presence of another tone. *Journal of the Acoustical Society of America* 54:882–887.

Levinger, G., and Clark, J. (1961). Emotional factors in the forgetting of word associations. *Journal of Abnormal and Social Psychology* 62:99–105.

Levy, B. A. (1971). The role of articulation in auditory and visual short-term memory. *Journal of Verbal Learning and Verbal Behavior* 10:123–132.

———. (1975). Vocalization and suppression effects in sentence memory. *Journal of Verbal Learning and Verbal Behavior* 14:304–316.

Levy, B. A., and Craik, F.I.M. (1975). The coordination of codes in short-term retention. *Quarterly Journal of Experimental Psychology* 27:33–46.

Lewis, D. (1947). Positive and negative transfer in motor learning. *American Psychologist* 2:423 (abstract).

Lewis, D., McAllister, D. E., and Adams, J. A. (1951). Facilitation and interference in performance on the Modified Mashburn Apparatus. I: The effects of varying the amount of original learning. *Journal of Experimental Psychology* 41:247–260.

Lewis, D. J., Miller, R. R., and Misanin, J. R. (1969). Selective amnesia in rats produced by electroconvulsive shock. *Journal of Comparative and Physiological Psychology* 69:136–140.

Lewis, D. J., Misanin, J. R., and Miller, R. R. (1968). Recovery of memory following amnesia. *Nature* 220:704–705.

Liberman, I. Y., Shankweiler, D., Liberman, A. M., Fowler, C., and Fischer, F. W. (1976). Phonetic segmentation and recoding in the beginning reader. In A. S. Reber and D. Scarborough (eds.), *Reading: The CUNY Conference* (tentative title). New York: Erlbaum, forthcoming.

Light, L. L., and Carter-Sobell, L. (1970). Effects of changed semantic context on recognition memory. *Journal of Verbal Learning and Verbal Behavior* 9:1–11.

REFERENCES

Lindsay, P. H., and Norman, D. A. (1972). *Human Information Processing*. New York: Academic Press.
Locke, J. (1690). *An Essay Concerning Human Understanding*. Reprinted by Everyman's Library. London: Dent, 1961.
Loeb, M., and Holding, D. H. (1975). Backward interference by tones or noise in pitch perception as a function of practice. *Perception and Psychophysics* 18:205–208.
Loess, H. (1964). Proactive inhibition in short-term memory. *Journal of Verbal Learning and Verbal Behavior* 3:362–368.
————. (1968). Short-term memory and item similarity. *Journal of Verbal Learning and Verbal Behavior* 7:87–92.
Loess, H., and Waugh, N. C. (1967). Short-term memory and inter-trial interval. *Journal of Verbal Learning and Verbal Behavior* 6:455–460.
Loftus, E. F., and Palmer, J. C. (1974). Reconstruction of automobile destruction: an example of the interaction between language and memory. *Journal of Verbal Learning and Verbal Behavior* 13:585–589.
Lovatt, D. J., and Warr, P. B. (1968). Recall after sleep. *American Journal of Psychology* 81:253–257.
Luria, A. R. (1968). *The Mind of a Mnemonist*. New York: Basic Books.
Luttges, M. W., and McGaugh, J. L. (1967). Permanence of retrograde amnesia produced by electroconvulsive shock. *Science* 156:408–410.
Lynch, S., and Yarnell, P. R. (1973). Retrograde amnesia: delayed forgetting after concussion. *American Journal of Psychology* 86:643–645.
Lyons, J. (1970). *Chomsky*. London: Fontana/Collins.
McClean, P. D. (1969). Induced arousal and time of recall as determinants of paired-associate recall. *British Journal of Psychology* 60:57–62.
McGaugh, J. L., and Dawson, R. G. (1971). Modification of memory storage processes. *Behavioral Science* 16:45–63.
McGaugh, J. L., and Gold, P. E. (1974). Conceptual and neurobiological issues in studies of treatments affecting memory storage. In G. H. Bower (ed.), *The Psychology of Learning and Motivation*, vol. 8. New York: Academic Press.
McGaugh, J. L., and Hart, J. D. Cited in Dawson and McGaugh (1973).
McGeoch, J. A. (1932). Forgetting and the law of disuse. *Psychological Review* 39:352–370.
————. (1936). Studies in retroactive inhibition. VIII: Retroactive inhibition as a function of the length and frequency of the interpolated lists. *Journal of Experimental Psychology* 19:674–693.
McGeoch, J. A., and MacDonald, W. T. (1931). Meaningful relation and retroactive inhibition. *American Journal of Psychology* 43:579–588.
McGlaughlin, A., and Dale, H. C. A. (1971). Stimulus similarity and transfer in long-term paired associate learning. *British Journal of Psychology* 62: 37–40.
McGrath, J. J. (1963). Irrelevant stimulation and vigilance performance. In D. N. Buckner and J. J. McGrath (eds.), *Vigilance: A Symposium*. New York: McGraw-Hill.
Mackinnon, D. W., and Dukes, W. F. (1962). Repression. In L. Postman (ed.), *Psychology in the Making*. New York: Knopf, pp. 662–744.
Mackworth, J. F. (1963). The relation between the visual image and post-perceptual immediate memory. *Journal of Verbal Learning and Verbal Behavior* 2:75–85.
McNulty, J. A. (1966). The measurement of "adopted chunks" in free recall learning. *Psychonomic Science* 4:71–72.

REFERENCES

Mandler, G. (1967). Organization and memory. In K. W. Spence and J. T. Spence (eds.), *The Psychology of Learning and Motivation,* vol. 1. New York: Academic Press, pp. 327–372.
———. (1970). Words, lists and categories: an experimental view of organized memory. In J. L. Cowan (ed.), *Studies in Thought and Language.* Tucson: University of Arizona Press, pp. 99–131.
———. (1972). Organization and recognition. In E. Tulving and W. Donaldson (eds.), *Organization and Memory.* New York: Academic Press, pp. 146–167.
Mandler, G., and Dean, P. J. (1969). Seriation: development of serial order in free recall. *Journal of Experimental Psychology* 81:207–215.
Mandler, G., Pearlstone, Z., and Koopmans, H. S. (1969). Effects of organization and semantic similarity on a recall and recognition task. *Journal of Verbal Learning and Verbal Behavior* 8:410–423.
Marcel, A. J. (1974). Perception with and without awareness. Paper presented at the July meeting of the Experimental Psychology Society Stirling, Scotland.
———. (1976). Negative set effects in character classification: a response retrieval view of reaction times. *Quarterly Journal of Experimental Psychology.* (In Press.)
Marcel, A. J., and Steel, R. G. (1973). Semantic cueing in recognition and recall. *Quarterly Journal of Experimental Psychology* 25:368–377.
Margrain, S. A. (1967). Short-term memory as a function of input modality. *Quarterly Journal of Experimental Psychology* 19:109–114.
Marks, L. E., and Miller, G. A. (1964). The role of semantic and syntactic constraints in the memorization of English sentences. *Journal of Verbal Learning and Verbal Behavior* 3:1–5.
Marks, M. R., and Jack, O. (1952). Verbal context and memory span for meaningful material. *American Journal of Psychology* 65:298–300.
Marshall, G. R. (1967). Stimulus characteristics contributing to organization in free recall. *Journal of Verbal Learning and Verbal Behavior* 6:364–374.
Marshall, J. C., and Newcombe, F. (1966). Syntactic and semantic errors in paralexia. *Neuropsychologia* 4:169–176.
———. (1973). Patterns of paralexia: a psycholinguistic approach. *Journal of Psycholinguistic Research* 2:175–199.
Martin, D. W. (1970). Residual processing capacity during verbal organization in memory. *Journal of Verbal Learning and Verbal Behavior* 9:391–397.
Martin, E. (1971). Verbal learning theory and independent retrieval phenomena. *Psychological Review* 78:314–332.
———. (1973). Memory codes and negative transfer. *Memory and Cognition* 1:495–498.
Martin, E., and Roberts, K. H. (1966). Grammatical factors in sentence retention. *Journal of Verbal Learning and Verbal Behavior* 5:211–218.
Massaro, D. W. (1970). Preperceptual auditory images. *Journal of Experimental Psychology* 85:411–417.
———. (1972). Preperceptual images, processing time and perceptual units in auditory perception. *Psychological Review* 79:124–145.
Matthews, W. A. (1968). Transformational complexity and short-term recall. *Language and Speech* 11:120–128.
Mechanic, A. (1964). The responses involved in the rote learning of verbal materials. *Journal of Verbal Learning and Verbal Behavior* 3:30–36.
Mehler, J. (1963). Some effects of grammatical transformations on the recall of English sentences. *Journal of Verbal Learning and Verbal Behavior* 2:346–351.

REFERENCES

Melton, A. W. (1963). Implications of short-term memory for a general theory of memory. *Journal of Verbal Learning and Verbal Behavior* 2:1–21.
——. (1970). The situation with respect to the spacing of repetitions and memory. *Journal of Verbal Learning and Verbal Behavior* 9:596–606.
Melton, A. W., and Irwin, J. M. (1940). The influence of degree of interpolated learning on retroactive inhibition and the overt transfer of specific responses. *American Journal of Psychology* 53:173–203.
Merikle, P. M., Coltheart, M., and Lowe, D. G. (1971). On the selective effects of a patterned masking stimulus. *Canadian Journal of Psychology* 25:264–279.
Meyer, D. E. (1970). On the representation and retrieval of stored semantic information. *Cognitive Psychology* 1:242–299.
Meyer, D. E., and Ellis, G. B. (1970). Parallel processes in word-recognition. Paper presented at the annual meeting of the Psychonomic Society, San Antonio, Texas, November 1970.
Meyer, D. E., Schvaneveldt, R. W., and Ruddy, M. G. (1975). Loci of contextual effects on visual word-recognition. In P. M. A. Rabbitt and S. Dornic (eds.), *Attention and Performance V.* New York: Academic Press.
Miller, G. A. (1956). The magical number seven, plus or minus two: some limits of our capacity for processing information. *Psychological Review* 63:81–97.
——. (1958). Free recall of redundant strings of letters. *Journal of Experimental Psychology* 56:485–491.
——. (1962). Some psychological studies of grammar. *American Psychologist* 17:748–762.
——. (1968). Encoding the unexpected. *Proceedings of the Royal Society, B* 171:361–376.
Miller, G. A., Galanter, E., and Pribram, K. H. (1960). *Plans and the Structure of Behavior.* New York: Holt, Rinehart and Winston.
Miller, G. A., and Selfridge, J. A. (1950). Verbal context and the recall of meaningful material. *American Journal of Psychology* 63:176–185.
Miller, G. A., and Taylor, W. G. (1949). The perception of repeated bursts of noise. *Journal of the Acoustical Society of America* 20:171–182.
Miller, R. R., and Springer, A. D. (1972). Temporal course of amnesia in rats after electroconvulsive shock. *Physiology and Behavior* 8:645–651.
——. (1973). Amnesia, consolidation and retrieval. *Psychological Review* 80:69–79.
——. (1974). Implications of recovery from experimental amnesia. *Psychological Review* 81:470–473.
Miller, R. R., Springer, A. D., and Vega, D. C. (1972). Conditions for stimulus-induced recovery from experimental amnesia. Paper presented at the meeting of the Society for Neuroscience, Houston.
Milner, B. (1966). Amnesia following operation on the temporal lobes. In C. W. M. Whitty and O. L. Zangwill (eds.), *Amnesia.* London: Butterworth, pp. 109–133.
——. (1968). Visual recognition and recall after right temporal-lobe excision in man. *Neuropsychologia* 6:191–209.
——. (1970). Memory and the medial temporal regions of the brain. In K. H. Pribram and D. E. Broadbent (eds.), *Biology of Memory.* New York: Academic Press.
——. (1971). Interhemispheric differences in the localization of psychological processes in man. *British Medical Bulletin* 27:272–277.

References

Milner, B. and Taylor, L. (1972). Right-Hemisphere superiority in tactile pattern recognition after cerebral commisurotomy: evidence for non-verbal memory. *Neuropsychologia* 10:1–15.

Minami, H., and Dallenbach, K. M. (1946). The effect of activity upon learning and retention in the cockroach. *American Journal of Psychology* 59:1–58.

Misanin, J. R., Miller, R. R., and Lewis, D. J. (1968). Retrograde amnesia produced by electroconvulsive shock after reactivation of a consolidated memory trace. *Science* 160:554–555.

Mollon, J. D. (1970). Temporal factors in perception. Unpublished D.Phil. thesis, Oxford University.

Montague, W. E., and Hillix, W. A. (1968). Inter-trial interval and proactive interference in short-term motor memory. *Canadian Journal of Psychology* 22:73–78.

Moray, N. (1969). *Attention: Selective Processes in Vision and Hearing*. London: Hutchinson.

Moray, N., Bates, A., and Barnett, T. (1965). Experiments on the four-eared man. *Journal of the Acoustical Society of America* 38:196–201.

Morin, R. E., Derosa, D. V., and Stultz, V. (1967). Recognition memory and reaction time. In A. F. Sanders (ed.), *Attention and Performance. Acta Psychologica* 27:298–305.

Morton, J. (1964a). The effects of context upon speed of reading, eye movements and eye-voice span. *Quarterly Journal of Experimental Psychology* 16:340–354.

———. (1964b). A model for continuous language behavior. *Language and Speech* 7:40–70.

———. (1970). A functional model for memory. In D. A. Norman (ed.), *Models of Human Memory*. New York: Academic Press.

Morton, J., Crowder, R. G., and Prussin, H. A. (1971). Experiments with the stimulus suffix effect. *Journal of Experimental Psychology Monograph* 91: 169–190.

Mowbray, G. H., and Durr, L. B. (1964). Visual masking. *Nature* 201:277–278.

Moyer, R. S. (1973). Comparing objects in memory: evidence suggesting an internal psychophysics. *Perception and Psychophysics* 13:180–184.

Müller, G. E., and Pilzecker, A. (1900). Experimentelle Beiträge zur Lehre vom Gedächtnis. *Zeitschrift für Psychologie* (supplement no. 1).

Murdock, B. B., Jr. (1961). The retention of individual items. *Journal of Experimental Psychology* 62:618–625.

———. (1962). The serial position effect in free recall. *Journal of Experimental Psychology* 64:482–488.

———. (1965). Effects of a subsidiary task on short-term memory. *British Journal of Psychology* 56:413–419.

———. (1967). Auditory and visual stores in short-term memory. *Acta Psychologica* 27:316–324.

———. (1971). Short-term memory. In G. Bower (ed.), *The Psychology of Learning and Motivation,* vol. 5. New York: Academic Press, pp. 67–127.

———. (1974). *Human Memory: Theory and Data*. Potomac, Md.: Earlbaum.

Murdock, B. B., Jr., and Walker, K. D. (1969). Modality effects in free recall. *Journal of Verbal Learning and Verbal Behavior* 8:665–676.

Murray, D. J. (1965). The effect of white noise upon the recall of vocalized lists. *Canadian Journal of Psychology* 19:333–345.

———. (1968). Articulation and acoustic confusability in short-term memory. *Journal of Experimental Psychology* 78:679–684.

Nagge, J. W. (1935). An experimental test of the theory of associative interference. *Journal of Experimental Psychology* 18:663–682.

REFERENCES

Naidoo, S. (1970). The assessment of dyslexic children. In A. W. Franklin and S. Naidoo (eds.), *Assessment and Teaching of Dyslexic Children*. London: Invalid Children's Aid Association.

Neisser, U. (1963). Decision-time without reaction-time: experiments in visual scanning. *American Journal of Psychology* 76:376–385.

———. (1967). *Cognitive Psychology*. New York: Appleton-Century-Crofts.

———. (1974). Review of *Visual Information Processing*, ed. W. G. Chase. *Science* 183:402–403.

Neisser, U., and Kerr, N. (1973). Spatial and mnemonic properties of memory images. *Cognitive Psychology* 5:138–150.

Nemiah, J. C. (1969). Hysterical amnesia. In G. A. Talland and N. C. Waugh (eds.), *The Pathology of Memory*. New York: Academic Press, pp. 107–113.

Neumann, E., and Ammons, R. B. (1957). Acquisition and long-term retention of a simple serial perceptual-motor task. *Journal of Experimental Psychology* 53:159–161.

Nevelsky, P. B. (1970). Comparative investigation of the short-term memory and long-term memory span. In K. H. Pribram and D. E. Broadbent (eds.), *Biology of Memory*. New York: Academic Press, pp. 21–28.

Newcombe, F., Oldfield, R. C., and Wingfield, A. (1965). Object naming by dysphasic patients. *Nature* 207:1217–1218.

Newell, A. (1974). You can't play 20 questions with nature and win. In W. G. Chase (ed.), *Visual Information Processing*. New York: Academic Press.

Newman, S. E., and Saltz, E. (1958). Isolation effects: stimulus and response generalization as explanatory concepts. *Journal of Experimental Psychology* 55:467–472.

Nickerson, R. S. (1965). Short-term memory for complex meaningful visual configurations: a demonstration of capacity. *Canadian Journal of Psychology* 19:155–160.

———. (1968). A note on long-term recognition memory for picture material. *Psychonomic Science* 11:58.

———. (1972). Binary-Classification reaction time: a review of some studies of human information-processing capabilities. *Psychonomic Monograph Supplements* 4:275–318.

Noble, C. E. (1952). An analysis of meaning. *Psychological Review* 59:421–430.

———. (1961). Measurements of association value (*a*), rated associations (*a'*), and scaled meaningfulness (*m'*) for the 2100 CVC combinations of the English alphabet. *Psychological Reports* 8:487–521.

Noble, C. E., Stockwell, F. E., and Pryer, M. W. (1957). Meaningfulness (*m'*) and association value (*a*) in paired-associate syllable learning. *Psychological Reports* 3:441–452.

Norman, D. A. (1966). Acquisition and retention in short-term memory. *Journal of Experimental Psychology* 72:369–381.

———. (1969). *Memory and Attention*. New York: Wiley.

———. (1970*a*). Comments on the information structure of memory. In A. F. Sanders (ed.), *Attention and Performance III*. Amsterdam: North Holland Publishing Co., pp. 293–303.

———. (1970*b*). *Models of Human Memory*. New York: Academic Press.

Norman, D. A., and Wickelgren, W. A. (1965). Short-term recognition memory for single digits and pairs of digits. *Journal of Experimental Psychology* 70:479–489.

———. (1969). Strength theory of decision rules and latency in retrieval from short-term memory. *Journal of Mathematical Psychology* 6:192–208.

401

Novinski, L. S. (1969). Part-whole and whole-part free recall learning. *Journal of Verbal Learning and Verbal Behavior* 8:152–154.

O'Connell, D. C. (1970). Facilitation of recall by linguistic structure in nonsense strings. *Psychological Bulletin* 74:441–452.

O'Connell, D. C., Turner, E. A., and Onuska, L. A. (1968). Intonation, grammatical structure and contextual association in immediate recall. *Journal of Verbal Learning and Verbal Behavior* 7:110–116.

Oldfield, R. C. (1954). Memory mechanisms and the theory of schemata. *British Journal of Psychology* 45:14–23.

———. (1966). Things, words and the brain. *Quarterly Journal of Experimental Psychology* 18:340–353.

Oldfield, R. C., and Wingfield, A. (1965). Response latencies in naming objects. *Quarterly Journal of Experimental Psychology* 17:273–281.

Osgood, C. E. (1949). The similarity paradox in human learning: a resolution. *Psychological Review* 56:132–143.

———. (1953). *Method and Theory in Experimental Psychology*. New York: Oxford University Press.

Ovsiankina, M. (1928). Die Wiederaufnahme unterbrochener Handlungen. *Psychologisch Forschung* 11:302–379.

Paivio, A. (1969). Mental imagery in associative learning and memory. *Psychological Review* 76:241–263.

———. (1971a). Imagery and deep structure in the recall of English nominalizations. *Journal of Verbal Learning and Verbal Behavior* 10:1–12.

———. (1971b). Imagery and language. In S. J. Segal (ed.), *Imagery: Current Cognitive Approaches*. New York: Academic Press.

———. (1971c). *Imagery and Verbal Processes*. New York: Holt, Rinehart and Winston.

———. (1974). Language and knowledge of the world. *Educational Researcher* 3:5–12.

———. (1975). Perceptual comparisons through the mind's eye. *Memory and Cognition* 3:635–647.

Paivio, A., and Csapo, K. (1969). Concrete-image and verbal memory codes. *Journal of Experimental Psychology* 80:279–285.

Parks, T. E., Kroll, N. E. A., Salzberg, P. M., and Parkinson, S. R. (1972). Persistence of visual memory as indicated by decision time in a matching task. *Journal of Experimental Psychology* 92:437–438.

Patterson, K. E. (1971). Retrieval limitations in categorized free recall. Unpublished Ph.D. thesis, University of California, San Diego.

———. (1972). Some characteristics of retrieval limitation in long-term memory. *Journal of Verbal Learning and Verbal Behavior* 11:685–691.

Patterson, K. E., and Marcel, A. J. (1975). Some observations on aphasia and dyslexia: impairment in the phonological representation of written words. Paper read at the London meeting of the Experimental Psychology Society, December 1975.

Pepper, R. L., and Herman, L. M. (1970). Decay and interference effects in the short-term retention of a discrete motor act. *Journal of Experimental Psychology, Monograph Supp. 83,* pt. 2, 1–18.

Perfetti, C. A. (1969). Sentence retention and the depth hypothesis. *Journal of Verbal Learning and Verbal Behavior* 8:101–104.

Perfetti, C. A., and Goodman, D. (1971). Memory for sentences and noun phrases of extreme depth. *Quarterly Journal of Experimental Psychology* 23:22–33.

Perkins, N. L. (1914). The value of distributed repetitions in rote learning. *British Journal of Psychology* 7:253–261.

REFERENCES

Peterson, L. R. (1966). Short-term verbal memory and learning. *Psychological Review* 73:193–207.

———. (1969). Concurrent verbal activity. *Psychological Review* 76:376–386.

Peterson, L. R., and Gentile, A. (1965). Proactive interference as a function of time between tests. *Journal of Experimental Psychology* 70:473–478.

Peterson, L. R., and Johnson, S. F. (1971). Some effects of minimizing articulation of short-term retention. *Journal of Verbal Learning and Verbal Behavior* 10:346–354.

Peterson, L. R., and Peterson, M. J. (1959). Short-term retention of individual items. *Journal of Experimental Psychology* 58:193–198.

Phillipchalk, R. P., and Rowe, E. J. (1971). Sequential and nonsequential memory for verbal and nonverbal auditory stimuli. *Journal of Experimental Psychology* 91:341–343.

Phillips, W. A. (1974). On the distinction between sensory storage and short-term visual memory. *Perception and Psychophysics* 16:283–290.

Phillips, W. A., and Baddeley, A. D. (1971). Reaction time and short-term visual memory. *Psychonomic Science* 22:73–74.

Phillips, W. A., and Singer, W. (1974). The function and interaction of "on" and "off" transients in vision. I: Psychophysics. *Experimental Brain Research* 19:493–506.

Pickering, J. (1971). Unpublished dissertation, University of Sussex.

Piéron, H. (1913). Récherches expérimentales sur les phénomènes de mémoire. *L'Année Psychologique* 19:91–193.

Plath, O. E. (1924). Do anesthetized bees lose their memory? *American Naturalist* 58:162–166.

Plomp, R. (1964). Decay of auditory sensation. *Journal of the Acoustical Society of America* 36:277–282.

Pollack, I. (1952). The information of elementary auditory displays. *Journal of the Acoustical Society of America* 24:745–749.

———. (1959). Message uncertainty and message reception. *Journal of the Acoustical Society of America* 31:1500–1508.

Pollack, I., and Ficks, L. (1954). Information of multidimensional auditory displays. *Journal of the Acoustical Society of America* 26:155–158.

Posner, M. I. (1967). Short-term memory systems in human information processing. *Acta Psychologica* 27:267–284.

———. (1969). Representational systems for storing information in memory. In G. A. Talland and N. C. Waugh (eds.), *The Pathology of Memory*. New York: Academic Press.

———. (1970). Abstraction and the process of recognition. In J. T. Spence and G. H. Bower (eds.), *The Psychology of Learning and Motivation: Advances in Learning and Motivation*, vol. 3. New York: Academic Press.

Posner, M. I., Boies, S. J., Eichelman, W. H., and Taylor, R. L. (1969). Retention of name and visual codes of single letters. *Journal of Experimental Psychology* 79:1–16.

Posner, M. I., and Keele, S. W. (1967). Decay of visual information from a single letter. *Science* 158:137–139.

———. (1969). Attention demands of movements. In *Proceedings of the 16th International Congress of Applied Psychology*. Amsterdam: Swets and Zeitlinger.

Posner, M. I., and Konick, A. F. (1966). Short-term retention of visual and kinesthetic information. *Organizational Behavior and Human Performance* 1:71–86.

Posner, M. I., and Mitchell, R. F. (1967). Chronometric analysis of classification. *Psychological Review* 74:392–409.

REFERENCES

Posner, M. I., and Rossman, E. (1965). Effect of size and location of informational transforms on short-term memory. *Journal of Experimental Psychology* 70:496–505.

Postman, L. (1963). Does interference theory predict too much forgetting? *Journal of Verbal Learning and Verbal Behavior* 2:40–48.

―――. (1969). Mechanisms of interference in forgetting. In G. A. Talland and N. C. Waugh (eds.), *The Pathology of Memory*. New York: Academic Press, pp. 195–210.

―――. (1971). Transfer, interference and forgetting. In J. W. Kling and L. A. Riggs, *Experimental Psychology*. New York: Holt, Rinehart and Winston.

―――. (1972). A pragmatic view of organization theory. In E. Tulving and W. Donaldson (eds.), *Organization of Memory*. New York: Academic Press, pp. 3–48.

Postman, L., and Goggin, J. (1964). Whole versus part learning of serial lists as a function of meaningfulness and intralist similarity. *Journal of Experimental Psychology* 68:140–150.

―――. (1966). Whole versus part learning of paired-associate lists. *Journal of Experimental Psychology* 71:867–877.

Postman, L., and Keppel, G. (1969). *Readings in Verbal Learning and Memory*. Harmondsworth, Middlesex: Penguin.

Postman, L., and Phillips, L. W. (1965). Short-term temporal changes in free recall. *Quarterly Journal of Experimental Psychology* 17:132–138.

Postman, L., and Stark, K. (1969). The role of response availability in transfer and interference. *Journal of Experimental Psychology* 79:168–177.

Postman, L., Stark, K., and Fraser, J. (1968). Temporal changes in interference. *Journal of Verbal Learning and Verbal Behavior* 7:672–694.

Postman, L., and Underwood, B. J. (1973). Critical issues in interference theory. *Memory and Cognition* 1:19–40.

Potter, M. C., and Faulconer, B. A. (1975). Time to understand pictures and words. *Nature* 253:437–438.

Poulton, E. C. (1958). Time for reading and memory. *British Journal of Psychology* 49:230–245.

Prentice, W. C. H. (1954). Visual recognition of verbally labelled figures. *American Journal of Psychology* 67:315–320.

Prisko, L. H. (1963). Short-term memory in focal cerebral damage. Unpublished doctoral thesis, McGill University.

Prytulak, L. S. (1971). Natural language mediation. *Cognitive Psychology* 2:1–56.

Puff, C. R. (1970). Role of clustering in free recall. *Journal of Experimental Psychology* 86:384–386.

Quartermain, D., and McEwen, B. S. (1970). Temporal characteristics of amnesia induced by protein synthesis inhibitor: determination by shock level. *Nature* 228:677–678.

Quartermain, D., McEwen, B. S., and Azmitia, E. C., Jr. (1970). Amnesia produced by electroconvulsive shock or cycloheximide: conditions for recovery. *Science* 169:683–686.

Quillian, M. R. (1968). Semantic memory. In M. Minsky (ed.), *Semantic Information Processing*. Cambridge: MIT Press, pp. 227–270.

―――. (1969). The teachable language comprehender: a simulation program and theory of language. *Communications of the Association for Computing Machinery* 12:459–476.

Raser, G. A. (1972). Recoding of semantic and acoustic information in short-

REFERENCES

term memory. *Journal of Verbal Learning and Verbal Behavior* 11:692–697.
Raymond, B. (1969). Short-term storage and long-term storage in free recall. *Journal of Verbal Learning and Verbal Behavior* 8:567–574.
Reder, L. M., Anderson, J. R., and Bjork, R. A. (1974). A semantic interpretation of encoding specificity. *Journal of Experimental Psychology* 102:648–656.
Reitman, J. S. (1971). Mechanisms of forgetting in short-term memory. *Cognitive Psychology* 2:185–195.
———. (1974). Without surreptitious rehearsal, information in short-term memory decays. *Journal of Verbal Learning and Verbal Behavior* 13:365–377.
Riccio, D. C., and Stikes, E. R. (1969). Persistent but modifiable retrograde amnesia produced by hypothermia. *Physiology and Behavior* 4:649–652.
Richardson, J. T. E. (1975). Imagery and deep structure in the recall of English nominalizations. *British Journal of Psychology* 66:333–339.
Richardson, J. T. E., and Baddeley, A. D. (1975). The effect of articulatory suppression in free recall. *Journal of Verbal Learning and Verbal Behavior* 14:623–629.
Riley, D. A. (1962). Memory for form. In L. Postman (ed.), *Psychology in the Making*. New York: Knopf.
Rips, L. J., Shoben, E. J., and Smith, E. E. (1973). Semantic distance and the verification of semantic relations. *Journal of Verbal Learning and Verbal Behavior* 12:1–20.
Roberts, W. A. (1969). The priority of recall of new items in transfer from part-list learning to whole-list learning. *Journal of Verbal Learning and Verbal Behavior* 8:645–652.
Robinson, C. E., and Pollack, I. (1971). Forward and backward masking: testing a discrete perceptual-moment hypothesis in audition. *Journal of the Acoustical Society of America* 50:1512–1519.
Rock, I., and Engelstein, P. (1959). A study of memory for visual form. *American Journal of Psychology* 72:221–229.
Rohrmann, N. L. (1968). The role of syntactic structure in the recall of English nominalizations. *Journal of Verbal Learning and Verbal Behavior* 7:904–912.
Rothkopf, E. Z., and Coke, E. V. (1961). The prediction of free recall from word association measures. *Journal of Experimental Psychology* 62:433–438.
Rubenstein, H., and Aborn, M. (1958). Learning, prediction and readability. *Journal of Applied Psychology* 42:28–32.
Rumelhart, D. E., Lindsay, P. H., and Norman, D. A. (1972). A process model for long-term memory. In E. Tulving and W. Donaldson (eds.), *Organization and Memory*. New York: Academic Press, pp. 198–246.
Rundus, D. (1971). Analysis of rehearsal processes in free recall. *Journal of Experimental Psychology* 89:63–77.
———. (1973). Negative effects of using list items as recall cues. *Journal of Verbal Learning and Verbal Behavior* 12:43–50.
Rundus, D., and Atkinson, R. C. (1970). Rehearsal processes in free recall: a procedure for direct observation. *Journal of Verbal Learning and Verbal Behavior* 9:99–105.
Russell, R. W., and Hunter, W. S. (1937). The effect of inactivity produced by sodium amytal on the retention of the maze habit in albino rats. *Journal of Experimental Psychology* 20:426–436.
Russell, W. R. (1959). *Brain, Memory, Learning: A Neurologist's View*. London: Oxford University Press.
Sachs, J. S. (1967). Recognition memory for syntactic and semantic aspects

of connected discourse. *Perception and Psychophysics* 2:437–442.
———. (1974). Memory in reading and listening to discourse. *Memory and Cognition* 2:95–100.

Salzberg, P. M., Parks, T. E., Kroll, N. E. A., and Parkinson, S. R. (1971). Retroactive effects of phonemic similarity on short-term recall of visual and auditory stimuli. *Journal of Experimental Psychology* 91:43–46.

Santa, J. L., and Lamwers, L. L. (1974). Encoding specificity: fact or artifact? *Journal of Verbal Learning and Verbal Behavior* 13:412–423.

Saul, E. V., and Osgood, C. E. (1950). Perceptual organization of materials as a factor influencing ease of learning and degree of retention. *Journal of Experimental Psychology* 40:372–379.

Savin, H. B., and Perchonok, E. (1965). Grammatical structure and the immediate recall of English sentences. *Journal of Verbal Learning and Verbal Behavior* 4:348–353.

Schaeffer, B., and Wallace, R. (1969). Semantic similarity and the comparison of word meanings. *Journal of Experimental Psychology* 82:343–346.

———. (1970). The comparison of word meanings. *Journal of Experimental Psychology* 86:144–152.

Schiller, P. H. (1965). Monoptic and dichoptic visual masking by patterns and flashes. *Journal of Experimental Psychology* 69:193–199.

Schlesinger, I. M. (1966). *Sentence Structure and the Reading Process.* The Hague: Mouton.

Scripture, E. W. (1905). *The New Psychology.* London: Scott.

Segal, S. J., and Fusella, V. (1969). Effects of imaging on signal-to-noise ratio with varying signal conditions. *British Journal of Psychology* 60:459–464.

Sekuler, R., Rubin, E., and Armstrong, R. (1971). Processing numerical information: a choice time analysis. *Journal of Experimental Psychology* 90:75–80.

Selfridge, O. G., and Neisser, U. (1960). Pattern recognition by machine. *Scientific American* 203:60–68.

Shallice, T. (1967). Paper presented at NATO symposium on short-term memory, Cambridge, England.

———. (1975). On the contents of primary memory. In P. M. A. Rabbitt and S. Dornic (eds.), *Attention and Performance V.* London: Academic Press.

Shallice, T., and Warrington, E. K. (1970). Independent functioning of verbal memory stores: a neuropsychological study. *Quarterly Journal of Experimental Psychology* 22:261–273.

———. (1975). Word recognition in a phonemic dyslexic patient. *Quarterly Journal of Experimental Psychology* 27:187–200.

Shannon, C. E., and Weaver, W. (1949). *The Mathematical Theory of Communication.* Urbana: University of Illinois Press.

Sheehan, P. W., and Neisser, U. (1969). Some variables affecting the vividness of imagery in recall. *British Journal of Psychology* 60:71–80.

Shepard, R. N. (1967). Recognition memory for words, sentences and pictures. *Journal of Verbal Learning and Verbal Behavior* 6:156–163.

Shepard, R. N., and Metzler, J. (1971). Mental rotation of three-dimensional objects. *Science* 171:701–703.

Shiffrin, R. M. (1970). Forgetting: trace erosion or retrieval failure? *Science* 168:1601–1603.

———. (1973). Visual free recall. *Science* 180:980–982.

Shulman, H. G. (1970). Encoding and retention of semantic and phonemic information in short-term memory. *Journal of Verbal Learning and Verbal Behavior* 9:499–508.

REFERENCES

———. (1971). Similarity effects in short-term memory. *Psychological Bulletin* 75:399–415.

Sidman, M., Stoddard, L. T., and Mohr, J. P. (1968). Some additional quantitative observations of immediate memory in a patient with bilateral hippocampal lesions. *Neuropsychologia* 6:245–254.

Siegel, J. A. (1974). Sensory and verbal coding strategies in subjects with absolute pitch. *Journal of the Acoustical Society of America* 55:S9(A).

Siipola, E. M., and Hayden, S. D. (1965). Exploring eidetic imagery among the retarded. *Perceptual and Motor Skills* 21:275–286.

Silverstein, C., and Glanzer, M. (1971). Difficulty of a concurrent task in free recall: different effects of LTS and STS. *Psychonomic Science* 22:367–368.

Simpson, P. J. (1970). The organization of retrieval in the recognition of letters and digits. Ph.D. dissertation, University of Sussex.

———. (1972). High-speed memory scanning: stability and generality. *Journal of Experimental Psychology* 96:239–246.

Singer, W., and Phillips, W. A. (1974). The function and interaction of "on" and "off" transients in vision. II: Neurophysiology. *Experimental Brain Research* 19:507–523.

Slak, S. (1970). Phonemic recoding of digital information. *Journal of Experimental Psychology* 86:398–406.

Slamecka, N. J. (1960). Retroactive inhibition of connected discourse as a function of practice level. *Journal of Experimental Psychology* 59:104–108.

———. (1961). Proactive inhibition of connected discourse. *Journal of Experimental Psychology* 62:295–301.

———. (1968). An examination of trace storage in free recall. *Journal of Experimental Psychology* 76:504–513.

———. (1969). Testing for associative storage in multitrial free recall. *Journal of Experimental Psychology* 81:557–560.

———. (1972). The question of associative growth in the learning of categorized material. *Journal of Verbal Learning and Verbal Behavior* 11:324–332.

Slamecka, N. J., Moore, T., and Carey, S. (1972). Part-to-whole transfer and its relation to organization theory. *Journal of Verbal Learning and Verbal Behavior* 11:73–82.

Slobin, D. I. (1968). Recall of full and truncated passive sentences in connected discourse. *Journal of Verbal Learning and Verbal Behavior* 7:876–881.

Sperling, G. (1960). The information available in brief visual presentations. *Psychological Monographs* 74, whole no. 498.

———. (1963). A model for visual memory tasks. *Human Factors* 5:19–31.

———. (1967). Successive approximations to a model for short-term memory. *Acta Psychologica* 27:285–292.

———. (1970). Short-term memory, long-term memory, and scanning in the processing of visual information. In F. A. Young and D. B. Lindsley (eds.), *Early Experience and Visual Information Processing in Perceptual and Reading Disorders*. Washington, D.C.: National Academy of Sciences, pp. 198–218.

Sperling, G., and Speelman, R. G. (1970). Acoustic similarity and auditory short-term memory: experiments and a model. In D. A. Norman (ed.), *Models of Human Memory*. New York: Academic Press, pp. 152–202.

Springer, A. D., and Miller, R. R. (1972). Retrieval failure induced by electro-convulsive shock: reversal with dissimilar training and recovery agents. *Science* 177:628–630.

407

Squire, L. R. (1970). Physostigmine: effects on retention at different times after brief training. *Psychonomic Science* 19:49–50.

Standing, L., Conezio, J., and Haber, R. N. (1970). Perception and memory for pictures: single-trial learning of 2560 visual stimuli. *Psychonomic Science* 19:73–74.

Stelmach, G. E., and Wilson, M. (1970). Kinesthetic retention, movement extent, and information processing. *Journal of Experimental Psychology* 85:425–430.

Sternberg, S. (1966). High-speed scanning in human memory. *Science* 153: 652–654.

———. (1969). Memory-scanning: mental processes revealed by reaction-time experiments. *American Scientist* 57:421–457.

———. (1975). Memory scanning: new findings and current controversies. *Quarterly Journal of Experimental Psychology* 27:1–32.

Sternberg, S., Knoll, R. L., and Nasto, B. A. (1969). Retrieval from long-term vs. active memory. Paper presented at the annual meeting of the Psychonomic Society, St. Louis.

Stone, C. P., and Bakhtiari, A. B. (1956). Effects of electroconvulsive shock on maze relearning by albino rats. *Journal of Comparative and Physiological Psychology* 49:318–320.

Stones, M. J. (1974). Sleep and the storage and retrieval processes in humans. Unpublished Ph.D. thesis, University of Sheffield.

Strand, B. Z. (1970). Change of context and retroactive inhibition. *Journal of Verbal Learning and Verbal Behavior* 9:202–206.

Stromeyer, C. F., and Psotka, J. (1970). The detailed texture of eidetic images. *Nature* 225:346–349.

Studdert-Kennedy, M., and Shankweiler, D. (1970). Hemispheric specialization for speech perception. *Journal of the Acoustical Society of America* 48: 579–594.

Sullivan, E. V., and Turvey, M. T. (1972). Short-term retention of tactile stimulation. *Quarterly Journal of Experimental Psychology* 24:253–261.

Sutherland, N. S. (1968). Outlines of a theory of visual pattern recognition in animals and man. *Proceedings of the Royal Society, B* 171:297–317.

Theios, J. (1973). Reaction time measurements in the study of memory process: theory and data. In G. H. Bower (ed.), *The Psychology of Learning and Motivation,* vol. 7. New York: Academic Press, pp. 43–85.

Theios, J., Smith, P. G., Haviland, S. E., Traupman, J., and Moy, M. C. (1973). Memory scanning as a serial self-terminating process. *Journal of Experimental Psychology* 97:323–336.

Thorndike, E. L., and Lorge, I. (1944). *The Teacher's Word Book of 30,000 Words.* New York: Bureau of Publications, Teachers College.

Thune, L. E. (1951). Warm-up effect as a function of level of practice in verbal learning. *Journal of Experimental Psychology* 42:250–256.

Thurstone, L. L. (1930). The relation between learning time and length of task. *Psychological Review* 37:44–58.

Townsend, J. T. (1971). A note on the identifiability of serial and parallel processes. *Perception and Psychophysics* 10:161–163.

Treisman, A. M. (1964). Monitoring and storage of irrelevant messages in selective attention. *Journal of Verbal Learning and Verbal Behavior* 3:449–459.

Treisman, M., and Rostron, A. B. (1972). Brief auditory storage: a modification of Sperling's paradigm applied to audition. *Acta Psychologica* 36:161–170.

Trumbo, D., Ulrich, L., and Noble, M. (1965). Verbal coding and display coding in the acquisition and retention of tracking skill. *Journal of Applied Psychology* 49:368–375.

REFERENCES

Tulving, E. (1962). Subjective organization in free recall of "unrelated" words. *Psychological Review* 69:344–354.

————. (1966). Subjective organization and effects of repetition in multi-trial free-recall learning. *Journal of Verbal Learning and Verbal Behavior* 5: 193–197.

————. (1967). The effects of presentation and recall of materials in free-recall learning. *Journal of Verbal Learning and Verbal Behavior* 6:175–184.

————. (1968). Theoretical issues in free recall. In T. R. Dixon and D. L. Horton (eds.), *Verbal Behavior and General Behavior Theory*. Englewood Cliffs, N.J.: Prentice-Hall.

————. (1972). Episodic and semantic memory. In E. Tulving and W. Donaldson (eds.), *Organization of Memory*. New York: Academic Press, pp. 381–403.

————. (1974). Recall and recognition of semantically encoded words. *Journal of Experimental Psychology* 102:778–787.

Tulving, E., and Colotla, V. A. (1970). Free recall of trilingual lists. *Cognitive Psychology* 1:86–98.

Tulving, E., and Hastie, R. (1972). Inhibition effects of intralist repetition in free recall. *Journal of Experimental Psychology* 92:297–304.

Tulving, E., and Osler, S. (1968). Effectiveness of retrieval cues in memory for words. *Journal of Experimental Psychology* 77:593–601.

Tulving, E., and Patkau, J. E. (1962). Concurrent effects of contextual constraint and word frequency on immediate recall and learning of verbal material. *Canadian Journal of Psychology* 16:83–95.

Tulving, E., and Pearlstone, Z. (1966). Availability versus accessibility of information in memory for words. *Journal of Verbal Learning and Verbal Behavior* 5:381–391.

Tulving, E., and Psotka, J. (1971). Retroactive inhibition in free-recall: inaccessibility of information available in the memory store. *Journal of Experimental Psychology* 87:1–8.

Tulving, E., and Thomson, D. M. (1973). Encoding specificity and retrieval processes in episodic memory. *Psychological Review* 80:352–373.

Turvey, M. T. (1973). On peripheral and central processes in vision: inferences from an information-processing analysis of masking with patterned stimuli. *Psychological Review* 80:1–52.

Turvey, M. T., Brick, P., and Osborn, J. (1970). Proactive interference in short-term memory as a function of prior-item retention interval. *Quarterly Journal of Experimental Psychology* 22:142–147.

Turvey, M. T., and Kravetz, S. (1970). Retrieval from iconic memory with shape as the selection criterion. *Perception and Psychophysics* 8:171–172.

Tversky, B. (1969). Pictorial and verbal encoding in a memory search task. *Perception and Psychophysics* 4:225–233.

Tzeng, O. J. L. (1973). Positive recency effect in delayed free recall. *Journal of Verbal Learning and Verbal Behavior* 12:436–439.

Underwood, B. J. (1945). The effect of successive interpolations on retroactive and proactive inhibition. *Psychological Monographs* 59, whole no. 273.

————. (1948a). Retroactive and proactive inhibition after five and forty-eight hours. *Journal of Experimental Psychology* 38:29–38.

————. (1948b). "Spontaneous recovery" of verbal associations. *Journal of Experimental Psychology* 38:429–439.

————. (1954). Speed of learning and amount retained: A consideration of methodology. *Psychological Bulletin* 51:276–282.

————. (1957). Interference and forgetting. *Psychological Review* 64:49–60.

————. (1965). False recognition produced by implicit verbal responses. *Journal of Experimental Psychology* 70:122–129.

Underwood, B. J., and Ekstrand, B. R. (1966). An analysis of some shortcomings in the interference theory of forgetting. *Psychological Review* 73:540–549.

Underwood, B. J., Ekstrand, B. R., and Keppel, G. (1964). Studies in distributed practice. XXIII: Variations in response-term interference. *Journal of Experimental Psychology* 68:201–212.

Underwood, B. J., and Postman, L. (1960). Extra-experimental sources of interference in forgetting. *Psychological Review* 67:73–95.

Underwood, B. J., and Schulz, R. W. (1960). *Meaningfulness and Verbal Learning*. Philadelphia: Lippincott.

Van Bergen, A. (1968). *Task Interruption*. Amsterdam: North Holland Publishing Co.

Van Ormer, E. B. (1932). Sleep and retention. *Psychological Bulletin* 30:415–439.

Von Békésy, G. (1971). Auditory inhibition in concert halls. *Science* 171:529–536.

Von Restorff, H. (1933). Über die Wirkung von Bereichsbildungen im Spurenfeld. *Psychologisch Forschung* 18:299–342.

Von Sybel, A. (1909). Über das Zusammenwirken verscheidener Simesgebiete bei Gadächtnisleistungen. *Zeitschrift für Psychologie* 53:257–360.

Von Wright, J. M. (1968). On selection in immediate visual memory. *Quarterly Journal of Experimental Psychology* 20:62–68.

Walker, E. C., and Tarte, R. D. (1963). Memory storage as a function of arousal and time with homogeneous and heterogeneous lists. *Journal of Verbal Learning and Verbal Behavior* 2:113–119.

Wallace, G. (1970). Reminiscence in recognition memory for faces. Unpublished M.A. thesis, Monash University.

Wanner, H. E. (1968). On remembering, forgetting and understanding sentences: a study of the deep structure hypothesis. Unpublished doctoral dissertation, Harvard University.

Ward, L. B. (1937). Reminiscence and rote learning. *Psychological Monographs* 49.

Warr, P. B. (1964). The relative importance of proactive inhibition and degree of learning in retention of paired-associate items. *British Journal of Psychology* 55:19–30.

Warrington, E. K., and Ackroyd, C. (1975). The effect of orienting tasks on recognition memory. *Memory and Cognition* 3:140–142.

Warrington, E. K., and Baddeley, A. D. (1974). Amnesia and memory for visual location. *Neuropsychologia* 12:257–263.

Warrington, E. K., Logue, V., and Pratt, R. T. C. (1971). The anatomical localization of selective impairment of auditory verbal short-term memory. *Neuropsychologia* 9:377–387.

Warrington, E. K., and Shallice, T. (1969). The selective impairment of auditory verbal short-term memory. *Brain* 92:885–896.

————. (1972). Neuropsychological evidence of visual storage in short-term memory tasks. *Quarterly Journal of Experimental Psychology* 24:30–40.

Warrington, E. K., and Taylor, A. M. (1973). Immediate memory for faces: long- or short-term memory. *Quarterly Journal of Experimental Psychology* 25:316–322.

Warrington, E. K., and Weiskrantz, L. (1973). An analysis of short-term and long-term memory defects in man. In J. A. Deutsch (ed.), *The Physiological Basis of Memory*. New York: Academic Press.

Wason, P. C., and Johnson-Laird, P. N. (1972). *Psychology of Reasoning: Structure and Content*. London: Batsford.

Watkins, M. J. (1972). Locus of the modality effect in free recall. *Journal of Verbal Learning and Verbal Behavior* 11:644–648.

Watkins, M. J., and Watkins, O. C. (1973). The postcategorical status of the modality effect in serial recall. *Journal of Experimental Psychology* 99: 226–230.

Watkins, O. C. (1975). The origin of the build-up of proactive inhibition effect. Paper presented at the meeting of the Experimental Psychology Society, London.

Wattenbarger, B. L., and Pachella, R. G. (1972). The effect of memory load on reaction time in character classification. *Perception and Psychophysics* 12: 100–102.

Waugh, N. C. (1970). Retrieval time in short-term memory. *British Journal of Psychology* 61:1–12.

Waugh, N. C., and Norman, D. A. (1965). Primary memory. *Psychological Review* 72:89–104.

———. (1968). The measure of interference in primary memory. *Journal of Verbal Learning and Verbal Behavior* 7:617–626.

Wearing, A. J. (1971). Vividness in the recall of English nominalizations. *Psychonomic Science* 22:121–122.

Weaver, G. E., Rose, R. G., and Campbell, N. R. (1971). Item-specific retroactive inhibition in mixed-list comparisons of the A-B, A-C and A-B, D-C paradigms. *Journal of Verbal Learning and Verbal Behavior* 10:488–498.

Webb, L. W. (1917). Transfer of training and retroaction: a comparative study. *Psychological Monographs* 24, whole no. 104.

Wechsler, D. (1944). *The Measurement of Adult Intelligence*, rev. ed. Baltimore: Williams and Wilkins.

Welford, A. T. (1967). *Fundamentals of Skill.* London: Methuen.

Wendon, L. (1972). *The Pictogram System: Set One.* Barton, Cambridge, England: Pictogram Supplies.

White, B. (1960). Recognition of distorted melodies. *American Journal of Psychology* 73:100–107.

Whorf, B. L. (1956). *Language, Thought, and Reality.* Cambridge: Technology Press.

Wickelgren, W. A. (1965). Acoustic similarity and intrusion errors in short-term memory. *Journal of Experimental Psychology* 70:102–108.

———. (1967). Exponential decay and independence from irrelevant associations in short-term memory for serial order. *Journal of Experimental Psychology* 73:165–171.

———. (1968). Sparing of short-term memory in an amnesia patient: implications for strength theory of memory. *Neuropsychologia* 6:235–244.

———. (1969). Auditory or articulatory coding in verbal short-term memory. *Psychological Review* 76:232–235.

———. (1970). Time, interference and rate of presentation in short-term recognition memory. *Journal of Mathematical Psychology* 7:219–235.

Wickelgren, W. A., and Norman, D. A. (1966). Strength models and serial position in short-term recognition memory. *Journal of Mathematical Psychology* 3:316–347.

Wickens, D. D. (1970). Encoding categories of words: an empirical approach to meaning. *Psychological Review* 77:1–15.

Wickens, D. D., Born, D. G., and Allen, C. K. (1963). Proactive inhibition and item similarity in short-term memory. *Journal of Verbal Learning and Verbal Behavior* 2:440–445.

Wickens, D. D., Shearer, W., and Eggemeier, T. (1971). Prerecognition process-

411

REFERENCES

ing of meaningful verbal material: an approach to successive multiple encoding. Paper presented to the Midwestern Psychological Association, Detroit.

Wiener, N. I., and Deutsch, J. A. (1968). Temporal aspects of anticholinergic-and anticholinesterase-induced amnesia for an appetitive habit. *Journal of Comparative and Physiological Psychology* 66:613–617.

Wilkins, A. J. (1971). Conjoint frequency, category size, and categorization time. *Journal of Verbal Learning and Verbal Behavior* 10:382–385.

Wilkins, A., and Stewart, A. (1974). The time course of lateral asymmetries in visual perception of letters. *Journal of Experimental Psychology* 102:905–908.

Williams, H. L., Beaver, W. S., Spence, M. T., and Rundell, O. H. (1969). Digital and kinesthetic memory with interpolated information processing. *Journal of Experimental Psychology* 80:530–536.

Wimer, R. (1964). Osgood's transfer surface: extension and test. *Journal of Verbal Learning and Verbal Behavior* 3:274–279.

Winograd, T. (1972). *Understanding Natural Language*. Edinburgh: Edinburgh University Press.

Wood, G. (1969). Retrieval cues and the accessibility of higher order memory units in multi-trial free recall. *Journal of Verbal Learning and Verbal Behavior* 8:782–789.

Wood, G., and Clark, D. (1969). Instructions, ordering and previous practice in free-recall learning. *Psychonomic Science* 14:187–188.

Woodhead, M. M. (1966). Varying the number of alternatives in short-term recall. *British Journal of Psychology* 57:45–52.

Woodward, A. E., Bjork, R. A., and Jongeward, R. H., Jr. (1973). Recall and recognition as a function of primary rehearsal. *Journal of Verbal Learning and Verbal Behavior* 12:608–617.

Woodworth, R. S. (1938). *Experimental Psychology*. New York: Holt, Rinehart and Winston.

Woodworth, R. S., and Schlosberg, H. (1954). *Experimental Psychology*. New York: Holt.

Wright, J. H. (1967). Effects of formal inter-item similarity and length of retention interval on proactive inhibition of short-term memory. *Journal of Experimental Psychology* 75:386-395.

Wright, P., and Barnard, P. (1975). Effects of "more than" and "less than" decisions on the use of numerical tables. *Journal of Applied Psychology* 60:606–611.

Wulf, F. (1922). Über die Veränderung von Vorstellungen. *Psychologisch Forschung* 1:333–373.

Wundt, W. (1905). *Grundriss der Psychologie*. Leipzig: Engelmann.

Yarnell, P. R., and Lynch, S. (1970). Retrograde memory immediately after concussion. *Lancet* 1:863–865.

Yates, F. A. (1966). *The Art of Memory*. London: Routledge and Kegan Paul.

Yerkes, R. M. (1907). *The Dancing Mouse*. New York: Macmillan.

Yin, R. (1969). Looking at upside-down faces. *Journal of Experimental Psychology* 81:141–145.

———. (1970). Face recognition by brain-injured patients: a dissociable ability? *Neuropsychologia* 8:395–402.

Yngve, V. (1960). A model and an hypothesis for language structure. *Proceedings of the American Philosophical Society,* 104:444–466.

Yuille, J. C., and Paivio, A. (1967). Latency of imaginal and verbal mediators as a function of stimulus and response concreteness-imagery. *Journal of Experimental Psychology* 75:540–544.

REFERENCES

Zacks, R. T. (1969). Invariance of total learning time under different conditions of practice. *Journal of Experimental Psychology* 82:441–447.

Zangwill, O. L. (1937). An investigation of the relationship between the process of reproducing and recognizing simple figures with special reference to Koffka's trace theory. *British Journal of Psychology* 27:250–276.

———. (1946). Some qualitative observations on verbal memory in cases of cerebral lesion. *British Journal of Psychology* 37:8–19.

Zeigarnik, B. (1927). Das Behalten erledigter und unerledigter Handlungen. In K. Lewin (ed.), Untersuchungen zur Handlungs und Affektpsychologie. *Psychologisch Forschung* 9:1–85.

Zeller, A. F. (1951). An experimental analogue of repression. III: The effect of induced failure and success on memory measured by recall. *Journal of Experimental Psychology* 42:32–38.

Zinkin, S., and Miller, A. J. (1967). Recovery of memory after amnesia induced by electroconvulsive shock. *Science* 155:102–104.

INDEX

415

8956